Compassion

Paul Gilbert brings together an international line-up of leading scholars and researchers in the field to provide a state-of-the-art exploration of key areas in compassion research and applications. Compassion can be seen as a core element of prosocial behaviour, and explorations of the concepts and value of compassion have been extended into different aspects of life including physical and psychological therapies, schools, leadership and business.

While many animals share abilities to be distress sensitive and caring of others, it is our newly evolved, socially intelligent abilities that make us capable of *knowingly and deliberately* helping others and purposely developing skills and wisdom to do so. This book generates many research questions whilst exploring the similarities and differences of human compassion to non-human caring and looks at how compassion changes the brain and body, affects genetic expression, manifests at a young age and is then cultivated (or not) by the social environment.

Compassion: Concepts, Research and Applications will be essential reading for professionals, researchers and scholars interested in compassion and its applications in psychology and psychotherapy.

Paul Gilbert, OBE, is Professor of Clinical Psychology, University of Derby, and has been actively involved in research and treating people with shame-based and mood disorders for over 30 years. He is a past President of the British Association for Cognitive and Behavioural Psychotherapy and a fellow of the British Psychological Society. He was awarded the OBE for contributions to mental health in 2011.

'This exciting collection of chapters will bring readers up-to-date with the latest developments in compassion research. Compassion has become an essential psychological concept with developmental, biological, and social roots as well as a wide variety of applications.'

Chris R. Brewin, Professor of Clinical Psychology,
University College London.

'Given the explosion of interest in compassion in many disciplines and professions, this overview of compassion is extremely timely. Paul Gilbert has assembled a stellar lineup of international experts, and the resulting book is essential for all who are interested in better understanding or fostering compassion. The book is remarkably comprehensive, addressing fundamental definitional and conceptual issues, the psychobiology of compassion, its origin in and impact on relationships, and its potential transformative role in leadership, health care, and psychotherapy. The book brilliantly summarizes the current state of compassion research and application and will serve as a catalyst for future explorations and developments.'

David C. Zuroff, Professor of Clinical Psychology,
McGill University, Montreal.

'This remarkable and powerful book links the practice of mindful compassion to basic science and theory effortlessly. Paul Gilbert has assembled and organized a truly excellent anthology of the essential elements regarding Compassion Focused Therapy and the applied research on compassion. Practitioners of evidence-based psychotherapy who wish to remain at the cutting edge of their science need this book. I give this my highest recommendation.'

Denis Tirch, Founding Director,
The Center for Compassion Focused Therapy, USA.

Compassion

Concepts, Research and Applications

Edited by Paul Gilbert

Routledge
Taylor & Francis Group

LONDON AND NEW YORK

First published 2017
by Routledge
2 Park Square, Milton Park, Abingdon, Oxon OX14 4RN

and by Routledge
711 Third Avenue, New York, NY 10017

Routledge is an imprint of the Taylor & Francis Group, an informa business

British Library Cataloguing in Publication Data
A catalogue record for this book is available from the British Library

Library of Congress Cataloging in Publication Data
A catalog record for this book has been requested

ISBN: 978-1-138-95718-3 (hbk)
ISBN: 978-1-138-95719-0 (pbk)
ISBN: 978-1-315-56429-6 (ebk)

Typeset in Times New Roman
by Swales & Willis Ltd, Exeter, Devon, UK
Printed and bound by CPI Group (UK) Ltd, Croydon, CR0 4YY

Contents

Illustrations

Figures

Tables

Contributors

Thorsten Barnhofer, PhD
Sir Henry Wellcome Mood Disorders Centre,
University of Exeter, United Kingdom

Rachna Chowla, PhD
Albion Street Group Practice, London, United Kingdom;
EIR INSEAD HMI, Fontainebleau, France

Valentina Colonnello, PhD
Department of Experimental, Diagnostic and Specialty Medicine,
University of Bologna, Italy

Christopher C. Conway, PhD
Department of Psychology, College of William and Mary
Integrated Science Center, Williamsburg, Virginia, United States

Pauline Favre, PhD,
Department of Social Neuroscience,
Max Planck Institute for Human Cognitive and Brain Sciences,
Leipzig, Germany

Barbara L. Fredrickson, PhD
Kenan Distinguished Professor, Director, Social Psychology
Doctoral Program,
Department of Psychology,
University of North Carolina, United States

Christopher Germer, PhD
Lecturer on Psychiatry,
Harvard Medical School, United States

Paul Gilbert, PhD OBE
Centre for Compassion Research and Training,
College of Health and Social Care Research Centre, University of Derby, United Kingdom

Yotam Heineberg, PhD
Palo Alto University/Stanford University Center for Compassion and Altruism, Research and Education (CCARE),
Stanford, United States

Markus Heinrichs, PhD
Department of Psychology, Laboratory for Biological and Personality Psychology, University of Freiburg, Germany;
Freiburg Brain Imaging Center, University Medical Center, University of Freiburg, Germany

Dacher Keltner, PhD
Department of Psychology,
University of California, Berkeley, United States

James N. Kirby, PhD,
Lecturer and Clinical Psychologist, School of Psychology,
University of Queensland, Australia

Daniel Martin, PhD
California State University, East Bay-Department of Management/Stanford University Center for Compassion and Altruism Research and Education (CCARE), Stanford, California, United States

Jennifer S. Mascaro, PhD,
Department of Family and Preventive Medicine
Emory University School of Medicine, Atlanta, Georgia

Mario Mikulincer
School of Psychology
Interdisciplinary Center (IDC) Herzliya, Israel

Darcia Narvaez, PhD
Professor of Psychology,
University of Notre Dame, Indiana, United States

Nicola Petrocchi, PhD
Department of Economics and Social Sciences, John Cabot University, Rome, Italy;
Compassionate Mind Italy Association, Rome, Italy

Charles L. Raison, MD,
Mary Sue and Mike Shannon Chair for Healthy Minds, Children and Families;
Professor at the School of Human Ecology;
Professor, Department of Psychiatry,
School of Medicine and Public Health, University of Wisconsin-Madison,
United States

Phillip R. Shaver, PhD
Department of Psychology,
University of California, United States

Daniel J. Siegel, PhD
Mindsight Institute,
Santa Monica, California, United States

Tania Singer, PhD
Director, Department of Social Neuroscience,
Max Planck Institute for Human Cognitive and Brain Sciences, Leipzig, Germany

George M. Slavich, PhD
Associate Professor of Psychiatry and Biobehavioral Sciences;
Research Scientist, Cousins Center for Psychoneuroimmunology;
Director, Laboratory for Stress Assessment and Research, Cousins Center for
Psychoneuroimmunology and Department of Psychiatry and Biobehavioral Sciences,
University of California, United States

Penny Spikins, PhD
Department of Archaeology,
University of York, United Kingdom

Jennifer E. Stellar, PhD
Assistant Professor,
University of Toronto, Canada

Dr Pascal Vrtička, PhD
Group Leader, Department of Social Neuroscience,
Max Planck Institute for Human Cognitive and Brain Sciences, Leipzig, Germany

Michael A. West, PhD
Senior Fellow, The King's Fund, London;
Lancaster University Management School,
Lancaster, United Kingdom

Preface

The last 20 years have seen some outstanding developments in research on prosocial behaviour, ranging over altruism, morality, caring and compassion. Studies have proliferated on how the brain and body respond to both receiving compassion and expressing compassion to self and others. These advances, along with evolutionary understanding, have helped us recognise how fundamentally so much of what we are as humans, even our genetic expressions, is influenced by the quality of care, affiliation and general friendliness there is in our social relationships. From the day we are born to the day we die the helpfulness, kindness and compassion of others will have a huge impact on the quality of our lives.

As with all vibrant areas of research, compassion research is not without its controversies. On the positive side controversies on definition, nature and function show that compassion is a fascinating area that is vigorous, vibrant and open to debate. On the negative side there can be a tendency to try to contain, restrain and limit definitions by adopting certain ones prematurely. In this edited book I have advised authors of my particular view about compassion but have not insisted that they adopt it. So you will find different definitions of compassion in different chapters. Often these reflect the particular focus or research interest of the author(s), which tend to vary.

For me though it has been a privilege to bring together some of the top thinkers and researchers in the field of prosocial behaviour and compassion to explore the array of different areas compassion research is now reaching. From understanding genetic expression, the choreography and architecture of our brains, through to our social relationships and psychotherapy, compassion is beginning to texture how we think about all of these topics. The book is divided into four parts exploring these different and exciting areas.

Part I considers the evolution and the nature of compassion with my opening piece on definitional issues and controversies. Chapter 2 by Penny Spikins offers fascinating reviews of the archaeological evidence for the gradual development of compassion in early human groups. She makes the point that prosocial, not antisocial, behaviour has been a driver of social intelligence. In (a rather extended) Chapter 3 I spell out a social mentalities approach to compassion. The argument here is that compassion can be understood as caring motivation textured by recently-evolved social intelligent competencies. One of these social intelligent competencies is self-awareness and capacities for intentional mindfulness which is explored in Chapter 4. Here Chris Germer and Thorsten Barnhorfer offer their extensive experience to explore the interactions between mindfulness and compassion.

Part II on the physiologies of compassion begins with Chapter 5 offering an overview of the field from Jennifer Mascaro and Charles Raison, highlighting the importance of many interacting sub-systems in compassion. Chapter 6 by Valentina Colonnello, Nicola Petrocchi and Markus Heinrichs illuminates particular neurophysiological systems, particularly the role of oxytocin, in compassion and prosocial behaviour in general. Chapter 7 by Jennifer Stellar and Dacher Keltner looks at a different aspect of the parasympathetic system and the vagus nerve associated with compassion. Chapter 8 by Pascal Vrtička, Pauline Favre and Tania Singer moves us into the brain with a review of how compassion and empathy are represented in the brain. This part is rounded off with Chapter 9 by Christopher Conway and George Slavich looking at the fast-developing field of epigenetics and prosocial compassionate behaviour, and in particular the importance of understanding socially guided methylation.

Part III takes us into the arena of social contexts. In Chapter 10 Darcia Narvaez highlights the importance of social context and early background for the development of a range of prosocial compassionate and moral behaviours. Chapter 11 by Mario Mikulincer and Philip Shaver provides a detailed overview of how early background experiences, particularly of attachment, impact subsequent compassionate and altruistic orientations. Chapter 12 by Barbara Fredrickson and Daniel Siegel provides a unique conversational chapter exploring the interactions between their different backgrounds in micro-moment and micro-interactional patterns with interpersonal neurobiology.

Part IV explores the importance and difficulties of applying compassion in the real world. Chapter 13 by Daniel Martin and Yotam Heineberg covers a wide-ranging literature on the conflict between prosocial and more antisocial types of leadership, and the challenges for compassion and leadership in organisations. Chapter 14 by Michael West and Rachna Chowla considers the importance of compassionate leadership in healthcare settings like the NHS. They explore some of the management styles that can facilitate or block compassion. Finally, Chapter 15 by James Kirby and myself explores the application of compassion focused approaches to mental health problems and psychotherapy. Our main theme is that as we learn more about the evolved role of affiliative emotions and motives on a range of physiological, psychological social processes, it makes sense that they should become centre ground to therapy.

I hope you find things in this book which will be useful to you and maybe even inspire you. The idea of developing a science for creating a more compassionate prosocial world is exciting and it's also exciting to see so many individuals making this the centre of their research.

Part I

Evolution and the nature of compassion

Chapter 1

Compassion

Definitions and controversies

Paul Gilbert

Compassion is clearly linked to the evolution of caring behaviour (Gilbert, 1989/2016, 2009, 2015a, 2015b; Keltner, Kogan, Piff & Saturn, 2014; Mayseless, 2016), altruism (Preston, 2013; Goetz, Keltner & Simon-Thomas, 2010; Ricard, 2015) and prosocial behaviour in general (Bierhoff, 2005; Brown & Brown, 2015; Penner, Dovidio, Piliavin & Schroeder, 2005). The last 20 years have seen increasing research into the nature and benefits of all these. For compassion, these include a range of effects on psychological processes (Jazaieri et al., 2013; Keltner et al., 2014; Singer & Bolz, 2012), social relationships (Cozolino, 2006; Crocker & Canevello, 2012; Penner et al., 2005) and physiological processes (Klimecki, Leiberg, Ricard & Singer, 2014; Kogan et al., 2014; Simon-Thomas et al., 2011; Weng et al., 2013) that extend to genetic expression (Slavich & Cole, 2013; Slavic & Conway, Chapter 9, this volume). Hoge et al. (2013) found that women with experience of loving-kindness meditation had longer relative telomere length than controls (see also Fredrickson et al., 2013). Compassionate motives benefit social relationships and well-being, whereas ego self-focused motives do not (Crocker & Canevello, 2012). Compassion has become the focus for psychotherapeutic interventions with increasing evidence for its effectiveness (Gilbert, 2000, 2010, 2015c; Hofmann, Grossman & Hinton, 2011; Kirby & Gilbert, Chapter 15, this volume; Leaviss & Uttley, 2015; Neff & Germer, 2013). In addition, all the chapters of this book address these themes too. However, despite this progress there remains controversy and discussion around the actual nature of compassion, its definition and constituents. This chapter explores some of these controversies.

Issues of definition: what's in a word?

We can only understand phenomena by agreeing a set of properties by which phenomena will be known. So, for example, we can distinguish between a chair, an elephant, a tiger and a cat by agreeing a set of qualities and properties that belong to each and those that are specific. Hence, they share qualities as four-legged things, but not of being living organisms. We can then distinguish between an elephant, a tiger and a cat and then finally between a tiger and a cat, and even different breeds of cat. Each subdivision has more and more overlapping features, but also more fine-grained distinctions. This is important in areas like compassion too which are easily fused with concepts such as altruism, benevolence, heartedness, prosociality, kindness and love. Sometimes it's the fine-grained distinctions that are important. Second, as the late Prof Kendell (1975) used to drum into us clinical trainees in Edinburgh in the 1970s, there is no such 'thing' as depression, anxiety or paranoia as rarefied states. Rather there are a set of phenomena (signs and symptoms) that we agree may cluster/fit together and we will give labels to, so that we can agree what we are discussing when we use the label. So too, the definition of compassion will depend upon the shared properties we give to this concept and its differentiation from similar concepts. Third, definition problems can plague psychological research because of the insufficient attention it gives to functions. For example, shame and guilt, envy and jealousy, are frequently used interchangeably when they are in fact very different, with very different evolutionary histories, competencies, functions and focus (Gilbert, 1989, 1998, 2005, 2009). So, as will be discussed, although there are many general ideas around what compassion is, currently there is no clear agreement about what the specific attributes of compassion are. Let's take a look at the range.

Defining compassion

One origin of the word compassion is from the Latin *compati*, meaning 'to suffer with'. However, words change their meanings with use over time and across cultures and this is certainly the case for the word compassion. For example, to 'suffer with' need not imply a compassionate motivation to do anything about it. Today 'to suffer with or on behalf of' might be more closely related to what we now call sympathy (Eisenberg, VanSchyndel & Hofer, 2015) or empathy (Batson, 2009). Aristotle argued that we only had compassion if we thought the suffering of another was nontrivial; to use one of his examples, 'we would not have compassion for the upset of an emperor who'd lost a shipment of Larks tongues he'd ordered for his party!' (Nassbaum, 2003). Aristotle also thought that a sense of deserve influenced compassion, and third that we would have to have some sense of that suffering; that we could imagine ourselves in their situation (Nassbaum, 2003). So the seriousness of suffering, sense of deserve and empathy texture compassion for Aristotle. Buddhist scholars would not see these qualities as central.

In regard to dictionary definitions there are quite a variety. The Oxford Dictionary (2016) suggests that compassion is 'Sympathetic pity and concern for the sufferings or misfortunes of others'. Teaching in France, Germany and Italy, colleagues inform me that 'compassion' is a difficult word to translate and can indeed be linked to pity. This is obviously a problem because pity is a very different process altogether and involves a sense of looking down on others (Nassbaum, 2003). This is a good example where misunderstanding about the use of a word can lead to heated debates and serious confusions. Schopenhauer (1788–1860), who was deeply influenced by Buddhist thought, and one of the first Western thinkers to introduce compassion into philosophy, argued that compassion was one of the highest and most important qualities of humanity. Neither self-interest, nor duty, social conformity nor fear of punishment could, in his view, be a source of genuine morality (Cartwright, 1988). However, Nietzsche wrote a number of significant critiques of Schopenhauer arguing that compassion is a poor source for moral development. The problem is, as Cartwright (1988) observed, these two philosophers were talking at cross purposes because of poor word definition:

> [B]ecause Schopenhauer and Nietzsche refer to two different emotions by the German noun 'Mitleid'; that it is best to understand Schopenhauer's conception of 'Mitleid' as 'compassion' and Nietzsche's as 'pity'. I shall argue that compassion is significantly (and morally) different from pity in ways that make Schopenhauer's Mitleids-Moral immune to this element of Nietzsche's critique.
>
> (p. 1)

This confusion of concepts remains, especially in translations, and may help explain why, at times, compassion is regarded as unhelpful (Who wants to be pitied?), or even as a weakness. In contrast, the Cambridge University Dictionary (2016) suggests compassion is 'a strong feeling of sympathy and sadness for the suffering or bad luck of others and a wish to help them'. Here, 'pity' is absent and is replaced with 'sympathy' and 'feelings of sadness', and the 'wish to be helpful' is also added. The concept of sympathy or 'natural sympathy', as David Hume called it, as underpinning human benevolence, is prevalent in many early philosophical texts. This definition also has the idea of a specific 'feeling' in compassion that stimulates motivated helping behaviour. In Goetz et al.'s (2010) major review of some of the evolutionary and historical origins of compassion they also place feeling centre stage:

> We define compassion as the *feeling that arises* in witnessing another's suffering and that motivates a subsequent desire to help. This definition con-ceptualizes compassion as an *affective state* defined by a specific subjective feeling, and it differs from treatments of compassion as an attitude . . . This definition also clearly differentiates compassion from empathy, which refers to the vicarious experience of another's emotions.
>
> (p. 351; italics added)

They also distinguish compassion from distress, sadness and love. As helpful and as detailed as this review is, there is a difference in defining compassion as a *feeling state* rather than a motivational state, and it is important not to confuse motives with emotions (Deckers, 2014; Gilbert, 2015a, Weiner, 1992). Indeed, Ekman (2016) surveyed researchers who study emotion. While 91% saw anger and 90% saw anxiety as basic emotions, compassion was rated one of the lowest with only 20% agreeing that compassion is an emotion. Without an evolved caring motiva-tion system there would be no emotions arising to signals of suffering/distress.

It is the motivation system that necessitates emotions in contexts, and those emotions may well then stimulate motivated actions (Gilbert, Chapter 3, this volume).

It is also unclear what the feeling state of compassion is. For example, what is the emotion when rushing into a burning house to save a child, consoling a recently bereaved or dying friend or fighting for human justice? It is likely that in the first case the feeling states/emotions are of urgency and anxiety, in the second sadness and sorrow, and in the third case a degree of anger at injustice. It's not the emotions that unite them, but the motivation to pay attention (on suffering and needs) and the motivation and intention to do something about it. That intention can be present even when people are not thinking about it or are not activated. Note too that compassion can represent blends of emotions. For example, a doctor is struck by the suffering of the Ebola virus and dedicates his/her life, working long hours, to finding a cure. Emotions here may be a *blend* of anger that such viruses exist in the world, sadness for the suffering caused and the way people die from it, and anxiety that if it gets out into the world it could even reach his/her own family. In addition, whereas emotions wax and wane, a motivation can guide behaviour for the whole of one's life.

The facial expressions of compassion can also differ according to context. The facial expressions we may have when consoling somebody in physical pain may be different to being with their grief or anger. The facial expression of a therapist meeting a patient for the first time and wishing to present themselves as compassionate, trustworthy and a safe listener will be different from compassionate expressions as different aspects of the story unfold. Whereas compassionate, kind and trustworthy faces are usually perceived as friendly, affiliative, happy and positive, such facial expressions may be less positively experienced when the viewer is in pain (Gerdes, Wieser, Alpers, Strack & Pauli, 2012; Godinho, Frot, Perchet, Magnin & Garcia-Larrea, 2008). When asked to pose compassion faces people automatically create soft expressions with gentle smiles of softness, friendliness and signals on being 'safe', kindness and gentleness (McEwan et al., 2014). Furthermore, it is now recognised that although compassion is seen as a positive act, it actually engages aversive emotions which arise when we are in touch with suffering (Condon & Barrett, 2013). So context is crucial.

The Free Dictionary definition (2016) suggests compassion is a 'Deep awareness of the suffering of another accompanied by the wish to relieve it'. In this definition there is no pity, sympathy or 'specific feeling' aspect like sadness or sorrow, but a focus on 'deep awareness' with (again) a motivation (the wish) to do something about it. This definition gets closer to the traditional philosophical and contemplative traditions of compassion, as we will see.

The contemplative traditions and the multifaceted approach: Many approaches to compassion see it as multifaceted, although they do not always agree on what those facets are. Buddhist scholar Geshe Thupten Jinpa (translator to the Dalai Lama) and colleagues, who developed the Stanford compassion cultivation training, define compassion as:

[A] multidimensional process comprised of four key components: (1) an awareness of suffering (cognitive/empathic awareness), (2) sympathetic concern related to being emotionally moved by suffering (affective component), (3) a wish to see the relief of that suffering (intention), and (4) a responsiveness or readiness to help relieve that suffering (motivational).

(Jazaieri et al., 2013)

Mindfulness and compassion thinkers Christina Feldman and Willem Kuyken (2011) also highlight the multifaceted textures of compassion. They suggest that:

Compassion is the acknowledgment that not all pain can be 'fixed' or 'solved' but all suffering is made more approachable in a landscape of compassion. Compassion is a multi-textured response to pain, sorrow and anguish. It includes kindness, empathy, generosity and acceptance. The strands of courage, tolerance, equanimity are equally woven into the cloth of compassion. Above all, compassion is the capacity to open to the reality of suffering and to aspire to its healing.

(p. 143)

They go on to add:

Compassion is an orientation of mind that recognises pain and the universality of pain in human experience and the capacity to meet that pain with kindness, empathy, equanimity and patience. While self-compassion orients to our own experience, compassion extends this orientation to others' experience.

(p. 145)

Kuyken and his colleagues offer a more specific listing from their major, more recent literature review (Strauss et al., 2016).

[W]e propose a new definition of compassion as a cognitive, affective, and behavioural process consisting of the following five elements that refer to both self – and other – compassion: (1) Recognizing suffering; (2) Understanding the universality of suffering in human experience; (3) Feeling empathy for the person suffering and connecting with the distress (emotional resonance); (4) Tolerating uncomfortable feelings aroused in response to the suffering person (e.g. distress, anger, fear) so remaining open to and accepting of the person suffering; and (5) Motivation to act/acting to alleviate suffering.

(p. 19)

Dutton, Workman and Hardin (2014), who have done considerable work on compassion in organisations, relate compassion to four core aspects that also touch on cognitive, affective and behavioural processes: (1) noticing/attending to another's suffering, (2) sensemaking or meaning making related to suffering; (3) feelings that resemble empathic concern, and (4) actions aimed at easing the suffering.

Emotions researcher Paul Ekman (2014), who worked with the Dalai Lama, suggests four dimensions of compassion: (1) empathic compassion (being in touch with the feelings of suffering of others); (2) action compassion (taking action to alleviate suffering); (3) concerned compassion (based on a motivation for helping); and (4) aspirational compassion (linked to a more cognitive desire to develop compassion).

Into the mix of what compassion is, Neff (2003) focused on *self*-compassion and defines it as follows:

> Self-compassion . . . involves being touched by and open to one's own suffering, not avoiding or disconnecting from it, generating the desire to alleviate one's suffering and to heal oneself with kindness. Self-compassion also involves offering nonjudgmental understanding to one's pain, inadequacies and failures, so that one's experience is seen as part of the larger human experience.
>
> (p. 87)

She also went on to suggest there are three bipolar dimensions that underpin self-compassion: self-kindness (in contrast to self-judgment and self-criticism); shared common humanity (in contrast to feeling isolated and alone and the only one); and mindfulness (in contrast to self-absorption and rumination). These constructs and resulting measures have not been without controversy (López et al., 2015; Muris & Petrocchi, 2016) as Neff herself recognises (Neff, Whittaker & Karl, in press). They are different to, say, a competencies focus (see Gilbert, Chapter 3, this volume). As Neff (2003, 2011) makes clear, what sits behind her approach is to consider a 'self-compassionate frame of mind' as a way to help people cope with difficult life circumstances and especially with self-criticism (see Germer & Barnhofer, Chapter 4, this volume).

Different again is Armstrong's (2011) focus on the roots of compassion in the golden rule of Confucius: 'Do unto others as you would be done to', or more negatively 'don't do things to other people you would not like them to do to yourself'. This has inspired the Charter for Compassion – designed to spread compassion values and behaviour through communitie – which is now a major world movement (see http://www.charterforcompassion.org).

Motivation approaches

Listing potential characteristics of compassion, a kind of diagnostic approach can be supported with a functional approach that focuses on motivation. Motivation is then not 'one of' the characteristics. 'It underpins signs or symptoms' of compassion; it is the main show that generates the core characteristics. Motivation underpins not just action but also being prepared to pay attention to suffering. Buddhist scholar Mathieu Ricard (2015) suggests that compassion is a form of altruism, made up of a range of sub-attributes, abilities and skills including sympathy, empathy and commitment. But at its heart, compassion is a *deeply felt wish* for others to be free of suffering, the causes of suffering, and to flourish and to find happiness (personal communication, 2012). This focus highlights motivation as 'the wish' (motive) for the alleviation of suffering.

Interestingly, compassion (motivation) hasn't been that clearly distinguished from altruism. For example, Preston (2013) suggests altruism as an almost identical process:

> Altruistic responding is defined as any form of helping that applies when the giver is motivated to assist a specific target *after perceiving their distress or need*... Altruistic responding further narrows these classifications to only include cases where the motivation to respond is fomented by direct or indirect perception of the other's distress or need . . . This excludes cases that emerged later in time or include diverse processes, such as cooperation or helping influenced by strategic goals, social norms, display rules, or mate signaling.
>
> (p. 1307; italics added)

Here, there has to be a cost of helping to the self that might not be the case for compassion. This also is a different take on altruism than say Ricard (2015). The Dalai Lama (2001) also links compassion to motivation (a wish):

> What is compassion? Compassion *is the wish that others be free of suffering.* It is by means of compassion that we aspire to attain enlightenment. It is compassion that inspires us to engage in the virtuous practices that lead to Buddhahood. We must therefore devote ourselves to developing compassion.
>
> (p. 91; italics added)

He also distinguishes between these wishes:

> Just as compassion is the wish that all sentient beings be free of suffering, loving-kindness is the wish that all may enjoy happiness.
>
> (p. 96)

So compassion also acts as an 'inspiration'. There is a clear distinction between loving-kindness (happiness focused) and compassion cultivation, as is captured in the concept of Bodhichitta (Gilbert & Choden, 2013; Tsering, 2005). Here again definitions are tricky because actually '*metta*' means friendliness or openheartedness, not 'love' as understood in Western psychology. These kinds of mistranslations and merging of concepts have caused difficulties for compassion, which can sometimes be confused with love (Gilbert & Choden, 2013; Goetz et al., 2010). In the West, love implies *liking trust and affection,* but in reality deep-courageous compassion is for those we may not know, may not like, trust or feel affection for. Indeed, the Dalai Lama (1995) suggests that if we just have compassion for people we love this is not real compassion! 'Your love and compassion towards your friends is in many cases actually attachment. This feeling is not based on the realization that all beings have an equal right to be happy and overcome suffering' (p. 63). When it comes to compassion for those whom we do not like, or who may threaten or harm us, then understanding courageous and assertive compassion, and its distinction from submissiveness and compliance, is crucial (Catarino, Gilbert, McEwan & Baião, 2014).

An insight that drives compassion in the Tibetan Buddhist traditions is insight into the fact that suffering naturally arises from the life process itself, including the impermanence of all things and our graspings and aversions (Dalai Lama, 1995; Tsering, 2005). Mindful compassion helps us to have insight into the illusory nature of the self, and our cravings and attachments that give rise to dukkha (suffering). The Dalai Lama (2001) suggests that if, via compassion, we cultivate 'our insight into the miserable nature of life we overcome that attachment' (p. 85). Schopenhauer also thought that life is pretty horrendous (miserable) which should inspire us to compassion. Many of the Gothic horror classics, including for example Mary Shelley's *Frankenstein*, were reflections on the horrors of life; being born without our consent, into bodies designed to age, decay and disease, in a world where our minds are set up for tribal and self-interest conflicts; yearning for love and acceptance, which, even if one gets them, are impermanent, with often painful death waiting in the wings for us and those we love. Death is the only escape. No wonder the Dalai Lama calls it 'a miserable life'.

Insight into this reality can lead either to dissonance, hopelessness, despair and anger, commonly dissociation (just keep these things out of mind and make the next dollar, plan the next holiday, buy better wine) or compassion, which is the bodhisattva insight and dedication. On leaving his Golden Palace, it was these insights (into decay, disease and death) which set Siddhartha on the path to enlightenment. So here, compassion arises for a deeper focus into the nature of our reality, and further, that all beings are struggling with this reality, not wanting to suffer (in a life inherently full of suffering) but be happy (Dalai Lama, 1995). In many ways some Buddhist concepts are major attacks on our natural tendencies to dissociate from the harsh realities of the suffering all around us in the very nature of biological life. In contrast, Western philosophers focus more on the search for meaning and morality, and medical solutions, rather than happiness and the illusions of the self (Sensky, 2010).

Compassion also implies the prevention of suffering (where we can), which means addressing needs. So, for example, if we don't feed our babies, or look after them they will die and hence suffer. So *compassion must involve* evaluating and providing for needs that prevent suffering; indeed we have a range of newly evolved, socially intelligent competencies that turn a caring motivation into a compassionate social mentality (see Gilbert, Chapter 3, this volume). To address needs requires empathic insight into, and taking an interest in, the needs of others. Now, of course, animals can address the needs of their offspring without having deep empathic insight, but empathic insight along with other socially intelligence competencies clearly aid our capacity to understand the needs of others and how to address them. For a bodhisattva 'a key need' is to provide conditions for enlightenment.

The point then is that compassion has many textures and definitions which emerge as partly guided by the functions to which they will be put. We can think of it as a particular feeling that arises, a motivation to be helpful, a listing of various attributes (of various types), and linked to personality traits. My own approach has been to focus on understanding these kinds of dispositions in a functional, evolutionary model and in particular the way evolved strategies (survival and reproduction) give rise to motives (see Gilbert, Chapter 3, this volume). In addition I have had an opportunity to work and meditate with colleagues at Samye Ling Monastery, including Lama Yeshee and the Buddhist Monk Choden with whom I wrote *Mindful Compassion* in 2013. Working within motivational theory (Gilbert 1989/2016) and the Mahayana tradition we have settled on a definition of compassion as '*a sensitivity to suffering in self and others with a commitment to try to alleviate and prevent it*'.

We added 'self' as well as 'others', and importantly the concept of 'prevention' which is implicit in most models. This actually has two types of psychology to it. The first is the motivation to attend and engage with suffering as opposed to avoiding it in various ways. How and why we turn towards or away from suffering is central to many psychological therapies and even political movements. Thus the aspect of motivation to engage is itself a complex area. Second, we may be motivated to engage but not have much idea of what to do. So compassion also requires us to think about how we are motivated to learn how to take action. This can involve courage and also dedication to understand the causes, prevention and alleviation of suffering so that we take wise (rather than impulsive or ignorant uninformed) actions. This is why the model outlined in Chapter 3 tries to identify specific competencies linked to specific motivation aspects of caring motivation.

In Mahayana tradition this motive underpins Bodhichitta and is supported by various paramitas – such as generosity, morality, wisdom, patience, energy and meditation. In the approach outlined in Chapter 3, the motivational approach to compassion gives a narrative of how it textures our minds. Compassion is rooted in a motivational care-focused system textured by recently evolved socially intelligent competencies and it is these competencies that elevate caring into compassion (see Gilbert, Chapter 3, this volume).

Conclusion

So where does this leave us? First we see the extraordinary, few thousand year history that sits behind the concepts of compassion, yet also the way we are reliant on language and cultural contexts to convey meaning. Consequently, different languages and cultures do not always have exactly the same meaning for the words they use, and heated debates can arise because people are actually talking at cross purposes. Hence, striving for precision and clarity are important, but we also recognise different definitions for different functions. To date, however, this precision remains elusive for compassion. There are different definitions, different listings of its qualities, with different implications for its study and training. As mentioned in the Preface we can see this as representing a vibrant, fascinating area of discussion and scientific enquiry with an agreement that all of us are a little bit like blind folk touching the elephant. It would therefore be unwise to prematurely settle on certain definitions without a better understanding of the processes that underpin compassion, the functions it serves, and allowing better and more comprehensive definitions to evolve. For example, the way a clinician may think about compassion might be different to how a lawyer thinks about compassion. This is not unusual. The way a medical, biologically orientated psychiatrist, wanting specific drugs for specific symptoms, thinks about depression and defines it is very different to how a psychodynamic therapist thinks about depression and defines it. Trying to categorise mental states in simple terms and lists is notoriously difficult. Anyone familiar with the controversies around psychiatric diagnosis of what 'is' depression, anxiety and paranoia will be very aware of these issues. What this chapter has tried to do is bring these issues to the fore.

References

Armstrong, R. (2011). *Twelve Steps to Lead a Compassionate Life*. London: Bodley.
Batson, C. D. (2009). These things called empathy: Eight related but distinct phenomena. In J. Decety and W. Ickes (Eds.) *The Social Neuroscience of Empathy* (pp. 3–15). Cambridge, MA: MIT Press.
Bierhoff, H.-W. (2005). The psychology of compassion and prosocial behaviour. In P. Gilbert (Ed.) *Compassion: Conceptualisations, Research and Use in Psychotherapy* (pp. 148–167). London: Routledge.
Brown, S. L., & Brown, R. M. (2015). Connecting prosocial behaviour to improved physical health: Contributions from the neurobiology of parenting. *Neuroscience and Biobehavioural Reviews, 55,* 1–17.
Cambridge Dictionary (2016). http://dictionary.cambridge.org/dictionary/english/compassion.
Cartwright, D. E. (1988). Schopenhauer's Compassion and Nietzsche's Pity. *Schopenhauer Jahrbuch, 69,* 557–567. http://www.schopenhauer.philosophie.uni-mainz.de/Aufsaetze_Jahrbuch/69_1988/Cartwright.pdf.
Catarino, F., Gilbert, P., McEwan, K., & Baião, R. (2014). Compassion motivations: Distinguishing submissive compassion from genuine compassion and its association with shame, submissive behavior, depression, anxiety and stress. *Journal of Social and Clinical Psychology, 33,* 399–412. doi: 10.1521/jscp.2014.33.5.399
Condon, P., & Barrett, L. F. (2013). Conceptualizing and experiencing compassion. *Emotion, 13,* 817–821.
Cozolino, L. (2006). *The Neuroscience of Human Relationships: Attachment and the Developing Social Brain*. New York: W. W. Norton.
Crocker, J., & Canevello, A. (2012). Consequences of self-image and compassionate goals. In P. G. Devine and A. Plant (Eds.) *Advances in Experimental Social Psychology* (pp. 229–277). New York: Elsevier.

Dalai Lama. (1995). *The Power of Compassion*. India: HarperCollins.

Dalai Lama. (2001). *An Open Heart*. London: Hodder and Stoughton.

Deckers, L. (2014). *Motivation: Biological, Psychological, and Environmental*. London: Routledge.

Dutton, J. E., Workman, K. M. & Hardin, A. E. (2014). Compassion at work. *Annual Review of Organizational Psychology and Organizational Behaviour, 1*, 277–304. doi: 10.1146/annurev-orgpsych-031413-091221

Eisenberg, N., VanSchyndel, S. K., & Hofer, C. (2015). The association of maternal socialization in childhood and adolescence with adult offsprings' sympathy/caring. *Developmental Psychology, 51*, 7–16. doi: 10.1037/a0038137

Ekman, P. (2014). *Moving Toward Global Compassion*. E-book available from www.paulekman.com.

Ekman, P. (2016). What scientists who study emotion agree about. *Perspectives on Psychological Science, 11*(1), 31–34.

Feldman, C., & Kuyken, W. (2011). Compassion in the landscape of suffering. *Contemporary Buddhism, 12*, 143–155: doi:10.1080/14639947.2011.564831

Fredrickson, B. L., Grewen, K. M., Coffey, K. A., Algoe, S. B., Firestine, A. M., Arevalo, J. M., . . . Cole, S. W. (2013). A functional genomic perspective on human well-being. *Proceedings of the National Academy of Sciences, 110*, 13684–13689. doi: 10.1073/pnas.1305419110

Free Dictionary (2016). http://www.thefreedictionary.com/compassion

Gerdes, A. B. M., Wieser, M. J., Alpers, G. W., Strack, F., & Pauli, P. (2012). Why do you smile at me while I'm in pain?—Pain selectively modulates voluntary facial muscle responses to happy faces. *International Journal of Psychophysiology, 85*, 161–167. doi: http://dx.doi.org/10.1016/j.ijpsycho.2012.06.002

Gilbert, P. (1989/2016). *Human Nature and Suffering*. London: Routledge.

Gilbert, P. (1998). What is shame? Some core issues and controversies. In P. Gilbert & B. Andrews (Eds.) *Shame: Interpersonal Behaviour, Psychopathology, and Culture* (pp. 3–38). New York: Oxford University Press.

Gilbert, P. (2000). Social mentalities: Internal 'social' conflicts and the role of inner warmth and compassion in cognitive therapy. In P. Gilbert & Bailey, K. G (Eds.) *Genes on the Couch: Explorations in Evolutionary Psychotherapy* (pp. 118–150). Hove: Psychology Press.

Gilbert, P. (2005). Compassion and cruelty: A biopsychosocial approach. In P. Gilbert (Ed.) *Compassion: Conceptualisations, Research and Use in Psychotherapy*, pp. 3–74. London: Routledge

Gilbert, P. (2009). *The Compassionate Mind: A New Approach to the Challenge of Life*. London: Constable & Robinson.

Gilbert, P. (2010). *Compassion Focused Therapy: The CBT Distinctive Features Series*. London: Routledge.

Gilbert, P. (2015a). The evolution and social dynamics of compassion. *Journal of Social & Personality Psychology Compass, 9*, 239–254. doi: 10.1111/spc3.12176

Gilbert. P. (2015b). An evolutionary approach to emotion in mental health with a focus on affiliative emotions. *Emotion Review* (special issues Normal and Abnormal Emotion. K. Scherer (Ed.) *7*, 230–237. doi: 10.1177/1754073915576552

Gilbert, P. (2015c). Affiliative and prosocial motives and emotions in mental health. *Dialogues in Clinical Neuroscience, 17*, 381–389.

Gilbert, P., & Choden (2013). *Mindful Compassion*. London: Constable & Robinson.

Godinho, F., Frot, M., Perchet, C., Magnin, M., & Garcia-Larrea, L. (2008). Pain influences hedonic assessment of visual inputs. *European Journal of Neuroscience*, *27*(9), 2219–2228. doi: 10.1111/j.1460-9568.2008.06196.x

Goetz, J. L., Keltner, D., & Simon-Thomas, E. (2010). Compassion: An evolutionary analysis and empirical review. *Psychological Bulletin*, *136*, 351–374. doi: 10.1037/a0018807

Hofmann, S. G., Grossman, P., & Hinton, D. E. (2011). Loving-kindness and compassion meditation: Potential for psychological interventions. *Clinical Psychology Review*, *31*(7), 1126–1132. doi: 10.1016/j.cpr.2011.07.003

Hoge, E. A., Chen, M. M., Orr, E., Metcalf, C. A., Fischer, L. E., Pollack, M. H., . . . Simon, N. M. (2013). Loving-Kindness Meditation practice associated with longer telomeres in women. *Brain, Behavior, and Immunity*, *32*, 159–163. doi: 10.1016/j.bbi.2013.04.005

Jazaieri, H., Jinpa, G. T., McGonigal, K., Rosenberg, E., Finkelstein, J., Simon-Thomas, E., . . . Goldin, P. R. (2013). Enhancing compassion: A randomized controlled trial of a compassion cultivation training program. *Journal of Happiness Studies*, *14*, 1113–1126. doi: 10.1007/s10902-012-9373-z

Keltner, D., Kogan, A., Piff, P. K., & Saturn, S. R. (2014). The sociocultural appraisals, values, and emotions (SAVE) framework of prosociality: Core processes from gene to meme. *The Annual Review of Psychology*, *65*, 425–460. doi: 10.1146/annurev-psych-010213-115054

Kendell, R. (1975). *The Role of Diagnosis in Psychiatry*. Edinburgh: Blackwell.

Klimecki, O. M., Leiberg, S., Ricard, M., & Singer, T. (2014). Differential pattern of functional brain plasticity after compassion and empathy training. *Social Cognitive & Affective Neuroscience*, *9*, 873–879. doi: 10.1093/scan/nst060

Kogan, A., Oveis, C., Carr, E. W., Gruber, J., Mauss, I. B., Shallcross, A., . . . Keltner, D. (2014). Vagal activity is quadratically related to prosocial traits, prosocial emotions, and observer perceptions of prosociality. *Journal of Personality and Social Psychology*, *107*, 1051–1063. doi: 10.1037/a0037509

Leaviss, J., & Uttley, L. (2015). Psychotherapeutic benefits of compassion-focused therapy: An early systematic review. *Psychological Medicine*, *45*, 927–945. doi: 10.1017/S0033291714002141

López, A., Sanderman, R., Smink, A., Zhang, Y., van Sonderen, E., Ranchor, A., & Schroevers, M. J. (2015). A reconsideration of the self-compassion scale's total score: Self-compassion versus Self-criticism. *PLOS ONE*, *10*(7): e0132940. doi:10.1371/journal.pone.0132940

McEwan, K., Gilbert, P., Dandeneau, S., Lipka, S., Maratos, F., Paterson, K. B., & Baldwin, M. (2014). Facial expressions depicting compassionate and critical emotions: The development and validation of a new emotional face stimulus set. *PLOS ONE*, *9*(2), e88783.

Mayseless, O. (2016). *The Caring Motivation: An Integrated Theory*. Oxford: Oxford University Press.

Muris, P., & Petrocchi, N. (2016). Protection or Vulnerability? A Meta-Analysis of the relations between the positive and Negative Components of Self-Compassion and Psychopathology. *Clinical Psychology and Psychotherapy* (advanced online). doi: 10.1002/cpp.2005

Nassbaum, M. C. (2003). *Upheavals of Thought: The Intelligence of Emotions*. Cambridge: Cambridge University Press.

Neff, K. D. (2003). Self-compassion: An alternative conceptualization of a healthy attitude toward oneself. *Self and Identity*, *2*, 85–102.

Neff, K. D. (2011). *Self-compassion*. New York: Morrow.

Neff, K. D., & Germer, C. K. (2013). A pilot study and randomized controlled trial of the mindful self-compassion program. *Journal of Clinical Psychology*, *69*, 28–44. doi: 10.1002/jclp.21923

Neff, K. D., Whittakar, T., & Karl, A. (in press). Evaluating the factor structure of the Self-Compassion Scale in four distinct populations: Is the use of a total self-compassion score justified? *Journal of Personality Assessment*.

Oxford Dictionary (2016) http://www.oxforddictionaries.com/definition/english/compassion.

Penner, L. A., Dovidio, J. F., Piliavin, J. A., & Schroeder, D. A. (2005). Prosocial behavior: Multilevel perspectives. *Annual Review of Psychology*, *56*, 365–392. doi: 10.1146/annurev. psych.56.091103.070141

Preston., S. D. (2013). The origins of altruism in offspring care. *Psychological Bulletin*, *139*, 1305–41.

Ricard, M. (2015). *Altruism. The Power of Compassion to Change Itself and the World*. London: Atlantic Books.

Sensky, T. (2010). Suffering. *International Journal of Integrated Care*, *10*, 66–68, ISSN 1568-4156 – http://www.ijic.org/.

Simon-Thomas, E. R., Godzik, J., Castle, E., Antonenko, O., Ponz, A., Kogan, A., & Keltner, D. J. (2011). An fMRI study of caring vs self-focus during induced compassion and pride. *Social Cognitive and Affective Neuroscience*, *7*, 635–648. doi: 10.1093/ scan/nsr045

Singer, T., & Bolz, M. (Eds.) (2012). *Compassion: Bridging Practice and Science*. http:// www.compassion-training.org/

Slavich, G. M., & Cole, S. W. (2013). The emerging field of human social genomics. *Clinical Psychological Science*, *1*(3), 331–348. doi: 10.1177/2167702613478594

Strauss, C., Taylor, B. L., Gu, J., Kuyken, W., Baer, R., Jones, F., & Cavanagh, K. (2016). What is compassion and how can we measure it? A review of definitions and measures. *Clinical Psychology Review*, *47*, 15–27.

Tsering, G. T. (2005). *The Four Noble Truths: The Foundation of Buddhist Thought (Volume 1)*. Boston, MA: Wisdom Publications.

Weiner, B. (1992). *Human Motivation: Metaphors Theories and Research*. London: Sage.

Weng, H. Y., Fox, A. S., Shackman, A. J., Stodola, D. E., Caldwell, J. K., Olson, M.C., . . . Davidson, R. J. (2013). Compassion training alters altruism and neural responses to suffering. *Psychological Science*, *24*(7), 1171–1180. doi:10.1177/0956797612469537

Chapter 2

Prehistoric origins

The compassion of far distant strangers

Penny Spikins

Introduction

Our compassion has a long history. Archaeological evidence suggests that sustained care for those in need was part of daily life from the emergence of the very first early humans, over one and half million years ago. Though barely on the path to 'humanity' in biological terms, and physically and cognitively unlike us, such groups were nonetheless capable of something which feels quintessentially *human* on an emotional level – sustained care for those in need. In later species such as Neanderthals vulnerable individuals could be looked after for almost their whole lifetimes, apparently irrespective of circumstances. A whole range of injuries, from physical conditions leaving people unable to walk to brain injuries which will have affected cognitive abilities were accommodated. Moreover, wherever we find sizeable groups of individuals we also find some amongst them who must have been supported by the others. This extent of care challenges our preconceptions about survival in the distant past, seeming *costly* in functional terms. However, far from being a weakness, emotional commitments to others seem to have been the basis for the in-depth collaboration which was the basis for evolutionary success as well as being the starting point for those changes, such as brain expansion, that made us human. A human dependence on emotional commitments was not without its own costs – felt in terms of vulnerability to social emotions such as shame, anxieties over one's social value, and vigilance over social threats. However, these in turn drove motivations to help and alleviate emotional as well as physical suffering.

Ignoring the uncomfortable?

Evidence for care is found *earlier* in our evolutionary past than evidence for interpersonal violence and is *more widespread*. However, such evidence receives remarkably little acknowledgement or attention (Hublin, 2009; Spikins, 2015a; Spikins, Rutherford & Needham, 2010; Tilley, 2015). Clear signs of extended care for illness or vulnerability is even more or less ignored, at best a short sentence in any lengthy paper (Tilley, 2015). Why this should be so is difficult to understand – we might think we should be proud of a willingness to help others. The only explanation seems to be that care and compassion feel like a *weakness*. In our modern cultures the deep-seated concept that success, and by implication evolutionary success, lies with selfish competition makes both the vulnerability of our ancestors, and their willingness to care for others, a strangely disturbing concept, one which is challenging to who we think we are. It is only over the last few years that we have begun to even recognise the compassion of these distant strangers and believe that it matters, and yet it does (see Mikulincer & Shaver, Chapter 11, this volume; Narvaez, Chapter 10, this volume).

This narrative of our distant past can influence who we feel we are and what we believe in subtle ways. Past cruelty instils a certain fear, and makes us some-what more lacking in trust about others' intentions, whilst acts of kindness in the far distant past have a certain power to inspire, especially if they took place in conditions in which compassion might be hard to find. Moreover, the sup-posed behaviours of our distant ancestors have a surprising influence on modern behaviours and beliefs through what is described as 'natural'. Descriptions of a heartless past, in which humanity was forged through violent competition, fed into justifications for the elimination of the disabled, epileptic or mentally ill that was the start of the Holocaust, for example. Even now many believe that care for the vulnerable is something new to modern societies and that natural selection would, and moreover should, favour the independent, hard-hearted and tough. Evidence for compassion, and the range of complex human social emotions in the past challenged perceptions of our ancestors as hard-hearted and even callous.

Archaeological evidence can also provide important clues to understanding the challenges and constraints of our own emotional minds (Gilbert, Chapter 3, this volume). We share a remarkable evolved capacity for compassion, however this same capacity to care can also be lacking in resilience – influenced by attachment (Mikulincer & Shaver, this volume; Narvaez, this volume), and frequently lost when faced with out-groups or compassion fatigue (Vrtička, Favre & Singer, Chapter 8, this volume). Equally our emotions, the product of many different evolutionary pro-cesses, each often in conflict, bind us to each other, and are a source of great comfort, yet also cause us much distress. Evidence for the evolution of past behaviours and the motivations which underlie them can help make sense of the minds we are left with.

The prehistory of compassion

Early transformations

The archaeological record from as far back as one and half million years ago dem-onstrates emotional bonds and motivations to relieve suffering which were already different in nature from those seen in our nearest relatives, chimpanzees and bono-bos, and which formed part of the key transformations which made us human.

Two exceptionally early examples of care are particularly significant. The first is a homo ergaster female (KNM ER 1808), one of the most complete skeletons of the time period found at Kobi Fora in Kenya, and dating to around 1.6 million years ago. Indications on her long bones are consistent with a severe and fatal case of hypervitaminosis A, identified through an abnormal outer layer on the bones which will have taken weeks or even months to form (Figure 2.1). She will have been in extreme and immobilising pain, often losing consciousness, for this time, leading to the conclusion that even at this date those around her must have fed her, given her water and protected her from predators whilst she was ill (Tilley, 2015, p.15; Walker & Shipman, 1997; Walker, Zimmerman & Leakey, 1982;). The second is even earlier, at 1.8 million years ago and from Dmanisi in Georgia. Here an individual had lost all but one of their teeth (Figure 2.2), and survived for probably months in this condition as the surrounding bone had reabsorbed (Lordkipanidze et al., 2005). It has been argued that they too must have been looked after by others (Lordkipanidze et al., 2005; Tilley, 2015).

What is distinctive in these early populations is not compassion per se, as compassion and a capacity to nurture are not unique to humans. Chimpanzees and bonobos, sharing a common ancestor with humans around 6–8 million years ago, are capable of a certain compassion. Chimpanzees console each other after a fight, for example, and sometimes provide fleeting, momentary care or assistance (de Waal, 2008). However, altruism in primates is limited (Silk & House, 2011). Their willingness to engage in extended care is limited to infants, and support for their closest allies is limited to moments of help and consolation structured by

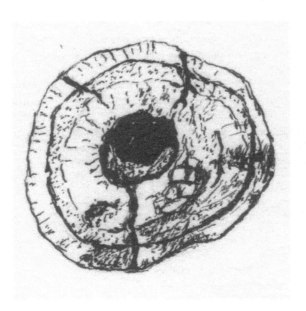

Figure 2.1 KNM-ER 1808 showing abnormal layer of bone on the femur.
Source: Author's own drawing.

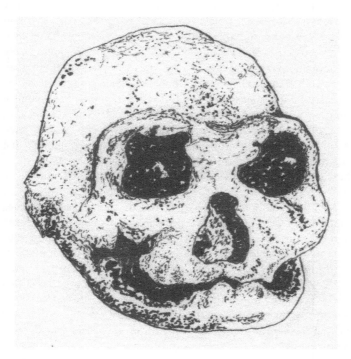

Figure 2.2 The 'toothless' Dmanisi hominin.
Source: Author's own drawing.

a reciprocal return of favours, albeit remembered over many months (Schino & Aureli, 2010). What is remarkable about examples of evidence for care in early humans is that care is *provided to adults*, and *for extended periods*.

These earliest cases of extended care coincide with other evidence for different and perhaps closer emotional bonds than we see in other species. Evidence for attention to individuals at death is also emerging by this time, for example. Pettitt has argued that the collection of 13 australopithecines at Hadar site AL-333 may be a case of deliberate deposition in a certain ritual location (Pettitt, 2013, p. 44). Moreover, the remains of potential contemporaneous individuals of Homo Naledi appear to represent some kind of mortuary location (Berger et al., 2015). Chimpanzees appear to grieve for the death of infants, with cases of mothers carrying around corpses for several weeks, but reactions to dead adults are fleeting, without the sense of a shared ritual we begin to see in human ancestors. Shared mortuary practice suggests the extent of grief felt at the passing of a loved one and perhaps even more significantly shared ritual practice implies shared feeling, and a shared drive to appease emotional suffering.

It seems to be no coincidence that at the same time as we see care for the ill or injured, and attention to the diseased, we also see evidence for extended 'care' in other ways. The most unusual is that of additional care and attention taken over stone tools. Artefacts created by early humans begin to mean more than merely functional items at around this time. Whilst earlier tools were merely functional, the appearance of handaxes show elements not only of aesthetics but also a certain generosity in making a tool pleasing to use, as well as emotional self-control in their production (Spikins, 2012); see Figure 2.3. Moreover, handaxes made of elephant bone ivory, a far less practical material than stone, have been interpreted as implying some kind of close connection to these highly empathetic animals that goes beyond seeing them as merely food (Zutovski & Barkai, 2015).

What drove these changes? From an evolutionary perspective there must have been distinct selection pressures.

The most obvious of the evolutionary pressures acting on human ancestors dates back at least 4 million years. Occupying more open ecological conditions exposed early human ancestors to unstable and unpredictable environments and numerous predators, and it is clear from the tell-tale marks on their bones that hominins were often prey. The first stages in the development of new ways of collaboration may thus have involved collaboratively defending themselves against predators, perhaps using tactics such as throwing stones as a group (Rose & Marshall, 1996). These abilities then opened up opportunities to scavenge meat from carcasses, and quite possibly to begin to share food, with evidence from the earliest stone tools use to cut meat appearing over 3 million years ago.

From these first collaborations, however, we see the development of strong selective pressures to be prosocial, and to collaborate in new, uniquely human ways. The context of early care lies within the timing of an important ecological transition occurring as early humans faced uniquely variable and unpredictable environments (Potts & Faith, 2015) as well as moving into a new niche of collaborative hunting (Domínguez-Rodrigo et al., 2014), actively competing with large predators. Social collaboration solved the problems that these challenges posed by allowing them to buffer risks through hunting, finding food and caring for infants *collaboratively*. Despite the challenges this is a time when the length of dependency of offspring increases, brain sizes increase and body shapes become larger.

To a great extent early human collaboration must have depended on evolving emotional capacities. Collaborative hunting, food sharing and shared parenting demanded an ability not only to invest in another's well-being above one's own, but also necessitated self control (and tolerance to emotional distress) to risk one's well-being when facing predators or dangerous prey on behalf of others, or in forgoing immediate gratification in saving and sharing food. These new emotional capacities and commitments transformed human society (Nesse, 2001), changing a group of individuals into a 'unique and highly competitive predatory organism' (Whiten & Erdal, 2012, p. 2119).

Figure 2.3 Olduvai handaxe, Lower Palaeolithic, about 1.2 million years old, Olduvai Gorge, Tanzania.

Source: Wikimedia Commons.

The role of social reputation

It isn't difficult to see how any individual benefits from being part of a highly cohesive collaborative group. However, *how* new emotional capacities evolved is a different issue. How would people *become* motivated to give up time or energy, or take risks for others? Why not avoid potentially life-threatening confrontations with predators or prey, or keep food to oneself? Most particularly why care about people too ill to ever repay one's care, or even the dead or even objects? Motivations to be concerned about the treatment of the dead, to identify with objects (take for example tendencies to infer motivations and feelings to moving shapes (Heider & Simmel, 1944)), are part of our complex human emotional minds, yet hardly seem to make sense in functional terms.

There is, of course, much debate. However, the material record provides a key explanation regarding the significance of tangible signals of *social or moral reputation* to early human selective success.

A positive social reputation plays a noticeable, if minor, role in the social dynamics of our nearest relatives. Chimpanzees don't need to collaborate to survive, nonetheless their understanding of fairness, and complex social dynamics based on remembered favours means that it *sometimes* pays in chimpanzee society to put others first. Even though chimpanzees mostly compete with those alpha males who intervene to break up conflicts and behave 'fairly' will stay dominant for longer. Overly aggressive, dominant males have even been known to be excluded by combined action of the other group members (Flack & De Waal, 2000). Our common ancestor with chimpanzees, living around 6–8 million years ago, is likely to have shared important cognitive and moral capacities to remember behaviours and make moral judgements of others.

Where collaboration *is key to survival* selection pressures change. Rather than the most powerful, it is the *best collaborators* who are selected as allies and mates, willingly helped and trusted to help out in turn, and whose genes are most likely to be passed on. Judgements of how likeable (Gilbert, 2015) or how trustworthy any individuals are to act in the interests of others (Nesse, 2001) become the major currency of selection. Selection pressures on the best collaborators are however much more complex than pressures on physical abilities. Where it may be easy to judge who is the strongest or most powerful (or for this to be evident through physical conflicts), judging who is the best collaborator is complex. It is not behaviour per se, but *motivations*, which are at stake. After all a shrewd and self-orientated individual might pretend to care deeply about the well-being of their ally or mate, and so elicit their support when they need it by *behaving* altruistically, but in reality be prepared to abandon them (as do chimpanzees) if they are no longer convenient. Detecting a genuine sensitivity to prosocial emotions is essential to the evolution of altruism and compassion, and in turn judgments of moral reputation need to use all the clues available and are built over many observations. Detecting and punishing cheats is also critically important, however doing so is cognitively demanding – if we see someone punishing someone else how do we know if there are being aggressive, or punishing an offender? Both making reliable signals of one's genuine motivations and trustworthy nature *and* being vigilant to such signals in others become all important (Hoffman, Yoeli & Nowak, 2015; Nowak & Sigmund, 2005).

Selection pressures genuinely emotionally motivated by the well-being of others can be seen operating amongst hunter-gatherers in modern contexts today. Amongst the Ache of Paraguay, for example, those who are judged to be most genuinely generous are looked after more willingly and extensively when ill or elderly (Gurven et al., 2000). Even adult males, the least dependent element of society, depend on this support, with hunters spending a third of their time too ill or injured to hunt. Amongst the Martu, those who are most generous are favoured as partners in collaborative hunts, and Bliege Bird and Power comment that 'prosocial generosity produces benefits indirectly, through the formation of trusting, cooperative partnerships' (Bliege Bird & Power, 2015, p. 389). Experiments show that equally in modern societies a reputation for caring about group well-being can have similar payoffs (Hardy & Van Vugt, 2006).

The importance of a good social or moral reputation may have driven much of human emotional and cognitive transformations. First, the complexities of making judgements of motivations prompted pressures on brain expansion and social understanding (Nowak & Sigmund, 2005). Second, we evolved to feel and signal our motivations in many different ways. Caring for the vulnerable is one way of displaying one's emotional credentials as a trustworthy ally, i.e. one that is both motivated to help others in need, and has the emotional self control to do so. However, the same capacities can also be signalled in other ways, such as how we treat the bodies of the dead or even objects, as well as through evolved physical signs such as blushing or crying. Our material world even plays a role – a finely made handaxe or other aesthetically pleasing object demonstrates a certain skill (i.e. social value), generosity and self-control in its production which has a repeated effect, with each use reminding others of the qualities of its maker. Lastly, we become highly sensitive to small signals of genuine intent, vigilant to tiny facial expressions which might indicate genuine emotions, alert to how ways in which people express themselves might indicate that they are *on our side*, and equally vigilant to what they think about us. As consciousness allows us to reflect upon ourselves, and collaborative morality (Tomasello & Vaish, 2013) brings selection pressures from combined group opinion, vigilance of our *social value* becomes ever prominent.

Group support for the vulnerable

Through time, failing to be moved by the needs of others or unwilling to help them is likely to have been increasingly damaging to one's moral reputation, against which the economic costs of assistance will have been a minor consideration. With mortuary practices involving larger collections of individuals appear after half a million years ago, we tend to find a variety of debilitating conditions which must have been supported not only by individual allies but by the shared moral imperative of the group as a whole.

The earliest example comes from the site of Sima de los Huesos in northern Spain dating to around 400,000 years ago. Here at least 28 individuals, closely related to *Homo heidelbergensis*, were deposited in a natural cavity as some form of mortuary ritual. Several of these suffered from conditions which will have required support. One elderly man had a damaged pelvis and would only have been able to walk slowly and with a stick (Bonmatí et al., 2011). One individual has ear hyperostosis that probably caused deafness, and another a severe dental abscess (Pérez et al., 1997). A child mostly likely aged between five and eight years old at death suffered from craniosyntosis (Gracia et al., 2009).

A similar range of vulnerabilities amongst Neanderthals is found at the later site of Shanidar Cave in Iraq. Here ten individuals were buried within a cave between 60,000 and 45,000 years ago. Of these the most famous is an old man, aged around 35–45 years old, who had multiple pathologies which appeared to have occurred in childhood and made any mobility very difficult. These included damage to his left eye and probable blindness (as well as damage to the left cerebral cortex), right arm paralysis, fractures of right humerus, osteomyelitis of the right clavicle, fracture to the right foot and degenerative joint disease of the right knee and ankle (Solecki, 1971; Tilley, 2015, p.16; Trinkaus & Zimmerman, 1982). His care must have involved the whole group, over at least a decade. Another male, aged 35–50, suffered from severe osteoarthritis of the right foot, which is also likely to have much limited his mobility. He also survived injury to his left lung which must have involved having been immobilised for several weeks (Tilley, 2015, p. 16).

Far from being unusual, care for illness and injury is so common that many authors conclude that amongst Neanderthals those who were vulnerable must have been routinely cared for (Hublin, 2009; Solecki, 1971; Spikins, 2015a; Spikins et al., 2010); see Tilley (2015) for a detailed review. Other cases include that of an adult woman from Salé, in Morocco with congenital torticollis from birth, leading to cranial distortion and muscular trauma, as well possible limitations on limb movement, hip displacement and club foot (Hublin, 2009); that of a man from La Chapelle aux Saints in France with significant disability relating to degenerative joint disease in the back, shoulder, hip and foot (Tilley, 2015); and also an individual from La Ferrassie who recovered from a severe leg fracture, as well as being cared for for a substantial time whilst suffering from a severe systemic disease, most likely a pulmonary infection (Tilley, 2015). Such care can never have been easy, with skeletal records showing frequent famines as well as demanding lifestyles, yet most remains of Neanderthals show signs of healed pathologies.

Evidence for shared care continues to be found in ice-age Europe after the arrival of our own species. Cases include those such as a man with dwarfism from Romito in Italy (Frayer et al., 1987; Tilley, 2015), and an individual from Dolni Vestonice in the Czech Republic with chrondrodysplasia calcificans punctata, causing severe developmental abnormalities (Trinkaus et al., 2001).

Responses to mental and emotional suffering

Part and parcel of the way that emotions evolve to foster collaboration is a certain sensitivity, even a *vulnerability*, to our social emotions, alongside a greater vigilance of others, and greater anxieties over what individuals and the whole group feel about us or perceive our social value to be (see Gilbert, 2015 regarding Old Brain and New Brain mentalities). In consequence mental and emotional suffering, and a drive to alleviate it, seems to also have been part of the human condition as much as were physical stresses and caring responses.

Emotional suffering and mental disorder is, of course, harder to identify archaeologically than physical illnesses and injuries. Nonetheless we can identify an early willingness to accommodate those who were cognitively different, and who struggled with that difference. Cognitive disabilities were likely to be part of the symptoms of the 450,000bp child with craniosyntosis found at Atapuerca (Gracia et al., 2009). Equally a 90–100,000bp child found at Quafzeh, who had suffered a traumatic brain injury leading to reduced brain volume also probably suffered neurological problems (Coqueugniot et al., 2014). Both were clearly cared for. Difference can at times even confer a certain status. A woman, likely to have suffered epilepsy due to a malformation at the base of her skull received a rare elaborate burial in Mesolithic Germany, and has been interpreted as a shaman (Porr & Alt, 2006). Equally the ethnographic record highlights that modern hunter-gatherers tend to be very accommodating of difference or emotional distress. Whitley describes how those with bipolar disorder and other conditions, particularly those suffering from terrifying hallucinations, tend to take on roles as shaman in hunter-gatherer societies for example (Whitley, 2009). The unique talents of those with autism can be also be appreciated and socially valued, compensating for any lack of social understanding (Spikins, 2009).

Sometimes we can identify particular practices designed to alleviate emotional and mental suffering. An increasing attention to shared mortuary practices from interments in natural pits or crevices to burials themselves seems to be a response to a need to validate or alleviate feelings of grief through shared expressions (Pettitt, 2013). We can however also see the emergence of specific treatments which appear to be a response to severe mental or emotional distress. Practices such as trepanation are recorded from 12,000bp. Given how widespread trepanation is in later prehistory (found in between 2–8% of individuals in some regions of Neolithic Europe (Robb, 2002)), this seems likely to be not only a response to physical ailments of the brain (such as hydrocephaly) but also an attempt to treat other kinds of mental suffering or disorder. Tilley speculates that trepanation involves a great deal of trust between the surgeon and the individual being treated (Tilley, 2015, p. 34).

When written texts appear we see recorded descriptions of mental suffering and attempts to find ways to alleviate such suffering. Whilst the Babylonians lacked full understanding of the neurological basis of disorders, they constructed a careful study of symptoms and attempted to classify and treat mental disorders. Treatments for depression, involving creating an image made of clay, imagining it as themselves and wishing themselves happiness are even evocative of compassion-focused imagery exercises (Reynolds & Wilson, 2013, pp. 478–9). Barre discusses symptoms of depression in the third century AD in the Far East

(Barre, 2001), Kruger describes depression in the Hebrew Bible (Kruger, 2005) and Greaves discusses post-natal depression in Ancient Greece (Greaves, 2009).

That being cared for, and responding to emotional, mental and physical suffering, has been part of the human condition since the earliest remotely 'human' species explains why these responses are so integral to our neurological make-up. Far from an impediment to efficiency, widespread collaborative care is part of survival – only through a visible willingness to care *come what may* would the emotional context be created which prompted uniquely human collaboration.

Complex emotional minds

We can see in the archaeological record a trajectory of increasing *motivations to care* for and support other group members, and also to unconsciously display one's emotional credentials in different ways. However, beyond this general direction of change many cognitive-emotional transformations which have taken place are more challenging to fully understand.

Trust of others' emotional commitments is complex (Nesse, 2001). We may *trust* those who are *compassionate to the vulnerable* to have our interests and those of the whole group at heart. However, trust is also placed in individuals who *punish* those who appear to be dominators or cheats, risk their lives to *kill prey* to provide food, and even to be willing to take risks to *defend us against outsiders*. Relationships based on emotional commitments thus create complex conflicting motivations and have a darker side. Potential conflict between being compassionate to the vulnerable and protecting one's loved ones when faced with outsiders may explain why tolerance towards out-groups appears very late in human evolution.

It is only after around 100,000 years ago, beginning in Africa, and in broad association with the emergence of Homo sapiens that we see good evidence for sustained inter-group collaboration. Raw materials are more regularly sourced from what must have been well outside the usual ranges of groups, and non-functional items, such as shell beads like those found in north Africa over 80,000 years (Bouzouggar et al., 2007), are created and moved around in what seem to be large scale networks of gift-giving. Similar networks are seen in modern hunter-gatherers such as the Jo-huansi, and play a key role in survival through providing distant friends in times of need. Wiessner notes for example that in a time of food shortages following high winds and destruction of the mongongo nuts in /Xai/xai, half of the population moved in with distant exchange partners, and would not have survived if this social support was not possible (Wiessner, 2002). Collaborations between groups make modern human populations more resilient to fluctuations in resources than archaics. At the same time human populations disperse, rapidly occupying the whole globe, where previous species stayed within familiar ecological contexts (Spikins, 2015b).

Transformations since 100,000 years ago clearly reflect significant changes in social relationships. An increasing social tolerance, perhaps influenced by neurological changes, may be part of developments. However other changes in emotional capacities must also be playing a role in allowing large scale networks to emerge. Gift giving suggests an emphasis on complex emotional responses, depending on a high level of theory of mind ability, such as gratitude. Equally there may have been changes in emotional and cognitive responses to objects, with gifts perhaps increasingly sparking social memories, provoking affiliative hormones and representing others *as if they were there*. The association of a new level of collaboration with risky dispersals argues that the darker side of human emotions, with intents to harm those who fail to honour commitments, comes into play (Spikins, 2015b). It is equally clear that cultural changes may be playing an important role. Certainly the widespread 'demand sharing' (giving to any who are in need), egalitarianism and extraordinary willingness to support others at their own costs seen in modern small-scale hunter-gatherers is not merely a product of biology, but hard won through constant efforts to constrain ranked based mentalities and dominance (Boehm, 2012; Boehm et al., 1993). In contrast to in-group care and support we can almost see capacities to feel compassion for out-groups in an evolutionary sense as *only just evolving*.

The trajectory of the evolution of human social emotions has been complex in other ways besides. While it is tempting to see evolution as a simple progression towards ourselves, reality was evidently more complicated. It is clear that there is no *single human mind* but rather our genes code for *possible minds* depending on context. Sensitivity to social environments, for example, gives our minds a certain plasticity which seems to have been part of human success. By dropping back on self-orientated strategies individuals in emotionally harsh environments pay the psychological costs of a competitive mentality (Gilbert, 2005, 2015) but avoid being exploited and are more likely to survive. We can see this in the archaeological and ethnographic record: there are times and places where, despite whatever cultural controls discourage ranked mentalities, competition and violence rise to the fore (Spikins, 2008). Warfare is extremely rare in forager societies (Fry & Söderberg, 2013) and conflicts usually lead to movement rather than violence (Lee, 2014); however, sometimes changing environments or other causes lead to cultures of competition and aggression (Spikins, 2015a).

Furthermore, whilst we look back on the past and create a narrative of progression, there has never been *a set direction* along which compassionate responses evolved. Far from the pinnacle of evolution, we are, like other human species, an evolutionary experiment – a compromise between conflicting pressures which will have led in different directions in the past (and might equally in the future). Much as different primates show subtly different types of altruistic motivations (Silk & House, 2011) the compassionate response of our branching set of distant ancestors will have varied. Spikins, Rutherford and Needham (2010) argue, for example, that the highly internally supportive contexts of Neanderthals reflect a much more internally focused compassion. Our capacity for cruelty and inability to care for the environment calls into question in what sense we, as a species, can really be seen as *better* than alternatives. The more material evidence improves our understanding of how human compassion evolved, the more questions we raise.

Conclusions

We think of our ancestors as strong and invulnerable. However, the material record illustrates that they were vulnerable to injury, illness, famine and even emotional distress. Rather than independence it was a uniquely human emotional *interdependence*, based on compassionate responses and emotional commitments to each other, which was part of human evolutionary success. Widespread emotional commitments set in place transformations which included a widening of compassionate responses and increasingly complex social understanding as well as a greater *vulnerability* to our emotional motivations and greater vigilance of subtle signals of emotional competencies, expressed everywhere from personal interactions to treatment of objects. To be motivated to care for others, to respond to being cared for and to be somewhat anxious about one's social value made us human.

Whilst we are able to consider in analytical terms the large-scale evolutionary processes underlying the emergence of human compassion, our human capacities also allow us to reflect that the material evidence for the widespread willingness to care for others, despite the cost, in our far distant past, is nothing short of awe-inspiring.

References

Barre, M. L., 2001. 'Wandering about' as a topos of depression in ancient Near Eastern literature and in the Bible. *Journal of Near Eastern Studies*, 60(3), 177–187.

Berger, L. R. et al., 2015. Homo naledi, a new species of the genus Homo from the Dinaledi Chamber, South Africa. *eLife*, 4. Available online at: http://dx.doi.org/10.7554/eLife.09560

Bliege Bird, R., & Power, E. A., 2015. Prosocial signaling and cooperation among Martu hunters. *Evolution and Human Behavior*, 36(5), 389–397.

Boehm, C., 2012. *Moral Origins: The Evolution of Virtue, Altruism, and Shame*. New York: Basic Books.

Boehm, C. et al., 1993. Egalitarian behavior and reverse dominance hierarchy [and comments and reply]. *Current Anthropology*, 34(3), 227–254.

Bonmatí, A. et al., 2011. El caso de Elvis el viejo de la Sima de los Huesos. *Dendra médica. Revista de humanidades*, 10(2), 138–146.

Bouzouggar, A. et al., 2007. 82,000-year-old shell beads from North Africa and implications for the origins of modern human behavior. *Proceedings of the National Academy of Sciences of the United States of America*, 104(24), 9964–9969.

Coqueugniot, H. et al., 2014. Earliest cranio-encephalic trauma from the Levantine Middle Palaeolithic: 3D reappraisal of the Qafzeh 11 skull, consequences of pediatric brain damage on individual life condition and social care. *PLOS ONE*, 9(7), p.e102822.

Domínguez-Rodrigo, M. et al., 2014. On meat eating and human evolution: A taphonomic analysis of BK4b (Upper Bed II, Olduvai Gorge, Tanzania), and its bearing on hominin megafaunal consumption. *Quaternary International: The Journal of the International Union for Quaternary Research*, 322: 129–152.

Flack, J. C., & De Waal, F. B. M., 2000. 'Any animal whatever.' Darwinian building blocks of morality in monkeys and apes. *Journal of Consciousness Studies*, 7(1–2), 1–29.

Frayer, D. W. et al., 1987. Dwarfism in an adolescent from the Italian late Upper Palaeolithic. *Nature*, 330(6143), 60–62.

Fry, D. P., & Söderberg, P., 2013. Lethal aggression in mobile forager bands and implications for the origins of war. *Science*, 341(6143), 270–273.

Gilbert, P., 2005. Compassion and cruelty: A biopyschosocial approach. In P. Gilbert (Ed.) *Compassion: Conceptualisations, Research and Use in Pyschotherapy*. London: Routledge, pp. 9–74.

Gilbert, P., 2015. The evolution and social dynamics of compassion. *Social and Personality Psychology Compass*, 9(6), 239–254.

Gracia, A. et al., 2009. Craniosynostosis in the Middle Pleistocene human Cranium 14 from the Sima de los Huesos, Atapuerca, Spain. *Proceedings of the National Academy of Sciences of the United States of America*, 106(16), 6573–6578.

Greaves, A., 2009. Postnatal depression in Ancient Greece. *Midwives: Official Journal of the Royal College of Midwives*, 12(2), 40–41.

Gurven, M. et al., 2000. 'It's a wonderful life': Signaling generosity among the Ache of Paraguay. *Evolution and Human Behavior: Official Journal of the Human Behavior and Evolution Society*, 21(4), 263–282.

Hardy, C. L., & Van Vugt, M., 2006. Nice guys finish first: The competitive altruism hypothesis. *Personality & Social Psychology Bulletin*, 32(10), 1402–1413.

Heider, F., & Simmel, M., 1944. An experimental study of apparent behavior. *The American Journal of Psychology*, 57(2), 243–259.

Hoffman, M., Yoeli, E. & Nowak, M.A., 2015. Cooperate without looking: Why we care what people think and not just what they do. *Proceedings of the National Academy of Sciences of the United States of America*, 112(6), 1727–1732.

Hublin, J.-J., 2009. The prehistory of compassion. *Proceedings of the National Academy of Sciences of the United States of America*, 106(16), 6429–6430.

Kruger, P. A., 2005. Depression in the Hebrew Bible: An update. *Journal of Near Eastern Studies*, 64(3), 187–192.

Lee, R. B., 2014. Hunter-gatherers on the best-seller list: Steven Pinker and the 'Bellicose School's' treatment of forager violence. *Journal of Aggression, Conflict and Peace Research*, 6(4), 216–228.

Lordkipanidze, D. et al., 2005. Anthropology: The earliest toothless hominin skull. *Nature*, 434(7034), 717–718.

Nesse, R. M., 2001. Natural selection and the capacity for subjective commitment. In R. M. Nesse (Ed.) *Evolution and the Capacity for Commitment*. New York: Russell Sage Press, pp. 1–44.

Nowak, M. A., & Sigmund, K., 2005. Evolution of indirect reciprocity. *Nature*, 437(7063), 1291–1298.

Pérez, P. J. et al., 1997. Paleopathological evidence of the cranial remains from the Sima de los Huesos Middle Pleistocene site (Sierra de Atapuerca, Spain). Description and preliminary inferences. *Journal of Human Evolution*, 33(2–3), 409–421.

Pettitt, P., 2013. *The Palaeolithic Origins of Human Burial*. London: Routledge.

Porr, M., & Alt, K. W., 2006. The burial of Bad Dürrenberg, central Germany: Osteopathology and osteoarchaeology of a Late Mesolithic shaman's grave. *International Journal of Osteoarchaeology*, 16(5), 395–406.

Potts, R., & Faith, J. T., 2015. Alternating high and low climate variability: The context of natural selection and speciation in Plio-Pleistocene hominin evolution. *Journal of Human Evolution*, 87, 5–20.

Reynolds, E. H., & Wilson, J. V. K., 2013. Depression and anxiety in Babylon. *Journal of the Royal Society of Medicine*, 106(12), 478–481.

Robb, J., 2002. Time and Biography. In Hamilakis, Y., Pluciennik, M., & Tarlow, S. (Eds.) *Thinking Through the Body*. New York: Springer, pp. 153–171.

Rose, L., & Marshall, F., 1996. Meat eating, hominid sociality, and home bases revisited. *Current Anthropology*, 37(2), 307–338.

Schino, G., & Aureli, F., 2010. Primate reciprocity and its cognitive requirements. *Evolutionary Anthropology*, 19(4), 130–135.

Silk, J. B., & House, B. R., 2011. Evolutionary foundations of human prosocial sentiments. *Proceedings of the National Academy of Sciences of the United States of America*, 108 Suppl 2, pp. 10910–10917.

Solecki, R. S., 1971. *Shanidar, the First Flower People*. New York: Knopf.

Spikins, P., 2008. The bashful and the boastful. *Journal of World Prehistory*, 21(3–4), 173–193.

Spikins, P., 2009. Autism, the integrations of 'difference'and the origins of modern human behaviour. *Cambridge Archaeological Journal*, 19(02), 179–201.

Spikins, P., 2012. Goodwill hunting? Debates over the 'meaning' of lower Palaeolithic handaxe form revisited. *World Archaeology*, 44(3), 378–392.

Spikins, P., 2015a. *How Compassion Made Us Human: The Evolutionary Origins of Tenderness, Trust and Morality*. Barnsley, UK: Pen and Sword.

Spikins, P., 2015b. The geography of trust and betrayal: Moral disputes and Late Pleistocene dispersal. *Open Quaternary*, 1(1). Available online at: http://www.openquaternary.com/articles/10.5334/oq.ai/print/

Spikins, P., Rutherford, H., & Needham, A., 2010. From homininity to humanity: Compassion from the earliest archaics to modern humans. *Time and Mind*, 3(3), 303–325.

Spikins, P. et al., 2014. The cradle of thought: Growth, learning, play and attachment in Neanderthal children. *Oxford Journal of Archaeology*, 33(2), 111–134.

Tilley, L., 2015. *Theory and Practice in the Bioarchaeology of Care*. New York: Springer.

Tomasello, M., & Vaish, A., 2013. Origins of human cooperation and morality. *Annual Review of Psychology*, 64, 231–255.

Trinkaus, E. & Zimmerman, M. R., 1982. Trauma among the Shanidar Neandertals. *American Journal of Physical Anthropology*, 57(1), 61–76.

Trinkaus, E. et al., 2001. Dolní Věstonice 15: Pathology and persistence in the Pavlovian. *Journal of Archaeological Science*, 28(12), 1291–1308.

de Waal, F. B. M., 2008. Putting the altruism back into altruism: The evolution of empathy. *Annual Review of Psychology*, 59, 279–300.

Walker, A., & Shipman, P., 1997. *The Wisdom of the Bones: In Search of Human Origins*, New York: Vintage.

Walker, A., Zimmerman, M. R., & Leakey, R. E., 1982. A possible case of hypervitaminosis A in Homo erectus. *Nature*, 296(5854), 248–250.

Whiten, A., & Erdal, D., 2012. The human socio-cognitive niche and its evolutionary origins. *Philosophical Transactions of the Royal Society of London. Series B, Biological Sciences*, 367(1599), 2119–2129.

Whitley, D. S., 2009. *Cave Paintings and the Human Spirit: The Origin of Creativity and Belief*. New York: Prometheus Books.

Wiessner, P., 2002. Taking the risk out of risky transactions: A forager's dilemma. In Salter, F. (Ed.) *Risky Transactions: Trust, Kinship, and Ethnicity*. New York: Berghahn Books, pp. 21–43.

Zutovski, K., & Barkai, R., 2015. The use of elephant bones for making Acheulian handaxes: A fresh look at old bones. *Quaternary International*, 406, 227–238.

Chapter 3

Compassion as a social mentality
An evolutionary approach

Paul Gilbert

Introduction: from caring to compassion – the emergence of the social intelligences

My interest in compassion has been both personal and professional: as a clinician, I try to understand the core ingredients for compassion training as an antidote to some of the traumas, shames, hatreds, terrors, depressions and loneliness people suffer (Gilbert, 1989/2016, 2009, 2010; Gilbert & Choden, 2013). It is rooted in an evolution context that highlights the importance of (evolved) motivations. Motivations and intentions are crucial because people may behave in helpful ways for all kinds of reasons (Böckler, Tusche & Singer, 2016; Catarino, Gilbert, McEwan & Baião, 2014); although many of our are not always conscious to us (Huang & Bargh, 2014). We know too that intention is not enough for compassion because a lack of wisdom or skill can result in negative outcomes; the road to hell is paved with good intentions as they say.

As outlined in Chapter 1, compassion can be seen as an evolved motive, desire and intention to address suffering in self and others, hence giving the definition of 'a sensitivity to suffering in self and others with a commitment to try to alleviate and prevent it'. Although other animals certainly respond to distress, and express caring behaviours, we probably would not use the term 'compassion' to describe them. As noted elsewhere (Gilbert, 1989/2016, 2005a, 2005b, 2009) motives for caring evolved into capacities for compassion with the evolution of profound changes in social cognition and social intelligence during human evolution (Dunbar, 2007; Geary & Huffman, 2002; Gilbert, 2000, 2005a; Hrdy, 2011; Malle & Hodges, 2005; Suddendorf & Whitten, 2001). Consideration of the interaction, co-ordination and regulation between older brain motives and emotions with new brain competencies is central to understanding human morality (Krebs, 2008), compassion (Gilbert, 1989/2016, 2005a, 2009; Goetz, Keltner & Simon-Thomas, 2010) and indeed most human activities including culture, science and of course, prosocial behaviour (Hrdy, 2011; Jensen, Vaish & Schmidt, 2014). Thus human compassion extends to: an openness to the reality of suffering all around us and in the nature of biological life itself; an empathic awareness of suffering; a readiness to meet needs with a desire to work to prevent suffering;

a desire to acquire wisdom to do so and a desire not to be a cause of suffering. Many sub-motives are therefore embedded in the 'compassion motive'. Indeed, in the tradition of Bodhicitta, compassion is central to all actions and as lived in the eight-fold pathway and various paramitas (Gilbert, 2009). Compassion and altruism therefore infuse ethics and morality (Music, 2014). As the Buddha is reported to have said, 'What is the one thing, which when you possess, you have all the virtues? It's compassion' (Jinpa, 2015). So Bodhicitta intention is to see into the causes of suffering in order to work to release self and others from suffering. Geshe Tashi Tsering (2005) speaks about the meaning of *Bodhicitta* in the following way:

> *Bodhicitta* is the essence of all of Buddhist practise. The word *bodhicitta* itself explains so much: bodhi is Sanskrit for "awake," or "awakening" and *chitta* for "mind." As enlightenment is the state of being fully awakened, the precious mind of bodhicitta is the mind that is starting to become completely awakened in order to benefit all other beings. *There are two aspects to this mind: the aspiration to benefit others and the wish to obtain complete enlightenment in order to do that most skilfully.*
>
> (p. 1; italics added)

These *motives* and *intentions* are the focus for all practices, from mindfulness to actions. However as the Dalai Lama argues, enlightenment also comes from 'intention guided by wisdom' and science is a source of wisdom that reveals much about the brain nature has made for us and how compassion influences its patterns of activations.

Compassion and the emergence of human social intelligence

While we share many motivations with other animals, rooted in reproduction and survival strategies, such as harm avoidance, food seeking, sexual and reproduction, status seeking and care of offspring, the last 2 million years brought major evolutionary advances in a range of cognitive and self-aware abilities and competencies that now influence and regulate these motives: we are the 'thinking ape' (Byrne, 1995; Dunbar, 2007; Malle & Hodges, 2005). One always has to be extremely cautious in trying to draw clear distinctions between the competencies of one species and another and indeed many of the seeds of our social intelligences preexist human evolution. So the comparative arguments are less important than what actually operates for humans. The fact is though we have, for example, evolved capacities for *knowing awareness and deliberation*. We are 'aware that we are aware' with a 'conscious of consciousness'. Within limits (Huang & Bargh, 2014), humans have some awareness to not only 'feel', but 'know that they feel and often what they feel', not only to act 'but know what they are doing and why they are doing it': acting with *intentions*, in a way that no other animal probably can. For example, Goodall (1990) says of cruelty:

[A]lthough the basic aggressive patterns of the chimpanzee are remarkably similar to some of our own, their comprehension of the suffering they inflict on their victims is very different to ours. Chimpanzees, it is true are able to empathise, to understand at least to some extent the wants and needs of their companions. But only humans, I believe are capable of *deliberate* cruelty – acting with the intention of causing pain and suffering.

(p. 92)

This profoundly important *knowing awareness* enables a whole range of competencies, including mindfulness (Germer & Barnhofer, Chapter 4, this volume) and inner reflective competencies that facilitate new forms of planned, reasoned and deliberate thinking and action. Researchers have drawn a distinction between mindfulness, which is 'being aware on purpose' a deliberate focusing of attention, as neutral observation, versus our metacognition (mindful of our reactions) of what arises, and also how we choose to work with what arises (Goodall, Trejnowska & Darling, 2012). These in turn are linked to a basic sense of social security arising from caring, compassionate attachments (Goodall et al., 2012; Mikulincer & Shaver, Chapter 11, this volume; Siegel, 2011).

We have capabilities for languages and symbol use, which created profound new mechanisms for cognition and reasoning (Dunbar, 2007). Indeed, some theorists think that learnt symbol systems of communication profoundly influenced not only what we think but how we think (Fletcher & Hayes, 2005). This could only evolve in a species that had high motivation for interpersonal connectedness, communication, sharing and relating (Spikins, Chapter 2, this volume).

We have capacities for metacognition, the ability to think about thinking; and meta feeling, the ability to make a judgment about feeling and have feelings about feeling (we can be anxious by feeling angry or angry by feeling depressed). Although empathy and mind reading exist in simpler forms in other animals, we have capacities for a very different level of empathy, theory of mind and mentalisation (Jensen et al., 2014; Malle & Hodges, 2005: Whitten, 1999). Siegel (2011) calls it 'Mindsight' and highlights the enormous importance of affiliative and compassionate caring, especially in early life, for its development. We also have profound abilities for intersubjectivity, the ability to share perspectives, so that, for example, when a parent points to something, the child understands that they need to look to where the finger is pointing, not at the finger (Hrdy, 2011; Malle & Hodges, 2005; Trevarthan & Aitken, 2001). Intersubjectivity (different to empathy) is a core competency in relating to other minds, creating a sharing of experience and awareness, and it too is a competency that develops through childhood, especially compassionate ones (Cortina & Liotti, 2010; Malle & Hodges, 2005). Whitten (1999) argues that: 'Reading others' minds makes minds deeply social in that those minds interpenetrate each other.' (p. 177).

All these and other competencies have a profound effect on our capacities to have a sense of self and sense of a personal identity, a 'me-ness', as well as a 'we-ness', each of which are crucial in how motivations are recruited and played out in social relationships. Sedikides and Skowronski (1997) explored some of the possible origins and earlier precursors for a capacity to symbolise 'a self'. They point to three types of 'self': subjective, objective and symbolic. Symbolic self–other awareness is the ability to imagine the self (or other) as an object and to judge and give value to the self and other, to have self-esteem, pride or shame, or allocate positive or negative values to others (good and able, or worthless and useless). Central here too is self–other differentiation and understanding the minds of others (Malle & Hodges, 2005). For example, when we empathically connect to the suffering and needs of another we recognise them as in the other and not the self (Singer & Limecki, 2014), that self and other are different (Malle & Hodges, 2005; Nickerson, 1999). We also have competencies for (deliberately using) *imagination*, (imagining what it would be like to be, or 'to feel as' another person – central to Rogerian centered therapies). Imagination also enables us to play out different scenarios in our minds and imagine 'what would happen if . . . '. Indeed 'human play' provides important contexts for learning and practicing social behaviours – including prosocial ones. We can imagine consequences before we act, which offers huge evolved advantages. And we can imagine forms of thinking like, 'I think that Sally thinks that James thinks that Jim thinks. . .' (Suddendorf & Whitten, 2001).

These competencies support meaning-making and meaning-seeking; indeed, as argued elsewhere, we are a '*meaning-making and meaning-seeking species*', and that in itself is a complex issue that textures motives (Fletcher & Hayes, 2005; Gilbert, 1989/2016, 2005a; Yalom, 1980). Motives are core to meaning making (Neel et al., 2016). For example, we can put caring motives, and a desire to make a helpful difference, central to meaning in our lives, or a more self-focused desire for fame and fortune.

Integration and flexibility

Emerging with meaning-making is our capacity to use a range of competencies that enable us to think systemically and understand systemic relationships; we can have knowing 'insight'. We attribute causalities, learn from the past and predict the future. Such competencies give rise to what we call *wisdom*. Again, although animals can certainly learn from their experience, and even pass on their knowledge, wisdom is probably not a term we would apply in any depth to nonhumans, at least not our insightful, conscious faculty of wisdom. Wisdom and insight can be both drivers of compassion and a consequence of mindful compassion cultivation (Gilbert & Choden, 2013).

Another key aspect of wisdom is 'knowingly' being psychologically and contextually flexible. In Acceptance Commitment Therapy psychological flexibility is a core therapeutic target (Fletcher & Hayes, 2005). Tirch, Schoendorfe and Silberstein (2015) have been at the forefront of integrating motivational and compassion focused approaches into this therapy highlighting the interactions between creating compassion within and between individuals in the development of 'knowing flexibility' and distinguishing 'me and you', 'now and then', 'here and there'. Clearly, the evolution of the frontal cortex, the interaction of the two hemispheres and changes in neuronal connectivity played major roles in the evolution of these competencies (LeDoux, 2014; Singer & Bolz, 2012). In fact our minds can *flexibly integrate* information in unique and amazing ways – for example no animal could learn to drive a car and then coordinate their actions inside the car, and with other drivers in the fast-flowing streams in heavy traffic; or to play a Rachmaninov piano concerto from memory and experience appreciation of an audience who understand the talent and complexity of this dexterity. These are extraordinary specific feats of information integration and flexibility (Gilbert, 2009; Siegel, 2016). LeDoux (2014) suggests that the evolution of these conscious, cognitive abilities changes how we should understand emotion in general and the human regulation of it.

Compassion creates contexts for mental integration

Socially, while threat and feeling threatened can result in segregated and stereotypic responses (e.g. fight, flight, freeze inhibit), and in the extreme cause dis-integration and dissociation, compassion can provide for a sense of safeness (a secure base; see Mikulincer & Shaver, Chapter 11, this volume). This enables the integration of inherently disparate and segregated systems via open attention and exploration (Gilbert, 1993, 2005a, 2014a; Keltner, Kogan, Piff & Saturn, 2014; Kirby & Gilbert, Chapter 15, this volume; Siegel, 2011, 2016). This is linked in turn to the evolution of 'attachment' that creates a secure base for learning, exploration and integration (see Brown & Brown, 2015; Mikulincer & Shaver, Chapter 11, this volume), and in particular how caring behaviours regulate a range of processes (such as neurotransmitters and hormones, immune systems, the frontal cortex and autonomic nervous system) that are conducive to integration, psychological flexibility and confident social engagement in the receiver of care (Keltner, Kogan, Piff & Saturn, 2014; Porges, 2007).

In his new book on the nature of the 'Mind', Siegel (2016) develops work from his interpersonal neurobiology approach to suggest that we are such evolved *social beings,* we can think of the human mind more as an interacting field of shared processing: our brains are energy stimulating and information transferring rather than decontextualised autonomous units. Indeed, we have minds that create and generate new, novel social environments called *cultures* that we then adapt (even physiologically) our minds to in novel ways. Key for Siegel is how the energy flows between our minds create contexts for mental integration. Hence, although we have a Stone Age brain we live in very different minds to our Stone Age ancestors, created by cultural worlds of history, narratives, television, cars and social media. We have not yet learned how to regulate and create social cultures that harness well-being, social justice and equality, compassion and seeking the social good rather than personal and tribal advance.

Downsides of social intelligence

Unfortunately, our capacities to have a sense of an individualised self and abilities to think, imagine and reason as we do, also give rise to serious mental health problems and potentials for intense cruelty and violence (Gilbert, 2005a, 2009). Leary (2004) called it *The Curse of the Self?* Shame, self-criticism, rumination, self-absorption, (psychotic) voice hearing, narcissistic self-focus, a sense of hopelessness, forms of vengeance, sadistic (torture) inventions, tribal conquests, slavery and female genital mutilations also all spin out from these competencies. Modern cultures (only possible because of these competencies) are very distant from our small ancestral groups of mutuality. They can breed mental health and violent problems, and feed competitive motives, tribal and gendered identities, and narcissistic self-focus. Understanding that these arise because of the way the human brain evolved, how our socially intelligent competencies interact with earlier evolved motives (e.g. for harm avoidance, resource acquisition and control, status, sex, belonging) and that they can be choreographed by the social niche and culture in which our minds are embedded, helps us see that *much of the content of our minds is not our fault*: we are actors of slices of DNA, gene built and culturally scripted actors of archetypal dramas. Yet learning how to recognise this, become 'mindful,' de-personalise (seen in part as a common humanity issue; Barrett, Dunbar & Lycett, 2002; Yalom, 1980) and then take responsibility for how our mind's outputs (actions) is part of the compassionate (Bodhicitta) insight. This helps to address issues of shame and develop a compassionate orientation to one's own and others' suffering (see below; Gilbert, 2010; Gilbert & Irons, 2005; Kirby & Gilbert, Chapter 15, this volume).

Siddhartha's great insight on the road to enlightenment, sitting under the Bodhi tree, was almost exactly this, that our minds are full of chaotic desires, passions and motives that can take us over. According to Vessantara (1993) he regarded the unenlightened or 'unmindful mind' as almost insane, dangerously chaotic. But if we cultivate mindful awareness, married with compassion motivation, compassionate intention and wisdom, we can do much to take responsibility on how we function, the patterns of physiological activation we cultivate (and sustain through neuroplasticity) and what we bring into the world (Gilbert & Choden, 2013); this links to our intent. So *compassion is probably one of the most important antidotes (counteracting motives) to the downside and dark side of humanity.*

Social motives, social mentalities and compassion

Within evolutionary theory motives emerge from survival and reproductive strategies (the two driving forces of evolution) and fashion phenotypes according to the environments in which they mature (Barrett et al., 2002; Buss, 2014). The way this arises is that evolution builds physiological mechanisms that have stimulus detection functions (input-sensitive), so that when a stimulus is detected it triggers a cascade of physiological reactions that produce behaviour (outputs) appropriate to that motive; so a kind of 'if A do Y', but if 'B do R'. For example, detection of sudden movement or sound close by might trigger a threat response of freeze or flight; a dominant's threat signal triggers a submissive defense; an infant's distress call triggers patterns of physiological change in a parent setting in motion behaviours of searching, rescuing, soothing or feeding. The emotions that might be generated will be dependent upon the context, and pre-stimulus physiological state. It is known that there are a range of physiological processes that influence these 'stimulus-detection-response' mechanisms. For example, genetic polymorphisms influence the interest-attention-allocation and the response behaviours in question. Polymorphisms on the oxytocin 'gene' influence caring interest and helping behavior; polymorphisms on the testosterone 'gene' influence context-linked sexuality and aggressiveness (just two of very many). These variations are a source of genetic selection (see Conway & Slavich, Chapter 9, this volume). Very briefly then, survival and reproduction *strategies* give rise to motives which in turn give rise to physiologies for signal detection and response that are then influenced by history, context and current physiological states.

Evolution of caring

Reproductive strategies can be divided into r and K (r/K selection), which relate to the degree of parental investment (Geary, 2000). Some species in relatively resource abundant environments use strategies of producing large numbers but not investing in any of their offspring – r selection (e.g., many invertebrates follow this strategy). In more crowded environments and where there is greater competition for resources K selection strategies are for smaller numbers of offspring but investing in them after birth – caring (e.g. mammals → primates → humans). Over time parental investing K strategies can evolve that enable-infants to be born more and more vulnerable, looked after post birth, and with greater learning potential for phenotypic development, variation and niche exploitation. Hrdy (2011) has argued that in the pre-human primate transition to humans there were significant changes in caring which may even have partly driven the evolution of socially intelligent competencies. Key is that we are the only primate that allows and even encourages multiple care-givers. Pre and post birth, humans recruit kin and non-kin helpers in ways no other primate does. Indeed, the evolution of upright walking adversely influenced the birth canal (at a time when the babies head was evolving to be larger) such that humans may often need help in giving birth. Hence, one source of human compassion arose from the needs for multiple caring and investments for infants and children – which actually extend over a long period of childhood.

In males the challenge of caring in these contexts of infant helplessness and the long period of developmental dependency were (maybe) pressures to become more caring too. So caring males would be more attractive to females but also helpful to their offspring. Caring male parenting styles (in contrast to being aggressive) may have played an important role in maturation of competencies to build supportive alliances when adults. There are many reasons for caring also involving males.

Indeed, there is evidence of a feminisation of facial features perhaps indicative of the changing role of testosterone with increases in parental investment (Cieri, Churchill, Franciscus, Tan & Hare, 2014; Gilbert, 2015b). Partly due to the different investment strategies many women may have slightly different processes of caring (see Mayseless, 2016 for a review).

Babies born into a world of multiple caregivers (including males) are from day one interested in the human face, eye-to-eye contact and voice tones; they have a form of intersubjectivity that doesn't properly exist for other animals (Trevarthen & Aitken, 2001). This offers profoundly important new ways in which, from birth, we interact with the minds of others and empathically attune to them (Hrdy, 2011). It also offers infants the opportunities to receive empathic caring from a number of individuals rather than just one. This in turn requires competencies for multi-social relating, working out who is safe and helpful, which in turn builds capacities for social connectedness which is central for the regulation of emotion, a caring sense of self and psychological flexibility (Keltner et al., 2014; Porges, 2007). In fact, throughout our lives we are surrounded by multiple potential care-givers. Obvious ones are the medical professionals, but we look to many different types of individuals to perform different caring, relieving, protecting, preventing roles; police, rescue services, teachers and so on – all of whom are focused on helping us in one way or another. Our capacity to create divisions of labour around caring and support is unique and profound to our species, some requiring much courage. Individuals can have a sense of pride in the quality of helpfulness they can provide. We are embedded in a sea of interconnected help-giving others which we commonly take for granted without perhaps realising that to some extent the care motivational system underpins both desire to provide and the experiencing of these essential relationships.

Moreover, we show empathic and care-focused sensitivities from a very young age. Not only can young children have an interest in caring and helping others, but infants show preferences for toys that have been depicted as caring/helpful rather than uncaring (Warneken & Tomasello, 2009). So the evolution of human caring itself offers major insights into the origins of our interests and competencies for compassion. Reflecting on this, however, Hrdy (2011) also indicates how modern living may be undermining the nature of human care-giving-receiving relationships (see also Narvaez, Chapter 10, this volume). So being sensitive to the distress and needs of others, with an interest in helping (compassion), originates in K selected strategies. These strategies build motives with stimulus-detection responses for caring which are elaborated through evolution (e.g. adapted and used as a social signal of altruism and attractiveness), subject to genetic variation, and become modified and regulated through social intelligences. These create its phenotypes.

Motives, social mentalities and competencies

It is clear that caring is an evolved motive and that compassion is one of its derivatives (Gilbert, 1989/2016; Mayseless, 2016). The word and concept of *motivation* is derived from the Latin word motivus, meaning 'moving' or 'to move', motives are linked to desires, wishes and wants; they give rise to specific incentives and concerns, but differ from values and emotions (Klinger, 1977). They are the causes of behaviour (Deckers, 2014; Neel et al., 2016; Weiner, 1992). Specific motives evolve because they 'alert and move' the animal to achieve biosocial goals of supporting reproduction and survival (e.g. feeding, harm avoidance, status, sex-mate bonding, alliance formation, infant care); they guide animals on what to pay attention to, what to be emotionally aroused by, and choreograph behaviour (Bernard, Mills, Swenson & Walsh, 2005; Deckers, 2014; Dunbar, 2007; Gilbert, 1989/2016, 2014a; Weiner, 1992). There is increasing evidence that evolved motives are central to how people think and organise their lives, are a focus for a sense of meaning, value and self-identity, that they are a source of individual difference between people and that they are different from personality traits (Neel et al., 2016).

All motives require two basic processes, (Buss, 2014; Deckers, 2014) and so does compassion. *Stimulus detection* and *stimulus-meaning* is the first process, the second is appropriate *responding*. Each requires a number of competencies that are species specific and motive specific. For example, consider avoiding danger or seeking food or a sexual partner. The animal requires stimulus detection competencies, sensitivity to signals (indicative) of potential danger, food or a sexual opportunity. When the motive-linked stimulus is detected it triggers a number of physiologically processes to hone attention, generate emotion and cognitive processes (including recent human evolved ones), and primes arousal for motive appropriate action. Anxiety, for example, would not exist if there wasn't a motivational system to avoid harm and an ability to distinguish threat stimuli from non-threat stimuli; hence most theorists see harm avoidance as a basic motive that can recruit different emotions (such as anger, anxiety and disgust) according to context. Thus, anxiety arises in the post threat-detection phase to energise and guide behaviour. Similarly, *caring motivation* has to underpin the stimulus-detection aspect of compassion, giving rise to feelings and cognitive processing that are appropriate to the contexts for compassionate behaviour.

The second process is *stimulus-response-what action*. Animals that hunt need to know not only when and what to hunt, but 'how' to hunt. Sexuality requires being attuned to stimulus-informing opportunities as they arise, being aroused by them, but also guided in the enactment of appropriate, skillful courting and copulatory behaviour. So compassion as a motive also guides knowing 'when', 'what' and 'how to' care. Social motives, as social mentalities (Gilbert, 1989/2016, 2005b, 2014a), enable animals to be flexible in their processing of these domains, changing their behaviour almost moment-by-moment according to the impact their behaviour has on another – in an interactional dance between self and other/s. Empathy and intersubjectivity are crucially important for humans to do this effectively and appropriately (Cortina & Liotti, 2010; Gilbert, 2009). Compassionate interactions are clearly like this.

Interpersonal dances

In line with many evolution thinkers (Buss, 2014; Barrett et al., 2002; Neel et al., 2016) social mentality theory suggests a relatively limited number of social motives (Gilbert, 1989/2016). The main ones are depicted in Table 3.1 and indicate that they create self–other role relating patterns and organise *social behaviour into interpersonal dances* for the pursuit of biosocial goals. For example, the biosocial goal of human parental caring is the survival and flourishing of offspring, the social role (dance) of caring involves complex interactions between the care-giver (parent) and infant (care-seeker, elicitor and user), changing moment by moment according to how each of them is responding to the other. In contrast, the biosocial goal of securing resources in competition with others can involve inter-conspecific dances such as ritualised antagonistic behavior and dominate-subordinate displays such that fighting and injury are minimised. The sexual-courting behaviour of many species have specific dances signalling intent too; if the signals are wrong or 'misattuned' then one or other pulls out – moves or flies away.

In humans these dances recruit socially intelligent competencies. As relationships develop so do the dances; for example, in a bonded couple it is expected that

Table 3.1 A brief guide to social mentalities

	Self as	Other as	Fears
Caring eliciting/ seeking	Needing input from other(s): care, protection, safeness, reassurance, stimulation, guidance	Source of: care, nurturance, protection, safeness, reassurance, stimulus, guidance	Unavailable, withdrawn, withholding, exploitation, threatening, harmful
Care-giving	Provider of: care, protection, safeness, reassurance, stimulation, guidance	Recipient of: care, protection, safeness, reassurance, stimulation, guidance	Overwhelmed, unable to provide, threat, focused guilt
Cooperation	Of value to others, sharing, appreciating, contributing, helping	Valuing one's contribution, sharing, reciprocating, appreciating	Cheating, non-appreciating or non-reciprocating, rejecting/shame
Competitive	Inferior-superior, more/less powerful harmful/benevolent	Inferior superior, more/less powerful, harmful/ benevolent	Involuntary subordination, shame, marginalisation, abused
Sexual	Attractive/desirable	Attractive desirable	Unattractive rejected

Source: Adapted from Gilbert (1992), *The Evolution of Powerlessness*. London: Psychology Press.

each will help equally (reciprocity and fairness) and be caring. Threat emotions appear if these dances become mis-attuned. Imagine the interaction and dance of a couple who are highly caring *and* empathic in contrast to ones who care but neither is very empathic.

Because human social motives have these complexities to them I referred to them as *social mentalities*. A rough if somewhat clunky description might be: *A social mentality creates interpersonal dances for the formation of role relationships to pursue biosocial goals (e.g. status, mating, offspring care), recruiting socially intelligent competencies in the process* (Gilbert, 2005a, 2005b, 2014a). As noted, different social mentalities can have specific ways of processing social signals (Geary & Huffman, 2002). For example, in a status-seeking or resource-acquiring competitive social mentality (brain pattern), a preparedness to escalate (threaten) or de-escalate (submit and express submissive displays) conflicts gives rise to aggression, or social anxiety and submissiveness, and/or shame (Gilbert, 1989/2016). However, in a caring mentality none of these apply; we do not compare ourselves to others and we're not fearful of the judgments of others, nor do we engage in submissive or dominant aggressive behaviour. Consider too that the way we monitor and respond to (changes in) facial expressions, voice tones, body postures and verbal content, utilises specialised-focused processing systems that vary according to what social mentality is active. Seeing somebody cry could be pleasurable if I'm motivated to hurt them but distressing if I'm trying to care for them; seeing somebody joyful because of a success is pleasurable if I care for them but could create envious anger if I am in a competitive mentality. These ways of thinking help locate compassion as a social mentality arising from the caring motives, and choreographed by socially intelligent interpersonal dances. Intentionality is therefore crucial.

Dance of the phenotypes?

Social mentalities are in the service of survival and reproductive strategies and their phenotypes. What is crucial is how these play out, not only in our own minds but the minds around us. For example, aggressive dominant strategies will only work if they can stimulate fear and submissive defences in the minds of others around them; sexual attraction displays only work if they actually attract; friendship strategies only work if they create a sense of actual or likely reciprocal friendliness. Non-reciprocation undermines friendships for the self in the minds of others. *Social mentalities are therefore also working to create conditions in the minds of others conducive to their own strategic functioning and survival.* At the social cultural level too, different strategies and social mentalities will seek to create conditions (states of mind in others) conducive to their own enactment. In humans, this is partly regulated by the manipulation of beliefs, and by offering solutions to evolutionary challenges such as harm avoidance, tribal identities and belonging, resource access and distribution. So, for example, some politicians are able to stimulate fear 'of the other' in their followers, tribal loyalties and even violence. One way of thinking about some political philosophies is the degree to which they are vehicles for strategies which seek to create contexts that are focused on threat and resource accumulation, rather than sharing, and compassion for the human condition (Sachs, 2012). Individuals whose minds are focused on wanting to influence the minds of others on a large scale are trying to create social climates for those strategies to operate and be accepted. So the choreographers of our intimate, social and cultural dances are complex strategic and phenotypic processes; humans are not disconnected, autonomous beings but are influenced and influencing others, even at the physiological, non-conscious and phenotypic level all the time. If we are 'unmindful' then what is in competition here are strategies – minds being their vehicles (Huang & Bargh, 2014). Such ways of thinking have important implications for bringing and embedding compassion phenotypes into social discourse and culture formation.

Emotions, motives and intentions

The relationship between motives-intentions, feeling states and emotions are complex with major implications for compassion (Deckers, 2014; Weiner, 1992). Consider the fact that as men and women age they can lose androgens, and can lose sexual feelings and function, but not sexual motivation. Indeed, this loss of feeling (libido) can be a source of depression for some people, because they very much *want to feel* sexual and competent with loved partners. Depressed mothers can be very motivated to care and be compassionate to their children, but depression can block those 'affectionate and caring feelings states.' Again, this loss of feeling can be a source of sadness, depression and even self-criticism, a major problem in serious postnatal and other depressions. Nonetheless, they may continue *to behave* in caring ways *in the absence of feeling*, because of their motivation and identity of wanting to be a caring parent (see Gilbert, 1989/2016, p. 167 for a clinical case example). Indeed, in compassion focused therapy, training and guidance links intention to behaviour rather than to feeling, because the lack of feeling can be distressing. Although training mentally well people in loving kindness has neurophysiological effects (Singer & Klimecki, 2014), it can be hard for depressed people 'to experience compassionate and connectedness feelings with, for and from others' and that in itself can be a source of depression, because they would like to have these feelings.

In contrast, behaving in line with one's 'desires, wishes, intentions and values' even when depressed (and one has to work hard at them) can be helpful (Tirch et al., 2015). So there is an important distinction between wanting, desiring and being motivated, and being able 'to feel something'. This is clinically very important and why we caution against seeing compassion as a feeling state in the clinic; therapists should focus on developing *intention and behaviour* first (Gilbert, 2000, 2007, 2010). Indeed, other therapies, for example Acceptance Commitment Therapy, argue similarly (Tirch et al., 2015).

While emotions are important for the colours and textures of our lives, they are in the service of motives. For example, an emotion like anxiety may not say anything about either the situation or motivation that fuels it. We could be anxious for any number of threatened motives, such as failing an exam, breakup of a relationship or being chased by a predator. Emotion would be much less if we weren't that bothered about exams and quite happy for the relationship to end or were hunting. Emotions do not tell us much about the behaviour either, because anxiety may lead us to avoid or engage and address the issue in numerous ways.

Importantly, motives are powerful 'primes' creating a readiness for feeling and actions even when they are not actively stimulating emotion or are unconscious (Huang & Bargh, 2014). For example, one might not notice a child's attachment-motive until the bond is threatened which activates emotions (anxiety-crying) and behaviour (seeking). So one can have a high care-motive (compassion), whilst doing something else (e.g. cooking). A motivational system need not be changed by what one is doing in any moment, in the way an emotion is. The moment a stimulus arrives, that is linked to compassion motives (e.g. we hear the cry of someone in distress), it then triggers a range of emotions, thoughts and behaviours, and redirects us away from the cooking to searching for the distressed. Such switches of attention could not be triggered without the motivation. Without pre-existing motivation, we may be disinterested in the distress signal and continue cooking. In order for us to drop what we are doing (cooking), and immediately refocus our attention and action on helping, the compassion motivation system has to come online and turn off other motivational systems; it has to be given priority and generate, in that moment, emotions and behavioural dispositions. This is central because there is now considerable evidence that 'motivational readiness' can operate consciously and unconsciously, motives can conflict with each other and one motive can be given priority for action over others (Deckers, 2014; Huang & Bargh, 2014; Neel et al., 2016). This may explain individual differences in the degree to which compassion motives organise our minds, with some people having higher 'tonic' (readiness) activation or readiness and priority for compassion engagement than others (Crocker & Canevello, 2012; Neel et al., 2016); which in turn may link to various genetic polymorphisms and phenotypes (see Colonnello, Petrocchi & Heinrichs, Chapter 6, this volume; Conway & Slavich, Chapter 9, this volume). The degree to which individuals feel safe and secure also play an important role in the strength of prosocial motives and or their inhibitors, in that insecure individuals are more defensive and threat-focused and may struggle with compassion (Gilbert, 2009; Gilbert, McEwan, Matos & Rivis, 2011; Mikulincer & Shaver, Chapter 10, this volume; Narvaez, Chapter 9, this volume). Part of what compassion therapies and training may do is *prime* caring motives to be more accessible and active. To sum up then, in this approach, motivation underpins both the feelings that arise in observing suffering but also the feelings that direct actions and these are context dependent.

The flow of compassion

All social mentalities have a flow to them. For example, consider sexuality: there are the sexual feelings we have for others, the awareness of sexual feelings others have for us and those of our own (autoerotic) sexual fantasies and feelings (to which we may be open or ashamed); these are interdependent. We are more likely to feel ourselves to be sexually attractive if other people treat us as if we are. Social behaviour is played out in (the social mentality guided) interactional dances where individuals send signals to each other and respond to those signals according to the social roles being created between them using their socially intelligent competencies. Compassion too is a flow in that there is the compassion we feel for others, our openness and responsiveness to the compassion flowing from others, and our capacity to be self-compassionate. Figure 3.1 depicts this flow and their interactions, including the ways social contexts can inspire, flow or block it, as in the aforementioned 'dance of the phenotypes' (Gilbert & Mascaro, in press). For example, schools and families and even political parties can highlight and model the value of moral and compassionate behaviour or self-focused achievement, defensiveness and combativeness.

These require different competencies and attentional focus. For example, Van Doesum, Van Lange and Van Lange (2013) distinguish between what they call self-focused mindfulness and social mindfulness. Social mindfulness is where we become mindful of what is arising in the minds of others and here a whole range of socially intelligent competencies for empathy and mindreading are important and are used differently than for self-mindfulness.

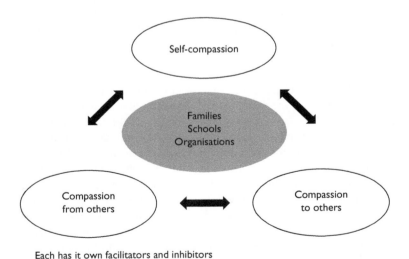

Each has it own facilitators and inhibitors

Figure 3.1 The interactive flow of compassion.

There is now considerable work showing that early experiences of socially intel-ligent, caring and compassion from others is crucial for developing a range of the child's own socially intelligent competencies and a compassionate and prosocial orientation to the world, and that it also supports self-compassion as a self-to-self relating style (Cortina & Liotti, 2010; Mikulincer & Shaver, Chapter 11, this volume; Siegel, 2011, 2016). Compassionate and affectionate caring has pro-found effects on a range on physiological developmental trajectories and even genetic expression (Keltner et al., 2014; Conway & Slavich, Chapter 9, this vol-ume; Narvaez, Chapter 10, this volume).

Being open to compassion from others stimulates emotions such as grati-tude and appreciation but also offers a sense that the world is safe rather than threatening. Feeling socially safe and connected, and able to turn to others for help, has major impacts on health and well-being because we are evolved for this to be so (Dunbar, 2007; Kelly, Zuroff, Leybman & Gilbert, 2012). These 'flows of compassion' are interdependent. In a test of social mentality theory Hermanto and Zuroff (2016), showed how the different orientations of compassion are related. High care-giving along with the ability to receive care predicted self-compassion, whereas high care-giving with low care-seeking (being less open and receptive to compassion) predicted poor self-compassion. This fits with Bowlby's notions of compulsive care-giving and also that care-giving can be defensive and submissive (Catarino et al., 2014). Gilbert et al. (2011) also found that fears of receiving compassion were strongly associated with fears and resistances associated with being self-compassionate, but much less so to being compassionate to others. Hermanto, Zuroff, Kopala, Sibley, Kelly and Gilbert (2016) also found that being open to compassion from others buffers the effect of self-criticism on depression. Such data highlights the fact that to understand how compassion manifests in the world we need to focus on both competencies for giving *and receiving*: that is, recognising compassion as a social mentality.

One core dimension relating to conflicts between motives is self-interest versus the interest of others – although these can overlap (Gilbert, 2009; Huang & Bargh, 2014; Neel et al., 2016). To what extent will we risk ourselves to save others; to what extent will we help others rather than hold onto resources for ourselves (Loewenstein & Small, 2007)? Whether or not compassion motives take priority depends upon how that motivational system interacts with all oth-ers in our repertoire of motives and 'fires up' emotions. In CFT (Gilbert, 1989, 2000 2009, 2014a , 2015a, 2015b) and Buddhist traditions, (especially via the eightfold pathway) training is focused on cultivating motivation of a personal, compassionate identity (Bodhichitta) and shift out of competitive self-focus. This leads to another key issue: to what extent does compassion training change the internal dynamics (physiological infrastructures) of our motivational pri-orities, our 'tonic readiness' and possibly phenotypes? Emerging early data suggest we may be able to (Fredrickson et al., 2013; Hoge et al., 2013; Singer & Klimecki, 2014).

Self compassion vs. the compassionate self

Cultivating the compassionate self is quite different to self-compassion. The compassionate self is linked to a self-identity based in intention and motivation that organises the mind. As noted above it is linked to the concept of Bodhichitta. The compassionate self facilitates the flow of comparison in the three orientations. Thus when training and cultivating our compassionate self we are creating a state of mind that develops insights and wisdom (e.g. into the nature of the human 'tricky' brain, the complexity of our emotions and belief formation), that stimulates the vagus nerve and improves heart rate variability, stimulates the hormonal bases for caring behaviour, and organises the frontal cortex in a way that facilitates inhibition of unhelpful impulsiveness and supports empathic insights. This mind state is an integrating state, whereas threat processing is a disintegrating or segregating state. As we cultivate the various competencies of a compassionate self (see Figure 3.3) then our capacity to facilitate compassion for others, be open to the compassion from others and have the wisdom for self-compassion improves. This is captured in Figure 3.2.

Extending compassion

Human social intelligences enable caring and compassion to extend beyond kin and reciprocal relationships and even be directed to animals and plants; we can anthropomorphise (Loewenstein & Small, 2007). For human relations though, social friendliness, altruism and helpfulness are attractors. Individuals who show altruistic traits are more attractive as friends, allies and sexual partners. A recent study by Arnocky, Pich, Albert, Ouellette and Barclay (2016) highlighted that although potentially costly, altruism has a range of beneficial effects on reproductive success in a number of species. In addition, because it is an attractor-signal individuals

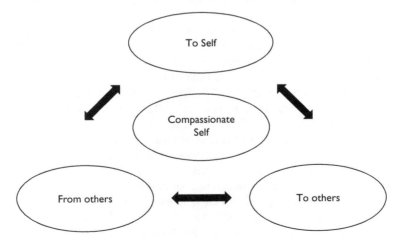

Figure 3.2 Relation of the compassionate self to the flows of compassions.

can compete to be the most desired and seen as the most altruistic (see Arnocky et al. (2016) for useful review of this literature). Being considerate of others and being liked carry many benefits (Crocker & Canevello, 2012; Goetz et al., 2010).

Nonetheless, whatever the benefits are, it is our socially intelligent competencies that make possible *Bodhicitta intention* (Jinpa, 2015; Ricard, 2015; Vessantara, 1993) such that compassion intention can underpin all other motives (Table 3.1). Hence (as with the eightfold pathway) our eating should not cause suffering (vegetarian or vegan); our sexualities should not cause suffering or be exploitive (so we stay sensitive to the other); our livelihoods and competitive behaviour should not cause suffering or be exploitative, but prevent it (Sachs, 2012), and our co-operative behaviour is not Machiavellian (Ricard, 2015). And we learn in CFT to follow the compassionate intention of not to cause suffering to ourselves. We therefore address self-criticism, shame, rumination, self-harm and trauma memory.

Sensitivity to distress/suffering

The concept of sensitivity to distress is central to compassion but this too is complicated. First, there is the focus of flow (Figures 3.1 and 3.2) – being sensitive to our own suffering, the suffering of others or awareness that others are sensitive to our suffering; we may be competent at one but not another (Gilbert et al., 2011). Second, as Panksepp and Panksepp (2013) point out, empathic sensitivity to the distress in others actually began as a defensive, threat awareness process. For example, when an animal hears another animal in distress or crying in pain, that may indicate a predator and danger, and trigger flight behaviour. So, here, signals of distress do not generate or motivate to care or to help.

There are many examples where signals of distress, which might be associated with disease or danger, trigger avoidance, and for good evolutionary reasons. Jane Goodall (1990) writes of how polio struck the chimpanzee population she was studying. Some of the chimpanzees became paralysed in their arms or legs. This seemed frightening to the other chimpanzees who carefully avoided them. Signals of disease often trigger avoidance, rather than approach behaviour. Indeed, from the work of Nancy Eisenberg and others, it has been known for a long time that being moved by the distress of others may simply cause personal distress and not motivate caring behaviour at all (Eisenberg, VanSchyndel & Hofer, 2015). The question is then: what enables us to overrule fear and avoidance, and then approach and help instead? Clearly, our human-evolved, socially intelligent competencies will play a major role in this, including the way we create our self-identities, the kind of person we think we are and want to be when confronted by certain types of suffering and the way we reason about distress; empathy will be crucial (Lowenstein & Small, 2007). This is probably why we admire so much those individuals who have the courage to work with people who are diseased, those who went to West Africa to fight the Ebola crisis in 2015, and have probably saved the world from a very nasty virus. Indeed, while there are also many examples of animals caring for sick or injured conspecifics, the archaeological record suggests that early humans were very caring of injured and sick individuals, and such caring marks our 'humanity' (see Spikins, Chapter 2, this volume). These behaviours were evolving alongside, or in tandem with, our evolving socially intelligent competencies that would support insight into what to do.

When it comes to our own internal suffering, as Freud observed long ago, things that we may feel ashamed about, see as something wrong with us, or cause us pain, we may try to avoid, repress, deny and dissociate from, rather than approach and engage with compassion. Indeed, the basis of many CFT (and other) therapies is to switch from inner avoidance into compassionate engagements with what is painful and avoided (Gilbert, 2000, 2010, 2014; Kirby & Gilbert, Chapter 15, this volume). As noted in Chapter 1, however, we need clarity on the meaning of suffering in the different traditions.

Shame, guilt and the compassionate social mentality

Shame and guilt are both important self-conscious emotions but they have very different evolutionary origins, underpinning motivational systems and links to compassion (Gilbert, 1989/2016, 2007). Shame evolved from competitive, social rank and status regulation motives (Gilbert, 1998; Gilbert & McGuire, 1998). Unfavourable social comparison, inferiority and being judged negatively by others and vulnerable to their exclusions, rejections or attacks is a major threat to primates in general, but especially humans. These social threats that arise in group, hierarchical living with competition for social space, sexual opportunities and status, when recruited into human social intelligent competencies (self-awareness), gives the potential for a sense of shame. *External* shame is marked by feeling that others view the self to be inferior, undesirable, rejectable, with a damaged reputation, to be cut off from the benefits of affiliative caring and sharing. *Internal* shame relates to our own self-evaluations, overlaid with self-criticism and negative self-monitoring. Developmentally, self-criticism is much more common in children from shaming and insecure backgrounds, and/or highly competitive ones, than from safe, caring ones. Growing up in environments where others are more powerful and potentially hostile and critical, adopting a submissive low rank/inferior, non-confident profile would be a safety strategy. Such strategies can pattern the sense of self so that, under threat, the defensive strategy of demobilisation is triggered along with the appropriate self-concept (and maybe emotional memory) of seeing oneself as worthless, inadequacy or useless. Compassion seeks to help individuals understand the nature of these safety strategies and shift to a caring strategy to self and others. There is no specific shame emotion because it can be different blends of primary emotions such as anxiety, anger, disgust, sadness and loss of positive affective tone (depression-like associated with the defeat and demobilisation defences) (Gilbert, 1998, 2007).

Non-human primates can certainly show submissive, and shame-*like* behaviours in the context of status threat because they're frightened of what more dominant others might do to them (Gilbert & McGuire, 1998), but it's unlikely that they ruminate or reflect on themselves with negative self judgements; they can be frightened by what others could do to them but not by their own thoughts, feelings or potential actions; they can't 'put themselves down' – as far as we know. Humans can do all these. Shame is intimately linked to the fear of disconnection and social rejection. Typical thoughts of people struggling with shame are: 'If you really knew what went on in my mind you wouldn't think I deserve compassion'. Some individuals can be very motivated to be helpful to others but this is not necessarily genuinely care focused, rather it is more shame avoidance and the desire to be accepted and not rejected (Catarino et al., 2014). Indeed, recently Böckler et al. (2016) identified a variety of motives behind caring behaviours. People who are more self-focused and defensive in their motives for helping might be more prone to shame than guilt.

The origins of guilt are entirely different. With the evolution of caring motivation and behaviour there also had to be a harm avoidance mechanism; one has to avoid harming the object of one's caring, e.g. the infant (Gilbert 1989/2016). As MacLean (1985) noted, first was kin recognition, so you don't eat the kids (as some fish do)! In addition, when inadvertently causing harm there needs to be a response that focuses the attention on reparation. Hence, in guilt the emotions are typically ones of sadness and remorse with a desire for reparation as soon as possible (the attention and focus is quite different to that of shame). The attention is focused on the other not on the self; there is no issue of social comparison, inferiority or being worried about being judged negatively by others. Empathy used from caring motivation is to understand the needs of others and be helpful, whereas empathy from a competitive social mentality is to work out what others will like or dislike about you and how you can repair your reputation and get them to like or accept you again. Demonstrations of guilt and genuine sadness and reparation are also important in victims accepting apologies and repairing relationships. Indeed, because supportive caring relationships are so important for well-being and survival, guilt can function as a compassionate repair and socially cohesive process. Importantly, a person expressing guilt doesn't need to assume a low status position with subordinate and submissive non-verbal communications as can be the case in shame. Again, since a compassionate motivation intends not to cause harm, inadvertently doing so is not an attack on the self but a regret: sadness and sorrow. Obviously, though, these are not mutually exclusive.

Viewing compassion as a social mentality, rooted in caring motivation, reveals the important differences between shame and guilt. Being in touch with sadness and remorse, if we have been hurtful, is important to help us stay on track with our compassionate intention and identity; but this can be blocked by shame focused defensive manoeuvres (Gilbert, 2009). In CFT one of the therapeutic steps can be to help people move out of self- and rank-focused shame and (in the context of hurting others) to experience guilt (Gilbert, in press). One way of doing this is to focus on the sadness and remorse of an event rather than whether one is a 'bad' self. These themes are also crucial in forms of moral thinking and distinctions of retributive (shame and shaming focused) and restorative (guilt-focused) justice and are discussed more fully in Gilbert (2009).

Individuals who have not processed sadness in themselves for their own traumas and care-receiving ruptures can find it difficult to process any kind of sadness including that necessary from guilt (Gilbert, in press; Gilbert & Irons, 2005). In a major review of the neurophysiology of empathy Shirtcliff et al. (2009) found evidence to support this view. They summarise their findings as follows:

> The review proposes neurobiological impairments in individuals who display little empathy are not necessarily due to a reduced ability to understand the emotions of others. Instead, evidence suggests individuals who show little arousal to the distress of others likewise show decreased physiological arousal to their own distress; one manifestation of reduced stress reactivity may be a dysfunction in empathy which supports psychopathic-like constructs (e.g., callousness).
>
> (p. 137)

So if one can't process one's own distress then the mechanisms for empathy, such as mirror neurons, are not going to work. People who are sadness-guilt blocked can be at risk of harming others. People with psychopathic traits can be sensitive to shame (their reputation) and humiliation but probably do not experience the sadness of others' pain, or the sad remorse if they are the cause, feelings that are so important for guilt. It is as if everyone is classed as an out-group, almost as potential enemies. We know that hurting our enemies also blocks sadness-guilt. The degree to which this is a combined genetic or acquired issue is unknown – but certainly to help them CFT suggests one should be very cautious about using threat-punitive measures as shame (unfortunately typical in some forensics settings). Rather the therapeutic focus is on their ability to experience sadness for themselves first and then for others. Without the ability to tolerate sadness they may struggle to experience guilt – although the degree to which this is possible is unresearched (Gilbert, in press; Shirtcliff et al., 2009).

Causing suffering

Shame and guilt also have different relations to a core issue of compassion which is the avoidance of *causing suffering*. The most obvious one is that people who have been shamed may well be vengeance orientated and have an *increased* desire to cause harm, whereas guilt never creates an increased desire to cause harm (Stuewig, Tangney, Heigel, Harty & McCloskey, 2010).

There is a word in German – *Schadenfreude* – which is 'taking pleasure in the misfortune and suffering of others' (Leach, Spears, Branscombe & Dossje, 2003), which is the exact opposite of compassion. Again we can look to evolution for why we have brains like this. Seeing others fall from grace and/or being 'brought down' via shame and humiliation can bring satisfaction depending on our relationship with them (common across competing tribes – even psychotherapy ones!). And we can be motivated to cause harm by vengeance or spite, or simply to gain competitive advantage. There is considerable evidence that people who have been shamed and humiliated can have an extraordinary desire to harm others and hence why we should avoid shame if we wish to stimulate compassionate motives. Hence compassion research needs to clarify these distinctions.

But of course it's not only shame that stimulates sadistic desire. Our human history of torture and violence is tragic, horrendous and legendary. Causing suffering is a common theme in our entertainments – be it at the Roman games or now films and TV shows (Nell, 2006). In addition, desires to cause or watch suffering are very much linked to the emotion of vengeance. Western films and television are now saturated with scripts of aggressive and rather unpleasant characters (mostly men) causing nasty harm (rapes and tortures) to others, so that the 'good guys' can fly in and kill them and make them suffer too – and it is all becoming more sadistic. But everyone can go home joyous – 'we stuffed those bastards' and now we are waiting for the next episode. Competitive TV shows are no longer a celebration of an Olympic ideal of enjoying excellence, but the weekly focus on who will be rejected – who is not good enough this week, always tinged with trying to increase anxiety by making people wait to hear whether they are in or out.

We can also become angry and vengeful to our own experiences of ourselves and want to hurt ourselves (self-harm) when we think there are parts of ourselves that are unwanted, hurtful or damaging to us. We can treat parts of ourselves as if they are alien or criminal. So 'sensitivity to suffering' by itself would not define compassion. It is the motivational systems that distress signals tap into that are crucial. In this context, the issue of forgiveness becomes crucial to the softening of vengeance – and forgiveness can arise from compassionate insight – a theme that Nelson Mandela sought to instigate in his reconciliation councils. We see therefore how vital it is to recognise that compassion also carries a desire *not to cause harm* or take pleasure from harm caused.

The key issue here there is that by understanding compassion as a social mentality, linked to caring motivation, we are able to advance insight into harm avoidance and harm repair and how compassion motivates it. Developing a deep desire to not be harmful or to participate in harmful actions (and focus on guilt not shame if we do) is central to a compassionate identity. Indeed, it was trying to find ways to help deeply ashamed and self-critical people experience and tolerate sadness that partly gave birth to CFT (Gilbert, 2000, 2010). Having an evolutionary focus (Gilbert 1989/2016), I was trying to find ways to switch people from a self-focused competitive social mentality (often recruited in threatening environments) into a caring one (more common in safe environments) and in that way help them reorganise a whole range of psychological processes –congruent with the social mentality of compassion (Gilbert 1993; 2000, 2010; Gilbert & Irons, 2005). A core question remains: Is it possible to change phenotypic expression?

The two psychologies of compassion

As noted above, all evolved motives have two aspects: stimulus detection and appropriate action. For compassion these are: (1) Motivated sensitivity to, appraisal of, and engagement with, (signals of) suffering in self and others; and (2) Motivated action to (try to) alleviate and prevent it (and in humans motivation to acquire the wisdom for skilled action). In the model presented in Figure 3.3, there are six competencies for engagement and six for alleviation and prevention – discussed in more detail elsewhere (Gilbert, 2009, 2014).

Any motivation without the competencies to fulfil it wouldn't be very useful. In the case of compassion many have identified a range of competencies including: attentional attunement, empathy, sympathy, generosity, openness, distress tolerance, patience, commitment and wisdom amongst others (see Gilbert, Chapter 1, this volume). Many of these competencies will be *shared by other motivational systems*. For example, empathy, like courage and distress tolerance, can be useful for many motives and are not specific to compassion (Zaki, 2014). Currently, however, there is no agreement on exactly what the competencies are that underpin compassion. Part of the problem is the lack of clarity of different elements. For example, sympathy and tenderness may be seen as part of compassion, but actually they're also quite different. We can be tender when we look into the face of the smiling baby – which is not compassion (Niezink, Siero, Dijkstra, Buunk & Barelds, 2012). Kindness too is often linked to compassion, but remembering your birthday might be kind, but is not compassionate and so it too is not identical to compassion (Phillips & Taylor, 2009). Love is also very different to compassion, because it involves liking in a way that compassion may not. Liking-others and self-liking should not be confused with compassion

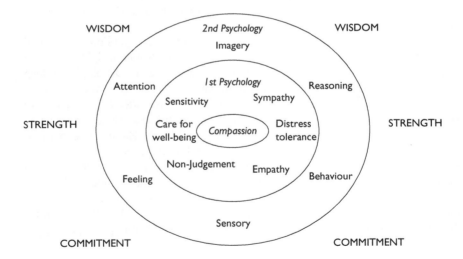

Figure 3.3 The motivation and competencies of compassion.

Source: Adapted From Gilbert (2009), *The Compassionate Mind*. With kind permission of Constable Robinson.

because compassion is about working with the suffering, distress and the dark side of ourselves and others, in order for us to more fully bring compassionate (Bodhichitta) intention into our lives and the world. The most powerful compassion is for what we do not like, do not love, and might be frightened of (Dalai Lama, 2001; Leowenstein & Small, 2007). Similarly for forgiveness, we do not need to like or love the people we forgive. Grouping all these positive social emotions into one process, 'compassion' is problematic.

Some of the socially intelligent competencies that create compassion from caring are outlined here. These are taken from what is now an extensive literature, so are not original at all, but are arranged in terms of the two psychologies of basic motives. Over time they may change or be added to and developed. The reader can judge for themselves if removing any one of them would make compassion stronger or weaker, or if others need to be added or refined. Note too that these are process variables or competencies not outcome variables.

First psychology: engagement with, and appraisal of, suffering

(Desire for) Compassionate well-being: As will be clear by now, in the contemplative conditions and from motivation theory the key focus of compassion training *is intention* – always being clear of one's motives and intention, and choosing intention wisely. Whether we are doing mindfulness, empathy or psychotherapy training, what is the intention and why? Clarifying the intention then gives rise to purpose and focus. With intention we set sail on the journey to engage suffering in order to find ways to understand, alleviate and prevent it (and certainly not carelessly or purposefully cause it). This is the way of Bodhicitta (Gilbert & Choden, 2013; Jinpa, 2015). In psychotherapy it's not enough that the client experiences the empathy of the therapist; they need to pick up on their intention. Some clients may have experienced empathy from others but with less than helpful intention (Kirby & Gilbert, Chapter 15, this volume).

Sensitivity

Most definitions start with some concept of *noticing* and *sensitive attention to suffering/distress*. As argued above, evolution only builds an attentional sensitivity competency to support a motivational and goal-seeking system. Attention sensitivity and subsequent processing, however, (as for any motivation) are subject to facilitators and inhibitors. For example, the dimension of *liking-disliking* runs through every motivational system – it is easier to eat the foods we like than those we don't (even if the latter are more healthy); it is easier to have sex with people we like than with people we don't; it is easier to cooperate with people we like than people we don't and of course it is easier to be compassionate to people we like than people we don't (Gilbert & Mascaro, in press; Loewenstein & Small, 2007). The one motivational system where it changes, is that it's harder to be competitive with people we like than people we dislike – disliking can make us insensitive to others' distress.

We are also more orientated to attend to and help friendly and happy people rather than distressed, unhappy people (we like happy-appreciative people more). Empathic awareness does not always result in compassionate actions to the most distressed (Hauser, Preston & Stansfield, 2014). Aristotle argued that we only have compassion if we think the suffering of another is nontrivial, that it is not deserved and we could imagine ourselves in their situation (Nassbaum, 2003). So the seriousness of suffering, sense of deservedness and empathy texture compassion-engagement and sensitivity for Aristotle.

The sense of deservedness is central in many religions too, which believe in the role of hell for the punishment of the sinner. Here, the compassion for the intense suffering of hell realms has to be blocked (we become *insensitive*) in favour of justification (Gilbert & Gilbert, 2015). In the Buddhist traditions, however, there is no sense of compassion being deserved or not – and deservedness probably is only relevant to hierarchical groups, that seek criteria to allocate or remove status and resources on some basis of deservedness and to punish cheaters (Gilbert 1989/2016). Compassion training can help us with these (evolved) sensitivity biases and develop the wisdom to extend our compassionate 'noticing' and engagement to those we may not like or know – even wishing to create a better world for those not yet born (Dalai Lama, 1995). So this is 'pay attention and note one's compassion inhibitors as they arise'.

Sympathy

Once the compassion motivation-intention and its attentional focusing is engaged, emotions and feelings arise from a direct (or sometimes imagined) experience of suffering. This is called sympathy (Eisenberg, Zhou & Koller, 2001; Eisenberg et al., 2015; Jensen et al., 2014). Whereas empathy requires us to have some capacity to feel similar feelings to another (feel/think as they do), in sympathy we are automatically emotionally drawn into the suffering of the other with feelings created in the self. The accuracy of *understanding* may be loose, however. The feelings and emotions ignited by sympathy may not match those of the object of sympathy. In extreme cases, the sympathiser may be more upset than the object of sympathy. As sympathy moves by the elicitation of feelings within oneself it can be elicited by projection, whereas projection reduces accurate empathy (Gilbert, 1989/2016, 2005a; Music, 2014). For example, we can feel distressed by somebody in a coma, even though clearly at that point they are not experiencing suffering, or somebody whose site of a stroke has made them indifferent to their loss; we can feel distress because we know how they used to be before the stroke. This is an example where again human evolved competencies have major impacts on sympathetic experience. However, if attention sensitivity to suffering creates sympathetic feelings that seem as threats or being overwhelmed, then rather than tuning into suffering we may tune out, disengage our attention, deny or dissociate. When sympathetic feelings seem intolerable (high personal distress as Eisenberg et al., 2015 note) we need the next competency of distress tolerance.

Distress tolerance

What's important for compassion to unfold then is that we are able to tolerate the feelings that arise when we engage with suffering (in ourselves or others), whatever those feelings might be. Core to distress tolerance is building *courage* – the courage to face and take action on suffering and the causes of suffering. *Courage* is at the heart of Buddhist approaches to compassion (Jinpa, 2014; Vessantara, 1993), although is not always referred to in more secular approaches. We need courage both to engage but also to act, and one might have one without the other. Hence, compassionate courage requires the capacity to *tolerate distress* rather than avoid or dissociate from it. Indeed, in many psychotherapies distress tolerance is a focus for therapeutic intervention (Gilbert, 2010; Linehan, 2014). Singer and Klimecki (2014) distinguish two neurophysiological systems they call empathy and personal distress. However, it is not so much low personal distress that motivates compassion but our ability to tolerate and override it. Nurses (I was one once as a holiday job) may have to clean up diarrhea and vomit, which is extremely unpleasant, but one overrides the sense of disgust and avoidance for the benefit of the patient. Also, in terms of a compassionate emotion and facial expressions (see Gilbert, Chapter 1, this volume), one's compassion expression is one of reassurance and even smiling 'Don't worry Mrs Smith, we will soon have this sorted; it's not your fault, you will be right as rain very soon'. Again emotion, actions and facial expression depend on context, and deliberate intention to address needs. So what helps us with tolerating distress is how we utilise our evolved competencies *knowingly*, choosing to stay with distress rather than avoid it.

In addition, we can 'deliberately knowingly and on purpose' choose to train ourselves to tolerate our own and others' distress. A simple example might be getting physically fit by exercising – not quitting when our heart is pumping, chest hurting and legs aching. It is *knowing intentionality* that enables this. Tolerating mental suffering can come from wise intention and focused purpose: the agoraphobic bears their anxiety, going further each day 'knowingly' to try to recover. A person tries to work with their anger, discovering and tolerating its dark side in order to develop compassion and Bodhichitta. Learning distress tolerance is often via graded tasks and practices and reducing shame. Tolerance builds acceptance but not necessarily liking. I can learn to be mindful of my anger, tolerate it (rather than repress or deny it) and take control of it, but I don't have to like it. Same with using the bathroom!

Empathy

Whereas the word compassion comes from the Latin *compati* implying 'suffering with', empathy comes from the Greek *empatheria* meaning 'to feel into' or 'to enter into the experience of another'. It does not imply suffering particularly, nor motivation particularly, *but a competency*. Empathy is multi-textured and multi-layered, with the earliest forms being emotional contagion which we may share with many animals (Jensen et al., 2014; Preston & de Waal, 2002). This also has its own ontogenetic development. For example, babies will cry to the sound of other babies crying rather than just noises; later, as young children, they may take a distressed child to their own mother; later still they take a distressed child to the child's mother. So we see here a gradual differentiation between self and another and improving competencies to understand 'needs'. In a major review, Batson (2009) identified eight basic definitions of empathy. The most common is to distinguish between cognitive empathy (or perspective taking) and emotional empathy (emotional mirroring, resonance or contagion) (Decety & Cowell, 2014; Decety & Ickes, 2011; Malle & Hodges, 2005; Preston & de Waal, 2002). The links between cognitive empathy, theory of mind, mentalising and intersubjectivity, and how they serve motives, is complex (Zaki, 2014).

There is a difference between the automatic, intuitive empathic response to another person, and an effortful process by which we deliberately try to imagine ourselves in the position of the other; to see the world through their eyes. The latter is key for psychotherapy training. Here, self–other differentiation is important (Malle & Hodges, 2005; Singer & Klimecki, 2014). We can distinguish between (1) trying to imagine what it would be like to actually be them, and (2) how we would feel (as ourselves) in that situation. The influential perception-action model (PAM) of Preston and de Waal (2002) suggests that mental states from a target activate representations of that state in observers. These representations are influenced not only by the observer's current state but also past experience, knowledge and motives (wanting to empathise). So, for example, empathising with somebody who likes hang gliding will be much easier if one is a hang glider oneself, and less so if one hates heights or with someone who has a problem with drugs if one also has that problem. However, sometimes, although people can empathise with others, if they dislike those traits in themselves they may dislike them in others and be less compassionate. In a fascinating study Mohr, Kross and Preston (2016) found that while distraught, depressed patients could empathise with distraught, depressed patients, they actually offered more support and help to more resilient depressed patients.

The link between empathy and compassion is complex in that we may well be able to understand people but not necessarily want to help, and we may not want to empathise too closely with what Jung called shadow material, our dark sides, and engage instead in projective identification. These processes, particularly unconscious empathic processes, are relatively unexplored (Huang & Bargh, 2014; Music, 2014) but could play a fundamental role in the facilitators and inhibitors of compassion. In an fMRI Hein, Silani, Preuschoff, Batson and Singer (2010) studied circuits associated with empathy while watching someone in (mild hand prick) pain. These circuits were less active if they were watching somebody who had previously been seen cheating or someone identified as belonging to a different group (football team). Even our empathic brain is selective on who it will light up to! Indeed, some of the moral dictates for in-groups are almost reversed for out-groups (killing the enemy is heroic, killing your friends is not). Part of the reason is because morality is evolved to serve in-group and much less out-group dynamics (Krebs, 2008; Music, 2014). So again, another reason to be cautious of compassion as a feeling is because of its out-groups biases (Loewenstein & Small, 2007).

Linked to this is how easy it is to make errors in how we think other people think or feel if we only use our own (egocentric) knowledge, experience and judgments (projections) rather than thinking about the perspective of the other: 'how I would be in that situation' (Nickerson, 1999). So our experience of empathy can be tinged by problems of projection. For example, a patient says 'It's been a difficult week because of the death of my father'. The therapist feels a sense of (what they take as empathic) sadness and reflects: 'So that's a very sad time for you'. The patient looks puzzled and says 'Hell no, I hated him – it's been difficult because of all the things I had to organise for the bloody funeral'. Sometimes it is important to recognise when a person may feel *differently* to us (Nickerson, 1999).

Interestingly, people with psychopathic disorders may lack sympathy and emotional attunement but have cognitive empathic abilities if they deliberately choose to employ them (Meffert, Gazzola, den Boer, Bartels & Keysers, 2013). What is crucial, though, is that caring interest and motivation seems lacking. Hence, capacities for feeling sadness and guilt for any harm they may do are also lacking. In contrast, not only might cognitive empathy relate to our personal experiences (Preston & de Waal, 2002) but some people might be very good mentalisers in some roles (social mentalities) but not others; e.g. poker players may have certain competencies that they do not use in care-requiring situations (Liotti & Gilbert, 2011). Mentalisation can be turned on and off by the degree of threat people feel in particular roles, their willingness to engage with it and the basic social mentality and relationship they are in (Liotti & Gilbert, 2011). A colleague I worked with was very empathic with patients but just thought her managers (authority figures) were 'callous' and had little interest 'mentalising from their position'. As a competency we can exert discerning choice of when and how we use empathy.

An important study that highlights the distinction between empathy as a competency and caring as motivation was provided by Winczewski, Bowen and Collins (2016). They asked couples to discuss personal and difficult relational issues and then looked at the combination of empathic accuracy with and without compassionate motivation and caring interest. Empathic accuracy without caring motivation was not helpful and possibly harmful whereas compassionate motivation associated with empathic accuracy was the most beneficial. In another study Koren-Karie, Oppenheim, Dolev, Sher and Etzion-Carasso (2002) explored three types of maternal interaction: Positively insightful, one-sided and disengaged. Positively insightful mothers try to see their child's experiences through the *child's eyes*, and accounting for them being a child. The one side-mother is keen to care for her child but has preset (adult) ideas of what a child needs and a 'undimensional' view of the child. Disengaged mothers lack emotional involvement. Even thinking about what might be going on in their child's mind was novel to them and not something they found pleasant. Once again the combinations of motive/intention with empathy are crucial. One without the other may flounder.

Non-judgment

The sixth competency is non-judgment in the sense of not condemning. Here is the ability to accept (though neither like or agree). Acceptance makes available information for the other competencies to process because we are not fighting with it or trying to push it away. So being motivated to develop an open acceptance aids distress tolerance and enables empathy, and empathy helps build motivation, but wise-discernment is always core to compassion too.

Second psychology: wise action

If we only have the competencies of the first psychology of compassion, we would be very limited. We could, for example, imagine going to the Accident and Emergency department with a broken arm and encountering a doctor who had all of the first psychologies. They were attentive to our pain, clearly emotionally moved by it, able to tolerate the sight of blood, had an insight into why we were in pain and did not judge us because we'd fallen over and broken arm, or because we were screaming! No matter how much the doctor demonstrated these wonderful qualities at some point we would want them to focus on action. The degree to which they had trained to ensure they had the skills to wisely and competently set the bone would be a mark of their full compassion. If they had been lazy and not bothered to study – that would be poor compassion. The first psychology of engagement is rarely enough. This is why commitment (to develop wisdom/ skills) is an important part of the definition of compassion given here and as used in compassion focused therapy (see Kirby & Gilbert, Chapter 15, this volume).

Helpful attention

In order to begin to address suffering and distress we need to switch our attention to bringing to mind our knowledge and wisdom of what is likely to be helpful. For example, our doctor might bring into mind his training. We can only attend to what is helpful if have learnt what is helpful. Empathy clearly plays a role here too.

Imagery

One of the major evolved competencies of modern humans is our ability to imagine – (even what doesn't actually exist); to be able to run scenarios in the mind (Singer, 2006). This is what makes humans hugely creative and fantastic problem solvers. In compassion training, imagery is used in many different ways. For example, we can imagine how to be compassionate but we can also imagine compassion coming to us, that is receiving compassion (Gilbert, 2010). Imagery also stimulates physiological systems in ways that verbal and symbolic processing may not. Imagery has very powerful physiological effects and this is used in CFT training. Indeed, there are many meditation techniques that guide people through different imagery practices in order to stimulate different states of mind and build compassion (Gilbert & Choden, 2013; Jinpa, 2015).

Reasoning

Some of the obvious major advances in human evolution from earlier ancestors are our capacities for reflection, reasoning and metacognition (Byrne, 1995; Suddendorf & Whitten, 2001). Compassion is not stupid or simply automatic but has a wisdom to it – the best compassion is rooted in wise insight and *wise* action (Germer & Siegel, 2012). Sometimes wisdom can take years to achieve. In DBT, therapists discuss the importance of cultivating a 'wise mind' (Linehan, 2014). Wisdom allows us to reason not about only the individual but the social contexts in which the individual is embedded, not only about the immediate now but also the future. What's important for compassion is that our reasoning is recruited for, and directed by, caring motivation/intention rather than, say, competitive self-interest. Being able to reason integrates competencies for language and symbolising, empathy and imagination.

Behaviours

We can of course engage in behaviours that appear to be linked to a motive but are not. People can express behaviours for strategic reasons. For example, we may appear cooperative when we don't feel cooperative or wish to fake it – sex workers do not feel sexy – and we may try to act with compassion and caring when really the main focus is to be liked and avoid rejection: what has been called submissive compassion (Catarino et al., 2014). So helpful behaviour can have a defensive intention or motive.

There are a number of different compassionate behaviours that depend on context and purpose. One is linked to capacity for *soothing* distress: being present, listening, validating and empathising, maybe stroking, hugging or hand holding. As I noted in Chapter 1 voice tones, body postures and facial expressions can play a key role here. Clients (and therapists) can be taught how to work with the body in order to bring better parasympathetic balance, which can then provide the context for them to start to think through difficulties or tolerate difficulties. Other behaviors might be more active as in driving someone to hospital, working on projects to help others and standing up against injustice.

Another aspect of behaviour is choosing to cultivate compassion – so for example one might choose to go on a meditation retreat in order to develop mindful compassion, or practice engaging in one compassionate act (that one wouldn't have done normally) each day. Choosing our actions wisely in order to develop motivation and competencies such as caring and compassion is part of behavioural development. Developing the competencies and capacities to follow through on intentions can be important because while we may have good intentions the necessary behaviours may not follow.

Compassionate behaviour can involve exposure to what is feared in order to alleviate and prevent suffering. This develops *courage*, cultivated through compassionate distress tolerance. Indeed, the role of courage for compassion is sometimes overlooked (Gilbert, 2005a). We need compassion to stand against unkind or harmful behavior. Interestingly, although friendliness and agreeableness are commonly associated with compassion, people who are friendly and agreeable may not necessarily be the most courageous. In fact, Bègue et al. (2014) note that these individuals may try to avoid conflict, can be submissive to avoid conflict, and may even be complicit in Milgram-like obedience experiments. Crucially then, for kind people 'looking after one's elderly neighbour or trying to treat others with kindness' may be relatively easy if this does not involve risks to themselves, but they may struggle to overcome fears, risks or injury in saving others or standing up against hostile authority. And those individuals that have that courage might not have a 'kindly temperament'. So while kindness serves compassion in some contexts, compassion is more than kindness; compassion requires courage to confront our own fears, blocks and resistances across contexts (Gilbert & Choden, 2013; Gilbert & Mascaro, in press; Jinpa, 2015; Vessantara, 1993).

Compassionate behaviour is also not without its moral dilemmas. Batson, Klein, Highberger and Shaw (1995) demonstrated that justice-fairness and care-compassion focused moral thinking and behaviours are different prosocial motives, which can produce different behaviours and even conflicts. Or consider saving people in say a war situation (e.g. Jewish people from the Nazis). That could be regarded as an heroic act but if you're caught your whole family will be killed. To what extent does putting one's children at risk count as a moral compassionate act? Importantly then, compassion can involve complex moral conflicts of judgment (Krebs, 2008; Music, 2014).

Sensory

Sensory focusing can be used to help people to be aware of body states and also cultivate body states that are conducive to the cultivation of compassion. For example, ways of breathing and feeling more grounded, with better parasympathetic tone, which in turn influences frontal cortex can be practised. Bornemann, Kok, Böckler and Singer (2016) found that helping people improve their heart-rate variability (HRV) had knock-on effects to prosocial behaviour. One reason for this may be that improving HRV influences threat processing (Stellar & Keltner, Chapter 7, this volume). Focusing on body states is increasingly important in a range of psychotherapies (Van der Kolk, 2015), including compassion focused ones (Gilbert, 2010, 2014a). Becoming mindful of how different thoughts, behaviours and feelings play out in the body is important for body and sensory focus work. Different types of mindfulness can utilise sensory experience, such as focusing on the breath or a particular sound (Germer & Barnhofer, Chapter 4, this volume; Gilbert & Choden, 2013). There are also a range of 'body' therapies and yoga and practices which are specifically designed to help the body create certain states of mind, insight and abilities.

Feelings

As noted in Chapter 1, feelings of compassion are associated with context. For example, they may be ones linked to sympathy that cluster around feelings of sadness. However, other blends of feelings can also arise; for example, anxiety and anger. In 1984 (Sir) Bob Geldolf became so angry at the inaction of governments over the Ethiopian famine crisis that he established Band-Aid which was to raise over £100 million. While obvious sadness and concern were part of his reaction he was clear that it was his also his anger that fuelled the urgency of his behaviour and focus. Moreover, an angry outburst on the BBC resulted in a big increase in donations. As Lowenstein and Small (2007) note, feelings are often part of compassion but we also need to use our rationality and sense of a moral compass when focusing on the alleviation and prevention of suffering.

Conclusion

The approach to compassion taken here links it with fundamental issues in human evolution that have profoundly important implications for how we live our lives both individually and collectively. For the contemplative traditions the core of compassion is *intentionality* (Bodhichitta), and the cultivation of *dedication and courage* to help others (Jinpa, 2015; Vessantara, 1993) which texture the multiple domains of living (as in the eightfold pathway). The same for CFT. However, these characteristics are sometimes less emphasised in some of the secular approaches.

Emerging from caring motivation, combined with human social intelligences, compassion is one of a range of prosocial processes which can be extended to kin and non-kin depending on context – but group boundaries can be an obstacle. The evolution of the motives to be caring of others probably has a number of different routes from infant care and multiple care-takers (Hrdy, 2011) to the value of supporting one's alliances and being supported, and being desired as an investing sexual mate (Goetz et al., 2010; Mayseless, 2016). In addition, many of the competencies that support compassion also support other motives and facilitate competent social agency in a world of minds influencing other minds (Malle & Hodges, 2005; Siegel, 2016).

What science is also beginning to indicate is that our capacities to be empathic to others (one of the core competencies of compassion) may depend to some degree on our capacities to be empathic to ourselves and in tune with our own emotions. If, for various reasons, we are not able to process our emotions but remain unconscious to our fears, rages and sadnesses, fearful of feeling vulnerable, despair or alone, this can be a block to empathy and compassion motivation and potentially breaks links with the concept of common humanity. How can I be emotionally attuned to your deep existential fear of death, for example, if I'm completely blocked out on it myself? Internal emotional disengagement can also significantly interfere with harm avoidance and experiences of guilt, sadness and remorse (Shiftcliff et al., 2009).

Compassion can be viewed as a *social mentality* which choreographs interpersonal dances utilising various social intelligences, including those depicted in Figure 3.2.

Indeed, these competencies are often the focus for therapeutic interventions and compassion cultivation (Gilbert, 2010). So, for example, we may help people develop and cultivate attention sensitivity, mindfulness, distress tolerance, empathy, mentalisation training, body awareness and grounding, emotion awareness, wise reasoning or courageous compassionate behaviour (see Kirby & Gilbert, Chapter 15, this volume). These are co-ordinated and recruited via generating an inner sense of one's best compassionate self (one's inner Bodichitta) and then, like an actor taking on a role or character, beginning to practice thinking and acting from this sense of self. Over time individuals can begin to distinguish between how (for example) angry self, or anxious self might deal with a situation in comparison to a deliberately cultivated compassionate self. This also goes for how compassion works internally in that it operates as a relation-forming aspect of mind – we can take a compassionate stance to our own angry, anxious, depressed or critical tendencies or selves for example. We can try to create internal roles of empathic understanding and support (see for example http://compassionforvoices.com/). It is thus an integrating process of mind.

As noted too, a social mentality can't be understood in terms of (just) the individual but has to be understood, rather, in terms of the interpersonal dances it creates and responds to (see also Siegel, 2016). A social mentality is relatively useless without a partner to enact it (although one can play them out in imagination).

What is crucial is *the intentionality* that lies behind the use of our competencies and the dances we seek to create in and with others. By having a better understanding of the competencies that support compassion we have better ways of designing therapies to cultivate and use compassion motives to stimulate brain systems therapeutically. We can also work with organisations and the political groups to promote compassion and prosocial values, motives and behaviour in the world (Ekman, 2014). We are seeking a more prosocial dance of the phenotypes.

References

Arnocky, S., Pich, T., Albert, G., Ouellette, D., & Barclay, P. (2016). Altruism predicts mating success in humans. *British Journal of Psychology* (advanced online). doi:10.1111/bjop.1220s.

Barrett, L., Dunbar, R., & Lycett, J. (2002). *Human Evolutionary Psychology*. London: Palgrave.

Batson, C.D. (2009). These things called empathy: Eight related but distinct phenomena. In J. Decety and W. Ickes (eds) *The Social Neuroscience of Empathy* (pp. 3–15). Cambridge, MA: MIT Press.

Batson, C. D., Klein, T. R., Highberger, L., & Shaw, L. L. (1995). Immorality from empathy-induced altruism: When compassion and justice conflict. *Journal of Personality and Social Psychology*, 68, 1042–1054.

Bègue, L., Beauvois, J. L., Courbet, D., Oberlé, D., Lepage, J., & Duke, A. A. (2014). Personality predicts obedience in a Milgram paradigm. *Journal of Personality*. Advanced online publication.

Bernard, C., Mills, M., Swenson, L., & Walsh, R. P. (2005). An evolutionary theory of human motivation. *Genetic, Social, and General Psychology Monographs*, 131, 129–184.

Böckler, A., Tusche, A. & Singer, T. (2016). The structure of human prosociality: Differentiating altruistically motivated, norm motivated, strategically motivated, and self-reported prosocial behaviour. *Social Psychological and Personality Science (advanced online)* doi: 10.1177/1948550616639650.

Bornemann, B., Kok, B. E., Böckler, A. & Singer, T. (2016). Helping from the heart: Voluntary upregulation of heart rate variability predicts altruistic behaviour. *Biological Psychiatry*, 119, 54–63.

Brown, S. L., & Brown, R. M. (2015). Connecting prosocial behavior to improved physical health: Contributions from the neurobiology of parenting. *Neuroscience and Biobehavioral Reviews*, 55, 1–17.

Buss, D. M., *Evolutionary Psychology: The New Science of Mind (5th edition)*. London. Routledge.

Byrne, R. (1995). *The Thinking Ape: The Evolutionary Origins of Human Intelligence.* New York: Oxford University Press.

Catarino, F., Gilbert, P., McEwan, K., & Baião, R. (2014). Compassion motivations: Distinguishing submissive compassion from genuine compassion and its association with shame, submissive behavior, depression, anxiety and stress. *Journal of Social and Clinical Psychology*, 33, 399–412. doi: 10.1521/jscp.2014.33.5.399.

Cieri, R. L., Churchill, S. E., Franciscus, R. G., Tan, J., & Hare, B. (2014). Craniofacial feminization, social tolerance, and the origins of behavioral modernity. *Current Anthropology*, 55, 419–443.

Cortina, M. & Liotti, G. (2010). Attachment is about safety and protection, intersubjectivity is about sharing and social understanding the relationship between attachment and intersubjectivity. The relationships between attachment and intersubjectivity. *Psychoanalytic Psychology*, 27, 410–441.

Crocker, J., & Canevello, A. (2012). Consequences of self-image and compassionate goals. In P. G. Devine and A. Plant (eds) *Advances in Experimental Social Psychology* (pp. 229–277). New York: Elsevier.

Dalai Lama (1995). *The Power of Compassion.* India: HarperCollins.

Dalai Lama (2001). *An Open Heart.* London: Hodder and Stoughton.

Decety, J., & Cowell, J. M. (2014). Friends or foes: Is empathy necessary for moral behavior? *Perspectives on Psychological Science*, 9, 525–537. doi: 10.1177/1745691614545130.

Decety, J., & Ickes, W. (2011). *The Social Neuroscience of Empathy.* Cambridge, MA: Bradford Press.

Deckers, L. (2014). *Motivation: Biological, Psychological, and Environmental.* London: Routledge.

Dunbar, R. I. M. (2007). Mind the bonding gap: Or why humans aren't just great apes. *Proceedings of the British Academy*, 154, 403–433.

Eisenberg, N., VanSchyndel, S. K., & Hofer, C. (2015). The association of maternal socialization in childhood and adolescence with adult offsprings' sympathy/caring. *Developmental Psychology*, 51, 7–16. doi: 10.1037/a0038137.

Eisenberg, N., Zhou, Q., & Koller, S. (2001). Brazilian adolescents' prosocial moral judgment and behavior: Relations to sympathy, perspective taking, gender-role orientation, and demographic characteristics. *Child Development*, 72, 518–534. doi:10.1111/1467-8624.00294.

Ekman, P. (2014). *Moving Toward Global Compassion.* E-book available from www.paule kman.com.

Fletcher, L., & Hayes, S. C. (2005). Relational frame theory, acceptance and commitment therapy, and a functional analytic definition of mindfulness. *Journal of Rational-emotive and Cognitive-behavior Therapy*, 23(4), 315–336.

Fredrickson, B. L., Grewen, K. M., Coffey, K. A., Algoe, S. B., Firestine, A. M., Arevalo, J. M. G., . . . Cole, S. W. (2013). A functional genomic perspective on human well-being. *Proceedings of the National Academy of Sciences*, 110, 13684–13689. doi: 10.1073/pnas.1305419110.

Geary, D. C. (2000). Evolution and proximate expression of human parental investment. *Psychological Bulletin*, 126, 55–77.

Geary, D. C., & Huffman, K. J. (2002). Brain and cognitive evolution: Forms of modularity and functions of the mind. *Psychological Bulletin*, 128, 667–698.

Germer, C. K., & Siegel, R. D. (2012). *Wisdom and Compassion in Psychotherapy*. New York: Guilford.

Gilbert, P. (1989/2016). *Human Nature and Suffering*. London: Routledge.

Gilbert, P. (1993). Defence and safety: Their function in social behaviour and psychopathology. *British Journal of Clinical Psychology*, 32, 131–153

Gilbert, P. (1998). What is shame? Some core issues and controversies. In P. Gilbert & B. Andrews (eds) *Shame: Interpersonal Behaviour, Psychopathology, and Culture* (pp. 3–38). New York: Oxford University Press.

Gilbert, P. (2000). Social mentalities: Internal 'social' conflicts and the role of inner warmth and Compassion in cognitive therapy. In P. Gilbert & Bailey, K. G. (eds) *Genes on the Couch: Explorations in Evolutionary Psychotherapy* (pp. 118–150). Hove: Psychology Press.

Gilbert, P. (2005a). Compassion and cruelty: A biopsychosocial approach. In P. Gilbert (ed.) *Compassion: Conceptualisations, Research and Use in Psychotherapy* (pp. 3–74). London: Routledge.

Gilbert, P. (2005b). Social mentalities: A biopsychosocial and evolutionary reflection on social relationships. In M. Baldwin (ed) *Interpersonal Cognition* (pp. 299–333). New York: Guilford.

Gilbert, P. (2007). *Psychotherapy and Counselling for Depression (3rd Edition)*. London: Sage.

Gilbert, P. (2009). *The Compassionate Mind: A New Approach to the Challenge of Life*. London: Constable & Robinson.

Gilbert, P. (2010). *Compassion Focused Therapy: The CBT Distinctive Features Series*. London: Routledge.

Gilbert, P. (2014a). The origins and nature of compassion focused therapy. *British Journal of Clinical Psychology*, 53, 6–41. doi: 10.1111/bjc.12043.

Gilbert, P. (2014b). Negotiating in a world of mixed beliefs and value systems: A compassion-focused model. In M. Gallucio (ed.) *International Negotiations*. New York: Springer.

Gilbert, P. (2015a). The evolution and social dynamics of compassion. *Journal of Social & Personality Psychology Compass*, 9, 239–254. doi: 10.1111/spc3.12176.

Gilbert, P. (2015b). An evolutionary approach to emotion in mental health with a focus on affiliative emotions. *Emotion Review* (special issues Normal and Abnormal Emotion). K. Scherer (ed.) 7, 230–237. doi: 10.1177/1754073915576552.

Gilbert, P. (2015c). Affiliative and prosocial motives and emotions in mental health. *Dialogues in Clinical Neuroscience*, 17, 381–389.

Gilbert, P. (in press). Exploring compassion focused therapy in forensic settings: An evolutionary and social-contextual approach. In J. Davies & C. Nagi (eds) *Individual Psychological Therapies in Forensic Settings*. London: Routledge.

Gilbert, P. & McGuire, M. (1998). Shame, status and social roles: The psychobiological continuum from monkeys to humans. In P. Gilbert & B. Andrews (eds) *Shame:*

Interpersonal Behavior, Psychopathology and Culture (pp. 99–125). New York: Oxford University Press.

Gilbert, P., Catarino, F., Duarte, C., Matos, M., Kolts, R., Stubbs, J., Ceresatto, L., Duarte, J., & Pinto-Gouveia, J. (in press). Three orientations of compassion: The development of self-report measures and their link to depression. *Frontiers in Psychiatry.*

Gilbert, P., & Choden (2013). *Mindful Compassion.* London: Constable & Robinson.

Gilbert, P., & Gilbert, H. (2015). Cruelty, evolution, and religion: The challenge for the new spiritualities. In T. G. Plante (ed.) *The Psychology of Compassion and Cruelty: Understanding the Emotional, Spiritual and Religious Influences* (pp. 1–15). Oxford: Praeger.

Gilbert, P., & Irons, C. (2005). Focused therapies and compassionate mind training for shame and self-attacking. In P. Gilbert (ed) *Compassion: Conceptualisations, Research and Use in Psychotherapy* (pp. 263–325). London: Routledge.

Gilbert, P., & Mascaro, J. (in press). Compassion: Fears, blocks, and resistances: An evolutionary investigation. In E. Sappla & J. Doty (eds) *Handbook of Compassion.* New York: Oxford University Press.

Gilbert, P., McEwan, K., Matos, M., & Rivis, A. (2011). Fears of compassion: Development of three self-report measures. *Psychology and Psychotherapy: Theory, research and practice,* 84, 239–255. doi: 10.1348/147608310X526511.

Goetz, J. E., Keltner, D., & Simon-Thomas, E. (2010). Compassion: An evolutionary analysis and empirical review. *Psychological Bulletin,* 136, 351–374.

Goodall, J. (1990). *Through a Window: My Thirty Years with the Chimpanzees of Gombe.* New York: Penguin.

Goodall. K., Trejnowska, A., & Darling, S. (2012). The relationship between dispositional mindfulness, attachment security and emotion regulation. *Personality and Individual Differences,* 52, 622–626.

Hauser, D. J., Preston, S. D., & Stansfield, R. B. (2014). Altruism in the wild: When affiliative motives to help positive people overtake empathic motives to help the distressed. *Journal of Experimental Psychology: General,* 143, 1295–1305.

Hein, G., Silani, G., Preuschoff, K., Batson, C. D., & Singer, T. (2010). Neural responses to ingroup and outgroup members' suffering predict individual differences in costly helping. *Neuron,* 68, 149–160.

Hermanto, N., & Zuroff, D. C. (2016). The social mentality theory of self-compassion and self-reassurance: The interactive effect of care-seeking and caregiving. *Journal of Social Psychology* (advanced online). doi:10.1080/00224545.2015.1135779.

Hermanto, N., Zuroff, D. C., Kopala-Sibley, D. C., Kelly, A. C., Matos, M., & Gilbert, P. (2016). Ability to receive compassion from others buffers the depressogenic effect of self-criticism: A cross-cultural multi-study analysis. *Personality and Individual Differences,* 98, 324–332. doi.org/10.1016/j.paid.2016.04.055.

Hoge, E. A., Chen, M. M., Orr, E., Metcalf, C. A., Fischer, L. E., Pollack, M. H., . . . Simon, N. M. (2013). Loving-Kindness meditation practice associated with longer telomeres in women. *Brain, Behavior, and Immunity,* 32, 159–163. doi: 10.1016/j.bbi.2013.04.005.

Hrdy, S. B. (2011). *Mothers and Others: The Evolutionary Origins of Mutual Understanding.* Boston, MA: Harvard University Press.

Huang, J. Y., & Bargh, J. A. (2014). The selfish goal: Autonomously operating motivational structures as the proximate cause of human judgment and behavior. *Behavioral and Brain* Sciences, 37, 121–175.

Jensen, K., Vaish, A., & Schmidt, M. F. (2014). The emergence of human prosociality: Aligning with others through feelings, concerns, and norms. *Frontiers in Psychology*, 5, 822.

Jinpa, T. (2015). *A Fearless Heart: Why Compassion is the Key to Greater Well-Being*. London: Little Brown.

Kelly, A, C., Zuroff, D.C., Leybman, M. J., & Gilbert, P. (2012). Social safeness, received social support, and maladjustment: Testing a tripartite model of affect regulation. *Cognitive Therapy and Research*, 36, 815–826. doi: 10.1007/s10608-011-9432.

Keltner, D., Kogan, A., Piff, P. K., & Saturn, S. R. (2014). The sociocultural appraisals, values, and emotions (SAVE) framework of prosociality: Core processes from gene to meme. *The Annual Review of Psychology*, 65, 425–460. doi: 10.1146/annurev-psych-010213-115054 .

Klinger, E. (1977). *Meaning and Void*. Minneapolis, MN: University of Minnesota Press.

Koren-Karie, N., Oppenheim, D., Dolev, S., Sher, S., & Etzion-Carasso, A. (2002). Mothers' insightfulness regarding their infants' internal experience: Relations with maternal sensitivity and infant attachment. *Developmental Psychology*, 38, 534–542.

Krebs, D. L. (2008). Morality: An evolutionary account. *Perspectives on Psychological Science*, 3, 149–172.

Leach, C. W., Spears, R., Branscombe, N. R., & Dossje, B. (2003). Malicious pleasure. Schadenfreude at the suffering of another group. *Journal of Personality and Social Psychology*, 84, 932–943.

Leary, M. R. (2004). *The Curse of the Self: Self-awareness, Egotism and the Quality of Human Life*. Oxford: Oxford University Press.

LeDoux, J. E. (2014). Coming to terms with fear. *Proceedings of the National Academy of Sciences*, 111, 2871–2878.

Linehan, M., M. (2014). *The DBT Skills Training Book*. New York: Guilford Press.

Liotti, G., & Gilbert, P. (2011). Mentalizing, motivations and social mentalities: Theoretical considerations and implications for psychotherapy. *Psychology and Psychotherapy*, 84, 9–25.

Loewenstein, G., & Small, D. A. (2007). The scarecrow and the tin man: The vicissitudes of human sympathy and caring. *Review of General Psychology*, 11, 112–126. doi: 10.1037/1089-2680.11.2.112.

MacLean, P. (1985). Brain evolution relating to family, play and the separation call. *Archives of General Psychiatry*, 42, 405–417.

Malle, B. F., & Hodges, S. D (2005). *Self and Others: How Humans Bridge the Divide between Self and Others*. New York: Guilford Press.

Mayseless, O. (2016). *The Caring Motivation: An Integrated Theory*. Oxford: Oxford University Press.

Meffert, H., Gazzola, V., den Boer, J. A., Bartels, A. A. J., & Keysers, C. (2013). Reduced spontaneous but relatively normal deliberate vicarious representations in psychopathy. *Brain*, 136, 2550–2562.

Mohr, A. H., Kross, K., & Preston, S. D. (2016). Devil in the details: Effects of depression on the prosocial response depend on timing and similarity. *Adaptive Human Behavior and Physiology*, 2, 281–297. doi: 10.1007/s40750-016-0044-x.

Music, G. (2014). *The Good Life: Well Being and the Neuroscience of Altruism Selfishness and Immorality*. London: Routledge.

Nassbaum, M. C. (2003). *Upheavals of Thought: The Intelligence of Emotions*. Cambridge: Cambridge University Press.

Neel, R., Kenrick, D. T., White, A. E., & Neuberg, S. L. (2016). Individual differences in fundamental social motives. *Personality and Individual Differences*, 110, 887–907. doi.org/10.1037/pspp0000068.supp.

Nell, V. (2006). Cruelty's rewards: The gratifications of perpetrators and spectators. *Behavioral and Brain Sciences*, 29, 211–257.

Nickerson, R. S. (1999). How we know – and sometimes misjudge – what others know: Imputing one's own knowledge to others. *Psychological Bulletin*, 125(6), 737–759. doi: 10.1037/0033-2909.125.6.737.

Niezink, L. W., Siero, F. W., Dijkstra, P., Buunk, A. P., & Barelds, D. P. H. (2012). Empathic concern: Distinguishing between tenderness and sympathy. *Motivation and Emotion*, 36, 544–549. doi: 10.1007/s11031-011-9276-z.

Panksepp, J., &. Panksepp, J. B. (2013). Toward a cross-species understanding of empathy. *Trends in Neurosciences*, 36, 489–496. doi: 10.1016/j.tins.2013.04.009.

Phillips, A., & Taylor, B. (2009). *On Kindness*. London: Hamish Hamilton Press.

Porges, S.W. (2007). The polyvagal perspective. *Biological Psychology*, 74, 116–143.

Preston, S. D., & de Waal, F. B. M. (2002). Empathy: Its ultimate and proximate bases. *The Behavioral and Brain Sciences*, 25, 1–71. doi:10.1017/S0140525X02510013.

Ricard, M. (2015). *Altruism: The Power of Compassion to Change Itself and the World*. London Atlantic Books.

Sachs, J. (2012). *The Price of Civilization: Economics and Ethics After the Fall*. New York: Vintage.

Sedikides, C., & Skowronski, J. J. (1997). The symbolic self in evolutionary context. *Personality and Social Psychology Review*, 1, 80–102.

Shirtcliff, E. A., Vitacco, M. J., Graf, A. R., Gostisha, A. J., Merz, J. L. & Zahn-Waxler, C. (2009). Neurobiology of empathy and callousness: Implications for the development of antisocial behavior. *Behavior Sciences and the Law*, 27: 137–171. doi: 10.1002/bsl.862.

Siegel, D. J. (2011). *Mindsight: Transform Your Brain with the New Science of Kindness*. New York: One World Publications.

Siegel, D. J. (2016). *Mind: A Journey to the Heart of Being Human*. New York: Norton.

Singer, J. (2006). *Imagery in Psychotherapy*. Washington: American Psychological Press.

Singer, T., & Bolz, M. (eds) (2012). *Compassion: Bridging Practice and Science*. http://www.compassion-training.org/.

Singer, T., & Klimecki, O. M. (2014). Empathy and compassion. *Current Biology*, 24, 875–878.

Stuewig, J., Tangney, J. P., Heigel, C., Harty, L., & McCloskey, L. (2010). Shaming, blaming, and maiming: Functional links among the moral emotions, externalization of blame, and aggression. *Journal of Research in Personality*, 44, 91–102.

Suddendorf. T., & Whitten, A. (2001). Mental evolutions and development: Evidence for secondary representation in children, great apes and other animals. *Psychological Bulletin*, 127, 629–650.

Tirch, D., Schoendorfe, B., & Silberstein, L. R. (2015). *ACT Practitioner's Guide to the Science of Compassion: Tools for Fostering Psychological Flexibility*. California: New Harbinger.

Trevarthen, C., & Aitken, K. (2001). Infant intersubjectivity: Research, theory, and clinical applications. *Journal of Child Psychology and Psychiatry*, 42, 3–48.

Tsering, G. T. (2005). *The Four Noble Truths: The Foundation of Buddhist Thought (Volume 1)*. Boston, MA: Wisdom Publications.

Van Der Kolk (2015). *The Body Keeps the Score: Mind, Brain and Body in the Transformation of Trauma*. New York: Penguin.

Van Doesum, N. J., Van Lange, D. A., & Van Lange, P. A. M. (2013). Social mindfulness: Skill and will to navigate the social world. *Journal of Personality and Social Psychology*, 105, 86–103. doi: 10.1037/a0032540.

Vessantara (1993). *Meeting the Buddhas: A Guide to Buddhas, Bodhisattvas and Tantric Deities*. Cambridge: Windhorse Publications.

Warneken, F. & Tomasello, M. (2009). The roots of human altruism. *The British Journal of Psychology*, 100, 455–471.

Weiner, B. (1992). *Human Motivation: Metaphors Theories and Research*. London: Sage.

Whitten, A. (1999). The evolution of deep social mind in humans. In M. C. Corballis, S. E. G. Lea (eds) *The Descent of Mind: Psychological Perspectives on Humanoid Evolution* (pp. 173–193). New York: Oxford University Press.

Winczewski, L. A., Bowen, J. D., & Collins N. L. (2016). Is empathic accuracy enough to facilitate responsive behaviour in dyadic Interaction? Distinguishing ability from motivation. *Psychological Science*, 27, 394–404. doi: 10.1177/0956797615624491.

Yalom, I. D. (1980). *Existential Psychotherapy*. New York: Basic Books.

Zaki, J. (2014). Empathy: A motivated account. *Psychological Bulletin*, 140, 1608–1647. doi: 10.1037/a0037679.

Chapter 4

Mindfulness and compassion
Similarities and differences

Christopher Germer and Thorsten Barnhofer

In the last 25 years, mindfulness training has found its way into many aspects of modern society including psychology, medicine, business, education, and the military (Williams & Kabat-Zinn, 2013). Compassion training is following close on the heels of mindfulness, emphasizing the attitudinal and relational aspects of mind training. In this chapter, we will explore ancient and modern meanings of *mindfulness* and how compassion fits or doesn't fit in with those concepts, and how we currently teach mindfulness. Then we will do the reverse – consider the multidimensional meaning of *compassion* and the role mindfulness plays in compassion theory and practice, followed by a discussion of the unique features of self-compassion training. Finally, we will review some scientific evidence for considering mindfulness and compassion as converging or diverging psychological processes.

Compassion in mindfulness

Mindfulness as we currently know it has its roots in Buddhist psychology and is considered the "heart of Buddhist psychology" (Nyanaponika Thera, 1965) in the Theravada ("Elder Vehicle") Buddhist tradition. Mindfulness derives from the Pali word *sati*. In ancient times, *sati* meant "memory" in the usual sense, but the Buddha applied it in a special way to describe "lucid awareness of present happenings," especially awareness of the impermanent, interdependent nature of experience (Bodhi, 2013). Sati also connotes meta-cognitive awareness, or being aware of knowing itself. Mindfulness occupies a less central role in the Mahayana ("Great Vehicle") tradition (usually including Tibetan and Zen Buddhism), but is considered nonetheless essential for cultivating the stable, focused attention required for more demanding meditations on compassion and emptiness.

In both the Theravada and Mahayana traditions, the fruit of mindfulness depends on the intention behind a person's practice (Wallace, 2008). For example, mindfulness is only possible when we are free from the grip of greed, aversion, and delusion (spacing-out). As meditation teacher Jack Kornfield (2011) once quipped, "You can't meditate after a day of killing and stealing. It just doesn't work" (p. 276). Mindfulness has always been part of a broader agenda that is essentially compassionate – dedicated to the alleviation of suffering, one's own and others.

In our modern understanding of mindfulness, the elements of kindness and compassion are implied in the words "non-judgment" or "acceptance." The most common definition of mindfulness is "the awareness that emerges through paying attention, on purpose, in the present moment, and non-judgmentally to the unfolding of experience moment by moment" (Kabat-Zinn, 2003, p. 145). A stripped-down version of that definition is "awareness of present experience, with acceptance" (Germer, 2013, p. 7). In a consensus opinion among experts, Bishop and colleagues (2004) proposed a two-component model of mindfulness: "The first component involves the self-regulation of attention so that it is maintained on immediate experience, thereby allowing for increased recognition of mental events in the present moment. The second component involves adopting a particular orientation towards one's experience that is characterized by curiosity, openness, and acceptance" (p. 232).

Our modern, scientific understanding of mindfulness emphasizes awareness itself more than the *qualities* of mindful awareness such as loving-kindness and compassion. Loving-kindness is "the wish that all sentient beings be happy," and compassion is "the wish that all sentient beings be free from suffering" (Dalai Lama, 2003, p. 67). The emphasis on awareness in mindfulness practice probably stems from the Theravada tradition which is a wisdom tradition concerned primarily with lucid awareness of things as they are, especially impermanence, the universality of suffering, and the insubstantiality of "self." In the Mahayana tradition, particularly Tibetan Buddhism, the point of mindfulness is to become enlightened for the sake of all beings so compassion cultivation is of greater importance. Ultimately we need both wisdom and compassion, known in the Tibetan tradition as "two wings of the bird."

Language can also skew our understanding of mindfulness. The ancient Pali word for mind, *citta*, literally means heart/mind. Mindfulness could just as easily be called "heartfulness" or "kindfulness" (Brahm, 2016). We don't have a single word in the English language that encompasses both the intellective and emotional sides of lucid awareness. A simple way of defining mindfulness that does not leave out the qualities of loving-kindness and compassion is "loving awareness" or "compassionate awareness."

Compassion within mindfulness training

There are currently three types of meditation that are typically taught under the umbrella of "mindfulness meditation" in the West, namely (1) focused attention; (2) open monitoring; and (3) loving-kindness and compassion (Salzberg, 2011). *Focused attention* (or concentration) is bringing your attention back, again and again, to the breath or another focal object. Focused attention calms the mind and is how people practice mindfulness meditation most of the time. *Open monitoring* (or choiceless awareness) is closer to what was originally understood as mindfulness per se, or insight (*vipassana*) meditation. The instruction for open monitoring is to notice what is most salient and alive in your field of awareness, moment-to-moment.

Open monitoring is present-moment awareness of multiple, successive objects. For people without extensive training, this practice is rather difficult to do for more than a few seconds at a time without returning to a focal object like the breath. Open monitoring develops the capacity for relaxed awareness among the changing elements of our lives. The third type of meditation, *loving-kindness* or *compassion* meditation, warms up our awareness with goodwill. An example of loving-kindness and compassion meditation is repeating phrases such as "May all beings be happy and free from suffering." It is loving-kindness meditation when we intentionally cultivate *happiness* and it is compassion meditation when we cultivate *goodwill in the face of suffering* (Germer & Siegel, 2102). Goodwill is likely to blossom into positive attributes such as joy, warmth, courage, and commitment.

Focused attention and open monitoring meditations have been emphasized in our scientific exploration of mindfulness meditation. However, the practices of loving-kindness and compassion have received more interest in recent years (Hofmann, Grossman, & Hinton, 2011). Neurological evidence suggests that the mental skills cultivated by these three meditation types represent overlapping, yet distinct, brain processes (Brewer et al., 2011; Desbordes et al., 2012; Lee et al., 2012; Lippelt, Hommel, & Colzato, 2014; Lutz, Slagter, Dunne, & Davidson, 2008). The common element in all mindfulness meditation techniques is non-judgmental, moment-to-moment awareness.

Meditation practices may be grouped into three families: *attentional, constructive*, and *deconstructive* (Dahl, Lutz, & Davidson, 2015). Focused attention and open monitoring are attentional practices. Loving-kindness meditation is "constructive" insofar as we are building new mental and emotional habits derived from the motivation to promote universal well-being. The third category, deconstructive meditation, is what is commonly understood as insight (Pali: *vipassana*) meditation and has been blended with mindfulness in Western parlance. Insight meditation is the cultivation of metacognitive awareness of how we construct a "self" through distinguishing its component parts (perception, emotion, cognition, intention), much like laying the parts of a car on the floor of a repair shop (Olendzki, 2013).

A constructive meditation like compassion and loving-kindness may seem diametrically opposed to the agenda of attentional or deconstructive meditations. Although our brains evolved to construct a sense of a separate self, with intentions and emotions geared to pursue survival and reproduction, in Buddhist psychology the "self" is considered the cause of most unnecessary suffering because we spend so much time protecting and promoting our "self" against emotional and physical threats. Dismantling the "self" into moment-to-moment experience (attentional approach) or its component parts (deconstructive approach) frees us from the prison of a separate self.

In contrast, loving-kindness and compassion meditation usually require a "self" as the object of practice. Shouldn't focusing on a "self," especially our own, increase suffering by reifying the illusion of separateness? Paradoxically, in actual practice, when we offer compassion to a suffering "self," it begins to dissolve.

(Just consider for a moment how much less self-absorbed you were after a dear friend listened compassionately to your sorrows.) Therefore, the different types of meditation actually support a common goal. Attentional and deconstructive meditations *dismantle* the self and constructive meditation *melts* the self.

The most widely disseminated mindfulness training today is the Mindfulness-Based Stress Reduction (MBSR) program (Kabat-Zinn, 2013). MBSR instructors teach loving-kindness and compassion implicitly by embodying those qualities in how they interact with their students and by encouraging a friendly attitude toward all experience. Loving-kindness meditation is also usually taught during the daylong retreat, but the primary purpose of MBSR is developing the skill of moment-to-moment awareness.

Compassion training can be tricky for beginning mindfulness practitioners because compassion training is designed not only to enhance present moment awareness but also to *warm up* our awareness. The added element of "warming things up" can seduce practitioners into striving to feel better. Practised correctly, compassion training may be more *intentional* than mindfulness training but it isn't more *effortful*. When we open to suffering with compassion, our instinctive efforts to resist discomfort are no longer needed. The heart melts in the heat of suffering. The paradox is, "When we struggle, we practise compassion *not to feel better* but *because* we feel bad." Opening to suffering in this way also requires courage based on clear understanding and an open heart.

Overall, mindfulness training appears to increase compassion for oneself (Kuyken et al., 2010) and others (Condon, Desbordes, Miller, & DeSteno, 2013). This does not imply, however, that compassion training is redundant with mindfulness training. For example, preliminary research by Neff and Germer (2013) found that the mindful self-compassion (MSC) training program raised participants' self-compassion levels by 43% compared to an average increase of 19% in 5 MBSR studies and 9% in 3 MBCT studies. As compassion training programs develop alongside mindfulness programs, the relative capacity of each program to meet the needs of individual students should be carefully investigated.

Mindfulness in compassion

The English word *compassion* derives from the Latin roots *pati* (to suffer) and *com* (with), so compassion means to "suffer with" another person. Compassion is an elusive concept that has been defined in various ways (see Gilbert, Chapter 1). Compassion is also at the core of the world's great religions (Armstrong, 2010). For example, Confucius wrote, "Never do to others what you would not like them to do to you" and Jesus said, "Love your neighbor as yourself" (Mark 12:31). Ancient definitions of compassion were usually prescriptions for how people should relate to others. Our modern scientific understanding of compassion suggests that compassion is also: (1) an inner strength that improves psychological well-being (Germer & Siegel, 2012); (2) a skill that can be enhanced through practice (Lutz, Brefczynski-Lewis, Johnstone, & Davidson, 2008); and (3) an emotional resource that can be directed toward oneself (Germer, 2009; Neff, 2011). Compassion appears to be the next step after mindfulness in the convergence of Buddhist psychology and modern, scientific psychology.

Paul Gilbert elegantly defines compassion as "a sensitivity to suffering in self and others with a commitment to try to alleviate and prevent it" (see Chapter 1, this volume). Various attributes and skills of compassion may be organized on two dimensions: (1) engaging with suffering, and (2) alleviating suffering (Gilbert, 2015). To *engage* with suffering, we need the attributes of distress tolerance, non-judgment, sensitivity, empathy, sympathy, and care. To *alleviate* suffering, we need the skills of focusing, imagining, reasoning, feeling, sensing, and acting.

Thupten Jinpa, translator for the Dalai Lama, offers the following definition of compassion:

> [A] multidimensional process comprised of four key components: (1) an awareness of suffering (cognitive/empathic awareness), (2) sympathetic concern related to being emotionally moved by suffering (affective component), (3) a wish to see the relief of that suffering (intention), and (4) a responsiveness or readiness to help relieve that suffering (motivational).
>
> (Jazaieri et al., 2013)

It appears that a variety of personal qualities and capacities need to be active in order for compassion to arise.

Beth Lown (2016) identified additional skills involved in the compassion process in her effort to train compassionate physicians: attending, listening, recognizing and responding to emotions, perspective-taking, self–other boundaries, valuing others, regulation of emotions, self-compassion, self-care, communication skills, reflection, and meta-cognition. Each of these components suggests a specific training, such as mindfulness training for attention, skills training for better listening, cultural sensitivity training for valuing others, and wellness curricula for self-care (see Chapter 1 for Gilbert's own inventory of competencies required for compassionate engagement and action).

It is likely that all these aspects of compassion may be supported by mindfulness. For example, some components of compassion that may be enhanced by mindfulness are empathy (Shapiro & Izett, 2008), listening (Kramer, Meleo-Myer, & Turner, 2008), recognizing emotions (Wachs & Cordova, 2007), perspective-taking (Kingsbury, 2009), emotion regulation (Tang, Hölzel, & Posner, 2015), distress tolerance (Lotan, Tanay, & Bernstein, 2013), and meta-cognition (Jankowski & Holas, 2014).

Perhaps the key contribution of mindfulness to compassion training is *awareness of suffering*. One definition of mindfulness is "knowing what you are experiencing *while* you are experiencing it." How often do we have the presence of mind to say, "This is a moment of suffering" while it's happening? When difficulties appear, our natural tendency is to review the past for related problems or to anticipate future threats and try to avoid them. We go on autopilot. Mindfulness affords us the perspective we need to disengage from our personal reactions and to choose a compassionate response.

Mindfulness is so fundamental to compassion training that Kristin Neff (2003) built it into her definition of self-compassion. Neff suggests that taking a self-compassionate approach has three components: (1) self-kindness versus self-criticism; (2) common humanity versus isolation; and (3) mindfulness versus overidentification. Overidentification (or cognitive fusion) is when we are engaged in our experience with little awareness of being engaged, like watching a movie and forgetting it is only a movie. Mindfulness affords us the perspective we need to step back from our emotional reactions and to choose a compassionate response.

Mindfulness within compassion training

Our current interest in compassion training appears to have grown out of the widespread appeal of mindfulness training. Some mindfulness students discovered the transformative power of loving-kindness and compassion in their mindfulness practice and began looking for opportunities to explicitly cultivate those qualities. Other students noticed that loving-kindness and compassion were difficult to sustain when they were no longer in contact with their teachers or were confronted with challenging and new life circumstances.

There are currently five empirically supported compassion training programs in the psychological literature, most notably Compassion Focused Therapy (Gilbert, 2010); Mindful Self-Compassion (Germer & Neff, 2013; Neff & Germer, 2013); Compassion Cultivation Training (Jazairi et al., 2015); Cognitively Based Compassion Training (Pace et al., 2009); and Mindfulness-Based Compassionate Living (Bartels-Velthuis et al., 2016; van den Brink & Koster, 2015). Each of these programs has a different origin and emphasis, and may vary in format and target audience, but they all share the common goal of cultivating compassion towards self and others.

Mindfulness is woven into each of these programs and each program contains at least a few hours of explicit mindfulness training. For example, participants of Mindfulness-Based Compassionate Living (MBCL) are expected to have some familiarity with mindfulness practice before applying for MBCL, preferably by taking a MBSR or MBCT course. MBCL includes mindfulness practices like the Three-Minute Breathing Space, adapted from MBCT, but focuses mostly on cultivating compassion itself. Compassion Focused Therapy (CFT) is the only compassion-based *therapy* program and it doesn't follow the 6–8 week group training structure of the other programs, although a structured program is currently under development for non-clinical populations with promising early evidence of effectiveness. In CFT, mindfulness is used to stabilize attention for the work of compassion training and to "shine a spotlight" on how our minds function, especially in response to threat. Cognitively Based Compassion Training (CBCT) derived from Tibetan mind training and dedicates two of its six sessions to mindfulness training; one session is pure mindfulness training and the other employs mindfulness to recognize our common humanity and open the door to self-compassion. Compassion Cultivation Training (CCT), also developed from the Tibetan perspective, teaches mindfulness to settle the mind in preparation for compassionate reflection.

To further illustrate how mindfulness may be integrated into compassion training, we will take a closer look at the Mindful Self Compassion (MSC) program because one of the authors of this chapter (Christopher Germer) is a co-developer of MSC, along with Kristin Neff. Mindfulness has four key roles in MSC:

1   Knowing that we're suffering while we're suffering. We cannot have a compassionate response if we don't know we're suffering.
2   Anchoring and stabilizing awareness in ordinary, present-moment experience when a person is emotionally overwhelmed. Compassion training is warming and mindfulness training is cooling, or calming.
3   Managing difficult emotions by finding them in the body and relating to them with spacious, affectionate awareness. It is easier to connect with the felt sense of difficult emotions in the body rather than in fleeting thoughts.
4   Balancing compassion with equanimity. We need equanimity to create room for compassionate choices.

MSC is considered "mindfulness-based compassion training" – a hybrid of mindfulness and compassion training. The second of eight MSC sessions is dedicated entirely to the theory and practice of mindfulness. Additionally, mindfulness is taught throughout the program in formal and informal practices such as "affectionate breathing," "compassionate body scan," "soles of the feet," "sense and savor walk," "compassionate movement," "soften-soothe-allow," and "savoring food." The qualities of kindness and compassion are emphasized in those practices more than in typical mindfulness training. For example, while practising affectionate breathing, participants are encouraged to savor the gentle rhythm of breathing– the "internal caress" of the breath – and to feel how the breath nourishes the body on each in-breath and relaxes the body on each out-breath. During the compassionate body scan, the practitioner may send loving-kindness to different body parts or gently touch a part that may be experiencing discomfort. In the inquiry process that follows all meditations and exercises, teachers open the conversation with the mindfulness question, "What did you notice?" Mindfulness is the first step in learning to be more self-compassionate – turning with loving awareness toward difficult experience (thoughts, emotions, and sensations). Self-compassion comes next – responding with loving awareness toward *ourselves* when we suffer, fail, or feel inadequate.

In spite of the important role of mindfulness in MSC, the main agenda of MSC is to give participants a felt-sense of self-compassion and skills to evoke self-compassion in daily life. Two of three core meditations in MSC are compassion meditations ("Loving-Kindness for Ourselves" and "Giving and Receiving

Compassion") and class exercises were developed to evoke self-compassion in challenging situations (e.g. "Finding Your Compassionate Voice" and "Meeting Unmet Needs"). At least seven practices in MSC activate compassion for *others* as a precursor to including oneself in the circle of compassion. For example, in the Loving-Kindness for a Loved One meditation, the practitioner begins with loving-kindness toward a living being who naturally evokes a smile (e.g. a grandparent, a pet) and then moves to loving-kindness for *both* oneself and the loved one, and finally to oneself. In this manner, practitioners learn to tuck themselves into the circle of their compassion even if they initially feel unworthy of compassion.

In sum, mindfulness training is the mostly implicit foundation of MSC just as compassion training is assumed and mostly implicit in MBSR. Since it is impossible to offer students everything they need in a single, structured, eight-week program, the development of diverse training programs is a welcome evolution in the field of empirically supported contemplative training.

Distinctive features of self-compassion training

As documented throughout this book, compassion is inherently beneficial to individuals and to society. Compassion training has some unique features that may expand our understanding of contemplative training beyond awareness-based mindfulness approaches. In particular, the practice of *self*-compassion offers unique opportunities for emotional growth and healing.

Compassion training has a distinctly personal touch. We cannot be compassionate toward an *emotion* such as despair or shame, but we can be compassionate toward a *person* who suffers from those emotions. Whereas mindfulness training orients the practitioner to moment-to-moment *experience*, compassion training focuses on an *experiencer*. Mindfulness asks, "What am I *experiencing* right now?" and self-compassion asks, "What do I *need* right now?" When we're suffering, mindfulness asks, "Can you *make room* for your suffering?" and self-compassion asks, "Can you *be kind* to yourself in the midst of your suffering?"

Self-compassion training puts us squarely in the world of relationships. Most of the pain that we experience in our lives occurs in relationship and is healed in relationship. This is because, as many authors in this volume describe, human beings are highly social animals that regulate one another through a range of hormonal and neurophysiological systems. Emotional pain, in particular, is embedded in the relational matrix of our lives, often because relationships in which we sought care and comfort caused us disappointment and pain. A corrective healing relationship can be either *self-to-other* or *self-to-self*. An example of self-to-self healing is when a compassionate part of ourselves has the capacity to empathize with a wounded part and offer care, comfort, strength, and support.

Most mindfulness practitioners discover that self-compassion training is more emotionally activating than mindfulness training. This is because of "backdraft," or the process of rediscovering old relational wounds when we give ourselves kindness and compassion (Germer, 2009). For example, when we say, "May I be kind to myself" we're likely, at least at first, to remember times that others were unkind to us or we were unkind to ourselves. Another way of stating this is that "when we give ourselves unconditional love (positive regard, caring, affection), we discover the conditions in which we were unloved." Self-compassion opens old wounds as it provides the resources to meet old wounds from a position of courage, comfort, and care. Thupten Jinpa (in Shonin & van Gordon, 2016) described this process as "reparenting." Self-compassion isn't necessarily a therapy but it can be profoundly therapeutic.

Self-compassion works with our attachment patterns (see Chapter 10). Gilbert and Irons (2005) suggest that self-compassion deactivates the threat system that is associated with insecure attachment and activates the caregiving system associated with safeness and secure attachment. People who lack self-compassion are more likely to have critical mothers, come from dysfunctional families and have insecure attachment (Neff & McGeehee, 2010).

Self-compassion training is uniquely helpful for dealing with *shame* (Gilbert & Proctor, 2006). Shame is an innocent emotion insofar as it emerges from the wish to be loved and the fear of being unloved. The first task of a newborn baby is to be loved, and when it succeeds, all the necessities of life are likely to be provided (Lieberman, 2013). As human beings, we never grow out of the need to be loved. It's a matter of survival. The threat of being unloved because of a perceived imperfection – "I'm defective," "I'm incompetent" – is shame. It is very difficult to be mindful of the experience of shame because the observer is under siege – assaulted with self-criticism, riddled with fear, and desperately trying to flee the experience of shame. That's when we need self-compassion in addition to mindfulness – the capacity to hold *ourselves* in a loving embrace until we are strong enough to turn toward shame with curiosity and non-judgmental awareness.

Another distinctive feature of compassion training is that it is *goodwill* training. Much like mindfulness, compassion works with intention, especially moving toward or away from our experience. Compassion adds an element of warmth and kindness. Compassion makes us feel safe and connected enough to meet difficult experience with not only curiosity, but with tenderness and love. Compassion is an "inclination of heart" similar to the bending forward of a parent toward a newborn child.

Compassion is frequently associated with positive emotions (Klimecki, Leiberg, Lamm, & Singer, 2013). Compassion is also likely to generate positive feedback cycles in which positive emotions lead to positive interactions with others which reciprocally reinforce well-being in all concerned (Fredrickson, 2012).

Converging or diverging psychological processes?

Even though in the Tibetan Buddhist traditions mindfulness and compassion are seen as two wings of a bird, supporting one another, we will now consider some scientific evidence, albeit limited, that might help to compare and contrast the practices of mindfulness and compassion and their effects. As described above, mindfulness and compassion have much in common. Research into the brain signatures and psychological effects of mindfulness and compassion can provide helpful information to illuminate their respective characteristics.

Evidence from recent brain imaging research supports the assumption that compassion is more emotionally engaging than mindfulness. Compassion practice increases positive emotions, reflected in activation of regions of the positive affect system such as the medial orbitofrontal cortex, nucleus accumbens, and the ventral striatum (Engen & Singer, 2015; Klimecki, Leiberg, Ricard, & Singer, 2013; Klimecki, Leiberg, Lamm, & Singer, 2013). In response to empathic distress, a study comparing compassion meditation to cognitive reappraisal (deliberately changing how we think) found that compassion meditation activated brain systems related to *positive* emotion and motivation whereas cognitive reappraisal engaged cognitive control regions and reduced activity in regions of the *negative* affect system, including the amygdala and the anterior insula (Engen & Singer, 2015). Evidence also suggests that mindfulness practitioners show reduced activation and structural changes in the amygdala (Taren, Creswell, & Gianaros, 2013; Taren et al., 2014; Hölzel et al., 2013). In other words, the effect on the brain of mindfulness training and cognitive reappraisal appears to be similar despite their differing mechanisms – mindfulness changes perspective and cognitive reappraisal changes meaning.

The idea that mindfulness and compassion seem to address different affect systems – reduced negative affect for mindfulness and increased positive affect for compassion – is in line with the idea that mindfulness and compassion are complementary practices and can work in mutually reinforcing ways. Recent cognitive studies illustrate the benefit of combining compassion with mindfulness practice. A study investigating the effects of different emotion-regulatory strategies in patients with major depressive disorder found that a brief induction of self-compassion enhanced the effects of mindfulness on mood (Diedrich, Hofmann, Cuipers, & Berking, 2016). Other research has demonstrated that brief priming of self-compassion can increase the willingness to continue with mindfulness following an initial introductory mindfulness exercise (Rowe, Shepstone, Carnelley, Cavanagh, & Millings, in press). There is also evidence that compassion practices may facilitate a stronger commitment to meditation practice and more lasting effects (May, Weyker, Spengel, Finkler, & Hendrix, 2014).

Mindfulness/insight and compassion practices have been described as deconstructive and constructive practices, respectively (Dahl, Lutz, & Davidson, 2015). Through mindful observation of the dynamics of perceptions, cognitions, and emotions, the self is deconstructed in its component parts. In contrast, compassion is explicitly aimed at constructing or cultivating more caring attitudes and feelings. Because of the emphasis in mindfulness practice on the observation of inner processes, mindfulness seems particularly helpful in preventing the escalation of negative mood – countering tendencies to be carried away by harmful automatic responses and maladaptive patterns of thinking. Research indicates that increases in the ability to decentre or disentangle from our experience represent one of the main mechanisms of action of mindfulness-based interventions (Bieling et al., 2012). A study comparing effects of brief mindfulness and loving-kindness meditation in novice meditators found that only mindfulness practice was able to decouple repetitive thoughts from negative reactions to those thoughts (Feldman, Greeson, & Senville, 2010).

Increasingly, research is investigating the effects of mindfulness on the *default mode network* (DMN), or the neural processes and brain regions underlying spontaneous thought and the wandering mind. There is now considerable evidence that emotional disorders such as depression are associated with aberrations in the connectivity and resting state dynamics of the DMN (Whitfield-Gabrieli & Ford, 2012). Patients and individuals at risk from emotional disorders show increased and altered connectivity within the DMN and an increased tendency to engage the DMN even during rest. Dominance of the DMN at the expense of other networks represents a risk factor underlying the development and maintenance of emotional disorders (Marchetti, Koster, Sonuga-Barke, & De Raedt, 2012).

Research on expert mindfulness meditators suggests that simple breathing meditations allow practitioners to flexibly engage non-DMN brain systems (Hasenkamp, Wilson-Mendenhall, Duncan, & Barsalou, 2012) and that consistent practice can lead to changes in connectivity of the DMN. In particular, research has found that expert mindfulness meditators show reductions in connectivity between the DMN and regions involved in self-related cognitions such as the medial prefrontal cortex (Taylor et al., 2013). Furthermore, there is evidence that mindfulness training can lead to changes in the *salience network* (SN) that coordinates the switching between the DMN and other networks (Grant, Courtemanche, Duerden, Duncan, & Rainville, 2010; Tang, Lu, Feng, Tang, & Posner, 2015). The anterior cingulate cortex, a central region in the SN, seems to be particularly activated in meditations that require persistent monitoring of the focus of attention. There is evidence for changes in white matter integrity in the anterior cingulate after only several hours of practice as well as significant increased brain density in expert practitioners (Tang et al., 2010). Mindfulness practices thus seem well-suited to address imbalances in DMN dynamics as well as enhance our ability to flexibly switch between brain networks.

Does the research imply that other meditation techniques are *not* likely to have effects on DMN dynamics and connectivity? Just like mindfulness practices, compassion practices require practitioners to maintain attention on a particular object and are thus incompatible with spontaneous thought and mind wandering. Research by Brewer and colleagues has demonstrated relative deactivation of main nodes in the DMN in expert meditators across a range of different meditation practices including loving-kindness meditation (Brewer et al., 2011). Novice meditators also showed significant reductions in frequency of mind wandering after only a few weeks of compassion training (Jazaieri et al., 2015). It appears that although the focus of compassion training is on the cultivation of compassion rather than regulating attentional processes, compassion training still has an impact on attentional processes involved in DMN dynamics.

A key aspect of compassion training is that it is inherently relational and interpersonal. The research is still in its infancy, but we might hypothesize that compassion meditation would alter brain structure and function related to basic perceptual and motor simulation processes, simulation of another's affective body state, slower and higher-level perspective-taking, modulatory processes such as emotion regulation, and discrimination of self and other (Mascaro, Darcher, Negi, & Raison, 2015).

The relational nature of compassion practices is also important from a clinical perspective. There is evidence that compassion practice can directly address negative core beliefs (e.g. I am unworthy, unlovable, defective) that are associated with many emotional disorders, and that the practice can serve as an important antidote against self-criticism (Neff, 2003; Neff, Kirkpatrick, & Rude, 2007), one of the strongest predictors of anxiety and depression.

Perhaps the most compelling research question is "what for whom" – matching a practitioner with either mindfulness or compassion training. Toward that end, one of the authors of this chapter (Thorsten Barnhofer) conducted a small study with individuals at risk for depression relapse (Barnhofer, Chittka, Nightingale, Visser, & Crane, 2010). We compared the effects of brief practices of breathing meditation and loving-kindness meditation on the affective and motivational state of the participants by measuring prefrontal alpha asymmetry in resting EEG, a parameter that reflects differences in resting state activity in right and left prefrontal regions of the brain that has been found to indicate differences in global affective style. Relatively increased activation on the left side of the prefrontal cortex has been reliably associated with increased positive affect and approach motivation whereas relatively increased activation on the right side is associated with increased negative affect and withdrawal motivation. Participants received either breathing or loving-kindness meditation and prefrontal asymmetry was measured before and after training. Given the focus of loving-kindness meditation on generating positive affect, we assumed that loving-kindness meditation would lead to stronger left-sided activation than the breathing meditation. However, results showed that both meditations had similar effects on alpha asymmetry. Interestingly, when we differentiated between those previously depressed participants who reported relatively high tendencies towards rumination compared to those who reported relatively low tendencies towards rumination, a different pattern emerged. Those with high levels of rumination significantly benefited from breathing meditation – their prefrontal asymmetry showed significant changes towards a more positive state – whereas those with low levels of rumination significantly benefited from loving-kindness meditation. In other words, when asked to engage in meditation without much prior preparation, those who were more vulnerable to depression derived little benefit from loving-kindness meditation but seemed to respond well to simple breathing meditation.

These findings are consistent with the clinical observation that old relational wounds can be activated in some people (fear of compassion, backdraft) as they begin to give themselves kindness and compassion (Miron, Seligowski,

Boykin, & Orcutt, 2016). Paradoxically, it seems that people in a state of vulnerability may be most in need of what is least accessible to them. A study investigating the characteristics of previously depressed patients who had dropped out of a course of mindfulness-based cognitive therapy for suicidal depression found that the best predictors of drop-out were ruminative tendencies and cognitive reactivity, the very processes that mindfulness-based cognitive therapy for depression is designed to target. People who showed high levels of rumination and the strongest negative responses to subtle changes in mood were also those who were most likely to discontinue the course (Crane & Williams, 2010).

How, then, should we start to practice? Should individuals be encouraged to practice in their areas of vulnerability or encouraged to choose the path of least resistance? For example, should highly ruminative, depressed individuals practice mindfulness rather than self-compassion to decrease rumination (Barnhofer et al., 2010) even though self-compassion is strongly associated with uncoupling from depressed thinking (Kuyken et al., 2010)? But perhaps compassion is too emotionally activating for some people (Gilbert, McEwan, Matos, & Rivis, 2011) even though it seems to enhance commitment to meditation and mindfulness practice (May et al., 2014; Rowe et al., 2016)? Would focusing on fears, blocks and resistances to compassion be a helpful way to engage with clients for whom compassion is too activating, as we do in CFT? And should mindfulness and compassion be practised separately, at least at the beginning, or creatively blended by each practitioner? These decisions may always be more art than science, but additional research into the emerging field of compassion training will go a long way toward informing wise choices.

Summary

In summary, it appears that mindfulness and compassion are multidimensional states of mind that significantly overlap but also have unique characteristics. The historical traditions of Theravada (mindfulness) and Tibetan (compassion) Buddhism place varying emphasis on mindfulness and compassion, but it appears that both are essential for practice. For example, we cannot be compassionate if we don't know what we are feeling and we cannot be mindful without a friendly attitude toward our experience, especially when we suffer. Conceptual differences such as dismantling the "self" into moment-to-moment experience versus embracing the "self" with compassion appear to be in conflict, but they both seem to produce a more flexible, adaptive sense of self. Compassion training programs have been developing over the past 5–10 years whereas secular mindfulness training started gaining momentum 20 years earlier, in the early 1980s. We can expect an abundance of compassion research in the coming decade that will help us discover the mechanisms by which mindfulness and compassion training work. Preliminary research suggests that compassion activates positive emotions and, relatively speaking, mindfulness deactivates negative emotions. Both practices appear to downregulate or decouple the brain's default mode network, our wandering mind. Perhaps the most distinctive aspect of compassion training may be how we can regulate emotion through *affiliation* rather than through *attention*, and this arena of study is promising both for researchers and for clinicians trying to navigate the complex terrain of human relationships safely and effectively.

References

Armstrong, K. (2010). *Twelve Steps to a Compassionate Life.* New York: Knopf.

Barnhofer, T., Chittka, T., Nightingale, H., Visser, C., & Crane, C. (2010). State effects of two forms of meditation on prefrontal EEG asymmetry in previously depressed individuals. *Mindfulness, 1,* 21–27.

Bartels-Velthuis, A., Schroevers, M., van der Ploeg, K., Koster, F., Fleer, J. & van den Brink, E. (2016). A mindfulness-based compassionate living training in a heterogeneous sample of psychiatric outpatients: A feasibility study. *Mindfulness,* doi: 10.1007/s12671-016-0518-8

Bieling, P. J., Hawley, L. L., Bloch, R. T., Corcoran, K. M., Levitan, K. M., Young, T. L., MacQueen, G. M., & Segal, Z. V. (2012). Treatment-specific changes in decentering following mindfulness-based cognitive therapy versus antidepressant medication or placebo for prevention of depressive relapse. *Journal of Consulting and Clinical Psychology, 80,* 365–372.

Bishop, S. R., Lau, M., Shapiro, S., Carlson, L., Anderson, N. D., Carmody, J., . . . Devins, G. (2004). Mindfulness: A proposed operational definition. *Clinical Psychology: Science and Practice, 11*(3), 230–241.

Bodhi, B. (2013). What does mindfulness really mean? A canonical perspective. In J. M. Williams & J. Kabat-Zinn (Eds.), *Mindfulness: Diverse Perspectives on its Meaning, Origins, and Applications.* New York: Routledge.

Brahm, A. (2016). *Kindfulness.* Somerville, MA: Wisdom Publications.

Brewer, J. A., Mallik, S., Babuscio, T. A., Nich, C., Johnson, H. E., Deleone, C. M., . . . Rounsaville, B. J. (2011). Mindfulness training for smoking cessation: Results from a randomized controlled trial. *Drug and Alcohol Dependence, 119*(1–2), 72–80.

Brewer, J. A., Worhunsky, P. D., Gray, J. R., Tang, Y.-Y., Weber, J., & Kober, H. (2011). Meditation experience is associated with differences in default mode network activity and connectivity. *Proceedings of the National Academy of Sciences of the United States of America, 108,* 20254–20259.

Condon, P., Desbordes, G., Miller, W., & DeSteno, D. (2013). Meditation increases compassionate responses to suffering. *Psychological Science OnlineFirst.* doi: 10.1177/0956797613485603

Crane, C., & Williams, J. M. G. (2010). Factors associated with attrition from mindfulness-based cognitive therapy in patients with a history of suicidal depression. *Mindfulness, 1,* 10–20.

Dahl, C., Lutz, A., & Davidson, R. (2015). Reconstructing and deconstructing the self: Cognitive mechanisms in meditative practice. *Trends in Cognitive Sciences, 19*(9), 515–523.

Dalai Lama (2003). *Lighting the Path: The Dalai Lama Teaches on Wisdom and Compassion.* South Melbourne, Australia: Thomas C. Lothian.

Desbordes, G., Negi, L., Pace, T., Wallace, A., Raison, C., & Schwartz, E. (2012). Effects of mindful-attention and compassion meditation training on amygdala response to emotional stimuli in an ordinary, non-meditative state. *Frontiers in Human Neuroscience, 6,* 292.

Diedrich, A., Hofmann, S. G., Cuijpers, P., Berking, M. (2016). Self-compassion enhances the efficacy of explicit cognitive reappraisal as an emotion regulation strategy in individuals with major depressive disorder. *Behaviour Research and Therapy, 82,* 1–10.

Engen, H. G., & Singer, T. (2015). Compassion-based emotion regulation up-regulates experienced positive affect and associated neural networks. *Social, Cognitive, and Affective Neuroscience, 10,* 1291–1301.

Feldman, G., Greeson, J., & Senville, J. (2010). Differential effects of mindful breathing, progressive muscle relaxation, and loving-kindness meditation on decentering and negative reactions to repetitive thoughts. *Behaviour Research and Therapy, 48,* 1002–1011.

Fredrickson, B. (2012). Building lives of wisdom and compassion. In C. Germer & R. Siegel (Eds.), *Mindfulness and Psychotherapy* (pp. 48–58). New York: Guilford Press.

Germer, C. (2009). *The Mindful Path to Self-Compassion: Freeing Yourself From Destructive Thoughts and Emotions.* New York: Guilford Press.

Germer, C. (2013). Mindfulness: What is it? What does it matter? In C. Germer & R. Siegel (Eds.), *Mindfulness and Psychotherapy, 2nd edition* (pp. 3–35). New York: Guilford Press.

Germer, C., & Neff, K. (2013). Self-compassion in clinical practice. *Journal of Clinical Psychology, 69*(8), 856–867.

Germer, C., & Siegel, R. (2012). *Wisdom and Compassion in Psychotherapy.* New York: Guilford Press.

Gilbert, P. (2010). *Compassion Focused Therapy: Distinctive Features.* New York: Routledge.

Gilbert, P. (2015). The evolution and social dynamics of compassion. *Social and Personality Psychology Compass,* 1–16. doi: 10.1111/spc3.12176

Gilbert, P., & Irons, C. (2005). Focused therapies and compassionate mind training for shame and self-attacking. In P. Gilbert (Ed.), *Compassion: Conceptualisations, Research and Use in Psychotherapy* (pp. 263–325). London: Routledge.

Gilbert, P., McEwan, K., Matos, M., & Rivis, A. (2011). Fears of compassion: Development of three self-report measures. *Psychology and Psychotherapy: Theory, Research and Practice,* 239–255.

Gilbert, P., & Procter, S. (2006). Compassionate mind training for people with high shame and self-criticism: Overview and pilot study of a group therapy approach. *Clinical Psychology and Psychotherapy, 13,* 353–379.

Grant, J. A., Courtemanche, J., Duerden, E. G., Duncan, G. H., & Rainville, P. (2010). Cortical thickness and pain sensitivity in Zen meditators. *Emotion, 10,* 43–53.

Hasenkamp, W., Wilson-Mendenhall, C. D., Duncan, E., & Barsalou, L. W. (2012). Mind wandering and attention during focused meditation: A fine-grained temporal analysis of fluctuating cognitive states. *NeuroImage, 59,* 750–760.

Hofmann, S., Grossman, P., & Hinton, D. (2011). Loving-kindness and compassion meditation: Potential for psychological interventions. *Clinical Psychology Review, 31,* 1126–1132.

Hölzel, B. K., Hoge, E. A., Greve, D. N., Gard, T., Creswell, J. D., Brown, K. W., . . . Lazar, S. W. (2013). Neural mechanisms of symptom improvements in generalized anxiety disorder following mindfulness training. *NeuroImage: Clinical, 2,* 448–458.

Jankowski, T., & Holas, P. (2014). The metacognitive model of mindfulness. *Consciousness and Cognition: An International Journal, 28,* 64–80.

Jazaieri, H., Lee, I., McGonigal, K., Jinpa, T., Doty, J., Gross, J. J., & Golding, P. R. (2013). A randomized controlled trial of compassion cultivation training: Effects on mindfulness, affect, and emotion regulation. *Motivation and Emotion, 38*, 23–35. doi: 10.1007/s11031-013-9368-z

Kabat-Zinn, J. (2003). Mindfulness-based interventions in context: Past, present, and future. *Clinical Psychology: Science and Practice, 10*(2), 144–156.

Kabat-Zinn, J. (2013). *Full Catastrophe Living.* New York: Bantam.

Kingsburg, E. (2009). The relationship between empathy and mindfulness: Understanding the role of self-compassion. *Dissertation Abstracts International: Section B: The Sciences and Engineering, Vol 70(*5-B), pp. 3175.

Klimecki, O. M., Leiberg, S., Lamm, C., & Singer, T. (2013). Functional neural plasticity and associated changes in positive affect after compassion training. *Cerebral Cortex, 23*, 1552–1561. doi:10.1093/cercor/bhs142

Klimecki, O. M., Leiberg, S., Ricard, M., & Singer, T. (2013). Differential pattern of functional brain plasticity after compassion and empathy training. *Social, Cognitive, and Affective Neuroscience, Article number nst060*, 873–879.

Kornfield, J. (2011). *Bringing Home the Dharma.* Boston, MA: Shambhala Publications.

Kramer, G., Meleo-Meyer, F., & Turner, M. (2008). Cultivating mindfulness in relation: Insight dialogue and the interpersonal mindfulness program. In S. Hick & T. Bien (Eds.), *Mindfulness and the Therapeutic Relationship* (pp. 195–214). New York: Guilford Press.

Kuyken, W., Watkins, E., Holden, E., White, K., Taylor, R., Byford, S., . . . Dalgleish, T. (2010). How does mindfulness-based cognitive therapy work? *Behaviour Research and Therapy, 48*, 1105–1112.

Lee, T., Leung, M., Hou, W., Tang, J., Yin, J., So, K., . . . Chan, C. (2012). Distinct neural activity associated with focused-attention meditation and loving-kindness meditation. *PLOS ONE, 7*(8), e40054.

Lieberman, M. (2013). *Social: Why Our Brains Are Wired to Connect.* New York: Broadway Books.

Lippelt, D., Hommel, B., & Colzato, L. (2014). Focused attention, open monitoring and loving kindness meditation: Effects on attention, conflict monitoring and creativity – A review. *Frontiers in Psychology, 5*, 1083. doi:10.3389/fpsyg.2014.01083

Lotan, G., Tanay, G., & Bernstein, A. (2013). Mindfulness and distress tolerance: Relations in a mindfulness perspective. *International Journal of Cognitive Therapy, 6*(4), 371–385.

Lown, B. (2016). A social neuroscience-informed model for teaching and practicing compassion in health care. *Medical Education, 60*, 332–342.

Lutz, A., Brefczynski-Lewis, J., Johnstone, T., & Davidson, R. J. (2008). Regulation of the neural circuitry of emotion by compassion meditation: Effects of meditative expertise. *Public Library of Science, 3*(3), 1–5.

Lutz, A., Slagter, H. A., Dunne, J. D., & Davidson, R. J. (2008). Attention regulation and monitoring in meditation. *Trends in Cognitive Sciences, 12*(4), 163–169.

Marchetti, I., Koster, E. H. W., Sonuga-Barke, E. J., & De Raedt, R. (2012). The default mode network and recurrent depression: A neurobiological model of cognitive risk factors. *Neurospsychology Review, 22*, 229–251.

Mascaro, J. S., Darcher, A., Negi, L. T., & Raison, C. L. (2015). The neural mediators of kindness-based meditation: A theoretical model. *Frontiers in Psychology, 6*, Article number 109.

May, C. J., Weyker, J. R., Spengel, S. K., Finkler, L. J., & Hendrix, S. E. (2014). Tracking longitudinal changes in affect and mindfulness caused by concentration and loving-kindness meditation with hierarchical linear modeling. *Mindfulness, 5*, 249–258.

Miron, L. R., Seligowski, A. V., Boykin, D. M., & Orcutt, H. K. (2016). The potential indirect effect of childhood abuse on posttrauma pathology through self-compassion and fear of self-compassion. *Mindfulness, 7*, 596–605.

Neff, K. D. (2003). Development and validation of a scale to measure self-compassion. *Self and Identity, 2*, 223–250.

Neff, K. D. (2011). *Self-compassion: Stop Beating Yourself Up and Leave Insecurity Behind.* New York: William Morrow.

Neff, K., & Germer, C. (2013). A pilot study and randomized controlled trial of the mindful self-compassion program. *Journal of Clinical Psychology, 69(1)*, 28–44.

Neff, K., Kirkpatrick, K. L., & Rude, S. S. (2007). Self-compassion and adaptive psychological functioning. *Journal of Research in Personality, 41*, 139–154.

Neff, K., & McGeehee, P. (2010). Self-compassion and psychological resilience among adolescents and young adults. *Self and Identity, 9*, 225–240.

Nyanaponika, Thera (1965). *The Heart of Buddhist Meditation.* York Beach, ME: Red Wheel/Weiser.

Olendzki, A. (2013). The construction of mindfulness. In J.M. Williams & J. Kabat-Zinn, (Eds.), *Mindfulness: Diverse Perspectives on its Meaning, Origins, and Applications.* New York: Routledge.

Pace, T., Negi, T., Adame, D., Cole, S., Sivilli, T., Brown, T. D., . . . Raison, C. (2009). Effect of compassion meditation on neuroendocrine, innate immune and behavioral responses to psychosocial stress. *Psychoneuroendocrinology, 34*, 87–98.

Rowe, A. C., Shepstone, L., Carnelley, K. B., Cavanagh, K., & Millings, A. (in press). Attachment security and self-compassion priming increase the likelihood that first-time engagers in mindfulness meditation will continue with mindfulness training. *Mindfulness.*

Salzberg, S. (2011). *Real Happiness: The Power of Meditation.* New York: Workman.

Shapiro, S. L., & Izett, S. (2008). Meditation: A universal tool for cultivating empathy. In S. Hick & T. Bien (Eds.), *Mindfulness and the therapeutic relationship* (pp. 161–175). New York: Guilford Press.

Shonin, E., & van Gordon, W. (2016). Thupten Jinpa on compassion and mindfulness. *Mindfulness, 7*, 279–283.

Tang, Y., Hölzel, B., & Posner, M. (2015). The neuroscience of mindfulness. *Nature Reviews/Neuroscience, 16*, 213–235.

Tang, Y.-Y., Lu, Q, Feng, H., Tang, R., & Posner, M. I. (2015). Short-term meditation increases blood flow in anterior cingulate cortex and insula. *Frontiers in Psychology, 6*, article number 212.

Tang, Y.-Y., Lu, Q., Geng, X., Stein, E. A., Yang, Y., & Posner, M. I. (2010). Short-term meditation induces white matter changes in the anterior cingulate. *Proceedings of the National Academy of Sciences of the United States of America, 107*, 15649–15652.

Taren, A. A., Creswell, J. D., & Gianaros, P. J. (2013). Dispositional mindfulness co-varies with smaller amygdala and caudate volumes in community adults. *PLOS ONE, 8*, e64574.

Taren, A. A., Gianaros, P. J., Greco, C. M., Lindsay, E. K., Fairgrieve, A., Brown, K. W., . . . Creswell, J. D. (2014). Mindfulness meditation training alters stress-related amygdala resting state functional connectivity: A randomized controlled trial. *Social, Cognitive, and Affective Neuroscience, 10*, 1758–1768.

Taylor, V. A., Daneault, V., Grant, J., Scavone, G., Breton, E., Roffe-Vidal, S., . . . Beauregard, M. (2013). Impact of meditation training on default mode network during a restful state. *Social Cognitive and Affective Neuroscience*, *8*, 4–14.

van den Brink, E. & Koster, R. (2015). *Mindfulness-based Compassionate Living*. London: Routledge.

Wachs, K., & Cordova, J. (2015). Mindful relating: Exploring mindfulness and emotion repertoires in intimate relationships. *Journal of Marital and Family Therapy*, *33*(4), 464–481.

Wallace, B. A. (Spring, 2008). A mindful balance. *Tricycle* magazine.

Whitfield-Gabrieli, S., & Ford, J. M. (2012). Default mode network activity and connectivity in psychopathology. *Annual Review of Clinical Psychology*, *8*, 49–76.

Williams, J. M., & Kabat-Zinn, J. (2013). *Mindfulness: Diverse Perspectives on its Meaning, Origins, and Applications*. London: Routledge.

Part II

Compassion and its physiologies

Chapter 5

The body of compassion

Jennifer S. Mascaro and Charles L. Raison

Introduction

Charles Darwin's *The Expression of the Emotions in Man and Animals* (Darwin, Ekman, & Prodger, 1998) shaped the study of emotions with the basic assertion that they are best understood as evolved and adaptive processes that facilitate communication and connection. Of all human emotions and behaviors, compassion may be the best exemplar of Darwin's claim. Or said more exactly, many scientific studies find strong evidence that compassion and its constituent components, such as empathy, are engendered by body and brain systems shaped by natural selection to facilitate social connection. It is these body and brain systems underpinning compassion that are the focus of this chapter.

Defining relevant terms

A crucial starting place for understanding the bodily basis for compassion is with clear definitions and descriptions of the social cognitive skills and traits in question (for discussions of the importance of accurate construct definition see Batson, 2009). While not in complete agreement, social cognitive neuroscientists and social psychologists generally converge on a definition of empathy as an affective response that arises from the comprehension of another's emotional state and that is similar to what the other person is feeling (de Vignemont & Singer, 2006; Eisenberg, Shea, Carlo, & Knight, 2014). Early research on empathy often used the term *empathic concern* to denote an emotional reaction to the suffering of another akin to empathy, but also including the accompanying motivated response (for example, Batson, Eklund, Chermok, Hoyt, & Ortiz, 2007). More recently, social cognitive neuroscientists have turned their attention to *compassion*, defined by many as the deep wish that self and others be free from suffering, coupled with the motivation to alleviate and prevent suffering (Gilbert, Chapter 3, this volume; Kim et al., 2009; Klimecki, Leiberg, Lamm, & Singer, 2013). Social cognitive neuroscientists generally argue that both empathy and compassion can lead to *prosocial behavior* or *altruism*, helping behavior directed at another in need (De Waal, 2008). Notably, empathy may also lead to *personal distress*.

To explore a putative "body" of compassion requires a bird's eye view of the primary neural and peripheral systems at work during social connection. We take an approach that considers the central and peripheral nervous system as well as the hormonal and immune factors that regulate them. Classically, hormones were understood to be produced by specialized glands in the body from whence they moved through the blood to impact a number of different bodily tissues. However, hormones in the body can also function as neurotransmitters in the central nervous system (CNS). A classic example is the peptide hormone oxytocin, which is produced primarily in the hypothalamus. For many years, oxytocin was known for its role in childbirth and lactation In this respect, oxytocin is a hormone; however, oxytocin also helps organize maternal brain systems to respond to offspring (Numan and Stolzenberg, 2009), and discoveries over the last 15 years have demonstrated that oxytocin has profound effects on the brain directly related to social behavior, including empathy and compassion, in humans and other mammals. In this role oxytocin behaves more like a neurotransmitter than a classic hormone (Colonnello, Petrocchi, & Heinrichs, Chapter 6, this volume; Ross & Young, 2009).

Oxytocin is not the only hormone with multiple functions. For example, another important hormone discussed in this chapter relevant to compassion is cortisol, which has so many effects on the immune system that one could almost consider it to be an immune molecule as much as an endocrine one. These endocrine, immune, and central nervous systems are best thought of as interacting systems that facilitate bi-directional communication between the external social world and the brain and body. These are the mechanisms of embodiment by which a person's world – or, more accurately, their interpretation of their world – gets under the skin and impacts the body. And these are the bodily mechanisms that, in turn, shape the way a person interprets and interacts with their world.

With this brief survey of terms, we turn now to examining associations between compassion and empathy and the neural systems most related to them. Following this we focus on the neuromodulatory systems that serve as the bi-directional drivers of these neural systems. To this end, we will review the evidence that alteration of these systems impact social connection on the one hand, and that changes in social connection impact these systems, on the other.

Neuroscientific explorations of compassion

As noted above empathy is often a central competency for the enactment of compassion. The empathic process is thought to have two crucial constituents: (1) an affective dimension that involves a shared affective experience sometimes called emotional contagion; and (2) a cognitive dimension that is often called perspective taking and mentalizing. These two dimensions can function quite differently and depend on different neurological systems (de Vignemont & Singer, 2006; Eisenberg & Eggum, 2009; Vrtička, Favre & Singer, Chapter 8, this volume). Elsewhere, we have synthesized over a decade of functional neuroimaging research into a mechanistic model that situates *three* major components underlying the neural bases of empathy and trace the possible relationship of empathy to compassion and helping behavior. These core components include early and fast perceptual and motor simulation processes, affective simulation, and slower, cognitive processing (Mascaro, Darcher, Negi, & Raison, 2015). In addition to these core processes, empathy may require a self–other distinction and emotion regulation. Importantly, the model specifies that these three components are not a necessary progression for compassion. Rather, we, in agreement with many others (De Waal, 2008; Decety & Cowell, 2014; Preston & Hofelich, 2012), note that they are one possible route by which a perception of suffering trigger the motivation for compassionate action. With this caveat in mind, we briefly review this model below.

Perceptual/motor

Though not consistently activated by functional neuroimaging studies (Fan, Duncan, De Greck, & Northoff, 2011; Lamm, Decety, & Singer, 2011), the amygdala is arguably a core structure for empathy and compassion. The first evidence supporting its importance for empathy came from studies of psychopaths, whose deficits in empathy form a diagnostic symptom of their disorder and who consistently have altered amygdala structure and function (Blair, 2008; Marsh et al., 2013; Rilling et al., 2007). Beyond its potential causal role in psychopathy, recent studies also support the amygdala's role in empathy in healthy populations. For example, a recent study found that extreme altruists have greater amygdala volume and activity when viewing others' distressed faces (Marsh et al., 2014), and another study found that individuals that self-report high levels of emotional empathy have greater functional connectivity between the amygdala and other limbic structures consistently implicated in empathic processing (anterior insula) (Cox et al., 2012).

However, the amygdala's implication in empathy rests in large part on correlational studies such as those referenced above (though see Leigh et al., 2013 for the effects of acute amygdala lesion on affective empathy) and its exact role remains unclear. Some have argued that the importance of the amygdala in this context stems from its role in detecting the salience of, and learning about, social information based on sensory cues (Blair, 2008), which may be critical in the affective dimension of empathy (Hurlemann et al., 2010b). For example, the amygdala plays a crucial role in detecting social information from others' eyes (Mosher, Zimmerman, & Gothard, 2014) and in emotional processing of visual information (Pessoa & Adolphs, 2010; Wang et al., 2014), and it is well-placed to translate incoming sensory information into changes in arousal (Davis, 1992).

A second early system that is often implicated in empathy is the putative 'mirror neuron system', composed of the anterior part of the inferior parietal lobe and the inferior frontal cortex (Iacoboni & Dapretto, 2006). This system is thought to facilitate emotional understanding by mapping the target's emotive facial expression onto the observer's premotor system. As such, neural activity related to motor simulation supports the ability to read emotional facial expressions (Carr, Iacoboni, Dubeau, Mazziotta, & Lenzi, 2003; Jabbi & Keysers, 2008), and there is evidence that activity in this system precedes and may be causal to activity in the affective system described below (Jabbi & Keysers, 2008).

Affective

A second component of empathy and its role in compassion is often referred to as affective simulation, or emotional contagion, a process of matching limbic system activity with that of the target. Both the perception (auditory and visual) and contemplation of the suffering of another consistently elicits activation in the anterior mid-cingulate cortex (aMCC), as well as bilateral anterior insula (AI) and ventral frontal operculum, particularly on the right side (Lamm, Decety, & Singer, 2010). Activity in the AI is thought to represent a simulated mapping of the observed individual's body state onto one's own (Bernhardt & Singer, 2012; Fan et al., 2011). Two studies have linked subsequent prosocial behavior with anterior insula activity when viewing another's suffering (Hein, Silani, Preuschoff, Batson, & Singer, 2010; Masten, Morelli, & Eisenberger, 2011). Importantly, these results were consistent despite the use of divergent methodologies, with one study inducing empathy in subjects by leading them to believe others were being excluded in a ball-tossing game (Masten et al., 2011) and the other had subjects watch others receive painful shocks and then gave them the choice to endure painful shocks on behalf of the other (Hein et al., 2010). In both cases, the finding that altruistic behavior was predicted by anterior insula activity supports the idea that affective simulation is, at least in some cases, causal to compassion and prosocial behavior.

Cognitive

The third component of empathy is the cognitive element, often referred to as perspective-taking or mentalizing, which allows the observer to understand that his or her affective state is related to someone else's affective state. Mentalizing consistently activates the medial and dorsomedial prefrontal cortex and the temporoparietal junction, systems that are thought to subserve relatively controlled, reflective cognition (Lieberman, 2007). These neural regions are also activated by a diverse array of empathy-inducing tasks (Lamm et al., 2011; Morelli, Rameson, & Lieberman, 2012). Mentalizing enables us to see behind the scenes as it were, to not only understand what somebody is feeling but why they might be feeling what they are feeling; it allows us insight into motivation and intent. Supporting the idea that mentalizing is distinct from those components described above, several studies now indicate that individuals diagnosed with psychopathy have no trouble mentalizing (Dolan and Fullam, 2004; Richell et al., 2003).

Emotion regulation

Research from social and developmental psychology has demonstrated a difference, both in subjective feeling and in resultant behavior, between *empathy* and the related but distinct experience of *personal distress* (Batson, Oquin, Fultz, Vanderplas, & Isen, 1983; Eisenberg et al., 1998). Batson explains personal distress: "This state does not involve feeling distressed *for* the other or distress *as* the other. It involves feeling distressed *by* the state of the other" (Batson, 2009). Personal distress begins early; for example, when young babies hear the cries of another baby they will cry themselves, an example of emotional contagion based purely on the distress in the receiver. With maturation, the distress may be displaced by empathy such that helping behavior occurs. As evidence, cross-cultural studies (Germany, Israel, Indonesia, and Malaysia) in preschool-aged children consistently reveal a positive relationship between empathy (e.g. child shows features of sadness and has a soft voice toward an experimenter whose balloon had popped) and prosocial helping behavior. However, there was a negative relationship between self-focused distress (child turns away from victim, interpreted as avoidance of the distressing stimuli) and prosocial behavior (Trommsdorff, Friedlmeier, & Mayer, 2007). Taken together, these data suggest that becoming overly distressed is distinct from empathy and impairs prosocial behavior. It is likely, then, that emotion regulation plays an integral role in determining an individual's response to viewing another's suffering.

Defined as the initiation of new, or modulation of ongoing, emotional responses, emotion regulation varies in method and speed of processing from changes in attention to more cognitive reappraisal strategies (Ochsner & Gross, 2005). For example, simply shifting attention toward or away from social cues can up- or down-regulate empathic processes (Zaki, 2014), a regulatory process that arguably involves the amygdala, in some cases relying on it (Todd, Cunningham, Anderson, & Thompson, 2012), in other cases modulating it (Larson et al., 2013). In addition to attention-shifting, cognitive reappraisal may modulate empathy by altering emotional responding. Zaki presents a detailed model of empathy-specific appraisals that are influenced by approach and avoidance motivations to determine empathy across contexts (Zaki, 2014). In general, cognitive strategies activate the lateral (Ochsner, Bunge, Gross, & Gabrieli, 2002) and ventromedial (Urry et al., 2006) prefrontal cortex. Interestingly, cognitive reappraisal strategies, involving prefrontal regions, are generally linked with *reduced* activation of the amygdala (e.g. Banks, Eddy, Angstadt, Nathan, & Phan, 2007), suggesting that, while cognitive reappraisal is certainly not mutually exclusive with attention-shifting, the two different types of emotion regulation may have differing functional profiles in the amygdala. In addition to the prefrontal cortex, cognitive reappraisal strategies also engage the vagus nerve's parasympathetic influence over heart rate, as reflected by respiratory sinus arrhythmia (RSA) (Butler, Wilhelm, & Gross, 2006; Segerstrom & Nes, 2007). Porges's Polyvagal theory posits that it is this vagal brake, shaped by evolutionary pressures for parental caregiving, that supports affiliative interactions (Porges, 2003, 2007; Stellar & Keltner, Chapter 7, this volume). Researchers have found that compassionate responses appear to rely on parasympathetic dampening of the emotional response of witnessing another's suffering (Rockliff, Gilbert, McEwan, Lightman, & Glover, 2008).

Self/other distinction

Nearly two decades of research from social psychology shows that excessive overlap between self and other may render the perceiver mired in personally oriented distress that, rather than leading to prosocial behavior, leads to disengagement from the sufferer (Batson, 1998; Batson, Fultz, & Schoenrade, 1987). In addition to this cross-sectional research, Hoffman cites developmental research in support of the same idea. While young children display "egocentric empathic distress" causing them to seek personal comfort when they witness another in distress (for example, by crawling into their parent's lap), the development of a self-concept is concomitant with a child's tendency to make helpful advances toward the victim (Hoffman, 2001). Several studies have found that mirror-self recognition in children predicts later helping behavior during empathic distress (Bischoff-Kohler, 1991; Johnson, 1982; Zahn-Waxler, Radke-Yarrow, & King, 1979). Based on these data, social cognitive neuroscientists have persuasively argued for the importance for empathy of a rigid self/other distinction (Decety & Grèzes, 2006), and experimental induction of a self-oriented versus other-oriented perspective reveals that taking the perspective of another who is suffering activates the posterior cingulate cortex and temporoparietal junction [TPJ] (Jackson, Brunet, Meltzoff, & Decety, 2006).

Compassion

Clarifying the distinction between compassion as a care-focused motive and empathy as a social processing competency typifies the promise of functional neuroimaging methods, as recent studies of these discrete processes reveal distinctly different patterns of brain activation. In fact, one of the first neuroimaging studies that purported to probe the neural correlates of compassion likely evoked empathy, and as such, the neural response to the empathy-inducing stimuli was characteristic of the core network described above (Immordino-Yang, McColl, Damasio, & Damasio, 2009). However, Kim and colleagues found that adopting a true compassionate stance when viewing photographs of others suffering activated the mesolimbic dopamine system (ventral tegmental area and ventral striatum) implicated in reward and motivation (Kim et al., 2009). A more recent study found that activity in the septal nuclei, another area important for reward and motivation, was commonly activated by several different empathy-inducing tasks and predicted helping behaviors (Morelli et al., 2012).

Interestingly, the research on compassion is consistent with that emerging from the investigation of the neurobiology of the parental brain. Animal models have long implicated both the septal area (Francis, Champagne, & Meaney, 2000) and the mesolimbic dopamine (DA) system in supporting the motivation to proactively nurture offspring, with DA-producing cell bodies in the ventral tegmental area (VTA) projecting to the nucleus accumbens (NA) to motivate caregiving (Numan & Stolzenberg, 2009). Recent neuroimaging research suggests that this system may support human parents' motivation to nurture their offspring

(Mascaro, Hackett, & Rilling, 2013; Rilling, 2013), which raises the intriguing possibility that it is this system that underlies the motivational quality of compassion (Preston & Hofelich, 2012). Researchers have long argued that compassion co-opts the systems in the brain and body that evolved for maternal attachment and caregiving (Gilbert, 1989; Preston & De Waal, 2002), and these data provide both support and a neural mechanism for such a view.

In summary, the model presented here proposes that empathy is composed of basic attentional, perceptual and motor simulation processes, simulation of another's affective body state, and slower and higher-level perspective-taking. These components are modulated by emotion regulation and self/other discrimination, and when infused with a motivational component, may become a compassionate response. Important for the current discussion, all of these neural processes take place in, and are influenced by, a neuromodulatory milieu that, as we will see, directly relates to that bi-directional social communication of which Darwin theorized. For, if our Darwinian approach to compassion is correct in as much as compassion is an emotional signal that facilitates connection, then we would expect it to be malleable, to change in response to a changing social environment. And if internal and external contextual factors influence compassion, brain and peripheral physiology should mediate this variability.

Neuromodulatory backdrop

While we are moving towards an understanding of the neural and physiological networks of compassion and its competencies we can also recognize that different brain states will influence the activation and engagement of these systems. Here we turn our attention to these modulatory systems that may influence the core systems detailed above.

Stress physiology

Studies often confirm what most of us know from personal experience: stress can create brain states that undermine compassion. What we often refer to as *stress* from a subjective sense relates to an evolved coordinated neurohormonal response by the sympathetic nervous system and hypothalamic pituitary adrenocortical (HPA) axis, and early research supported the idea that this system is antithetical to caring. For example, people who are socially excluded in an experimental paradigm show less subsequent prosocial behavior toward others (DeWall & Baumeister, 2006; Twenge, Baumeister, Dewall, Ciarocco, & Bartels, 2007). At a mechanistic level, this effect appears to be tied to stress responsivity in the HPA axis. For example, in both humans and mice, blocking HPA axis activity promotes emotional contagion among strangers (Martin et al., 2015). Linking with the model detailed above, this finding might suggest that cortisol and other stress mediators dampen a core competency of compassion and in that way are "anti-compassion" molecules. However, the truth is more complex and interesting.

In fact, just as we noted above that the amygdala plays an important role in compassion, significant data show that people who are unable to effectively activate stress responses, either in response to social stressors or in response to the distress of others, are at increased risk for a trait called callousness, which is diametrically opposed to empathy and other core components of compassion in general and with social threats in particular (Shirtcliff et al., 2009). In children, adolescents, and adults, lower levels of cortisol have been repeatedly associated with a lack of empathy and other traits that contribute to psychopathy, which includes an inability to love or establish meaningful personal relationships among its diagnostic elements. These reductions have been observed at rest and for cortisol responses to social stressors (reviewed in Shirtcliff et al., 2009).

How are we to make sense of these apparently conflicting bodies of research? One explanation is hinted at by research that acute stressors shift a person into a faster, more habitual and less flexible decision-making process, which can be promotive of compassion and altruistic behavior (Buchanan & Preston, 2014). If the habitual response has been shaped by a lifetime of altruism-promoting experiences (for example, experiences conferring the self-efficacy to believe one has the skills to help another whom is suffering), then acute stress may promote compassionate behavior. From a wider lens and consistent with our Darwinian framework, some posit that strengthening compassion as a response to life's slings and arrows may be an adaptive mechanism for enhancing social support and capital (Lim & DeSteno, 2016). Taken together, these studies suggest that there may be an inverse U-shaped relationship between stress and compassion, such that, given the right environment, acute and chronic stress may translate into compassionate action. Better understanding of the biological basis for this "sweet spot" is a challenge for social cognitive neuroscientists.

Innate immune system

To understand the relationship between the immune system and social connection, it is important to know that the mammalian immune system has two large interacting sub-systems: (1) a fast acting and non-specific one that is often referred to as innate immunity and is characterized by inflammation; and (2) a slow acting and specific system often referred to as acquired immunity, which is characterized by T cell activity and the production of antibodies that clear pathogens from the body. Studies in psychoneuroimmunology have made great strides with the discovery that chronic social isolation biases an individual's immune system toward the fast-acting innate immune response, characterized by deleterious pro-inflammatory signaling (Cole, 2009, 2014). At the same time, isolation down-regulates the slower acting acquired immune system. Relatedly, increases in inflammatory biomarkers are also documented in states of chronic stress and anxiety (Miller, Haroon, Raison, & Felger, 2013). These may act as compassion inhibitors. For example, enhanced signaling in the innate immune system has been shown to increase feelings of isolation and enhances amygdala responses to threatening social stimuli (Inagaki, Muscatell,

Irwin, Cole, & Eisenberger, 2012; Savitz et al., 2013). Moreover, it is crucial here to note the coordination of the inflammatory response with the stress response detailed above, with the acute inflammatory response triggering both the HPA axis and the sympathetic nervous system (Dantzer, Konsman, Bluthé, & Kelley, 2000). Taken together, these studies reveal a powerful cycle whereby isolation and depression enhance inflammation, which then further enhances subjective isolation and decreases empathy and compassion.

The optimistic outlook on such a negative cycle is that it renders particularly powerful those interventions that target the cycle at multiple sites by augmenting both subjective feelings of social connectivity and the biological systems that support it (Pace et al., 2009; Pace et al., 2013). This positive viewpoint is supported by the growing body of research showing that enhanced social connection optimizes immune function, stress physiology, and health more generally. For example, one study showed that individuals who report high levels of compassion receive more stress-buffering benefit (reduced cortisol and autonomic reactivity) when they receive social support (Cosley, McCoy, Saslow, & Epel, 2010). Other observational research indicates that providing social support decreases mortality (Brown, Nesse, Vinokur, & Smith, 2003), and that compassion mediates the consistent relationship between religiosity and health outcomes (Steffen & Masters, 2005).

Oxytocin

Increasing evidence suggests that oxytocin plays an important role in social processes in general (see Colonnello, Petrocchi, & Heinrichs, Chapter 6, this volume). Intranasal oxytocin delivery, which allows the neuropeptide to bypass the blood brain barrier, increases generosity toward others (Zak, Stanton, & Ahmadi, 2007); feelings of trust (Kosfeld, Heinrichs, Zak, Fischbacher, & Fehr, 2005); time spent in gazing at the eyes of other people (Guastella, Mitchell, & Dadds, 2008); and the ability to accurately read the emotional states signaled by facial expressions of other people (Domes, Heinrichs, Michel, Berger, & Herpertz, 2007; Lischke et al., 2012). Oxytocin administration increases people's sense of empathic concern for crime victims without increasing the desire to punish the criminal offenders (Krueger et al., 2012) and, in response to hearing the crying of infants, induces changes in brain activity that have been repeatedly associated with empathy (Riem et al., 2011). Intranasal oxytocin administration directly enhances feelings of empathy in both men and women (Hurlemann et al., 2010a), and is arguably most relevant to the emotional, or affective, components of empathy in comparison to the more cognitive aspects of understanding others' mental states (Frith & Singer, 2008).

In addition to studies relying on administration of intranasal OT, several studies have shown that genetic polymorphisms related to the oxytocin receptor are associated with prosocial behavior and empathy, as well as with neurological/psychiatric conditions such as autism. The later are characterized by deficits or abnormalities in social behavior and empathy (Rodrigues, Saslow, Garcia, John, & Keltner, 2009; Tost et al., 2010; Wu, Li, & Su, 2012). Interestingly, these same genetic variants appear to impact the structure and functional coupling of brain areas, including the hippocampus and amygdala that are essential for coping with stress and danger, especially when these threats are of a social nature (Tost et al., 2010).

But recent research has revealed a potential dark side to oxytocin relating to group dynamics. People tend to favor other individuals belonging to their in-group. Oxytocin enhances the distinction between in-group and out-group by making people more cooperative and caring toward in-group members but more competitive, even hostile, to out-group members (De Dreu, 2012). These findings have led some to suggest that rather than being the "love hormone," oxytocin should perhaps be characterized as the "tribal hormone." When placed in the evolutionary perspective in which the prosocial effects of oxytocin conferred an advantage, namely, maternal caregiving, it makes sense that oxytocin would bolster compassion and its constituent components as directed at close others (kin) at the same time as it would promote defensive aggression toward potential threats.

Summary and future directions

Evolution has created an integrated set of physiological systems that include the amygdala, frontal cortex, adaptations to autonomic nervous system (e.g. the myelinated vagal nerve) and a range of specific hormones like oxytocin that provide the infrastructures for caring, altruism and compassion. In addition we have seen how other systems, such as aspects of the immune system that impact on a range of psychological processes, also play a role in compassion's physiological infrastructures. As we noted early in this chapter, these endocrine, immune, and central nervous systems are best thought of as interacting systems that facilitate bi-directional communication between the external social world and the brain and body. The challenge for the future is to begin to understand the patterning and integrative functioning of these different systems, which is impossible when studying them in isolation. In addition, increasing research is exploring the genetic variations in these processes and in the way in which social contexts impact on those genetic dispositions (Conway & Slavich, Chapter 9, this volume). Understanding "the body of compassion" will greatly contribute to our ability to design interventions and programs to promote it.

References

Banks, S. J., Eddy, K. T., Angstadt, M., Nathan, P. J., & Phan, K. L. 2007. Amygdala–frontal connectivity during emotion regulation. *Social Cognitive and Affective Neuroscience*, 2, 303–312.

Batson, C. D. 1998. Altruism and prosocial behavior. In Gilbert, D., Fiske, S., & Lindzey, G. (Eds.) *The Handbook of Social Psychology*. Boston: McGraw-Hill.

Batson, C. D. 2009. These things called empathy: Eight related but distinct phenomena. In Decety, J. & Ickes, W. (Eds.) *The Social Neuroscience of Empathy.* Cambridge: The MIT Press.

Batson, C. D., Eklund, J. H., Chermok, V. L., Hoyt, J. L., & Ortiz, B. G. 2007. An additional antecedent of empathic concern: Valuing the welfare of the person in need. *Journal of Personality and Social Psychology,* 93, 65.

Batson, C. D., Fultz, J., & Schoenrade, P. A. 1987. Distress and empathy: 2 qualitatively distinct vicarious emotions with different motivational consequences. *Journal of Personality,* 55, 19–39.

Batson, C. D., Oquin, K., Fultz, J., Vanderplas, M. & Isen, A. M. 1983. Influence of self-reported distress and empathy on egoistic versus altruistic motivation to help. *Journal of Personality and Social Psychology,* 45, 706–718.

Bernhardt, B. C., & Singer, T. 2012. The neural basis of empathy. *Annual Review of Neuroscience,* 35, 1–23.

Bischoff-Kohler, D. 1991. The development of empathy in infants. In Lamb, M. E. & Keller, H. (Eds.) *Infant Development: Perspectives from German-Speaking Countries.* Hillsdale, NJ: Erlbaum.

Blair, R. J. R. 2008. The amygdala and ventromedial prefrontal cortex: Functional contributions and dysfunction in psychopathy. *Philosophical Transactions of the Royal Society B: Biological Sciences,* 363, 2557–2565.

Brown, S. L., Nesse, R. M., Vinokur, A. D. & Smith, D. M. 2003. Providing social support may be more beneficial than receiving it results from a prospective study of mortality. *Psychological Science,* 14, 320–327.

Buchanan, T. W., & Preston, S. D. 2014. Stress leads to prosocial action in immediate need situations. *Frontiers in Behavioral Neuroscience,* 8, 5.

Butler, E. A., Wilhelm, F. H. & Gross, J. J. 2006. Respiratory sinus arrhythmia, emotion, and emotion regulation during social interaction. *Psychophysiology,* 43, 612–622.

Carr, L., Iacoboni, M., Dubeau, M.-C., Mazziotta, J. C., & Lenzi, G. L. 2003. Neural mechanisms of empathy in humans: A relay from neural systems for imitation to limbic areas. *Proceedings of the National Academy of Sciences,* 100, 5497–5502.

Cole, S. W. 2009. Social regulation of human gene expression. *Current Directions in Psychological Science,* 18, 132–137.

Cole, S. W. 2014. Human social genomics. *PLoS Genet,* 10, e1004601.

Cosley, B. J., Mccoy, S. K., Saslow, L. R., & Epel, E. S. 2010. Is compassion for others stress buffering? Consequences of compassion and social support for physiological reactivity to stress. *Journal of Experimental Social Psychology,* 46, 816–823.

Cox, C. L., Uddin, L. Q., Di Martino, A., Castellanos, F. X., Milham, M. P., & Kelly, C. 2012. The balance between feeling and knowing: Affective and cognitive empathy are reflected in the brain's intrinsic functional dynamics. *Social Cognitive and Affective Neuroscience,* 7, 727–737.

Dantzer, R., Konsman, J.-P., Bluthé, R.-M., & Kelley, K. W. 2000. Neural and humoral pathways of communication from the immune system to the brain: Parallel or convergent? *Autonomic Neuroscience,* 85, 60–65.

Darwin, C., Ekman, P., & Prodger, P. 1998. *The Expression of the Emotions in Man and Animals.* New York: Oxford University Press.

Davis, M. 1992. The role of the amygdala in fear and anxiety. *Annual Review of Neuroscience,* 15, 353–375.

De Dreu, C. K. 2012. Oxytocin modulates cooperation within and competition between groups: An integrative review and research agenda. *Hormones and Behavior*, 61, 419–428.

De Vignemont, F., & Singer, T. 2006. The empathic brain: How, when and why? *Trends in Cognitive Sciences*, 10, 435–441.

De Waal, F. B. 2008. Putting the altruism back into altruism: The evolution of empathy. *Annual Review of Psychology*, 59, 279–300.

Decety, J., & Cowell, J. M. 2014. The complex relation between morality and empathy. *Trends in Cognitive Sciences*, 18, 337–339.

Decety, J., & Grèzes, J. 2006. The power of simulation: Imagining one's own and other's behavior. *Brain Research*, 1079, 4–14.

Dewall, C. N., & Baumeister, R. F. 2006. Alone but feeling no pain: Effects of social exclusion on physical pain tolerance and pain threshold, affective forecasting, and interpersonal empathy. *Journal of Personality and Social Psychology*, 91, 1–15.

Dolan, M. & Fullam, R. 2004. Theory of mind and mentalizing ability in antisocial personality disorders with and without psychopathy. *Psychological Medicine*, 34, 1093–1102.

Domes, G., Heinrichs, M., Michel, A., Berger, C., & Herpertz, S. C. 2007. Oxytocin improves "mind-reading" in humans. *Biological Psychiatry*, 61, 731–733.

Eisenberg, N., & Eggum, N. D. 2009. Empathic responding: Sympathy and personal distress. In Decety, J. & Ickes, W. (Eds.) *The Social Neuroscience of Empathy.* Cambridge, MA: The MIT Press.

Eisenberg, N., Fabes, R. A., Shepard, S. A., Murphy, B. C., Jones, S., & Guthrie, I. K. 1998. Contemporaneous and longitudinal prediction of children's sympathy from dispositional regulation and emotionality. *Developmental Psychology*, 34, 910–924.

Eisenberg, N., Shea, C. L., Carlo, G., & Knight, G. P. 2014. Empathy-related responding and cognition: A "chicken and the egg" dilemma. *Handbook of Moral Behavior and Development: Research*, 2, 63–88.

Fan, Y., Duncan, N. W., De Greck, M., & Northoff, G. 2011. Is there a core neural network in empathy? An fMRI based quantitative meta-analysis. *Neuroscience & Biobehavioral Reviews*, 35, 903–911.

Francis, D. D., Champagne, F. C., & Meaney, M. J. 2000. Variations in maternal behaviour are associated with differences in oxytocin receptor levels in the rat. *Journal of Neuroendocrinology*, 12, 1145–1148.

Frith, C. D., & Singer, T. 2008. The role of social cognition in decision making. *Philosophical Transactions of the Royal Society B: Biological Sciences*, 363, 3875–86.

Gilbert, P. 1989. *Human Nature and Suffering*. London: Psychology Press.

Guastella, A. J., Mitchell, P. B., & Dadds, M. R. 2008. Oxytocin increases gaze to the eye region of human faces. *Biological Psychiatry*, 63, 3–5.

Hein, G., Silani, G., Preuschoff, K., Batson, C. D., & Singer, T. 2010. Neural responses to ingroup and outgroup members' suffering predict individual differences in costly helping. *Neuron*, 68, 149–160.

Hoffman, M. L. 2001. *Empathy and Moral Development: Implications for Caring and Justice.* New York, Cambridge University Press.

Hurlemann, R., Patin, A., Onur, O. A., Cohen, M. X., Baumgartner, T., Metzler, . . . Kendrick, K. M. 2010a. Oxytocin enhances amygdala-dependent, socially reinforced learning and emotional empathy in humans. *The Journal of Neuroscience*, 30, 4999–5007.

Hurlemann, R., Patin, A., Onur, O. A., Cohen, M. X., Baumgartner, T., Metzler, . . . Maier, W. 2010b. Oxytocin enhances amygdala-dependent, socially reinforced learning and emotional empathy in humans. *The Journal of Neuroscience*, 30, 4999–5007.

Iacoboni, M., & Dapretto, M. 2006. The mirror neuron system and the consequences of its dysfunction. *Nature Reviews Neuroscience*, 7, 942–951.

Immordino-Yang, M. H., Mccoll, A., Damasio, H., & Damasio, A. 2009. Neural correlates of admiration and compassion. *Proceedings of the National Academy of Sciences*, 106, 8021–8026.

Inagaki, T. K., Muscatell, K. A., Irwin, M. R., Cole, S. W., & Eisenberger, N. I. 2012. Inflammation selectively enhances amygdala activity to socially threatening images. *Neuroimage*, 59, 3222–3226.

Jabbi, M., & Keysers, C. 2008. Inferior frontal gyrus activity triggers anterior insula response to emotional facial expressions. *Emotion*, 8, 775–780.

Jackson, P. L., Brunet, E., Meltzoff, A. N., & Decety, J. 2006. Empathy examined through the neural mechanisms involved in imagining how I feel versus how you feel pain. *Neuropsychologia*, 44, 752–761.

Johnson, D. B. 1982. Altruistic behavior and the development of the self in infants. *Merrill-Palmer Quarterly (1982–)*, 379–388.

Kim, J.-W., Kim, S.-E., Kim, J.-J., Jeong, B., Park, C.-H., Son, A. R., Song, J. E., & Ki, S. W. 2009. Compassionate attitude towards others' suffering activates the mesolimbic neural system. *Neuropsychologia*, 47, 2073–2081.

Klimecki, O. M., Leiberg, S., Lamm, C., & Singer, T. 2013. Functional neural plasticity and associated changes in positive affect after compassion training. *Cerebral Cortex*, 23, 1552–1561.

Kosfeld, M., Heinrichs, M., Zak, P. J., Fischbacher, U., & Fehr, E. 2005. Oxytocin increases trust in humans. *Nature*, 435, 673–676.

Krueger, F., Parasuraman, R., Moody, L., Twieg, P., De Visser, E., Mccabe, K., . . . Lee, M. R. 2012. Oxytocin selectively increases perceptions of harm for victims but not the desire to punish offenders of criminal offenses. *Social Cognitive and Affective Neuroscience*, 8(5), 494–498.

Lamm, C., Decety, J., & Singer, T. 2010. Meta-analytic evidence for common and distinct neural networks associated with directly experienced pain and empathy for pain. *Neuroimage*, 54, 2492–2502.

Lamm, C., Decety, J., & Singer, T. 2011. Meta-analytic evidence for common and distinct neural networks associated with directly experienced pain and empathy for pain. *Neuroimage*, 54, 2492–2502.

Larson, C. L., Baskin-Sommers, A. R., Stout, D. M., Balderston, N. L., Curtin, J. J., Schultz, . . . Newman, J. P. 2013. The interplay of attention and emotion: Top-down attention modulates amygdala activation in psychopathy. *Cognitive, Affective, & Behavioral Neuroscience*, 13, 757–770.

Leigh, R., Oishi, K., Hsu, J., Lindquist, M., Gottesman, R. F., Jarso, . . . Hillis, A. E. 2013. Acute lesions that impair affective empathy. *Brain*, 8, 2539–2549

Lieberman, M. D. 2007. Social cognitive neuroscience: A review of core processes. *Annual Review of Psychology*, 58, 259–289.

Lim, D. & Desteno, D. 2016. Suffering and compassion: The links among adverse life experiences, empathy, compassion, and prosocial behavior. *Emotion*, 16, 175.

Lischke, A., Berger, C., Prehn, K., Heinrichs, M., Herpertz, S. C., & Domes, G. 2012. Intranasal oxytocin enhances emotion recognition from dynamic facial expressions and leaves eye-gaze unaffected. *Psychoneuroendocrinology*, 37, 475–481.

Marsh, A. A., Finger, E. C., Fowler, K. A., Adalio, C. J., Jurkowitz, I. T. N., Schechter, J. C., . . . Blair, R. J. R. 2013. Empathic responsiveness in amygdala and anterior cingulate cortex in youths with psychopathic traits. *Journal of Child Psychology and Psychiatry*, 54, 900–910.

Marsh, A. A., Stoycos, S. A., Brethel-Haurwitz, K. M., Robinson, P., Vanmeter, J. W., & Cardinale, E. M. 2014. Neural and cognitive characteristics of extraordinary altruists. *Proceedings of the National Academy of Sciences*, 111(42), 15036–15041.

Martin, L. J., Hathaway, G., Isbester, K., Mirali, S., Acland, E. L., Niederstrasser, N., . . . Jeffrey S. 2015. Reducing social stress elicits emotional contagion of pain in mouse and human strangers. *Current Biology*, 25, 326–332.

Mascaro, J. S., Darcher, A., Negi, L. T., & Raison, C. L. 2015. The neural mediators of kindness-based meditation: a theoretical model. *Frontiers in Psychology*, 6.

Mascaro, J. S., Hackett, P. D., & Rilling, J. K. 2013. Testicular volume is inversely correlated with nurturing-related brain activity in human fathers. *Proceedings of the National Academy of Sciences*, 110, 15746–15751.

Masten, C. L., Morelli, S. A., & Eisenberger, N. I. 2011. An fMRI investigation of empathy for "social pain" and subsequent prosocial behavior. *Neuroimage*, 55, 381–388.

Miller, A. H., Haroon, E., Raison, C. L., & Felger, J. C. 2013. Cytokine targets in the brain: Impact on neurotransmitters and neurocircuits. *Depression and Anxiety*, 30, 297–306.

Morelli, S. A., Rameson, L. T., & Lieberman, M. D. 2014. The neural components of empathy: Predicting daily prosocial behavior. *Social Cognitive and Affective Neuroscience*, 9(1), 39–47

Mosher, C. P., Zimmerman, P. E., & Gothard, K. M. 2014. Neurons in the monkey amygdala detect eye contact during naturalistic social interactions. *Current Biology*, 24, 2459–2464.

Numan, M., & Stolzenberg, D. S. 2009. Medial preoptic area interactions with dopamine neural systems in the control of the onset and maintenance of maternal behavior in rats. *Frontiers in Neuroendocrinology*, 30, 46–64.

Ochsner, K. N., Bunge, S. A., Gross, J. J., & Gabrieli, J. D. E. 2002. Rethinking feelings: An fMRI study of the cognitive regulation of emotion. *Journal of Cognitive Neuroscience*, 14, 1215–1229.

Ochsner, K. N., & Gross, J. J. 2005. The cognitive control of emotion. *Trends in Cognitive Sciences*, 9, 242–249.

Pace, T. W., Negi, L. T., Dodson-Lavelle, B., Ozawa-De Silva, B., Reddy, S. D., Cole, . . . Raison, C. L. 2013. Engagement with cognitively-based compassion training is associated with reduced salivary C-reactive protein from before to after training in foster care program adolescents. *Psychoneuroendocrinology*, 38, 294–299.

Pace, T. W. W., Negi, L. T., Adame, D. D., Cole, S. P., Sivilli, T. I., Brown, . . . Raison, C. L. 2009. Effect of compassion meditation on neuroendocrine, innate immune and behavioral responses to psychosocial stress. *Psychoneuroendocrinology*, 34, 87–98.

Pessoa, L., & Adolphs, R. 2010. Emotion processing and the amygdala: From a "low road" to "many roads" of evaluating biological significance. *Nature Reviews Neuroscience*, 11, 773–783.

Porges, S. W. 2003. The polyvagal theory: Phylogenetic contributions to social behavior. *Physiology & Behavior*, 79, 503–513.

Porges, S. W. 2007. The polyvagal perspective. *Biological Psychology*, 74, 116–143.

Preston, S. D., & De Waal, F. 2002. Empathy: Its ultimate and proximate bases. *Behavioral and Brain Sciences*, 25, 1–20.

Preston, S. D., & Hofelich, A. J. 2012. The many faces of empathy: Parsing empathic phenomena through a proximate, dynamic-systems view of representing the other in the self. *Emotion Review*, 4, 24–33.

Richell, R. A., Mitchell, D. G. V., Newman, C., Leonard, A., Baron-Cohen, S. & Blair, R. J. R. 2003. Theory of mind and psychopathy: Can psychopathic individuals read the "language of the eyes"? *Neuropsychologia*, 41, 523–526.

Riem, M. M., Bakermans-Kranenburg, M. J., Pieper, S., Tops, M., Boksem, M. A., Vermeiren, R. R., . . . Rombouts, S. A. 2011. Oxytocin modulates amygdala, insula, and inferior frontal gyrus responses to infant crying: A randomized controlled trial. *Biological Psychiatry*, 70, 291–297.

Rilling, J. K. 2013. The neural and hormonal bases of human parental care. *Neuropsychologia*, 51, 731–747.

Rilling, J. K., Glenn, A. L., Jairam, M. R., Pagnoni, G., Goldsmith, D. R., Elfenbein, H. A., & Lilienfeld, S. O. 2007. Neural correlates of social cooperation and non-cooperation as a function of psychopathy. *Biological Psychiatry*, 61, 1260–1271.

Rockliff, H., Gilbert, P., Mcewan, K., Lightman, S., & Glover, D. 2008. A pilot exploration of heart rate variability and salivary cortisol responses to compassion-focused imagery. *Journal of Clinical Neuropsychiatry*, 5, 132–139.

Rodrigues, S. M., Saslow, L. R., Garcia, N., John, O. P., & Keltner, D. 2009. Oxytocin receptor genetic variation relates to empathy and stress reactivity in humans. *Proceedings of the National Academy of Sciences*, 106, 21437–21441.

Ross, H. E., & Young, L. J. 2009. Oxytocin and the neural mechanisms regulating social cognition and affiliative behavior. *Frontiers in Neuroendocrinology*, 30, 534–547.

Savitz, J., Frank, M. B., Victor, T., Bebak, M., Marino, J. H., Bellgowan, . . . Drevets, W. C. 2013. Inflammation and neurological disease-related genes are differentially expressed in depressed patients with mood disorders and correlate with morphometric and functional imaging abnormalities. *Brain, Behavior, and Immunity*, 31, 161–171.

Segerstrom, S. C., & Nes, L. S. 2007. Heart rate variability reflects self-regulatory strength, effort, and fatigue. *Psychological Science*, 18, 275–281.

Shirtcliff, E. A., Vitacco, M. J., Graf, A. R., Gostisha, A. J., Merz, J. L. & Zahn-Waxler, C. 2009. Neurobiology of empathy and callousness: Implications for the development of antisocial behavior. *Behavioral Sciences & the Law*, 27, 137–171.

Steffen, P. R., & Masters, K. S. 2005. Does compassion mediate the intrinsic religion-health relationship? *Annals of Behavioral Medicine*, 30, 217–224.

Todd, R. M., Cunningham, W. A., Anderson, A. K., & Thompson, E. 2012. Affect-biased attention as emotion regulation. *Trends in Cognitive Sciences*, 16, 365–372.

Tost, H., Kolachana, B., Hakimi, S., Lemaitre, H., Verchinski, B. A., Mattay, V. S., Weinberger, D. R., & Meyer-Lindenberg, A. 2010. A common allele in the oxytocin receptor gene (OXTR) impacts prosocial temperament and human hypothalamic-limbic structure and function. *Proceedings of the National Academy of Sciences*, 107, 13936–13941.

Trommsdorff, G., Friedlmeier, W., & Mayer, B. 2007. Sympathy, distress, and prosocial behavior of preschool children in four cultures. *International Journal of Behavioral Development*, 31, 284–293.

Twenge, J. M., Baumeister, R. F., Dewall, C. N., Ciarocco, N. J. & Bartels, J. M. 2007. Social exclusion decreases prosocial behavior. *Journal of Personality and Social Psychology*, 92, 56–66.

Urry, H. L., Van Reekum, C. M., Johnstone, T., Kalin, N. H., Thurow, M. E., Schaefer, . . . Alexander, A. L. 2006. Amygdala and ventromedial prefrontal cortex are inversely coupled during regulation of negative affect and predict the diurnal pattern of cortisol secretion among older adults. *The Journal of Neuroscience*, 26, 4415–4425.

Wang, S., Tudusciuc, O., Mamelak, A. N., Ross, I. B., Adolphs, R. & Rutishauser, U. 2014. Neurons in the human amygdala selective for perceived emotion. *Proceedings of the National Academy of Sciences*, 111, E3110–E3119.

Wu, N., Li, Z., & Su, Y. 2012. The association between oxytocin receptor gene polymorphism (OXTR) and trait empathy. *Journal of Affective Disorders*, 138, 468– 472.

Zahn-Waxler, C., Radke-Yarrow, M., & King, R. A. 1979. Child rearing and children's prosocial initiations toward victims of distress. *Child Development*, 319–330.

Zak, P. J., Stanton, A. A., & Ahmadi, S. 2007. Oxytocin increases generosity in humans. *PLOS ONE*, 2, e1128.

Zaki, J. 2014. Empathy: A motivated account. *Psychological Bulletin*, 140, 1608.

Chapter 6

The psychobiological foundation of prosocial relationships

The role of oxytocin in daily social exchanges

Valentina Colonnello, Nicola Petrocchi and Markus Heinrichs

Introduction

Caring and affiliative motivations are embedded in human nature and rooted in evolutionarily developed brain systems that we share with other mammals (MacLean, 1985; Panksepp & Biven, 2012). They are considered to be the root of compassion (Gilbert, 2009). Compassion can be considered the expression of the extended caregiving system, which is thought to have emerged from evolutionarily ancient motivations to detect and respond to the need of dependent offspring (Gilbert, Chapters 1 and 3). The caring motivation would extend, through evolution, to the welfare of all living beings and the formation of cooperative relations with non-kin (Goetz, Keltner, & Simon-Thomas, 2010; Wang, 2005).

As discussed by Gilbert in Chapter 1, despite growing interest in the subject of compassion, there is little consensus regarding the definition of the notion of compassion itself and its underlying psychobiological mechanisms. Compassion has been conceptualized as both an *affective state*, defined by a specific subjective feeling that arises while witnessing another's suffering (Goetz, Keltner, & Simon-Thomas, 2010), and a motivational state rooted in the evolution of caring emotional system and aimed at the prevention and relief of suffering and its causes. In the latter view, compassion encompasses a variety of characteristics and can give rise to a blend of emotions (Gilbert, 2015). Notably, in Gilbert's view, compassion is a motivational system, a social mentality that influences attention mechanisms towards the social world (Gilbert, Chapter 3, this volume). Thus, compassion relies on several emotions and it is not reducible to a single specific emotion.

Among the psychobiological systems involved in social bond formation and caring, the neuropeptide oxytocin plays a central role (Colonnello, Petrocchi, Farinelli, & Ottaviani, 2016; Donaldson & Young, 2008; Meyer-Lindenberg, Domes, Kirsch, & Heinrichs, 2011; Petrocchi & Couyoumdjian, 2015 for a review). Oxytocin is synthesized in the paraventricular and supraoptic nuclei of the hypothalamus and, through axonal projection, is processed to the posterior pituitary lobes and released for peripheral circulation (Meyer-Lindenberg et al., 2011, for a review). Oxytocin plays a key role in the expression of the caregiving motivation thanks to its receptors in several subcortical areas such as the anterior cingulated and the bed nucleus of the striaterminalis involved in parental behavior (Panksepp, 1998). In addition, the oxytocinergic system is very likely involved in approach/appetitive motivation thanks to its ability to facilitate interactions with the mesolimbic reward-seeking system (Shahrokh, Zhang, Diorio, Gratton, & Meaney, 2010) and its involvement with vagal dorsal motor nucleus regulation (Carter, 2014; Porges, 2003).

As several human studies indicate, the oxytocinergic system is involved in several aspects of social interactions as, for example, social bond formation (Galbally, Lewis, IJzendoorn, & Permezel, 2011) conflict resolution (Ditzen et al., 2009), understanding of others' feelings (Schulze et al., 2011), and self-related and other-related processing (Colonnello, Chen, Panksepp, & Heinrichs, 2013; Colonnello, Domes, & Heinrichs, 2016; Colonnello & Heinrichs, 2014). Given the key role of oxytocin in several aspects of positive social behavior, there is increased interest in studying this system's potential involvement in compassion motivation and compassion-related feelings and behaviors.

Compassionate behaviors rely on the understanding of other's emotions while maintaining self/other distinction and regulating personal distress – all aspects found to be modulated by oxytocin. Thus, we will focus on the effects of oxytocin administration on these central components for experiencing compassion, and will consider the possible mediating role of individual traits on oxytocin reception. Throughout this contribution to the field, we will highlight potential links and implications of oxytocin studies with regards to compassion.

Oxytocin involvement in caring behavior and distress regulation

Several studies have demonstrated that the oxytocinergic system plays a key role in the activation of caregiving approach motivation (Meyer-Lindenberg et al., 2011, for a review). For example, Feldman and colleagues (2007) reported that high peripheral oxytocin levels during pregnancy and the early postpartum period are positively associated with gazing at, affectionately touching and checking the infant, typical initial manifestations of maternal care (Feldman, Weller, Zagoory-Sharon, & Levine, 2007). Furthermore, mother–infant behavioral synchrony has been found to correlate positively with maternal salivary and plasma oxytocin levels (Feldman, Gordon, Schneiderman, Weisman, & Zagoory-Sharon, 2010; Feldman, Gordon, & Zagoory-Sharon, 2011).

Independent studies investigating the causal relationship between central oxytocin levels and caregiving behavior reveal that enhanced central levels of oxytocin increase sensitive parenting behaviors. In men, oxytocin administration increases respiratory sinus arrhythmia (an index of parasympathetic activity and readiness to willingly engage in social activity) along with affectionate touch and episodes of social reciprocity during interactions with their infants (Weisman, Zagoory-Sharon, & Feldman, 2012). In addition, the increase in central oxytocin levels promotes feelings of acceptance and other-oriented behaviors: men who received oxytocin revealed less hostile behavior than placebo-treated fathers during play sessions with their toddlers (Naber, van IJzendoorn, Deschamps, van Engeland, & Bakermans-Kranenburg, 2010). Moreover, following oxytocin administration, fathers have been found to be more sensitive to a disruption in the interaction with their infants, as seen by increased cortisol levels during the face-to-face-still-face paradigm.

One of the mechanisms by which oxytocin is thought to facilitate prosocial care-giving behaviors is by reducing avoidance and the fear of novelty while enhancing acceptance of the infant (Carter, 1998). The study by Riem and colleagues provides some support for this hypothesis: men and women were administered oxytocin or a placebo and were then exposed to an infant's signals of distress (crying sounds). The authors found that oxytocin administration reduced amygdala activation, a neural circuitry involved in aversion behaviors, and increased activation of the insula and inferior frontal gyrus, regions involved in empathic responses (Riem et al., 2011). In addition, the oxytocinergic system likely facilitates the initiation of caring motivation (Rilling, 2013) and promotes the protection of offspring (Rilling & Young, 2014) by virtue of its facilitating interactions with the reward-seeking mesolimbic dopaminergic neurons (Feldman, 2012).

Likewise, oxytocinergic-dopaminergic interactions might be central for creating caring compassionate motivation (Preston & Hofelich, 2012); ventral tegmental and ventral striatum dopamine areas have been found to activate when subjects adopt a compassionate stance when viewing photographs of others suffering (Kim et al., 2009). In addition, compassion-based meditation such as Loving Kindness Mediation (LKM) enhance neural responses to vignettes of others suffering in conjunction with ventral tegmental area activation (Klimecki, Leiberg, Lamm, & Singer, 2013).

The expression of compassionate behaviors relies on an increase in approach motivation in conjunction with reduced defensive avoidance motivation (Gilbert, 2010, 2014; see Chapter 3). The inclination to be caring and compassionate may be stronger in people we perceive as being pleasant than in those we perceive as being unpleasant. Oxytocin seems to impact this dimension. For example, intra-nasal administration of oxytocin appears to increase the attractiveness of infant faces (Marsh et al., 2012) and to enhance the attractiveness of unfamiliar faces (Theodoridou, Rowe, Penton-Voak, & Rogers, 2009). One possible underlying mechanism by which oxytocin could exert such an impact on the perception of pleasantness is in regulating amygdala activity and reducing the perceived ambiguity regarding the valence of social stimuli, and promoting approach behavior, thus facilitating affiliation (Domes et al., 2007).

Furthermore, central oxytocin regulates bodily functions associated with the parasympathetic nervous system by modulating output from the vagal dorsal motor nucleus (Carter, 2014). Vagus nerve activity is of particular importance to emotional regulation and social engagement (Porges, 2003). Oxytocin administration has been found to increase heart-rate variability (HRV) in humans at rest in the absence of any external demands on participants (Kemp et al., 2012). These vagal and oxytocin mediated mechanisms, by which withdrawal-related behaviors are inhibited and approach-related social behaviors (social engagement) are enhanced, may contribute to the expression of compassionate responses.

Caring compassion motivation leads to prosocial behaviors that may contribute to preventing and alleviating others' suffering. The instrumental support is one of the expressions of compassionate prosocial behavior (Gilbert, 2010). Oxytocin has been found to influence instrumental social support. Specifically, a single administration of oxytocin nasal spray increases a person's willingness to share their own economic resources with a deprived child, with no expectation for reciprocation. Interestingly, these effects were mediated by levels of parental love-withdrawal. Participants reporting supportive backgrounds were more willing to act in a prosocial manner than women reared in more families that were less supportive emotionally (Van IJzendoorn, Huffmeijer, Alink, Bakermans-Kranenburg, & Tops, 2011).

In line with the findings of Van IJzendoorn and colleagues, a study by Riem and colleagues (Riem, Bakermans-Kranenburg, Huffmeijer, & van IJzendoorn, 2013) found that oxytocin facilitates compassionate prosocial behavior toward socially excluded individuals in a Cyberball social exclusion game. The tendency to compensate for other players' ostracism was enhanced after oxytocin administration, but only in participants with low levels of maternal love withdrawal (Riem et al., 2013).

Oxytocin's role in feelings of safeness, and the mediating role of attachment style

Compassion Focused Therapy enhances feelings of comfort and safeness, and the associated inclination to positively relate to oneself, while feeling socially safe with others (Gilbert, 2010; Petrocchi, Ottaviani, & Couyoumdjian, 2016). The oxytocinergic system has been found to be involved in the expression of such feelings; specifically, oxytocin administration reduces feelings associated with separation distress (Panksepp, 2009), increases a positive view of oneself (Colonnello & Heinrichs, 2014) and promotes a positive perception of social aspects of the self (Cardoso, Ellenbogen, & Linnen, 2012). In addition, oxytocinergic system activation is associated with feelings of safeness and belonging, typical of secure attachment bonds. For example, in a study by Buchheim and colleagues (2009), men with insecure attachment patterns were asked to view pictures representing attachment-related events (e.g. a girl looking outside a window) accompanied by several statements representing the established attachment categories: secure, insecure-dismissing, insecure-preoccupied and unresolved trauma or loss. Each picture was accompanied by four statements, one for each attachment category. The participants were instructed to rank the statement based on its appropriateness to the picture. Participants reported a greater experience of attachment security following oxytocin, but not upon placebo administration. Notably, most but not all (69%) of the participants benefited from oxytocin administration, which highlights the individual variability in the oxytocinergic system's activity. Would oxytocin induce similar effects when the individuals with insecure attachment style were asked to recollect their own personal memories of caregiving figures or to imagine, *hic et nunc*, interactions with a positive caregiving figure? The study by Bartz and colleagues suggests that this is not the case. While oxytocin facilitates the recollection of positive maternal care and closeness in individuals with less anxious attachment patterns, it enhances the recollection of the mother *as less caring* after oxytocin (*versus* the placebo) in individuals with higher anxious attachment patterns (Bartz et al., 2010).

Notably, the effects of the increase in central oxytocin levels via nasal administration are dependent on context and the individual's attachment style (Bartz, Zaki, Bolger, & Ochsner, 2011). The availability of a perceived positive caring environment during throughout the individual's development contributes to shaping the brain's oxytocinergic system in humans and the body's sensitivity/ responses to oxytocin administration in adulthood. In conjunction, the availability and quality of parental care in childhood contributes to the organization of long-term oxytocinergic function. For example, Fries and colleagues (2005) found a relationship between social experience in infancy and urinary oxytocin levels in childhood: compared to children reared by their biological parents, children who had been institutionalized or adopted had lower oxytocin levels (Fries, Ziegler, Kurian, Jacoris, & Pollak, 2005).

It has been suggested that epigenetic processes might lead to lowered oxytocin sensitivity: parental rejection might raise methylation levels and thereby suppress genetic expression in areas related to the oxytocinergic system, thus decreasing receptiveness to intranasal oxytocin administration (van IJzendoorn, Bakermans-Kranenburg, & Ebstein, 2011). These findings form a good link with attachment studies showing that insecure attachment style is associated with reduced prosocial behavior (Mikulncher, Orbach, & Iavnieli, 1998; Mikulincer & Shaver, Chapter 11, this volume) and with compassion studies reporting the moderating role of attachment style on the effects of imagining a compassionate figure.

Rockliff et al. (2011) explored the effects of oxytocin on compassion-focused imagery (CFI) – that is, imagining another person being deeply compassionate to oneself – and the interaction of these effects with attachment security, self-criticism and feeling socially safe with others. Oxytocin increased the ease of imagining compassionate qualities; however, participants lower in attachment security, self-reassurance and social safety, and higher in self-criticism, had less-positive CFI experiences with oxytocin than with a placebo, indicating that the effects of oxytocin on affiliation may depend on one's attachment and self-evaluative style. In line with the "social salience hypothesis," oxytocin alters the perceptual salience and processing of social cues, thus creating a different effect on individuals depending on their dispositional traits and interpersonal situation (Bartz et al., 2011; Shamay-Tsoory & Abu-Akel, 2016).

Taken together, these findings suggest that a single dose of oxytocin may facilitate the encoding of specific attachment-related events and the recollection, acceptance and sharing of one's own negative memories, imagery and feelings, rather than modifying the attachment representation itself. Thus, high oxytocin levels would be relevant in a clinical context because oxytocin would give patients access to neglected or suppressed emotional memories and open the individual to the possibility of sharing. This sheds light on a phenomenon observed by Bowlby and described by Gilbert (2009, 2010) whereby positive feelings generated by caring interactions (for example a therapist being kind and reassuring with the client) might be experienced by the client as extremely frightening, thus activating a defensive response. It is possible that increased oxytocin generated by cues of kindness from the therapist would facilitate the activation of negative attachment-related memories in subjects with insecure attachment patterns. This is congruent with findings from recent studies indicating that oxytocin increases the ability to express one's own emotions (Lane et al., 2013), such as self-reported feelings of sadness in postnatally depressed mothers (Mah, Van IJzendoorn, Smith, & Bakermans-Kranenburg, 2013), while increasing the salience of social stimuli, as discussed in the next section.

Oxytocin and emotional understanding

Compassionate behavior is the ultimate output of the processing of information regarding one's own resources and feelings of safeness and the understanding of another person's perspective. To provide the kind of support that is more efficient to the care-elicitor, understanding another person's emotions and perspective is crucial. Notably, the emotion-recognition ability has been linked to prosocial behavior (Marsh, Kozak, & Ambady, 2007).

Several studies indicate that the neuropeptide oxytocin enhances the ability to detect other people's emotional expressions and recognize them accurately (Shahrestani, Kemp, & Guastella, 2013). For example, in the study by Schulze et al. (2011), participants were asked to indicate the presence or absence of target angry and happy faces versus neutral distractors. These were presented for 18, 35, or 53 ms and then subsequently masked by neutral faces. The authors found that oxytocin enhances the accuracy of detecting emotional faces, especially happy faces. Oxytocin has consistently been found to increase the shift of attention towards happy facial expressions at the early stage of face processing (100 ms) on a dot-probe paradigm, without affecting overt visual attention (Domes et al., 2013). Moreover, oxytocin administration reduced the activity of the anterior amygdala laterally and dorsally for fearful emotional faces, while increasing the activity for happy facial expressions on an emotion classification task (Gamer, Zurowski, & Büchel, 2010).

The facilitating effect of oxytocin for detecting positive social cues, such as happy facial expressions, is coupled with reduced reactivity to threatening social cues. For example, intranasal oxytocin administration weakens neural correlation of early arousal while viewing threat cues from the eyes (Kanat, Heinrichs, Schwarzwald, & Domes, 2015). Apparently, the enhanced ability to recognize positive emotions seems to contradict the thesis that compassionate behavior is based on recognizing another's suffering. However, this apparent paradox could easily be understood if one considers that the final goal of compassionate motivation is not only to *approach* suffering (modulating the level of arousal induced by negative emotions without impairing their recognition), but also to *promote* and sustain other's positive emotions. The early detection of positive emotions, facilitated by the oxytocinergic system, is important to bond formation and to guide, positively reinforce and maintain compassion-focused behavior.

As highlighted above, the effects of oxytocin administration depend on an individual's traits. For example, oxytocin administration increases a person's attention to facial stimuli, as indicated by relative greater pupil dilation in participants with low emotional sensitivity (Leknes et al., 2012). Riem and colleagues (2014) found that oxytocin increases the ability to recognize another's emotion in the Reading the Mind in the Eyes Test (RMET), a task in which participants are presented with emotions revealing varying difficulty of degrees to be recognized. This effect was stronger in participants reporting higher levels of maternal love withdrawal.

Polymorphisms of the OX gene

The effects of oxytocin administration on emotion recognition ability are also influenced by the oxytocin receptor gene's variation (see Conway & Slavich, Chapter 9, this volume). Polymorphisms have been identified for a number of neurotransmitter systems and one impact of them is contribute to individual sensitivity to the environment. For example, a six-marker haplotype block (the TTCGGG haplotype comprising single-nucleotide polymorphisms rs237917–rs2268498–rs4564970–rs237897–rs2268495–rs53576) is associated with increased emotion recognition ability following oxytocin compared with placebo administration. By contrast, the CCGAGA haplotype showed the opposite pattern (Chen et al., 2015).

A crucial ability found to be influenced by oxytocin administration is the ability to represent, interpret, and understand the mental states of others, that is, the Theory of Mind (ToM). It has been suggested that a better ToM ability helps individuals account for others' feelings and desires and therefore leads to more compassionate behavior (Chapter 3, this volume; Gilbert, 2010; Goldstein & Winner, 2012). Interestingly, twin studies suggest that large variance in children's ToM and prosocial behavior could be attributed to genetic factors (Hughes, Jaffee, Taylor, Caspi, & Moffit, 2005). The oxytocin receptor gene (OXTR) is one of the major candidates in explaining different subtypes of prosocial behavior. In a recent study on children (Wu & Su, 2015), oxytocin receptor (OXTR) variations were able to predict the difference in both prosocial behaviors and ToM ability: individuals homozygous for the G allele (GG; OXTR rs53576 genotype) exhibited more prosocial behaviors (increased helping and comforting, but not sharing) and better ToM ability than other genotypes.

The link between oxytocin and ToM has also been reported in mothers. A recent longitudinal study on pregnant women found that the level of plasma oxytocin during late pregnancy predicted increased ToM abilities, which in turn was associated with less remote and less depressive maternal interactive behavior during the first post-partum trimester (MacKinnon et al., 2014). Thus, alterations in the oxytocinergic system during the perinatal period may contribute to the awareness of social cues, which in turn has an impact on maternal interactive behavior. We also know that intranasal administration of oxytocin improves ToM in healthy men (Domes, Heinrichs, Michel, Berger, & Herpertz, 2007) and individuals with autism spectrum disorders (Guastella et al., 2010).

These findings suggest endogenous oxytocin may be a biomarker of social motivation and of individual sensitivity to social cues (Bartz et al., 2011), and could explain variability in the efficacy of compassion focus therapies.

Oxytocin and self/other distinction

Compassionate behavior is characterized by a prosocial approach, which implies the ability to tune or synchronize with others while maintaining the self/other distinction. In fact, as suggested by research from social psychology, excessive overlap between the "self" and "other" may produce personally oriented distress that leads to emotional disengagement, rather than compassionate behavior (Batson & Shaw, 1991). The development of a distinct self-concept is connected with a child's propensity to make helpful advances toward others (Hoffman, 2001).

Based on this data, social cognitive neuroscience research identifies the self/other distinction as a key component of empathy (Lamm, Bukowski, & Silani, 2016) and compassion. Oxytocin administration has been found to increase the tendency to synchronize one's own behavior with another's behavior (De Coster, Mueller, T'Sjoen, De Saedeleer, & Brass, 2014), while it increases the tendency to distinguish from self- and other-related stimuli (Colonnello et al., 2013). High central oxytocin levels facilitate the recognition of the self/other distinction. Specifically, compared to placebo administration, intranasal oxytocin administration shortened the time it took to recognize the identity in a self/other recognition task in which the photo of the participant's face morphed into the photo of an unfamiliar individual's face and vice versa. Regardless of the morphing direction, participants who received oxytocin demonstrated an advantage in recognizing their own and unfamiliar facial features. Notably, participants who received oxytocin were also more likely than placebo-treated participants to evaluate others positively (Colonnello et al., 2013). By dampening fear responses and enhancing dopaminergic-mediated seeking motivation, oxytocin may facilitate the recognition and acceptance of self/other differences.

Other studies have continued to explore the idea that oxytocin might be involved in self/other distinction processing. For example, Zhao et al. (2016) investigated the effect of oxytocin administration on judgment and the recollection of self (and other) (mother, classmate, or stranger) traits. Oxytocin has been found to accelerate the speed of decisions for the self versus other trait judgments. Thus, the work by Zhao and colleagues, expanding upon previous results on oxytocin effects on the self/other distinction, suggests that the effects of oxytocin on self/other distinction judgments are specific to the initial phases of self/other approach/interactions (Zhao et al., 2016).

In another analysis that aimed to study the link between oxytocin, the self/other distinction and empathic ability, participants received oxytocin or placebo and then were asked to imagine themselves (self-condition) and other individuals (other condition) in painful and non-painful situations. While no differences between the self and other conditions were found following placebo administration, oxytocin administration increased empathy to pain when imaging others, but not the self, in a painful condition (Abu-Akel, Palgi, Klein, Decety, & Shamay-Tsoory, 2015). Taken together, these results suggest that oxytocin might contribute to promoting feelings of compassion by reducing personal distress, sharpening the self/other distinction, and enhancing the understanding of others' needs.

Appearing to contrast with these studies on oxytocin's effect on sharpening self/other distinction, some have found that oxytocin administration increases self/other integration performance during a joint/social Simon task (Ruissen & de Bruijn, 2015) and decreases the control over automatic imitative behavior in a motor simulation task (De Coster et al., 2014). It is possible that one of the mechanisms by which oxytocin facilitates the recognition of self/other differences and the understanding of another's perspective is by increasing self/other motor tuning. From an evolutionary perspective, oxytocin-driven caring behavior relies on the caregiver's ability to both tune into the infant/care-elicitor and maintain the self/other distinction to realize effective caring behaviors. However, the temporal processing of self/other merging and distinguishing under increased oxytocin levels is unknown.

Interestingly, mindfulness and compassion-based psychotherapy approaches such as Compassion Focused Therapy (Gilbert, 2010) highlight the importance of helping patients to positively relate to others and to recognize and accept the presence of "multiple selves," that is, the different patterns of cognitive, emotional and motivational processing in oneself that can be "observed" with a curious, kindly observing stance, as if the personality of another, distinct individual were being manifested. This practice seems to facilitate a better understanding of, and healthy distinction from, difficult mental states that can be experienced and held in a more compassionate and less self-critical and distressing manner. In fact, there is evidence that the soothing effect of self-compassion practices can be strengthened with the use of a mirror that "externalizes" the object of the compassion practice (Petrocchi et al., 2016). Whether oxytocin promotes the soothing effect of this kind of compassion-focused practices remains unexplored.

Oxytocin's effects on the self/other distinction extend to the social ingroup-outgroup. Several studies by De Dreu and colleagues corroborate the role of this neurohormone in mediating the self/other distinction. Such a distinction does not necessarily lead to outgroup withdrawal. For example, oxytocin administration enhances cooperative behaviors within and between groups (Israel, Weisel, Ebstein, & Bornstein, 2012), increases social conformity under implicit social pressure (Huang, Kendrick, Zheng, & Yu, 2015), and facilitates care for individuals considered to be self-related (ingroup members), without necessarily inducing outgroup derogation (De Dreu, Greer, Van Kleef, Shalvi, & Handgraaf, 2011) or withdrawal to antagonists (Ten Velden, Baas, Shalvi, Kret, & De Dreu, 2014).

Oxytocin may, by enhancing self-confidence (Colonnello & Heinrichs, 2014), regulate prosocial behavior by limiting it to cooperative outgroup members (De Dreu, Shalvi, Greer, Van Kleef, & Handgraaf, 2012), facilitate approach motivation and the affiliation towards individuals perceived as physically strong (Chen, Mayer, Mussweiler, & Heinrichs, 2015; DeDreu, Greer, Handgraaf, Shalvi, & Van Kleef, 2012) and enhance ingroup-bias in individuals with a cognitive style characterized by inclination toward intuition rather than reflection (Ma, Liu, Rand, Heatherton, & Han, 2015).

Conclusion

Compassion is considered the expression of the extended caregiving system that motivates individuals to regulate their own self-defense mechanisms to approach others in distress, and promotes the well-being of non-kin members in society. The oxytocinergic system appears involved in modulating certain aspects of compassion motivation and compassion-related feelings and behaviors. As reviewed here, oxytocin promotes caring inclination and enhances the ability to understand another's perspective while maintaining the self/other distinction. In addition, oxytocin administration promotes social support towards socially excluded individuals which – from the perspective of compassion studies – is particularly relevant considering that (as Goetz et al., 2010, highlighted) the appraisal of vulnerability seems to be central to triggering the motivational state of compassion.

All this evidence suggests that the activation of this system is likely to be involved in the expression of compassion-related feelings and behaviors. However, several questions need to be addressed to better understand the role of oxytocin in compassion motivation. For example, it would be worth investigating whether increased oxytocin levels enhance the ability to adopt compassionate approach behavior despite perceived self/other differences. In addition, the temporal processing of self/other merging and distinction under increased oxytocin levels during compassion-focused therapy deserves research attention.

Furthermore, future research should investigate whether oxytocin, facilitating the self/other distinction, has a role to play in promoting accepting feelings towards the rejected aspects of self during compassion-focused practices, and to what extent this is mediated by an individual's personality traits and genetic variations in the oxytocin system. Compassion is obviously a complex phenomenon that most likely relies on the activation of more than one system and whose behavioral expressions are dependent on context. Thus, future studies should investigate the interactions between oxytocinergic, dopaminergic, and opiodergic systems in enhancing feeling of safeness in compassion-focused therapies.

References

Abu-Akel, A., Palgi, S., Klein, E., Decety, J., & Shamay-Tsoory, S. (2015). Oxytocin increases empathy to pain when adopting the other- but not the self-perspective. *Social Neuroscience, 10*, 7–15.

Bartz, J. A., Zaki, J., Bolger, N., & Ochsner, K. N. (2011). Social effects of oxytocin in humans: Context and person matter. *Trends in Cognitive Sciences, 15*, 301–309.

Bartz, J. A., Zaki, J., Ochsner, K. N., Bolger, N., Kolevzon, A., Ludwig, N., & Lydon, J. E. (2010). Effects of oxytocin on recollections of maternal care and closeness. *Proceedings of the National Academy of Sciences, 107*, 21371–21375.

Batson, C. D., & Shaw, L. L. (1991). Evidence for altruism: Toward a pluralism of prosocial motives. *Psychological Inquiry, 2*, 107–122.

Buchheim, A., Heinrichs, M., George, C., Pokorny, D., Koops, E., Henningsen, P., . . . Gündel, H. (2009). Oxytocin enhances the experience of attachment security. *Psychoneuroendocrinology, 34*, 1417–1422.

Cardoso, C., Ellenbogen, M. A., & Linnen, A. M. (2012). Acute intranasal oxytocin improves positive self-perceptions of personality. *Psychopharmacology, 220*, 741–749.

Carter, C. S. (1998). Neuroendocrine perspectives on social attachment and love. *Psychoneuroendocrinology, 23*, 779–818.

Carter, C. S. (2014). Oxytocin pathways and the evolution of human behavior. *Annual Review of Psychology, 65*, 17–39.

Chen, F. S., Kumsta, R., Dvorak, F., Domes, G., Yim, O. S., Ebstein, R. P., & Heinrichs, M. (2015). Genetic modulation of oxytocin sensitivity: a pharmacogenetic approach. *Translational Psychiatry, 5*, 664.

Chen, F. S., Mayer, J., Mussweiler, T., & Heinrichs, M. (2015). Oxytocin increases the likeability of physically formidable men. *Social Cognitive and Affective Neuroscience, 10*, 797–800.

Colonnello, V., Chen, F. S., Panksepp, J., & Heinrichs, M. (2013). Oxytocin sharpens self-other perceptual boundary. *Psychoneuroendocrinology, 38*, 2996–3002.

Colonnello, V., Domes, G., & Heinrichs, M. (2016). As time goes by: Oxytocin influences the subjective perception of time in a social context. *Psychoneuroendocrinology, 68*, 69–73.

Colonnello, V., & Heinrichs, M. (2014). Intranasal oxytocin enhances positive self-attribution in healthy men. *Journal of Psychosomatic Research, 77*, 415–419.

Colonnello, V., Petrocchi, N., Farinelli, M., & Ottaviani, C. (2016). Positive social interactions in a lifespan perspective with a focus on opioidergic and oxytocinergic systems: Implications for neuroprotection. *Current Neuropharmacology*, in press.

De Coster, L., Mueller, S. C., T'Sjoen, G., De Saedeleer, L., & Brass, M. (2014). The influence of Oxytocin on automatic motor simulation. *Psychoneuroendocrinology, 50*, 220–226.

De Dreu, C. K., Greer, L. L., Handgraaf, M. J., Shalvi, S., & Van Kleef, G. A. (2012). Oxytocin modulates selection of allies in intergroup conflict. *Proceedings of the Royal Society B, 279*, 1150–1154.

De Dreu, C. K., Greer, L. L., Van Kleef, G. A., Shalvi, S., & Handgraaf, M. J. (2011). Oxytocin promotes human ethnocentrism. *Proceedings of the National Academy of Sciences, 108*, 1262–1266.

De Dreu, C. K., Shalvi, S., Greer, L. L., Van Kleef, G. A., & Handgraaf, M. J. (2012). Oxytocin motivates non-cooperation in intergroup conflict to protect vulnerable in-group members. *PLOS ONE, 7*, e46751.1.

Ditzen, B., Schaer, M., Gabriel, B., Bodenmann, G., Ehlert, U., & Heinrichs, M. (2009). Intranasal oxytocin increases positive communication and reduces cortisol levels during couple conflict. *Biological Psychiatry, 65*, 728–731.

Domes, G., Heinrichs, M., Glascher, J., Buchel, C., Braus, D. F., & Herpertz, S. C. (2007). Oxytocin attenuates amygdala responses to emotional faces regardless of valence. *Biological Psychiatry, 62*, 1187–1190.

Domes, G., Heinrichs, M., Michel, A., Berger, C., & Herpertz, S. C. (2007). Oxytocin improves "mind-reading" in humans. *Biological Psychiatry, 61*, 731–733

Domes, G., Sibold, M., Schulze, L., Lischke, A., Herpertz, S. C., & Heinrichs, M. (2013). Intranasal oxytocin increases covert attention to positive social cues. *Psychological Medicine, 43*, 1747–1753.

Donaldson, Z. R., & Young, L. J. (2008). Oxytocin, vasopressin, and the neurogenetics of sociality. *Science, 322*, 900–904.

Feldman, R. (2012). Oxytocin and social affiliation in humans. *Hormones and Behavior, 61*, 380–391.

Feldman, R., Gordon, I., Schneiderman, I., Weisman, O., & Zagoory-Sharon, O. (2010). Natural variations in maternal and paternal care are associated with systematic changes in oxytocin following parent–infant contact. *Psychoneuroendocrinology, 35*, 1133–1141.

Feldman, R., Gordon, I., & Zagoory-Sharon, O. (2011). Maternal and paternal plasma, salivary, and urinary oxytocin and parent–infant synchrony: Considering stress and affiliation components of human bonding. *Developmental Science, 14*, 752–761.

Feldman, R., Weller, A., Zagoory-Sharon, O., & Levine, A. (2007). Evidence for a neuroendocrinological foundation of human affiliation plasma oxytocin levels across pregnancy and the postpartum period predict mother-infant bonding. *Psychological Science, 18*, 965–970.

Fries, A. B. W., Ziegler, T. E., Kurian, J. R., Jacoris, S., & Pollak, S. D. (2005). Early experience in humans is associated with changes in neuropeptides critical for regulating social behavior. *Proceedings of the National Academy of Sciences of the United States of America, 102*, 17237–17240.

Galbally, M., Lewis, A. J., IJzendoorn, M. V., & Permezel, M. (2011). The role of oxytocin in mother-infant relations: a systematic review of human studies. *Harvard Review of Psychiatry, 19*, 1–14.

Gamer, M., Zurowski, B., & Büchel, C. (2010). Different amygdala subregions mediate valence-related and attentional effects of oxytocin in humans. *Proceedings of the National Academy of Sciences, 107*, 9400–9405.

Gilbert, P. (2009). Introducing compassion-focused therapy. *Advances in Psychiatric Treatment, 15*, 199–208.

Gilbert, P. (2010). An introduction to compassion focused therapy in cognitive behavior therapy. *International Journal of Cognitive Therapy, 3*, 97–112.

Gilbert, P. (2014). The origins and nature of compassion focused therapy. *British Journal of Clinical Psychology, 53*, 6–41.

Gilbert, P. (2015). The Evolution and Social Dynamics of Compassion. *Social and Personality Psychology Compass, 9*, 239–254.

Goetz, J. L., Keltner, D., & Simon-Thomas, E. (2010). Compassion: An evolutionary analysis and empirical review. *Psychological Bulletin, 136*, 351–374

Goldstein, T. R., & Winner, E. (2012). Enhancing empathy and theory of mind. *Journal of Cognition and Development, 13*, 19–37.

Guastella, A. J., Einfeld, S. L., Gray, K. M., Rinehart, N. J., Tonge, B. J., Lambert, T. J., & Hickie, I. B. (2010). Intranasal oxytocin improves emotion recognition for youth with autism spectrum disorders. *Biological Psychiatry, 67*, 692–694.

Hoffman, M. L. (2001). *Empathy and Moral Development: Implications for Caring and Justice.* New York: Cambridge University Press.

Huang, Y., Kendrick, K. M., Zheng, H., & Yu, R. (2015). Oxytocin enhances implicit social conformity to both in-group and out-group opinions. *Psychoneuroendocrinology, 60*, 114–119.

Hughes, C., Jaffee, S. R., Taylor, A., Caspi, A., & Moffit, T. E. (2005). Origins of individual difference in theory of mind: From nature to nurture? *Child Development, 76*, 356–370.

Israel, S., Weisel, O., Ebstein, R. P., & Bornstein, G. (2012). Oxytocin, but not vasopressin, increases both parochial and universal altruism. *Psychoneuroendocrinology, 37*, 1341–1344.

Kanat, M., Heinrichs, M., Schwarzwald, R., & Domes, G. (2015). Oxytocin attenuates neural reactivity to masked threat cues from the eyes. *Neuropsychopharmacology, 40*, 287–295.

Kemp, A. H., Quintana, D. S., Kuhnert, R. L., Griffiths, K., Hickie, I. B., & Guastella, A. J. (2012). Oxytocin increases heart rate variability in humans at rest: Implications for social approach-related motivation and capacity for social engagement. *PLOS ONE, 7*, e44014.

Kim, J.-W., Kim, S.-E., Kim, J.-J., Jeong, B., Park, C.-H., Son, A. R., . . . Ki, S.W. (2009). Compassionate attitude towards others' suffering activates the mesolimbic neural system. *Neuropsychologia, 47*, 2073–2081.

Klimecki, O.M., Leiberg, S., Lamm, C., & Singer, T. (2013). Functional neural plasticity and associated changes in positive affect after compassion training. *Cerebral Cortex, 23*, 1552–1561.

Lamm, C., Bukowski, H., & Silani, G. (2016). From shared to distinct self–other representations in empathy: Evidence from neurotypical function and socio-cognitive disorders. *Philosophical Transactions of the Royal Society B, 371*(1686), 20150083.

Lane, A., Luminet, O., Rimé, B., Gross, J. J., de Timary, P., & Mikolajczak, M. (2013). Oxytocin increases willingness to socially share one's emotions. *International Journal of Psychology, 48*, 676–681.

Leknes, S., Wessberg, J., Ellingsen, D. M., Chelnokova, O., Olausson, H., & Laeng, B. (2012). Oxytocin enhances pupil dilation and sensitivity to "hidden" emotional expressions. *Social Cognitive and Affective Neuroscience, 8*, 741–749.

Ma, Y., Liu, Y., Rand, D. G., Heatherton, T. F., & Han, S. (2015). Opposing oxytocin effects on intergroup cooperative behavior in intuitive and reflective minds. *Neuropsychopharmacology, 40*, 2379–2387.

MacKinnon, A. L., Gold, I., Feeley, N., Hayton, B., Carter, C. S., & Zelkowitz, P. (2014). The role of oxytocin in mothers' theory of mind and interactive behavior during the perinatal period. *Psychoneuroendocrinology, 48*, 52–63.

MacLean, P. D. (1985). Brain evolution relating to family, play, and the separation call. *Archives of General Psychiatry, 42*, 405–417.

Mah, B. L., Van IJzendoorn, M. H., Smith, R., & Bakermans-Kranenburg, M. J. (2013). Oxytocin in postnatally depressed mothers: Its influence on mood and expressed emotion. *Progress in Neuro-Psychopharmacology and Biological Psychiatry, 40*, 267–272.

Marsh, A. A., Henry, H. Y., Pine, D. S., Gorodetsky, E. K., Goldman, D., & Blair, R. J. R. (2012). The influence of oxytocin administration on responses to infant faces and potential moderation by OXTR genotype. *Psychopharmacology*, *224*, 469–476.

Marsh, A. A., Kozak, M. N., & Ambady, N. (2007). Accurate identification of fear facial expressions predicts prosocialbehavior. *Emotion*, *7*, 239–251.

Meyer-Lindenberg, A., Domes, G., Kirsch, P., & Heinrichs, M. (2011). Oxytocin and vasopressin in the human brain: Social neuropeptides for translational medicine. *Nature Reviews Neuroscience*, *12*, 524–538.

Mikulincer, M., Orbach, I., & Iavnieli, D. (1998). Adult attachment style and affect regulation: Strategic variations in subjective self–other similarity. *Journal of Personality and Social Psychology*, *75*, 436.

Naber, F., van IJzendoorn, M. H., Deschamps, P., van Engeland, H., & Bakermans-Kranenburg, M. J. (2010). Intranasal oxytocin increases fathers' observed responsiveness during play with their children: A double-blind within-subject experiment. *Psychoneuroendocrinology*, *35*, 1583–1586.

Panksepp, J. (1998). *Affective neuroscience: The foundations of human and animal emotions*. New York: Oxford University Press.

Panksepp, J. (2009). Primary process affects and brain oxytocin. *Biological Psychiatry*, *65(9)*, 725–727.

Panksepp, J., & Biven, L. (2012). *The archaeology of mind: Neuroevolutionary origins of human emotions (Norton series on interpersonal neurobiology)*. New York: W. W. Norton.

Petrocchi, N., & Couyoumdjian, A. (2015). The impact of gratitude on depression and anxiety: The mediating role of criticizing, attacking, and reassuring the self. *Self and Identity*, *15(2)*, 191–205.

Petrocchi, N., Ottaviani, C., & Couyoumdjian, A. (2016). Compassion at the mirror: Exposure to a mirror increases the efficacy of a self-compassion manipulation in enhancing soothing positive affect and heart rate variability. *The Journal of Positive Psychology*, 1–12.

Porges, S. W. (2003). The polyvagal theory: Phylogenetic contributions to social behavior. *Physiology & Behavior*, *79*, 503–513.

Preston, S. D., & Hofelich, A. J. (2012). The many faces of empathy: Parsing empathic phenomena through a proximate, dynamic-systems view of representing the other in the self. *Emotion Review*, *4*, 24–33.

Riem, M. M., Bakermans-Kranenburg, M. J., Huffmeijer, R., & van IJzendoorn, M. H. (2013). Does intranasal oxytocin promote prosocialbehavior to an excluded fellow player? A randomized-controlled trial with Cyberball. *Psychoneuroendocrinology*, *38(8)*, 1418–1425.

Riem, M. M., Bakermans-Kranenburg, M. J., Pieper, S., Tops, M., Boksem, M. A., Vermeiren, R. R., van Ijzendoorn, M. H., & Rombouts, S. A. (2011). Oxytocin modulates amygdala, insula, and inferior frontal gyrus responses to infant crying: A randomized controlled trial. *Biological Psychiatry*, *70*, 291–297.

Riem, M. M., Bakermans-Kranenburg, M. J., Voorthuis, A., & van IJzendoorn, M. H. (2014). Oxytocin effects on mind-reading are moderated by experiences of maternal love withdrawal: An fMRI study. *Progress in Neuro-Psychopharmacology and Biological Psychiatry*, *51*, 105–112.

Rilling, J. K. (2013). The neural and hormonal bases of human parentalcare. *Neuropsychologia*, *51*, 731–747.

Rilling J. K, & Young L. J. (2014). The biology of mammalian parenting and its effect on offspring social development. *Science, 345*, 771–776.

Rockliff, H., Karl, A., McEwan, K., Gilbert, J., Matos, M., & Gilbert, P. (2011). Effects of intranasal oxytocin on 'compassion focused imagery'. *Emotion, 11*, 1388–1396.

Ruissen, M. I., & de Bruijn, E. R. (2015). Is it me or is it you? Behavioral and electrophysiological effects of oxytocin administration on self-other integration during joint task performance. *Cortex, 70*, 146–54.

Schulze, L., Lischke, A., Greif, J., Herpertz, S. C., Heinrichs, M., & Domes, G. (2011). Oxytocin increases recognition of masked emotional faces. *Psychoneuroendocrinology, 36*, 1378–1382.

Shahrestani, S., Kemp, A. H., & Guastella, A. J. (2013). The impact of a single administration of intranasal oxytocin on the recognition of basic emotions in humans: A meta-analysis. *Neuropsychopharmacology, 38*, 1929–1936.

Shahrokh, D. K., Zhang, T. Y., Diorio, J., Gratton, A., & Meaney, M. J. (2010). Oxytocin-dopamine interactions mediate variations in maternal behavior in the rat. *Endocrinology, 151*, 2276–2286.

Shamay-Tsoory, S. G., & Abu-Akel, A. (2016). The social salience hypothesis of oxytocin. *Biological Psychiatry, 79*, 194–202.

Ten Velden, F. S., Baas, M., Shalvi, S., Kret, M. E., & De Dreu, C. K. (2014). Oxytocin differentially modulates compromise and competitive approach but not withdrawal to antagonists from own vs. rivaling other groups. *Brain Research, 1580*, 172–179.

Theodoridou, A., Rowe, A. C., Penton-Voak, I. S., & Rogers, P. J. (2009). Oxytocin and social perception: Oxytocin increases perceived facial trustworthiness and attractiveness. *Hormones and Behavior, 56*, 128–132.

van IJzendoorn, M., Bakermans-Kranenburg, M., & Ebstein, R. (2011). Methylation matters in child development: Toward developmental behavioral epigenetics. *Child Development Perspectives, 5*, 305–310.

Van Ijzendoorn, M. H., Huffmeijer, R., Alink, L. R., Bakermans-Kranenburg, M. J., & Tops, M. (2011). The impact of oxytocin administration on charitable donating is moderated by experiences of parental love-withdrawal. *Frontiers in Psychology, 2*, 258.

Wang, S. (2005). A conceptual framework for integrating research related to the physiology of compassion and the wisdom of Buddhist teachings. *Compassion: Conceptualisations, research and use in psychotherapy*, 75–120.

Weisman, O., Zagoory-Sharon, O., & Feldman, R. (2012). Oxytocin administration to parent enhances infant physiological and behavioral readiness for social engagement. *Biological Psychiatry, 72*, 982–989.

Wu, N., & Su, Y. (2015). Oxytocin receptor gene relates to theory of mind and prosocial-behavior in children. *Journal of Cognition and Development, 16*, 302–313.

Zhao, W., Yao, S., Li, Q., Geng, Y., Ma, X., Luo, L., . . . Kendrick, K. M. (2016). Oxytocin blurs the self-other distinction during trait judgments and reduces medial prefrontal cortex responses. *Human Brain Mapping, 37*, 2512–2527.

Chapter 7

Compassion in the autonomic nervous system

The role of the vagus nerve

Jennifer E. Stellar and Dacher Keltner

Compassion in the autonomic nervous system: The role of the vagus nerve

One of the defining characteristics of the human species is our intensely social nature. We spend approximately 70–80% of our waking hours in the presence of others (Burger, 1995; Larson & Csikszentmihalyi, 1978) and healthy social relationships are a primary contributor to well-being and physical health (Cacioppo & Patrick, 2008; Cohen & Wills, 1985). As a consequence of our intense sociality, we care deeply about the welfare of others and when their welfare is threatened it elicits powerful emotional and, we argue, biological responses in us.

Although research has examined how compassion is experienced and expressed, its biological underpinnings in the autonomic nervous system are less well understood. In this chapter we explore the relationship between compassion and the autonomic nervous system. We begin by wrestling with fundamental questions about the definition of compassion and the functions of the autonomic nervous system. We propose that compassion is associated with activity in the parasympathetic branch of the autonomic nervous system, namely the vagus nerve. We review supporting evidence for this claim grounded in theoretical work on the vagus nerve's role in social engagement and caretaking as well as empirical findings that demonstrate its association with prosociality, social connection, and compassion. We explore whether feeling compassion may activate a larger network of integrated biological systems (autonomic, neural, and hormonal). Finally, we consider the benefits offered by applying psychophysiological methods to the study of compassion and future directions for this work.

Understanding compassion in the autonomic nervous system

As the first chapter notes, there are many approaches to defining compassion. It has been treated as a disposition or attitude toward others (Ricard, 2015; Shiota, Keltner, & John, 2006), an emotion or feeling state (e.g. Goetz, Keltner, & Simon-Thomas, 2010; Stellar & Keltner, 2014), and a cognitive or motivational state

(Gilbert & Choden, 2013) and it is likely all of these. Compassion can represent an enduring concern for the welfare of others, but also a momentary response to an instance of suffering. Characterizing compassion as both enduring and momentary raises the question of whether it is possible, with such a broad definition, to find a reliable association with specific physiological measures. We argue that it is, but in order to identify these physiological measures we need to understand the primary functions of the autonomic nervous system.

The autonomic nervous system functions to deploy attention and prepare the body for action. Therefore, when we explore what physiological systems are associated with dispositional and momentary compassion the goal should be to identify what features of compassion are relevant to these two functions of the autonomic nervous system. In other words, what are the attentional and behavioral features of compassion that manifest in reliable autonomic responses? We claim there are two. The first is social attunement, which would require a person to focus their attention on another person rather than on themselves or the broader environment. The second is preparing the body for approach-related affiliative behaviors, more specifically caretaking (e.g. soothing, comforting, or helping or rescuing). These two characteristics of compassion are heavily influenced by perceptions of safety. The autonomic nervous system prioritizes threat detection, which catalyzes a cascade of autonomic changes aimed at self-protection. In the case of compassion we believe it is important that individuals make the distinction that a threat is to another's well-being and not to the self. If a person feels she is under a direct threat, it will make it harder, though not impossible, to attune to the needs of others and engage in caretaking behaviors. As a result one would expect a person whose defense system is activated (e.g. someone who is chronically anxious or feeling a great deal of momentary distress) to be less compassionate, a point we will return to later. Therefore, it is compassion's ability to attune us to the needs of others and motivate caretaking behavior that we believe represent recurring themes when examining its autonomic correlates, features, which are present regardless of whether compassion is conceptualized as an enduring trait and a momentary state.

As a cautionary note, there are almost no components of the autonomic nervous system that are exclusively associated with one function, that level of modularity is not how the autonomic nervous system is designed. Therefore, we warn against assuming too strict an association between any one autonomic physiological measure and a phenomenon like compassion. For example, increases in heart rate are characteristic of fear, but also other emotional states like anger (Levenson, 1992), appetitive motivations (Fowles, Fisher, & Tranel, 1982), or exercise. This is because increased heart rate functions to make more resources available for physical mobilization, whatever the reason may be—to flee, to get a reward, or because we are trying to get in shape. If the context is narrowly defined, for example if an experimenter is showing a participant a scary video or someone is walking through a haunted house, one could more confidently claim that in this context greater increases in heart rate correspond to greater fear, but it would be incorrect to say that increased heart rate always indicates feeling threat, a person could be exercising, enjoying sex, or feel joyful at the news their child has passed their exams. We can be in activated states for both threat and positive reasons. In summary, it is grounded in a conceptualization of compassion as both an enduring and momentary experience defined by social attunement and caretaking that we now turn to its relationship to specific physiological measures in the autonomic nervous system.

Compassion and the vagus nerve

We propose that compassion is associated with greater activity of the vagus nerve, a component of the parasympathetic branch of the autonomic nervous system. The vagus nerve is the tenth cranial nerve, originating in the brain stem and innervating the palate, larynx, and pharynx, as well as the heart and digestive organs (see Figure 7.1). Notably, it innervates the Sinoatrial node of the heart, controlling the frequency with which the heart beats. Without constant vagal innervation the human heart would beat around 100 times per minute rather than the observed range of 60–80 beats per minute. This chronic vagal control over the heart is called vagal tone. Just as each person has a stable resting heart rate, we also have a stable resting vagal tone (although consistent exercise can change both). Therefore, vagal tone varies between individuals and can be interpreted much like a trait or dispositional measure. The vagus nerve also increases or decreases its activation in response to different contexts in a more phasic fashion. This type of vagal activation is often called vagal reactivity. Again, just as a person can show changes in heart rate to a given context, we can also experience changes in vagal activation.

Researchers measure vagal tone and vagal reactivity through the non-invasive indices of respiratory sinus arrhythmia (RSA) and high frequency heart rate variability (HF-HRV). RSA and HF-HRV represent the variability in heart rate as a function of respiration (Berntson, Cacioppo, & Quigley, 1993). In each respiration cycle vagal control over the pace of the heart changes; during inhalation, vagus nerve activity is suppressed, leading to heart rate acceleration, whereas during exhalation, vagus nerve activity increases, resulting in heart rate deceleration. This natural process leads to variation in heart rate, which acts as an index of the current activity of the vagus nerve.

There is converging evidence from theoretical and empirical work for a relationship between compassion, both enduring and momentary experiences, and vagal activation. The Polyvagal Theory offers theoretical support for claims that compassion is related to vagal activation by demonstrating its potential origins in facilitating social connection and engagement, and promoting caretaking and bonding (Porges, 2001, 2007). This argument claims that the myelinated portion of the vagus nerve emerged with the advent of mammals, and particularly attachment, which facilitates proximity seeking, as opposed to disbursement (as for most reptiles) at birth. The capacity to inhibit the fight-flight system and experience soothing and safeness in the context of relating helps facilitate increased sociality, a defining feature for mammals (see Grossman & Taylor, 2007 for a critique of this argument).

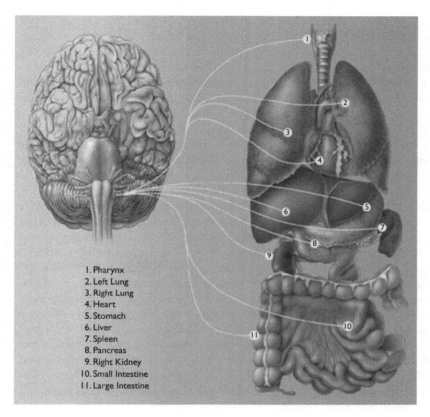

1. Pharynx
2. Left Lung
3. Right Lung
4. Heart
5. Stomach
6. Liver
7. Spleen
8. Pancreas
9. Right Kidney
10. Small Intestine
11. Large Intestine

Figure 7.1 Vagus nerve innervation.

According to this theory the vagus nerve can lead to quick changes in heart rate in response to non-threatening contexts, without activation of the more costly sympathetic or hypothalamic-pituitary-adrenal systems. Importantly, vagal activation slows the heart, producing calm states that could encourage affiliation and bonding. In support of this claim the neural origins of the vagus nerve are critical to social communication and engagement behaviors. These pathways innervate facial muscles required for emotional expression, such as the muscles involved in nodding the head (a key signal of engagement; see Kogan et al., 2014; Porges, 2001), orienting the head and gaze toward others, talking and vocalizing, and extracting the human voice from other noises (Porges, 2001). Fundamentally compassion is rooted in social connection and engagement, in particular sensitivity and responsiveness to distress signals (Gilbert, Chapter 1, this volume) as well as affiliation with others (Goetz et al., 2010). Thus greater activity of the vagus nerve, which supports these ends, could accompany compassion.

In addition, this theory ties vagal activation to the most basic form of sociality, caretaking, which also lies at the heart of compassion (Bowlby, 1988; Porges, 2003). Porges agues that the vagus nerve, along with other physiological responses such as the release of oxytocin, may have coopted defensive systems involved in freezing for immobilization during nursing, reproduction, and social bonding more generally. Compassion is also thought to be rooted in caretaking (for a summary of this argument see Gilbert 2014 and Chapter 3, this volume; Goetz et al., 2010; Narvaez, Chapter 10, this volume; Spikins, Chapter 2, this volume). Human infants have a longer period of vulnerability and require more parental investment than any other species. There is good evidence that strong emotional, cognitive, and physiological systems evolved to help attune parents to the distress of infants and promote caretaking behaviors. In sum, the Polyvagal Theory ties the vagus nerve to two fundamental aspects of compassion: social engagement and caretaking behaviors.

Support for a relationship between compassion and the vagus nerve also comes from empirical work. Recent studies suggest that individuals with higher vagal tone are more compassionate, prosocial, and feel greater social connection with others. Children with higher vagal tone exhibit greater sympathy to another in need (Fabes, Eisenberg, & Eisenbud, 1993). In addition, in one study, adolescents with higher vagal tone showed greater empathic accuracy with their mothers during a conversation (Diamond, Fagundes, & Butterworth, 2012). In adults vagal tone predicts higher scores on the personality trait of agreeableness, which is characterized by a kind, warm, cooperative, and considerate disposition toward others (Oveis et al., 2009). In multiple studies, observers rated those with higher vagal tone as more prosocial (though for adults this relationship was quadratic; Eisenberg et al., 1995; Eisenberg et al., 1996; Kogan et al., 2014). On the other hand, clinical samples defined by deficits in social attunement, such as those with autism, have chronically lower levels of vagal activation than healthy comparison groups (Ming, Julu, Brimacombe, Connor, & Daniels, 2005; Porges, 2007). Finally, in a nine-week longitudinal study where participants reported on their social interactions, those who started the study with higher vagal tone reported greater increases in feelings of connection to others, compared with those who had lower vagal tone (Kok & Fredrickson, 2010). In another study greater vagal tone predicted higher reports of social-support seeking, social integration, and social acceptance (Geisler, Kubiak, Siewert, & Weber, 2013). These studies suggest a potential link between higher vagal tone and a compassionate disposition, but what about momentary experiences of compassion?

Very few studies have measured physiological activity associated with compassion in response to witnessing another suffer, but the little work that has been done in this area appears to converge with findings on dispositional compassion. As mentioned previously, heart rate slows during increased vagal activation. Self-reports and expressive displays of compassion covary with heart rate deceleration (Eisenberg et al., 1991; Stellar, Cohen, Oveis, & Keltner, 2015) and the magnitude of heart rate deceleration distinguishes between those who report more or less compassion toward another's suffering (Stellar, Manzo, Kraus, & Keltner, 2012).

These findings on heart rate deceleration during compassion could be interpreted to represent increased vagal activation during compassion, which actively slows the heart. However, heart rate is affected by both the parasympathetic and sympathetic systems, so caution must be exercised in interpreting these data, highlighting the importance of measuring vagal activation more directly.

Our lab has found that vagal activation increases during inductions of compassion compared to neutral controls or other positive states such as pride or inspiration (Stellar et al., 2015). These findings generalized across a variety of compassion inductions in which participants watched videos of families of children with cancer, clips of past participants discussing the death of their grandparent, or pictures of individuals who were suffering. In addition, increases in vagal activation during compassion inductions predicted greater ratings of observed compassion by blind coders and greater self-reports of compassion by participants using a continuous self-report measure of emotion. These findings provide initial support that feelings of compassion are accompanied by increases in vagal activation.

While this emergent relationship between compassion and vagal activity is provocative, more work is needed to isolate the active ingredients of compassion that increase vagal activation (i.e. social engagement and activation of caretaking behaviors). In addition, greater attention must be paid to potential moderating factors that may influence the relationship between compassion and increased vagal activation such as the characteristics of the observer (their personal distress in response to seeing another suffer), the sufferer (the nature of that person's suffering), and the context (the ability to take action).

A biological network involved in compassion

In conjunction with greater vagal activation in the autonomic nervous system, individuals feeling compassion also exhibit changes in neural and hormonal systems. We propose that compassion activates an integrated network of biological responses. In the brain, increased activation in the periaqueductal gray (PAG) accompanies the experience of compassion. In one study, PAG activation increased when participants viewed pictures of others suffering; self-reported compassion, in combination with distress, also predicted levels of PAG activation (Simon-Thomas et al., 2012). Though this research suggests PAG activation is part of the experience of compassion, more work is needed to rule out alternative explanations and isolate this relationship.

Compassion has also been associated with the hormone oxytocin (e.g. Barraza & Zak, 2009), though some of these findings are controversial (Nave, Camerer, & McCullough, 2015) and may be moderated by important factors like group membership (De Dreu, 2012). Intranasal delivery of oxytocin increased compassion toward vulnerable targets (Palgi, Klein, & Shamay-Tsoory, 2015), empathic accuracy and emotional empathy especially for observers who are less socially proficient (Bartz et al., 2010; Hurlemann et al., 2010), and prosociality

(Zak, Stanton, & Ahmadi, 2007). Feelings of empathy also increased plasma levels of oxytocin suggesting the relationship may be causal in both directions (Barraza & Zak, 2009).

Importantly, the PAG and oxytocin have anatomical connections with the vagus nerve, suggesting that these systems may communicate with one another. The PAG has important projections to the part of the brain stem where the vagus nerve originates, the dorsal motor nucleus and nucleus ambiguus (Farkas, Jansen, & Loewy, 1997), offering the possibility that the vagus nerve and PAG may communicate directly with one another. In addition, new work has revealed that oxytocin levels are associated with vagal activity. In animal models, oxytocin injections lead to increased vagal activity (McCann & Rogers, 1990) and electrical stimulation of the vagus nerve also increases the release of oxytocin (Stock & Uvnäs-Moberg, 2008). In humans, individuals who were given intranasal oxytocin exhibited greater heart rate variability (a measure of vagal activation) compared to a placebo group (Kemp et al., 2012). Additionally, when fathers were administered oxytocin intranasally, they showed increases in vagal activity during play with their five-month olds compared to controls (Weisman, Zagoory-Sharon, & Feldman, 2012). The anatomical and observed relationships between the vagus nerve, PAG, and oxytocin suggest the potential for an integration of autonomic, neural, and hormonal responses during compassion.

Implications and future directions

Psychophysiology is uniquely positioned to offer important insights into compassion. At a broad level, identifying associations between the autonomic nervous system and compassion helps build support for evolutionary claims of a biological basis for altruism. If we have physiological systems that help us attune to the needs of others and promote caring for those in need then we can argue that prosociality may be as deeply embedded as selfishness. More specific to compassion, psychophysiological work can elucidate the process by which dispositional or momentary compassion translates to action. Although we know a great deal about how the body prepares to respond to threats in the environment, we know much less about how it facilitates approach-related behaviors, such as offering comfort, soothing, giving support, or even offering aid (e.g. Batson, Fultz, & Schoenrade, 1987; Eisenberg et al., 1989).

Identifying autonomic responses associated with momentary compassion will also help establish compassion as a discrete emotion. Despite disagreement among affective scientists as to whether compassion represents an emotional state (Ekman, 2016), compassion shows many of the qualities necessary to meet the definition of an emotion. It is universally experienced; it has been documented in a variety of cultures, including pre-historical and pre-industrialized cultures and even in our closest primate ancestors (de Waal, 1996; Eibl-Eibesfeldt, 1989; Hublin, 2009). It has reliable expressions in the form of touch and vocalizations that are universally recognized across radically different cultures (Cordaro, Keltner, Tshering, Wangchuk, & Flynn, 2016; Hertenstein, Keltner, App, Bulleit, & Jaskolka, 2006). It has clear evolutionary functions including caretaking of offspring (Gilbert, 2014; Goetz et al., 2010; Mikulincer, & Shaver, 2005; Stellar & Keltner, 2014) and promoting reciprocal cooperation among non-kin (Stellar & Keltner, 2014; Trivers, 1971). However, it has not been clear whether compassion evokes reliable physiological changes, which some scholars consider a necessary precondition for claiming a particular state is an emotion (e.g. Ekman, 1992; Lazarus, 1991; Panksepp, 1992).

Finally, at the practical level, this work offers researchers a method for assessing compassion that is free from social desirability since autonomic physiology is near impossible to control. Often researchers show individuals videos, photos, or stories of others who are suffering and ask participants how much compassion they feel (e.g. Oveis, Horberg, & Keltner, 2010; Stellar et al., 2012; Stellar et al., 2015). In many studies this method creates a strong demand to report high levels of compassion. In our work we find this demand is particularly powerful for women, who may feel cultural norms dictate that they report high levels of compassion. As a result, our studies and those of other researchers (for a review of this issues see Eisenberg & Lennon, 1983; LaFrance & Banaji, 1992) often find identical physiological responses to suffering among male and female observers, but differences in self-reports.

Future work in psychophysiology can help resolve questions about how to define this complex phenomenon. Notably, this method gives researchers the opportunity to unpack the mixed nature of compassion by exploring it as it unfolds in the body. Compassion combines positive feelings of warmth and tenderness with negative feelings of sadness or distress. The balance between these states is crucial. While a small amount of distress or anxiety is a signal that an individual cares about another's welfare, and may be necessary to compassion, when too pronounced, distress can overwhelm the more positive aspects of compassion that generate social connection and caretaking (Batson, 1987). In support of this claim research has shown that personal distress in response to another's suffering is less predictive of prosociality than feelings of compassion (Eisenberg et al., 1989). Physiological indicators in response to another's suffering like heart rate acceleration or increased cardiac output could signal the balance of affect is tipped toward distress. In addition, better temporal resolution in physiological studies may reveal initial physiological indicators of distress as one becomes aware that another is suffering followed by increased vagal activation as the individual transitions to feeling compassion and social connection to the sufferer. These findings would support arguments that compassion requires a tolerance of distress or perhaps a regulation of one's own negative feelings when seeing another suffer in order to produce a positive state of social connection (e.g. Stellar et al., 2015). Self-reports do not allow for enough clarity to disentangle the time course of these responses, but psychophysiological studies could help uncover how compassion unfolds over time.

Psychophysiological studies may also be able to differentiate between various responses to another's suffering that are currently all categorized as compassion. To take an example from Gilbert (Chapter 1, this volume), compassion may be felt when one sees a child trapped in a burning house or for someone who is grieving the loss of a loved one. Although these two types of suffering elicit compassion, they evoke very different behavioral responses that would be served by different physiological patterns of activity. Many studies on compassion focus on witnessing another's *emotional* suffering, rather than *physical* suffering (e.g. injury). Our lab has found that, in response to emotional suffering, individuals report behaviors consistent with giving social support or soothing the sufferer, whereas in response to physical suffering they report behaviors centered on mobilizing to provide emergency aid (e.g. binding a wound, getting help; Stellar et al., in press). While both types of suffering elicit heightened compassion, emotional suffering elicited more sadness, warmth, and tenderness, whereas physical suffering elicited more vicarious distress and anxiety. Unlike emotional suffering, which elicited parasympathetic activation primarily, physical suffering generated co-activation of the parasympathetic sympathetic systems, which would be important to mobilize an individual to act quickly. Despite colloquial usage of the word compassion to describe responses to both emotional and physical suffering, psychophysiological work demonstrates they may be experienced quite differently in the body. In sum, we believe that future psychophysiological studies have the capacity to challenge traditional definitions and offer a more nuanced understanding of compassion.

Future work should consider whether feeling compassion reduces physiological stress, promoting better health. Some accounts of the vagus nerve suggest it may be part of a soothing affect system (Rockliff, Gilbert, McEwan, Lightman & Glover, 2008) and that low vagal activation is a marker of threat and stress (Thayer, Åhs, Fredrikson, Sollers, & Wager, 2012). Activation of the vagus nerve reduces heart rate and levels of pro-inflammatory cytokines, an immune marker associated with stress (Johnston & Webster, 2009; Maes et al., 1998; Slavich, Way, Eisenberger, & Taylor, 2010; Steptoe, Willemsen, Natalie, Flower, & Mohamed-Ali, 2001; Tracey, 2002). In one study, when compassion focused imagery led to greater vagal activation, as assessed by heart rate variability, it was associated with reduced cortisol (Rockliff et al., 2008). In addition, decreased vagal function is a risk factor for cardiac disease and mortality (Thayer & Lane, 2007). Some work indicates that compassion is also associated with the release of oxytocin. Oxytocin inhibits the stress-induced activity of the hypothalamic–pituitary–adrenal axis in rats (e.g. Uvnas-Moberg, Ahlenius, Hillegaart, & Alster, 1994). In humans, intranasal oxytocin, especially when combined with social support, suppressed cortisol during a stressful task (Heinrichs, Baumgartner, Kirschbaum, & Ehlert, 2003) and in another study intranasal oxytocin reduced salivary cortisol levels after a conflict between romantic partners (Ditzen et al., 2009). The important inhibitory effects of vagal activation and oxytocin on physiological stress responses (e.g. heart rate, pro-inflammatory cytokines, and cortisol) suggest the potential anxiolytic power of compassion in the body.

Understanding the physiological changes associated with compassion may also allow researchers to develop novel compassion interventions that are physiologically based. Although emotions typically evoke physiological responses, there is an enduring debate about whether physiological responses may also evoke emotional states (Cannon, 1927; James, 1894; Lange, 1885). This debate raises the question of whether increasing vagal activation can promote compassion. Although no empirical research has addressed this question, there are a variety of possible methods for influencing vagal activation. Most notably, slowing one's breathing and taking deeper breaths. Many forms of meditation utilize this breathing technique and meditation has been found to increase both vagal activation (Ditto, Eclache, & Goldman, 2006) and compassion (Condon, Desbordes, Miller, & DeSteno, 2013). Future research should examine whether pacing one's breathing during meditation increases momentary compassion in response to suffering and whether this effect is explained by vagal activation. As technology progresses, alternative methods for increasing vagal activation have emerged. Currently, surgical implantation of a vagus nerve stimulator, which directly activates the vagus nerve by electric stimulation, is being employed for drug-resistant epilepsy (Handforth et al., 1998) and depression (Rush et al., 2000). In both disorders implantation of the vagus nerve stimulator led to increased positive mood and decreased negative mood (Elger, Hoppe, Falkai, Rush, & Elger, 2000; George et al., 2005; Harden et al., 2000), though this work is still nascent. Finally, in the past few months a new company claims they can activate the vagus nerve through an electrical pulse in the ear. Although these technologies may hold promise it remains to be seen whether increases in vagal activation do lead to notable increases in compassion.

Conclusion

In this chapter we have noted that the evolution of care-giving between infant and parent, alliance formation, and other forms of altruism were supported by a range of evolutionary adaptations to the body and brain. Among these was the ability for individuals to operate in close proximity to each other, feel safe (rather than threatened), and physiologically regulate each other. A capacity to pay attention to distress and be motivated to respond to distress is part of this evolution and is the root of our capacities for compassion. Clues to the physiological underpinnings of compassion can be found in the mechanisms and support caring behavior, particularly in the vagal nerve (Porges, 2003).

We have proposed that the higher vagal tone may be associated with more compassionate individuals and that vagal activation may increase activity during momentary experiences of compassion. Theoretical claims that the myelinated portion of the vagus nerve emerged with the advent of mammals has an important autonomic facilitator of social interaction and caretaking, suggest that the vagus nerve would be crucial to encouraging calm approach-related states characteristic of compassion in which individuals could offer support to, soothe, and comfort another in need. Empirical findings also support a relationship between vagal activity and compassion. This work highlights two essential elements of compassion, such as social attunement and behavioral responses like caregiving, which would be served by activation of particular physiological systems, and offers a new perspective to an enduring debate about the nature of compassion. We believe the ability to detect traces of compassion in our biological systems counters long-held notions that individuals are designed only to be selfish and demonstrates a deeply embedded tendency to be compassionate and concerned with the welfare of others.

References

Barraza, J. A., & Zak, P. J. (2009). Empathy toward strangers triggers oxytocin release and subsequent generosity. *Annals of the New York Academy of Sciences, 1167*(1), 182–189.

Bartz, J. A., Zaki, J., Bolger, N., Hollander, E., Ludwig, N. N., Kolevzon, A., & Ochsner, K. N. (2010). Oxytocin selectively improves empathic accuracy. *Psychological Science, 21*(10), 1426–1428.

Batson, C. D. (1987). Prosocial motivation: Is it ever truly altruistic? In L. Berkowitz (Ed.), *Advances in Experimental Social Psychology* (Vol. 20, pp. 65–122). New York: Academic Press.

Batson, C. D., Fultz, J., & Schoenrade, P. A. (1987). Distress and empathy: Two qualitatively distinct vicarious emotions with different motivational consequences. *Journal of Personality, 55*(1), 19–39.

Berntson, G. G., Cacioppo, J. T., & Quigley, K. S. (1993). Respiratory sinus arrhythmia: Autonomic origins, physiological mechanisms, and psychophysiological implications. *Psychophysiology, 30*, 183–196.

Bowlby, J. (1988). Attachment, communication, and the therapeutic process. *A Secure Base: Parent-child attachment and healthy human development*, 137–157.

Burger, J. M. (1995). Individual differences in preference for solitude. *Journal of Research in Personality, 29*(1), 85–108.

Cacioppo, J. T., & Patrick, W. (2008). *Loneliness: Human nature and the need for social connection.* New York: W. W. Norton.

Cannon, W. B. (1927). The James-Lange theory of emotions: A critical examination and an alternative theory. *The American Journal of Psychology, 39*(1/4), 106–124.

Cohen, S., & Wills, T. A. (1985). Stress, social support, and the buffering hypothesis. *Psychological Bulletin, 98*(2), 310–357.

Condon, P., Desbordes, G., Miller, W. B., & DeSteno, D. (2013). Meditation increases compassionate responses to suffering. *Psychological Science, 24*(10), 2125–2127.

Cordaro, D. T., Keltner, D., Tshering, S., Wangchuk, D., & Flynn, L. M. (2016). The voice conveys emotion in ten globalized cultures and one remote village in Bhutan. *Emotion, 16*(1), 117.

De Dreu, C. K. (2012). Oxytocin modulates cooperation within and competition between groups: an integrative review and research agenda. *Hormones and Behavior, 61*(3), 419–428.

Diamond, L. M., Fagundes, C. P., & Butterworth, M. R. (2012). Attachment style, vagal tone, and empathy during mother–adolescent interactions. *Journal of Research on Adolescence, 22*, 165–184.

Ditto, B., Eclache, M., & Goldman, N. (2006). Short-term autonomic and cardiovascular effects of mindfulness body scan meditation. *Annals of Behavioral Medicine*, *32*(3), 227–234.

Ditzen, B., Schaer, M., Gabriel, B., Bodenmann, G., Ehlert, U., & Heinrichs, M. (2009). Intranasal oxytocin increases positive communication and reduces cortisol levels during couple conflict. *Biological Psychiatry*, *65*(9), 728–731.

Eibl-Eibesfeldt, I. (1989). *Human Ethology*. New York: De Gruyter.

Eisenberg, N., Fabes, R. A., Karbon, M., Murphy, B. C., Wosinski, M., Polazzi, L., . . . Juhnke, C. (1996). The relations of children's dispositional prosocial behavior to emotionality, regulation, and social functioning. *Child Development*, *67*, 974–992.

Eisenberg, N., Fabes, R. A., Miller, P. A., Fultz, J., Shell, R., Mathy, R. M., & Reno, R. R. (1989). Relation of sympathy and personal distress to prosocial behavior: A multimethod study. *Journal of Personality and Social Psychology*, *57*(1), 55–66.

Eisenberg, N., Fabes, R. A., Murphy, B., Maszk, P., Smith, M., & Karbon, M. (1995). The role of emotionality and regulation in children's social functioning: A longitudinal study. *Child Development*, *66*, 1360–1384.

Eisenberg, N., Fabes, R. A., Schaller, M., Miller, P., Carlo, G., Poulin, R., . . . Shell, R. (1991). Personality and socialization correlates of vicarious emotional responding. *Journal of Personality and Social Psychology*, *61*, 459–470.

Eisenberg, N., & Lennon, R. (1983). Sex differences in empathy and related capacities. *Psychological Bulletin*, *94*(1), 100–131.

Ekman, P. (1992). An argument for basic emotions. *Cognition and Emotion*, 6, 169–200.

Ekman, P. (2016). What scientists who study emotion agree about. *Perspectives on Psychological Science*, *11*(1), 31–34.

Elger, G., Hoppe, C., Falkai, P., Rush, A. J., & Elger, C. E. (2000). Vagus nerve stimulation is associated with mood improvements in epilepsy patients. *Epilepsy Research*, *42*(2), 203–210.

Fabes, R. A., Eisenberg, N., & Eisenbud, L. (1993). Behavioral and physiological correlates of children's reactions to others in distress. *Developmental Psychology*, *29*, 655–663.

Farkas, E., Jansen, A. S., & Loewy, A. D. (1997). Periaqueductal gray matter projection to vagal preganglionic neurons and the nucleus tractus solitarius. *Brain Research*, *764*(1), 257–261.

Fowles, D. C., Fisher, A. E., & Tranel, D. T. (1982). The heart beats to reward: The effect of monetary incentive on heart rate. *Psychophysiology*, *19*(5), 506–513.

Geisler, F. C., Kubiak, T., Siewert, K., & Weber, H. (2013). Cardiac vagal tone is associated with social engagement and self-regulation. *Biological Psychology*, *93*(2), 279–286.

George, M. S., Rush, A. J., Marangell, L. B., Sackeim, H. A., Brannan, S. K., Davis, S. M., . . . Dunner, D. (2005). A one-year comparison of vagus nerve stimulation with treatment as usual for treatment-resistant depression. *Biological Psychiatry*, *58*(5), 364–373.

Gilbert, P. (2014). The origins and nature of compassion focused therapy. *British Journal of Clinical Psychology*, *53*(1), 6–41.

Gilbert, P., & Choden (2013). *Mindful Compassion*. London: Constable & Robinson.

Goetz, J. L., Keltner, D., & Simon-Thomas, E. (2010). Compassion: An evolutionary analysis and empirical review. *Psychological Bulletin*, *136*(3), 351–374.

Grossman, P., & Taylor, E. W. (2007). Toward understanding respiratory sinus arrhythmia: relations to cardiac vagal tone, evolution and biobehavioral functions. *Biological Psychology*, *74*(2), 263–285.

Handforth, A., DeGiorgio, C. M., Schachter, S. C., Uthman, B. M., Naritoku, D. K., Tecoma, E. S., . . . Labar, D. R. (1998). Vagus nerve stimulation therapy for partial-onset seizures: A randomized active-control trial. *Neurology*, *51*(1), 48–55.

Harden, C. L., Pulver, M. C., Ravdin, L. D., Nikolov, B., Halper, J. P., & Labar, D. R. (2000). A pilot study of mood in epilepsy patients treated with vagus nerve stimulation. *Epilepsy & Behavior*, *1*(2), 93–99.

Heinrichs, M., Baumgartner, T., Kirschbaum, C., & Ehlert, U. (2003). Social support and oxytocin interact to suppress cortisol and subjective responses to psychosocial stress. *Biological Psychiatry*, *54*(12), 1389–1398.

Hertenstein, M. J., Keltner, D., App, B., Bulleit, B. A., & Jaskolka, A. R. (2006). Touch communicates distinct emotions. *Emotion*, *6*(3), 528.

Hublin, J. J. (2009). The prehistory of compassion. *Proceedings of the National Academy of Sciences*, *106*, 6429–6430.

Hurlemann, R., Patin, A., Onur, O. A., Cohen, M. X., Baumgartner, T., Metzler, S., . . . Kendrick, K. M. (2010). Oxytocin enhances amygdala-dependent, socially reinforced learning and emotional empathy in humans. *The Journal of Neuroscience*, *30*(14), 4999–5007.

James, W. (1894) Physical basis of emotion. *Psychological Review*, *101*, 205–210.

Johnston, G. R., & Webster, N. R. (2009). Cytokines and the immunomodulatory function of the vagus nerve. *British Journal of Anaesthesia*, *102*(4), 453–462.

Kemp A. H., Quintana D. S., Kuhnert R., Griffiths K., Hickie I. B., Guastella A. J. (2012). Oxytocin increases heart rate variability in humans at rest: Implications for social approach-related motivation and capacity for social engagement. *PLOS ONE*, 7, e44014.

Kogan, A., Oveis, C., Carr, E. W., Gruber, J., Mauss, I. B., Shallcross, A., . . . Keltner, D. (2014). Vagal activity is quadratically related to prosocial traits, prosocial emotions, and observer perceptions of prosociality. *Journal of Personality and Social Psychology*, *107*, 1051–1063.

Kok, B. E., & Fredrickson, B. L. (2010). Upward spirals of the heart: Autonomic flexibility, as indexed by vagal tone, reciprocally and prospectively predicts positive emotions and social connectedness. *Biological Psychology*, *85*, 432–436.

LaFrance, M., & Banaji, M. (1992). Toward a reconsideration of the gender-emotion relationship. *Emotion and Social Behavior*, *14*, 178–201.

Lange, C. G. (1885). The mechanism of the emotions. *The Classical Psychologist*, 672–685.

Larson, R., & Csikszentmihalyi, M. (1978). Experiential correlates of solitude in adolescence. *Journal of Personality*, *46*, 677–693.

Lazarus, R. S. (1991). Progress on a cognitive-motivational-relational theory of emotion. *American Psychologist*, *46*(8), 819.

Levenson, R. W. (1992). Autonomic nervous system differences among emotions. *Psychological Science*, *3*(1), 23–27.

McCann, M. J., & Rogers, R. C. (1990). Oxytocin excites gastric-related neurones in rat dorsal vagal complex. *The Journal of Physiology*, *428*(1), 95–108.

Maes, M., Song, C., Lin, A., De Jongh, R., Van Gastel, A., Kenis, G., . . . Demedts, P. (1998). The effects of psychological stress on humans: Increased production of pro-inflammatory cytokines and Th1-like response in stress-induced anxiety. *Cytokine*, *10*(4), 313–318.

Mikulincer, M., & Shaver, P. R. (2005). Attachment security, compassion, and altruism. *Current Directions in Psychological Science*, *14*(1), 34–38.

Ming, X., Julu, P. O., Brimacombe, M., Connor, S., & Daniels, M. L. (2005). Reduced cardiac parasympathetic activity in children with autism. *Brain and Development, 27*(7), 509–516.

Nave, G., Camerer, C., & McCullough, M. (2015). Does oxytocin increase trust in humans? A critical review of research. *Perspectives on Psychological Science, 10*(6), 772–789.

Oveis, C., Adam, B., Cohen, J., Gruber, M., Shiota, N., Haidt, J., & Keltner, D. (2009). Resting respiratory sinus arrhythmia is associated with tonic positive emotionality. *Emotion* 9, 2(2009), 265–270.

Oveis, C., Horberg, E. J., & Keltner, D. (2010). Compassion, pride, and social intuitions of self-other similarity. *Journal of Personality and Social Psychology, 98*(4), 618–630.

Palgi, S., Klein, E., & Shamay-Tsoory, S. G. (2015). Intranasal administration of oxytocin increases compassion toward women. *Social Cognitive and Affective Neuroscience, 10*(3), 311–317.

Panksepp, J. (1992). A critical role for "affective neuroscience" in resolving what is basic about basic emotions, *Psychological Review, 99*, 554–560.

Porges, S. W. (2001). The polyvagal theory: Phylogenetic substrates of a social nervous system. *International Journal of Psychophysiology, 42*, 123–146.

Porges, S. W. (2003). The polyvagal theory: Phylogenetic contributions to social behavior. *Physiology & Behavior, 79*(3), 503–513.

Porges, S. W. (2007). The polyvagal perspective. *Biological Psychology, 74*, 116–143.

Ricard, M. (2015). *Altruism: The power of compassion to change yourself and the world.* London: Atlantic Books.

Rockliff, H., Gilbert, P., McEwan, K., Lightman, S., & Glover, D. (2008). A pilot exploration of heart rate variability and salivary cortisol responses to compassion-focused imagery. *Clinical Neuropsychiatry, 5*(3), 132–139.

Rush, A., George, M., Sackeim, H., Marangell, L., Husain, M., Giller, C., . . . Goodman, R. (2000). Vagus nerve stimulation (VNS™) for treatment-resistant depressions: A multi-center study. *Biological Psychiatry, 47*, 276–286.

Shiota, M. N., Keltner, D., & John, O. P. (2006). Positive emotion dispositions differentially associated with Big Five personality and attachment style. *The Journal of Positive Psychology, 1*(2), 61–71.

Simon-Thomas, E. R., Godzik, J., Castle, E., Antonenko, O., Ponz, A., Kogan, A., & Keltner, D. J. (2012). An fMRI study of caring vs self-focus during induced compassion and pride. *Social Cognitive and Affective Neuroscience, 7*(6), 635–648.

Slavich, G. M., Way, B. M., Eisenberger, N. I., & Taylor, S. E. (2010). Neural sensitivity to social rejection is associated with inflammatory responses to social stress. *Proceedings of the National Academy of Sciences, 107*(33), 14817–14822.

Stellar, J. E., Anderson, C. A, Bai, Y., McNeil, G. D., Gordon, A., & Keltner, D. (in press). The experience of awe across cultures: Comparing awe in individualist and collectivist cultures.

Stellar, J. E., Cohen, A., Oveis, C. & Keltner, D. (2015). Affective and physiological responses to the suffering of others: Compassion and vagal activity. *Journal of Personality and Social Psychology, 108*(4), 572–585.

Stellar, J. E., & Keltner, D. (2014). Compassion. In M. Tugade, L. Shiota, & L. Kirby (Eds.), *Handbook of Positive Emotion.* New York: Guilford Press.

Stellar, J. E., Manzo, V. M., Kraus, M. W., & Keltner, D. (2012). Class and compassion: Socioeconomic factors predict responses to suffering. *Emotion, 12*, 449–459.

Steptoe, A., Willemsen, G., Natalie, O. W. E. N., Flower, L., & Mohamed-Ali, V. (2001). Acute mental stress elicits delayed increases in circulating inflammatory cytokine levels. *Clinical Science*, *101*(2), 185–192.

Stock, S., & Uvnäs-Moberg, K. (2008). Increased plasma levels of oxytocin in response to afferent electrical stimulation of the sciatic and vagal nerves and in response to touch and pinch in anaesthetized rats. *Acta physiologica scandinavica*, *132*(1), 29–34.

Thayer, J. F., Åhs, F., Fredrikson, M., Sollers, J. J., & Wager, T. D. (2012). A meta-analysis of heart rate variability and neuroimaging studies: Implications for heart rate variability as a marker of stress and health. *Neuroscience & Biobehavioral Reviews*, *36*(2), 747–756.

Thayer, J. F., & Lane, R. D. (2007). The role of vagal function in the risk for cardiovascular disease and mortality. *Biological Psychology*, *74*(2), 224–242.

Tracey, K. J. (2002). The inflammatory reflex. *Nature*, *420*(6917), 853–859.

Trivers, R. L. (1971). The evolution of reciprocal altruism. *Quarterly Review of Biology*, *46*, 35–57.

Uvnas-Moberg, K., Ahlenius, S., Hillegaart, V., & Alster, P. (1994). High doses of oxytocin cause sedation and low doses cause and anxiolytic-like effect in male rats. *Pharmacological Biochemical Behavior*, *49*, 101–106.

de Waal, F.B.M. (1996). *Good Natured: The origins of right and wrong in humans and other animals*. Cambridge, MA: Harvard University Press.

Weisman, O., Zagoory-Sharon, O., & Feldman, R. (2012). Oxytocin administration to parent enhances infant physiological and behavioral readiness for social engagement. *Biological Psychiatry*, *72*(12), 982–989.

Zak, P. J., Stanton, A. A., & Ahmadi, S. (2007). Oxytocin increases generosity in humans. *PLOS ONE*, *2*(11), e1128.

Chapter 8

Compassion and the brain

Pascal Vrtička, Pauline Favre and Tania Singer

Part I: Defining social emotions such as compassion and empathy

An important aspect of a balanced and compassionate way of living is an individual's ability to generate and be receptive to feelings of care, warmth, and benevolence towards oneself and others. Within this context, we refer to a definition of compassion that includes both an emotion and, more crucially, a motivation, namely "the emotion one experiences when feeling concern for another's suffering and the desire to enhance that individual's welfare" (Goetz, Keltner, & Simon-Thomas, 2010; Singer & Lamm, 2009). This definition accords with the etymology of the term *compassion*, which is derived from the Latin origins "com" (with/together) and "pati" (to suffer), and was introduced into the English language through the French word *compassion* (Klimecki, Leiberg, Ricard, & Singer, 2014). Within the last decade, the investigation of the putative underlying neural basis of compassion has continuously gained on interest within the field of social neuroscience, which aims at understanding how biological systems – and particularly the brain – implement social processes and behavior.

As described above, our definition of compassion embraces two different processes: a feeling of concern and a motivation to help. However, before these compassion-related processes can unfold, one first has to recognize that another person is suffering; only then can one develop a feeling of concern and generate and act out the motivation to help the person in need (see Figure 8.1a).

Within our compassion definition framework, we associate the recognition that somebody is suffering with *empathy*, which we characterize as a particular human capacity to share and understand other people's emotions without confusing them with one's own feelings (de Vignemont & Singer, 2006). In other words, we empathize with another human being when we vicariously share his/her affective state, but at the same time are aware that the other person's emotion is causing our response. Accordingly, we see empathy as part of a motivational-affective route for understanding others. Our social neuroscience research on empathy is guided by an influential "shared-networks hypothesis," which proposes that empathic experiences are driven by activation of the same neural networks that process first-person experiences of affective states (Gallese & Goldman, 1998; Singer & Lamm, 2009). Such a shared-networks account is mainly based on functional magnetic resonance imaging (fMRI) studies that investigated neural responses to empathy for pain (Jackson, Meltzoff, & Decety, 2005; Singer et al., 2004). In these studies, participants either received painful stimulation by themselves or witnessed another person experiencing pain – the other person was either sitting right next to the brain scanner or was shown to participants on pictures or in movie clips. As revealed by meta-analytic evidence summarizing the available neuroimaging work on empathy for pain, there is strong support for two areas playing a principal role: the anterior insula (AI) and the anterior mid cingulate cortex (aMCC; see Figure 8.1b) (Lamm, Decety, & Singer, 2011). Although there is still an ongoing debate about the exact nature of the neural representation in this empathy-related core network consisting of AI and aMCC (e.g. Zaki, Wager, Singer, Keysers, & Gazzola, 2016), these two areas are known to be reliably involved in the evaluation and experience of emotion and interoceptive awareness, as well as the integration of pain, negative affect, and cognitive control, respectively (Singer, Critchley, & Preuschoff, 2009). The AI and aMCC are therefore assigned the role of key structures for the shared-networks account because they appear to co-represent self-experienced pain and vicariously experienced negative affect on the brain level.

Besides empathy, two other processes may help in recognizing that another person is suffering. On the one hand, more automatic and primitive mechanisms associated with action understanding are proposed to support empathic responses. One of these action-understanding mechanisms is *mimicry*, described as an automatically elicited response mirroring another person's emotional expression conveyed by facial, vocal or postural expressions or by movements (Hatfield, Rapson, & Le, 2009). Relying upon mimicry, a second action understanding mechanism proposed is *emotion contagion*, which goes one step further because it is not only associated with an automatic imitation and synchronization of displayed emotions, but also thought to result in a convergence of the actual emotional experience (Hatfield et al., 2009). Taken together, mimicry and emotion contagion are proposed to contribute to empathy in the sense that (1) seeing another person express a certain emotion will also (2) make us express the same emotion, which in turn will (3) make us experience the same emotion. Because mimicry and emotion contagion can occur rather unconsciously without self–other distinction – the latter feature being necessary for empathy to arise – mimicry and emotion contagion are regarded as (ontogenetic) precursors of empathy (see Figure 8.1a) (Klimecki & Singer, 2013).

Emotion contagion and empathy (as well as compassion, as discussed later in this chapter) are phenomena related to feelings/emotions as well as to motivation, and thus related to a motivational-affective route for the understanding of others. Besides such a motivational-affective route, social neuroscience has identified a more cognitive route for the understanding of others, referring to our ability to infer thoughts, beliefs and intentions of others; an ability termed *mentalizing, perspective taking* or *Theory of Mind* (ToM; see Figure 8.1a) (Kanske, Boeckler, Trautwein, & Singer, 2015). Not surprisingly, ToM is known to involve a distinct neural network as compared to empathy, including the temporoparietal junction (TPJ), temporal pole (TP), medial prefrontal cortex (mPFC), and precuneus/posterior cingulate (PCC; see Figure 8.1b) (Bzdok et al., 2012; Saxe & Kanwisher, 2003; Schurz, Radua, Aichhorn, Richlan, & Perner, 2014).

Apart from differentiating a motivational-affective route from a cognitive route for the understanding of others, we make a crucial distinction between two empathic responses to the suffering of others within the motivational-affective route (see Figure 8.2).

In our view, an empathic response can be characterized by *empathic* or *personal distress*, which can also be seen as a negative consequence of empathy (Klimecki & Singer, 2013). Empathic or personal distress is an aversive and self-oriented emotional response to the suffering of others. It is often associated with withdrawal behavior thought to be motivated by the desire to protect oneself from prevalent negative emotional experiences. Although regarded as a possible negative consequence of empathy, empathic distress falls somewhere between emotion contagion and empathy because the self–other distinction becomes blurred as the secondary empathic experience caused by witnessing another person suffering becomes so overwhelming that it turns into personal distress. The concept of empathic distress is particularly relevant for health care workers who are repeatedly exposed to the suffering of others and therefore run the risk of developing burnout. It therefore appears vital to find alternate ways for dealing with the suffering of others (Klimecki & Singer, 2013).

Luckily, an empathic response does not necessarily have to involve empathic or personal distress. Instead, empathy can be transformed into more adaptive and positive emotions and motivation, which we associate with compassion – also conceptualized by other authors as *empathic concern* or *sympathy* (Batson, Duncan, Ackerman, Buckley, & Birch, 1981; Batson, Fultz, & Schoenrade, 1987; Eisenberg et al., 1989). Behavioral research has shown that short-term training of loving-kindness and compassion is associated with increases in daily positive affect (Kok et al., 2013), prosocial behavior (Leiberg, Klimecki, & Singer, 2011), and resilience (Fredrickson, Cohn, Coffey, Pek, & Finkel, 2008), as well as with altered emotions of an individual when confronted with the suffering of others by specifically increasing positive affect related to the experience of warmth and concern (Klimecki, Leiberg, Lamm, & Singer, 2013; Klimecki et al., 2014).

In the remainder of this chapter, we would like to elucidate on the available evidence regarding the neural basis of compassion (Part II), and to discuss how the understanding of compassion on the brain level could inform the development of new strategies to prevent and/or treat burnout and "compassion fatigue" (Part III).

Part II: Neural basis of compassion

Social neuroscience has already been investigating the neural basis of empathy for more than a decade (Singer et al., 2004; Wicker et al., 2003). Conversely, social neuroscience research on the concept of compassion is still in its infancy – despite the fact that psychological assessment of related concepts such as sympathy and empathic concern has already emerged much earlier (Batson et al., 1981; Batson et al., 1987; Eisenberg et al., 1989). As a consequence, the number of available studies directly manipulating and/or measuring brain activity related to compassion is still limited (see e.g. Beauregard, Courtemanche, Paquette, & St-Pierre, 2009; Engen & Singer, 2015; FeldmanHall, Dalgleish, Evans, & Mobbs, 2015; Kim et al., 2009; Klimecki, Leiberg, Lamm, & Singer, 2013; Klimecki et al., 2014; Lutz, Brefczynski-Lewis, Johnstone, & Davidson, 2008; Weng et al., 2013). Nonetheless, the available data provide preliminary evidence to answer the following questions: (1) Which brain areas show increased activity during compassion generation towards the suffering of others? (2) Can compassion be trained and induce plasticity on a neural level? (3) Could compassion be used as a coping strategy and alternative means for emotion regulation – mainly in comparison with classical, cognitive emotion regulation strategies such as re-appraisal? And finally, (4) Can the neural signature of compassion directly predict altruistic behavior? In the remainder of Part II, we will summarize the available results from fMRI studies on compassion pertaining to these four questions. In so doing, a special focus will be on differences in brain responses during compassion versus empathy, if applicable.

To start, we would like to turn our attention to the first question: (1) Which brain areas show increased activity during compassion generation towards the suffering of others? Two of the available fMRI studies can be drawn upon to answer this question. Kim and colleagues (Kim et al., 2009) asked healthy adult participants with no previous compassion meditation experience to adopt either a compassionate or a passive attitude while viewing sad (i.e. distressed) versus neutral faces. Their findings revealed a main effect of adopting a compassionate (versus passive) attitude towards both neutral and sad faces in terms of increased activity in a range of areas spanning regions likely involved in empathy (i.e. insula), ToM (i.e. medial and inferior frontal cortex), as well as midbrain areas implicated in reward as well as prosocial/social approach behaviors. Furthermore, when testing for an interaction between attitude and emotional facial expression, the authors observed increased activity within the midbrain (overlapping with the ventral tegmental area – VTA – and substantia nigra – SN) and ventral striatum (VS)/septal region (SR) specifically when participants adopted a compassionate attitude towards sad faces. Beauregard and colleagues (Beauregard et al., 2009) observed a very similar brain activation pattern in terms of increased VTA and pallidum activation in their study during which they asked compassion-meditation-naïve adult participants to adopt an attitude of unconditional love (versus a passive attitude) towards people with disabilities. Given the known implication of the midbrain and VS/SR in reward processing (Schultz, 2006), affiliation (Bartels & Zeki, 2004; Vrtička, Andersson, Grandjean, Sander, & Vuilleumier, 2008), and prosocial behavior (Harbaugh, Mayr, & Burghart, 2007; Krueger et al., 2007; Moll et al., 2011), these results suggest that compassion may be neurally characterized by increased reward-related activity when facing a person in distress, thereby promoting the generation of unconditional happiness and feelings of warmth, as well as an approach-motivation necessary for initiating helping behavior. Supporting the latter notion are previous results showing that activity in the subgenual frontal area, the midbrain, and the VS/SR is increased when people are making charitable donations, as well as during the experience of prosocial emotions such as unconditional trust (Harbaugh et al., 2007; Krueger et al., 2007; Moll et al., 2006). Taken together, the above data provide evidence that compassion generation in untrained participants may be neurally characterized by increased activity in brain areas associated with reward, affiliation, positive social feelings, and prosocial motivation in the context of human suffering.

We can then turn to the second question: (2) Can compassion be trained and induce plasticity on a neural level? With the help of the available literature, this question can be answered in two ways, relying either on cross-sectional studies in meditation novices versus expert practitioners, or on pre- versus post-intervention studies in naïve participants. Applying a cross-sectional experimental design, Lutz and colleagues (Lutz et al., 2008) only very briefly instructed meditation-naïve adult participants how to generate a meditative state of loving-kindness and compassion, and asked them to re-generate such a state while being exposed to emotionally positive, neutral, or negative (i.e. distressed) human vocalizations. Brain activity in those briefly instructed meditation-naïve participants was then compared to brain activity in expert contemplative-meditation practitioners having at least 10,000 hours of experience in a variety of meditation practices. The authors found increased activity in the anterior and middle insula for all human vocalizations in expert meditators versus novices, and the degree of insula activity was positively correlated with self-reported intensity of the loving-kindness and compassion meditation in both groups. In addition, activity in middle insula was specifically higher for distress (versus neutral) vocalizations in expert meditators versus novices. This activation pattern suggests that expert meditators showed a stronger affective response, particularly to distress vocalizations, as compared to novices during a state of compassion. Furthermore, expert meditators also showed increased activity in the amygdala – a region important for emotional processing and saliency detection (Adolphs, 2010) – as well as in the TPJ and superior temporal sulcus (STS) – two areas usually implicated in ToM (Bzdok et al., 2012; Schurz et al., 2014) – in response to all human vocalizations. These data imply that expert meditators were more receptive of vocalizations and showed an enhanced mentation towards them while engaging in loving-kindness and compassion meditation as compared to novices.

Brain activity related to compassion training can also be assessed pre- versus post-compassion intervention (versus control training) in initially meditation-naïve participants. Within this context, compassion training is usually relying upon the Buddhist concepts of loving-kindness (i.e. *Metta*) and compassion (i.e. *Karuna*). Whereas loving-kindness mainly implies the wish that others may be well and happy, compassion infers the will that others may be free from suffering (Salzberg, 1995), and compassion therefore is seen as the result of loving-kindness in the face of suffering (Ricard, 2008). Klimecki and colleagues employed such a pre- versus post-compassion-training approach in two of their studies (Klimecki et al., 2013; Klimecki et al., 2014) (see Figure 8.3). For both investigations, the authors applied a newly developed task during which participants watched negative video clips showing people in distress versus neutral videos showing everyday scenes, and asked participants to rate their subjective experiences of empathy as well as positive and negative affect after each video clip (Socio-affective Video Task – SoVT). In the first study (Klimecki et al., 2013), SoVT performance was measured pre- and post-compassion training and compared to memory training in a control group. In the second study (Klimecki et al., 2014), the training sequence was extended by adding empathy training before the compassion training and compared to two subsequent memory trainings in the control group, with the SoVT being administered three times. In both studies before training, videos of people suffering were associated with increased negative emotion and empathy ratings and with heightened AI and aMCC activity, the latter behavioral and brain activity pattern probably representing a strong spontaneous empathic response. In participants first undergoing empathy training, such characteristic negative affect and neural empathic responses in AI and aMCC further increased. Importantly, however, compassion training changed this response pattern in both studies: participants not only reported feeling more positive emotions towards the suffering of others, but they also showed increased mOFC, nucleus accumbens (NAcc), and VS/midbrain (putamen, pallidum, VTA / SN) activity. Interestingly, compassion training in both studies was found to increase self-reported positive emotions in response to neutral and distress videos, whereas it did not alter negative emotion ratings to the same videos. These findings imply that participants who trained compassion still shared negative emotions of depicted people in distress, but that they in addition experienced positive, prosocial emotions associated with heightened activity in a network systematically engaged in compassion including mOFC, VS, NAcc, globus pallidus, and VTA. Taken together, these data indicate that compassion can be trained on a neural level. Not only do experienced meditators appear to show a different brain activation pattern during a state of compassion, but brain activity can even be changed pre- versus post-intervention in meditation-naïve participants by specifically instructing them in loving-kindness and compassion practices.

Relying upon such findings of brain plasticity induced by compassion training, one may ask the question whether (3) compassion could be used as a coping strategy and alternative means for emotion regulation – mainly in comparison with classical, cognitive emotion regulation strategies like re-appraisal. Within the classical framework of emotion regulation, the principal goal of emotion regulation strategies, and particularly cognitive re-appraisal, is to reduce negative emotions (Buhle et al., 2014; Ochsner et al., 2009). While the above-mentioned work on the neural basis of compassion did not find reliable evidence for negative emotion reduction through compassion training, compassion was robustly and repeatedly observed to increase positive, prosocial emotions, and activity in an extended reward-related neural network. In order to further investigate the potential role of compassion as an alternative emotion regulation strategy, Engen & Singer (2015) used a task adapted from the SoVT in expert-meditators (Buddhist practitioners) who were explicitly asked to use compassion meditation versus cognitive re-appraisal to alter their emotional state while being exposed to videos of people in distress (versus depicting neutral scenes). In the compassion condition, expert-meditators were instructed to generate "a warm feeling of positive affect and caring toward the individuals depicted in the film." Conversely, in the re-appraisal condition, expert-meditators were instructed to "re-interpret the films with positive emphasis." On the behavioral level, the compassion strategy primarily led to increased positive affect, whereas re-appraisal primarily led to decreased negative affect, which is in accordance with above-mentioned studies (Kim et al., 2009; Klimecki et al., 2013; Klimecki et al., 2014). Furthermore, compassion, relative to re-appraisal, elicited increased activation in the afore-mentioned brain-network related to compassion including the NAcc and the globus pallidus as well as midline cortical structures such as mOFC and sub-genual ACC. Conversely, activity to distress scenes, notably in the amygdala, remained unchanged. These specific findings support the notion that compassion may reflect a distinct emotion regulation strategy characterized by the endog-enous generation of positive social emotions linked to reward and affiliation, not prominently affecting the experience of negative emotions. Interestingly, the compassion network was found to be already activated prior to stimulus presen-tation, suggesting that the regulatory mechanism of compassion may act through an endogenous generation of positive affect in a stimulus-independent manner in expert-meditators (Engen & Singer, 2015). All these data accord with the notion that empathy/empathic distress (i.e. negative emotions) and compassion (i.e. positive emotions) can be experienced simultaneously while being exposed to a suffering person, and that it is rather a question of which path is predomi-nantly activated that will determine whether negative or positive outcomes will be observed in the long run (Klimecki & Singer, 2011).

Finally, the question remains whether (4) the neural signature of compassion could directly predict altruistic behavior, an assumption immediately follow-ing from our aforementioned definition of compassion including an affective state of concern for others and, more importantly, a motivation to improve the welfare of others, that is to engage in other-related actions. If yes, train-ing compassion and/or using it as an alternative emotion regulation strategy may be beneficial for social interactions by enhancing prosocial motivation as well as approach and helping behavior. Two available fMRI studies have so far directly probed such possible relation. In the first investigation, Weng and colleagues (Weng et al., 2013) combined several of the aforementioned approaches with a monetary redistribution of funds task to assess prosocial behavior post-scanning. Meditation-naïve participants underwent two-week compassion versus re-appraisal training and were then scanned by means of fMRI while seeing images of people in distress (versus neutral scenes) with the instruction to apply their assigned emotion regulation strategy. After scanning, participants played a redistribution game, during which they first observed a "dictator" transfer an unfair amount of money to a "victim" who had no money. After witnessing this fairness violation, participants could choose to spend any amount of their own endowment to compel the dictator to give twice that amount to the victim. Participants were paid the amount that was left in their endowment after making the decision. The authors found that behaviorally, individuals who trained in compassion (versus re-appraisal) were more altruistic toward victims of an unfair social interaction. In terms of brain activity after compassion training, images depicting people in distress were associated with increased connectivity between the dorsolateral PFC – a region commonly linked to cognitive control including re-appraisal (Buhle et al., 2014; Ochsner & Gross, 2005) – and the NAcc – a central node in the reward network associated with positive affect, pleasure, and happiness (Kringelbach & Berridge, 2009). In addition, inferior parietal cortex activity specifically predicted greater re-distribution of funds in compassion trainees and not in re-appraisal trainees, which led the authors to suggest that inferior parietal cortex recruitment may be a good neural marker for altruistic behavior induced by compassion training. In the second investigation, FeldmannHall and colleagues (FeldmanHall et al., 2015) had participants complete a "Pain vs. Gain" (PvG) task. For this task, participants were endowed with a personal bank account and then probed across 20 trials about their willingness to increase their financial gain at the expense of applying a series of harmful electric shocks to a confederate whom they had met and interacted with. Brain activity was assessed throughout the PvG task and later on correlated with self-report questionnaires assessing trait empathic concern (i.e. compassion) versus personal distress. Results revealed that trait empathic concern best predicted brain activity within the aforementioned compassion-related brain network (including VTA, caudate, and subgenual ACC) during observation of the consequences of participants' (costly) altruistic responses. Data from the first and second study are corroborated by previous neuroimaging studies reporting activity in the ventral mPFC and VS to be positively associated with the size of charitable donations (Harbaugh et al., 2007; Hare, Camerer, Knoepfle, O'Doherty, & Rangel, 2010; Moll et al., 2006), decisions to give equitably (Zaki & Mitchell, 2011), and prosocial behavior towards socially excluded others (Masten, Morelli, & Eisenberger, 2011), as well as with previous behavioral reports of increased prosocial helping behavior after loving-kindness and compassion training (Leiberg et al., 2011). It therefore appears that a compassionate attitude, be it after compassion training or present as a trait in terms of high empathic concern, is characterized by activation of the "compassion-related network" and directly predicts (even costly) altruistic behavior.

In conclusion, the discussed studies, particularly investigations showing train-ability of social emotions and the associated plasticity in neuronal networks, demonstrate a clear dissociation between empathy and compassion on the behavioral as well as brain level. Empathy seems to be primarily characterized by increased negative affect and heightened AI and aMCC activity, which can result in empathic or personal distress (Singer & Klimecki, 2014). In contrast, compassion appears to be mainly characterized by increased prosocial and positive emotions, and height-ened activity within a brain network including VS, globus pallidus, and mOFC associated with positive affect, affiliation, and care (Engen & Singer, 2015). Indeed, this compassion-related network coincides with brain areas rich in oxytocin/vasopressin receptors that play a critical role in prosocial and social approach behavior such as attachment, maternal care, and social cooperation (Baumgartner, Heinrichs, Vonlanthen, Fischbacher, & Fehr, 2008; Kosfeld, Heinrichs, Zak, Fischbacher, & Fehr, 2005; Strathearn, Fonagy, Amico, & Montague, 2009; Vrtička & Vuilleumier, 2012). Consequently, compassion may serve as an alternative emotion regulation strategy, and compassion training could counteract feelings of burnout and social disconnection through the strengthening of feelings of warmth and care (Eisenberger & Cole, 2012; Singer & Klimecki, 2014).

Part III: Burnout and "compassion fatigue"

Within the compassion definition framework we employ here, a compassionate person is described as able to respond with feelings of concern to the observed suffering of another individual. Importantly, the compassionate person is at the same time able to regulate his/her own negative feelings caused by an empathic response and aware that it is the other person who is suffering (Klimecki & Singer, 2011). Such positive, altruistic reaction to an empathic response is particularly important in clinical settings. When caregivers are frequently and extensively exposed to the suffering of others, empathic distress can easily lead to burnout and so-called "compassion fatigue" (see below for a clarification of terms). Available numbers point to the fact that burnout and "compassion fatigue" in caregivers are very frequent, both ranging up to 80%, and that both have various adverse effects not only on people who experience them, but also on the caregiver-patient relationship (Hooper, Craig, Janvrin, Wetsel, & Reimels, 2010; Klimecki & Singer, 2011; McCray, Cronholm, Bogner, Gallo, & Neill, 2008; van Mol, Kompanje, Benoit, Bakker, & Nijkamp, 2015). What appears to be one prominent factor leading to "compassion fatigue" in caregiv-ers is the perceived suffering of the patient, which suggests that empathy for the patient contributes to "compassion fatigue" (Schulz et al., 2007). Klimecki and Singer (2011) have therefore argued that the term "compassion fatigue" should be replaced by "empathic distress fatigue," because the corresponding condition described by caregivers closely resembles the state of empathic distress, rather than a tiredness of feeling too much compassion. Accordingly, the authors also argue that, instead of abstaining from empathic responses altogether, caregivers should aim at maintaining high levels of empathy and learn how to transform empathy into compassion and loving-kindness before being trapped by empathic distress. Such claims are based on the aforementioned results showing that compassion training can reverse the negative consequences of increased distress when exposed to the suffering of others, even after previous empathy training (Klimecki et al., 2014).

However, it should be noted here that besides being related to empathy for the patient, "compassion fatigue" has also been shown to depend on other factors, amongst which are level of educational background, years in the profession, years in emergency or intensive care units, work shift length, adequate manager support at work, and recognition of caregivers' contributions to practice (Gleichgerrcht & Decety, 2014; Hunsaker, Chen, Maughan, & Heaston, 2015). Taken together, such evidence suggests that lower levels of "compassion fatigue" in caregivers are also more generally related to a healthy and happy work environment contributing to overall increased job satisfaction. Consequently, additional and differential research in clinical settings is needed to more precisely delineate the conditions under which compassion fatigue arises, how empathy turns into empathic distress, and how this process can be avoided.

Nonetheless, and despite the fact that compassion research is still in its infancy, the results gathered so far suggest that loving-kindness and compassion training may serve as one powerful coping strategy to protect caregivers in helping professions from burnout, "compassion fatigue," or other maladaptive outcomes associated with daily exposure to the suffering of others, and that the beneficial effects of such meditation training are likely to also extend to patients.

Conclusion

Empathy and compassion constitute two distinguishable social emotions that are elicited by the observation of others suffering, and are associated with two different networks at the brain level. Furthermore, targeted training interventions can specifically modulate activity within these two distinct networks. In the case of compassion, loving-kindness and compassion training can up-regulate activity in a brain network including VS, globus pallidus, mOFC, and brain stem areas associated with positive feelings of concern, warmth, and care, as well as altruistic motivation and prosocial behavior. Compassion could therefore be used as an alternative emotion regulation strategy fostering resilience, for example in clinical settings where caregivers run a high risk of developing empathic distress fatigue.

a

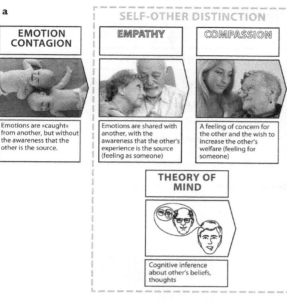

SELF-OTHER DISTINCTION

EMOTION CONTAGION	EMPATHY	COMPASSION	PROSOCIAL BEHAVIOR
Emotions are »caught« from another, but without the awareness that the other is the source.	Emotions are shared with another, with the awareness that the other's experience is the source (feeling as someone)	A feeling of concern for the other and the wish to increase the other's welfare (feeling for someone)	

THEORY OF MIND

Cognitive inference about other's beliefs, thoughts

b

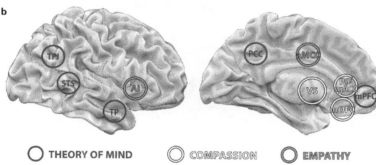

○ THEORY OF MIND   ○ COMPASSION   ○ EMPATHY

Figure 8.1 Two different routes for the understanding of others. (a) Two different routes for the understanding of others. The motivational-affective route encompasses action understanding processes such as emotion contagion, and social emotions like empathy and compassion. In turn, the cognitive route relies upon mental abilities to infer thoughts, beliefs and intentions of others also referred to as mentalizing, perspective taking or Theory of Mind. Both routes can lead to the emergence of prosocial behavior. (b) Differential neural networks underlying empathy, compassion and Theory of Mind. TPJ = temporo-parietal junction; STS = superior temporal sulcus; TP = temporal pole; AI = anterior insula; PCC = posterior cingulate cortex; aMCC = anterior midcingulate cortex; VS = ventral striatum; pg/sgACC = pregenual/subgenual anterior cingulate cortex; mOFC = medial orbitofrontal cortex; mPFC = medial prefrontal cortex.

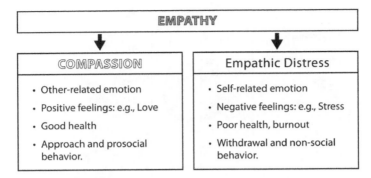

Figure 8.2 Two different responses to the suffering of others.

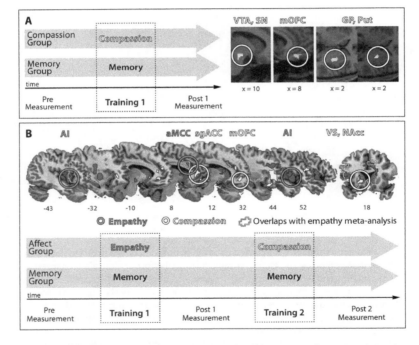

Figure 8.3 Evidence for differential functional brain plasticity after empathy and compassion training. (a) Compassion (compared to memory) training augments activation in ventral tegmental area/substantia nigra (VTA/SN), medial orbitofrontal cortex (mOFC) and striatum, the latter spanning globus pallidus (GP) and putamen (Put); (b) Empathy training leads to increased activation in anterior insula (AI) and anterior midcingulate cortex (aMCC), while subsequent compassion training augments activation in mOFC, subgenual anterior cingulate cortex (sgACC) and the ventral striatum/nucleus accumbens (VS/NAcc).

References

Adolphs, R. (2010). What does the amygdala contribute to social cognition? In A. Kingstone & M. B. Miller (Eds.), *Year in Cognitive Neuroscience 2010* (Vol. 1191, pp. 42–61).

Bartels, A., & Zeki, S. (2004). The neural correlates of maternal and romantic love. *Neuroimage, 21*(3), 1155–1166.

Batson, C. D., Duncan, B. D., Ackerman, P., Buckley, T., & Birch, K. (1981). Is empathic emotion a source of altruistic motivation. *Journal of Personality and Social Psychology, 40*(2), 290–302. doi:10.1037/0022-3514.45.3.706

Batson, C. D., Fultz, J., & Schoenrade, P. A. (1987). Distress and empathy: Two qualitatively distinct vicarious emotions with different motivational consequences. *Journal of Personality, 55*(1), 19–39. doi:10.1111/j.1467-6494.1987.tb00426.x

Baumgartner, T., Heinrichs, M., Vonlanthen, A., Fischbacher, U., & Fehr, E. (2008). Oxytocin shapes the neural circuitry of trust and trust adaptation in humans. *Neuron, 58*(4), 639–650.

Beauregard, M., Courtemanche, J., Paquette, V., & St-Pierre, É. L. (2009). The neural basis of unconditional love. *Psychiatry Research: Neuroimaging, 172*(2), 93–98.

Buhle, J. T., Silvers, J. A., Wager, T. D., Lopez, R., Onyemekwu, C., Kober, H., . . . Ochsner, K. N. (2014). Cognitive reappraisal of emotion: A meta-analysis of human neuroimaging studies. *Cerebral Cortex, 24*(11), 2981–2990.

Bzdok, D., Schilbach, L., Vogeley, K., Schneider, K., Laird, A. R., Langner, R., & Eickhoff, S. B. (2012). Parsing the neural correlates of moral cognition: ALE meta-analysis on morality, theory of mind, and empathy. *Brain Structure and Function, 217*(4), 783–796.

de Vignemont, F., & Singer, T. (2006). The empathic brain: How, when and why? *Trends in Cognitive Sciences, 10*(10), 435–441. doi:10.1016/j.tics.2006.08.008

Eisenberg, N., Fabes, R. A., Miller, P. A., Fultz, J., Shell, R., Mathy, R. M., & Reno, R. R. (1989). Relation of sympathy and personal distress to pro-social behavior: A multimethod study. *Journal of Personality and Social Psychology, 57*(1), 55–66. doi:10.1037//0022-3514.57.1.55

Eisenberger, N. I., & Cole, S. W. (2012). Social neuroscience and health: Neurophysiological mechanisms linking social ties with physical health. *Nature Neuroscience, 15*(5), 669–674.

Engen, H. G., & Singer, T. (2015). Compassion-based emotion regulation up-regulates experienced positive affect and associated neural networks. *Social Cognitive and Affective Neuroscience, 10*(9), 1291–1301.

FeldmanHall, O., Dalgleish, T., Evans, D., & Mobbs, D. (2015). Empathic concern drives costly altruism. *Neuroimage, 105*, 347–356. doi:10.1016/j.neuroimage.2014.10.043

Fredrickson, B. L., Cohn, M. A., Coffey, K. A., Pek, J., & Finkel, S. M. (2008). Open hearts build lives: Positive emotions, induced through loving-kindness meditation, build consequential personal resources. *Journal of Personality and Social Psychology, 95*(5), 1045–1062. doi:10.1037/a0013262

Gallese, V., & Goldman, A. (1998). Mirror neurons and the simulation theory of mind-reading. *Trends in Cognitive Sciences, 2*(12), 493–501. doi:10.1016/s1364-6613(98)01262-5.

Gleichgerrcht, E., & Decety, J. (2014). The relationship between different facets of empathy, pain perception and compassion fatigue among physicians. *Frontiers in Behavioral Neuroscience, 8*. doi:10.3389/fnbeh.2014.00243

Goetz, J. L., Keltner, D., & Simon-Thomas, E. (2010). Compassion: An evolutionary analysis and empirical review. *Psychological Bulletin, 136*(3), 351–374. doi:10.1037/a0018807

Harbaugh, W. T., Mayr, U., & Burghart, D. R. (2007). Neural responses to taxation and voluntary giving reveal motives for charitable donations. *Science, 316*(5831), 1622–1625.

Hare, T. A., Camerer, C. F., Knoepfle, D. T., O'Doherty, J. P., & Rangel, A. (2010). Value computations in ventral medial prefrontal cortex during charitable decision making incorporate input from regions involved in social cognition. *The Journal of Neuroscience, 30*(2), 583–590.

Hatfield, E., Rapson, R. L., & Le, Y.-C. L. (2009). Emotional contagion and empathy. *Social Neuroscience of Empathy,* 19–30.

Hooper, C., Craig, J., Janvrin, D. R., Wetsel, M. A., & Reimels, E. (2010). Compassion satisfaction, burnout, and compassion fatigue among emergency nurses compared with nurses in other selected inpatient specialties. *Journal of Emergency Nursing, 36*(5), 420–427. doi:10.1016/j.jen.2009.11.027

Hunsaker, S., Chen, H.-C., Maughan, D., & Heaston, S. (2015). Factors that influence the development of compassion fatigue, burnout, and compassion satisfaction in emergency department nurses. *Journal of Nursing Scholarship, 47*(2), 186–194. doi:10.1111/jnu.12122

Jackson, P. L., Meltzoff, A. N., & Decety, J. (2005). How do we perceive the pain of others? A window into the neural processes involved in empathy. *Neuroimage, 24*(3), 771–779. doi:10.1016/j.neuroimage.2004.09.006

Kanske, P., Boeckler, A., Trautwein, F.-M., & Singer, T. (2015). Dissecting the social brain: Introducing the EmpaToM to reveal distinct neural networks and brain-behavior relations for empathy and Theory of Mind. *Neuroimage, 122,* 6–19. doi:10.1016/j.neuroimage.2015.07.082

Kim, J.-W., Kim, S.-E., Kim, J.-J., Jeong, B., Park, C.-H., Son, A. R., . . . Ki, S. W. (2009). Compassionate attitude towards others' suffering activates the mesolimbic neural system. *Neuropsychologia, 47*(10), 2073–2081.

Klimecki, O. M., Leiberg, S., Lamm, C., & Singer, T. (2013). Functional neural plasticity and associated changes in positive affect after compassion training. *Cerebral Cortex, 23*(7), 1552–1561. doi:10.1093/cercor/bhs142

Klimecki, O. M., Leiberg, S., Ricard, M., & Singer, T. (2014). Differential pattern of functional brain plasticity after compassion and empathy training: Social cognitive and affective neuroscience, *9*(6), 873–879.

Klimecki, O., & Singer, T. (2011). Empathic distress fatigue rather than compassion fatigue? Integrating findings from empathy research in psychology and social neuroscience. In B. Oakley, A. Knafo, G. Madhavan, & D. S. Wilson (Eds.), *Pathological Altruism.* New York: Oxford University Press.

Klimecki, O., & Singer, T. (2013). *Empathy from the Perspective of Social Neuroscience.* Cambridge: Cambridge University Press.

Kok, B. E., Coffey, K. A., Cohn, M. A., Catalino, L. I., Vacharkulksemsuk, T., Algoe, S. B., . . . Fredrickson, B. L. (2013). How positive emotions build physical health: Perceived positive social connections account for the upward spiral between positive emotions and vagal tone. *Psychological Science, 24*(7), 1123–1132. doi:10.1177/0956797612470827

Kosfeld, M., Heinrichs, M., Zak, P. J., Fischbacher, U., & Fehr, E. (2005). Oxytocin increases trust in humans. *Nature, 435*(7042), 673–676.

Kringelbach, M. L., & Berridge, K. C. (2009). Towards a functional neuroanatomy of pleasure and happiness. *Trends in Cognitive Sciences, 13*(11), 479–487.

Krueger, F., McCabe, K., Moll, J., Kriegeskorte, N., Zahn, R., Strenziok, M., . . . Grafman, J. (2007). Neural correlates of trust. *Proceedings of the National Academy of Sciences, 104*(50), 20084–20089.

Lamm, C., Decety, J., & Singer, T. (2011). Meta-analytic evidence for common and distinct neural networks associated with directly experienced pain and empathy for pain. *Neuroimage*, *54*(3), 2492–2502.

Leiberg, S., Klimecki, O., & Singer, T. (2011). Short-term compassion training increases prosocial behavior in a newly developed prosocial game. *PLOS ONE*, *6*(3), e17798.

Lutz, A., Brefczynski-Lewis, J., Johnstone, T., & Davidson, R. J. (2008). Regulation of the neural circuitry of emotion by compassion meditation: Effects of meditative expertise. *PLOS ONE*, *3*(3), e1897.

McCray, L. W., Cronholm, P. F., Bogner, H. R., Gallo, J. J., & Neill, R. A. (2008). Resident physician burnout: Is there hope? *Family Medicine*, *40*(9), 626–632.

Masten, C. L., Morelli, S. A., & Eisenberger, N. I. (2011). An fMRI investigation of empathy for "social pain" and subsequent prosocial behavior. *Neuroimage*, *55*(1), 381–388.

Moll, J., Krueger, F., Zahn, R., Pardini, M., de Oliveira-Souza, R., & Grafman, J. (2006). Human fronto–mesolimbic networks guide decisions about charitable donation. *Proceedings of the National Academy of Sciences*, *103*(42), 15623–15628.

Moll, J., Zahn, R., de Oliveira-Souza, R., Bramati, I. E., Krueger, F., Tura, B., . . . Grafman, J. (2011). Impairment of prosocial sentiments is associated with frontopolar and septal damage in frontotemporal dementia. *Neuroimage*, *54*(2), 1735–1742.

Ochsner, K. N., & Gross, J. J. (2005). The cognitive control of emotion. *Trends in Cognitive Sciences*, *9*(5), 242–249.

Ochsner, K. N., Ray, R. R., Hughes, B., McRae, K., Cooper, J. C., Weber, J., . . . Gross, J. J. (2009). Bottom-up and top-down processes in emotion generation common and distinct neural mechanisms. *Psychological Science*, *20*(11), 1322–1331.

Ricard, M. (2008). *Meditation*. Munich: Nymphenburger.

Salzberg, S. (1995). *Loving-Kindness: The revolutionary art of happiness*. Boston, MA: Shambala.

Saxe, R., & Kanwisher, N. (2003). People thinking about thinking people: The role of the temporo-parietal junction in "theory of mind." *Neuroimage*, *19*(4), 1835–1842. doi:10.1016/s1053-8119(03)00230-1

Schultz, W. (2006). Behavioral theories and the neurophysiology of reward. *Annual Review of Psychology*, *57*, 87–115.

Schulz, R., Herbert, R. S., Dew, M. A., Brown, S. L., Scheier, M. F., & Beach, S. R. (2007). Patient suffering and caregiver compassion: New opportunities for research, practice, and policy. *Gerontologist*, *47*, 4–13.

Schurz, M., Radua, J., Aichhorn, M., Richlan, F., & Perner, J. (2014). Fractionating theory of mind: A meta-analysis of functional brain imaging studies. *Neuroscience & Biobehavioral Reviews*, *42*, 9–34.

Singer, T., Critchley, H. D., & Preuschoff, K. (2009). A common role of insula in feelings, empathy and uncertainty. *Trends in Cognitive Sciences*, *13*(8), 334–340.

Singer, T., & Klimecki, O. M. (2014). Empathy and compassion. *Current Biology*, *24*(18), R875–R878.

Singer, T., & Lamm, C. (2009). The social neuroscience of empathy. In M. B. Miller & A. Kingstone (Eds.), *Year in Cognitive Neuroscience 2009* (Vol. 1156, pp. 81–96).

Singer, T., Seymour, B., O'Doherty, J., Kaube, H., Dolan, R. J., & Frith, C. D. (2004). Empathy for pain involves the affective but not sensory components of pain. *Science*, *303*(5661), 1157–1162.

Strathearn, L., Fonagy, P., Amico, J., & Montague, P. R. (2009). Adult attachment predicts maternal brain and oxytocin response to infant cues. *Neuropsychopharmacology*, *34*(13), 2655–2666.

van Mol, M. M. C., Kompanje, E. J. O., Benoit, D. D., Bakker, J., & Nijkamp, M. D. (2015). The prevalence of compassion fatigue and burnout among healthcare professionals in intensive care units: A systematic review. *PLOS ONE*, *10*(8). doi:10.1371/journal.pone.0136955

Vrtička, P., Andersson, F., Grandjean, D., Sander, D., & Vuilleumier, P. (2008). Individual attachment style modulates human amygdala and striatum activation during social appraisal. *PLOS ONE*, *3*(8), e2868.

Vrtička, P., & Vuilleumier, P. (2012). Neuroscience of human social interactions and adult attachment style. *Frontiers in Human Neuroscience*, *6*. doi:10.3389/fnhum.2012.00212

Weng, H. Y., Fox, A. S., Shackman, A. J., Stodola, D. E., Caldwell, J. Z., Olson, M. C., . . . Davidson, R. J. (2013). Compassion training alters altruism and neural responses to suffering. *Psychological Science*, *24*(7), 1171–1180.

Wicker, B., Keysers, C., Plailly, J., Royet, J. P., Gallese, V., & Rizzolatti, G. (2003). Both of us disgusted in My Insula: The common neural basis of seeing and feeling disgust. *Neuron*, *40*(3), 655–664. doi:10.1016/s0896-6273(03)00679-2

Zaki, J., & Mitchell, J. P. (2011). Equitable decision making is associated with neural markers of intrinsic value. *Proceedings of the National Academy of Sciences*, *108*(49), 19761–19766.

Zaki, J., Wager, T. D., Singer, T., Keysers, C., & Gazzola, V. (2016). The anatomy of suffering: Understanding the relationship between nociceptive and empathic pain. *Trends in Cognitive Sciences*, *20*(4), 249–259. doi: http://dx.doi.org/10.1016/j.tics.2016.02.003

Chapter 9

Behavior genetics of prosocial behavior

Christopher C. Conway and George M. Slavich

Quantitative genetics of prosocial behavior

The field of quantitative genetics aims to understand how environmental and genetic factors independently and interactively shape behavioral traits in humans. This scientific approach has been applied to a wide variety of observed characteristics, or *phenotypes*, making this work relevant for all areas of psychology. To fully understand this body of work, we first need to introduce the quantitative genetic methodology and review the types of prosocial phenotypes that have been examined. Then, we can explain what the accumulating evidence reveals about the origins of prosocial behavior.

Overview of quantitative genetics

Quantitative genetics relies on samples of related individuals, called *genetically informative samples*. These samples include groups of adoptees, siblings, twins, and these probands' families. Twins have supplied the large majority of quantitative genetic data on compassion and related prosocial phenotypes, and so we focus heavily on them here. Twins are a sort of natural experiment. Identical, or *monozygotic* (MZ), twins share (for all intents and purposes) 100% of their genetic complement, whereas fraternal, or *dizygotic* (DZ), twins share 50% of their genetic complement. By comparing the resemblance of MZ versus DZ twins, behavior geneticists are able to estimate the degree to which genetic factors influence a given phenotype.

The primary objective of twin studies is to decompose variation in a trait into that which is caused by genetic versus environmental factors. In twin analysis, genetic effects are assumed to cause the heightened correspondence among MZ twins compared to DZ twins. In fact, the percentage of phenotypic variance that is due to genetics can be approximated by doubling the difference between the MZ and DZ twin correlations for a given trait (e.g. Falconer & MacKay, 1996). Environmental effects, in turn, are divided into two varieties in twin designs. The *shared environment* includes experiences that children reared in the same family have in common (e.g. parenting style, socioeconomic status) and that promote sibling similarity on a given trait. In contrast, the *unique environment* encompasses environmental exposures (e.g. peer groups, marital relationships) that cause siblings growing up in the same family to differ from one another. Accordingly, quantitative genetic studies that rely on twin samples typically report the proportion of variation in a particular trait that is due to genetics, the shared environment, and the unique environment.

Quantitative genetic studies of self-reported prosocial attitudes

Some of the first quantitative genetic studies on compassion and related prosocial behavior focused on self-reported attitudes that are related to these constructs. Early research on this topic asked over 500 pairs of MZ and DZ twins to answer questionnaires designed to assess altruism, empathy, and nurturance (Rushton, Fulker, Neale, Nias, & Eysenck, 1986). This research revealed an even split, whereby 50% of the variability in these traits was attributable to inherited genetics and 50% was attributable to environmental factors. Foreshadowing a consistent finding from subsequent studies in adults, this study reported that the shared environment—again, those elements of the child-rearing environment that cause siblings to resemble one another—had virtually no effect on prosocial outcomes. There are exceptions to this pattern, however, as a more recent study that used the University of London Institute of Psychiatry Adult Twin Register reported that 42% of the variability in prosocial behavior (e.g. civic responsibility, conscientiousness) was due to genetics, 35% to unique environment, and a full 23% to the common environment (Rushton, 2004).

Cooperativeness has also been shown to be partly under genetic influence. For example, 2,571 Australian twins over 50 years old completed the Cooperativeness scale on the Tridimensional Personality Questionnaire (Cloninger, Przybeck, & Svrakic, 1991), and analyses revealed that the percentage of variation due to genetic differences, called the *heritability estimate* (or h^2), was 27% (Gillespie, Cloninger, Heath, & Martin, 2003). The remaining variance was attributable to differences in the unique environment. A subsequent study of 617 Japanese adolescents and young adults who completed the Temperament and Character Inventory (TCI) found that the heritability for cooperativeness was estimated at 47%, and, again, no effect was detected for the shared environment (Ando et al., 2004). In this study, cooperativeness was among the most highly heritable personality traits (heritability range: .00–.49).

Several studies followed up on Rushton and colleagues' (1986) early genetic analysis of altruism. Krueger, Hicks, and McGue (2001), for example, reported surprising results from 673 adults in the Minnesota Twin Registry who completed the Self-Report Altruism Scale (Rushton, Chrisjohn, & Fekken, 1981), which inquires about altruistic actions toward strangers and organizations. Because the MZ twin correlation did not substantially exceed the DZ twin correlation for altruism, no genetic contribution to altruism was detected for those twin pairs. In contrast, a heritability estimate of 52% was reported for antisocial behavior in this sample. A subsequent study using an independent sample from the Minnesota Twin Registry also uncovered a small genetic influence (h^2 = 10%) on self-reported altruism (Koenig, McGue, Krueger, & Bouchard, 2007). Although this is a relatively small genetic effect, joint biometric analyses with reports of religiousness demonstrated a large correspondence (73%) between the genetic effects on altruism and religiousness.

Several other studies on adult twins are relevant to the genetic and environmental causes of prosociality. Consistent with results reported by Rushton et al. (1986), Matthews, Batson, Horn, and Rosenman (1981) reported that 72% of the variation on a self-report measure of empathy was due to genetic variation in middle-aged male twins. Also, Kendler (1996) asked over 1,000 adult twin pairs and their parents to describe the parenting they were exposed to as children, and he found that parental warmth was heritable (h^2 = 38%), whereas parental authoritarianism and protectiveness were not (see also Losoya, Callor, Rowe, & Goldsmith, 1997).

A small number of studies have examined the heritability of prosocial behavior in young people, in part to discern the relative importance of the rearing environment versus the inherited genetic complement to prosocial outcomes. In a sample of 183 seven-year-old twin pairs, Knafo-Noam and colleagues asked mothers to report on social behavior of their twin offspring in five areas: sharing, social concern, kindness, helping, and empathic concern (Knafo-Noam, Uzefovsky, Israel, Davidov, & Zahn-Waxler, 2015). These sub-domains of prosocial behavior were moderately inter-correlated (rs > .39). Moreover, evidence was found for a common prosociality factor that accounted for the correspondence among these sub-domains. Capitalizing on the twin design, the authors reported that much of the sample variation relate to this overarching factor was due to genetic causes (h^2 = 69%). In addition, the unique environment accounted for the remaining variance, leaving only a very small (perhaps nonexistent) role for the shared environment.

Taking a very similar approach, Scourfield, John, Martin, and McGuffin (2004) derived a common prosociality factor from parent and teacher ratings of child and adolescent prosocial behavior. This factor was moderately heritable (h^2 range: 46%–53%) in childhood (i.e. ≤ age 10) and even more so in adolescence. Furthermore, the small effect of the shared environment that was detected in childhood eroded completely as the youth transitioned into adolescence. The authors commented that this pattern of declining influence for the shared environment, and corresponding growing magnitude of genetic effects, resembles a pattern found in other substantive literatures, such as youth depression (e.g. Rice, Harold, & Thapar, 2002) and general intelligence (e.g. Briley & Tucker-Drob, 2017).

Quantitative genetic studies of self-reported prosocial behavior

Transitioning from studies designed to trace the genetic and environmental origins of prosocial attitudes, we now concentrate on the smaller number of quantitative genetic studies of self-reported prosocial behavior. In this context, Son and Wilson (2010) accessed twin data from the Midlife in the United States Study to evaluate genetic contributions to the number of hours per month that people spent doing volunteer work for organizations (e.g. youth education, healthcare work). They found that volunteering was mildly heritable for women ($h^2 = 30\%$), but not at all for men. For both sexes, there was no discernible shared environmental effect, meaning that the majority of the variance was accounted for by the unique environment. A second cleverly designed study used the Danish Twin Register to investigate the heritability of donating blood, which is thought to be motivated strongly by altruism (Pedersen et al., 2015). By linking the twin register to a national database of blood donors, the authors concluded that donating blood was jointly determined by genetic (53%) and shared environmental (28%) factors.

A pair of genetically informative studies has also been published on marital fidelity, which is a phenotype akin to pair bonding in animal research. One recent study of over 7,000 Finnish twins reported that much of the variation in self-reported fidelity (i.e. absence of extra-pair mating or, more colloquially, extramarital affairs) was due to genetics, although the percentage differed for males (62%) versus females (40%) (Zietsch, Westberg, Santtila, & Jern, 2015). Largely corroborating this result, an earlier study of female twin pairs in the United Kingdom estimated the heritability of marital fidelity at 41% (Cherkas, Oelsner, Mak, Valdes, & Spector, 2004). In a surprising twist, this same study found that *attitudes* toward infidelity, as compared to the act itself, were not at all heritable.

Experimental quantitative genetic studies of prosocial behavior

Finally, several studies have used the twin methodology in the context of experimental settings. An early study examined empathy among approximately 200 pairs of two-year-old twins (Zahn-Waxler, Robinson, & Emde, 1992). To induce empathic responses in the laboratory, these researchers asked experimenters to fake painful accidents, such as closing a finger in a suitcase or banging a knee on a table. The experimenters then simulated pain vocalizations and agonizing facial expressions. Children's facial expressions, vocalizations, and comforting actions were coded by independent raters. Ultimately, this study detected only modest evidence for the heritability of empathy insofar as the genetic effects were small and confined to only a few dimensions of empathy (e.g. affective facial expressions).

Using an almost identical methodology, a more recent study evaluated empathetic behavior in 400 twin pairs assessed four times between 14 and 36 months old (Knafo, Zahn-Waxler, Van Hulle, Robinson, & Rhee, 2008b). Over these four assessments, the heritability estimates for empathy were 0%, 0%, 34%, and 47%. For prosocial behavior (i.e. comforting actions, such as offering the experimenter a toy or getting a bandage), the corresponding estimates were 17%, 0%, 9%, and 24%. The influence of the shared environment declined over these intervals in concert with the rise of genetic factors such that, by the final time point, its influence on empathy was gone. Also, there was a moderate phenotypic association between empathic expressions and prosocial actions, but this relation was entirely due to overlapping environmental influences on these two outcomes. As such, the genetic factors involved in empathy and prosocial behavior were found to be entirely independent.

Summary of quantitative genetic studies

In summary, quantitative genetic techniques tell us about the proportion of sample variability that is attributable to genetic, shared environmental, and unique environmental factors. The methodology can thus give us unprecedented insight into the etiology of psychological phenotypes that is not available through traditional observational research designs. Twin studies are the workhorse of the quantitative genetic field, and most of the existing data that are relevant for understanding compassion come from twin samples.

To describe this literature, we reviewed evidence from studies in which respondents were (a) asked to report on prosocial attitudes, (b) asked to report on prosocial behavior, or (c) observed for evidence of prosociality in a laboratory setting. Although there are notable exceptions (e.g. Krueger et al., 2001), these studies generally confirm a partly genetic origin to compassion-related phenotypes. However, the magnitude of heritability estimates varies widely across studies, even among those that rely on the same sorts of samples and assessment tools. It is a truism that most personality and clinical traits have heritability estimates of approximately 50% in adulthood (Turkheimer, 2000). The studies reviewed here suggest that prosocial traits are similarly, or perhaps slightly less, heritable.

Consistent with patterns observed in other literatures, the heritability of prosociality appears to increase with age (Knafo et al., 2008b; Scourfield et al., 2004). Moreover, as genetic effects expand, shared environmental influences diminish. This increase in genetic influence has been attributed to the emergence of *gene-environment correlation*, or the process whereby genetically based preferences begin shaping the environments to which people are exposed (see Scarr & McCartney, 1983). For instance, compassionate young people may select into friendship groups of compassionate peers who further foster compassionate attitudes among their friends. Although it is tempting to label favorable social experiences as "environmental events," from a causal perspective, they are (distally) due to genetic influences. Therefore, as young people are able to exert more control over their environments, such as seeking out one's own social niche, the heritability estimates in behavior genetic studies rise.

Regardless of the reason for this increasing influence of genetic factors over time, the phenomenon raises interesting questions regarding the role the rearing environment plays in shaping long-term trajectories of prosocial behavior among offspring. Behavior genetic studies have indicated that the influence of the shared environment declines precipitously to point that, in adult samples, the influence of the shared environment is nil. These data suggest that the rearing environment, including parenting practices, may have little-to-no long-term effect on offspring prosocial behavior. Tackling this controversial issue is beyond the scope of this chapter, but interested readers can see Harris (1998) for an introduction.

Molecular genetics of prosocial behavior

Using the quantitative genetics paradigm to partition the origins of a phenotype into genetic, shared environmental, and unique environmental sources has many advantages. Unlike much social science research, for example, this methodology enables researchers to make strong inferences about what *causes* a given trait, as opposed to merely documenting statistical associations that may or may not be causal in nature. Moreover, quantitative genetics has been largely immune to the ongoing replication crisis in psychology (Plomin, DeFries, Knopik, & Neiderhiser, 2016). This is because within a given substantive domain, such as prosocial behavior, heritability estimates tend to be relatively consistent across studies.

At the same time, quantitative genetic studies have an important limitation: they do not identify the specific genes that give rise to phenotypes. Rather, these studies yield an omnibus genetic effect, meaning that researchers can discern the effect of individual differences in the entire genome on a trait; however, the genetic variants that drive these effects are not available for analysis. As a result, quantitative genetic methods alone cannot delineate the specific genes that are involved in shaping particular phenotypes, such as compassion or prosocial behavior.

This is where molecular genetics becomes useful. Molecular genetics is the set of methodologies that illuminates how individual genes are related to a phenotype. Since the completion of the Human Genome Project in the early 2000s, researchers have had access to the approximately 30,000 genes in the human genome, and variation at some genetic loci has been linked to psychological outcomes, including prosocial attitudes and behavior. In this section, then, we review the rapidly proliferating literature on how prosocial outcomes are related to measured genes, as opposed to the unmeasured genes that contribute to omnibus genetic effects that are revealed in behavior genetic designs.

Overview of molecular genetics

First, we need to introduce some fundamental terms and concepts in molecular genetics. For starters, genes are segments of DNA that contain instructions for making proteins. Proteins, in turn, are essential for the operation of countless psychological and biological processes that help sustain life. As an example, the serotonin transporter enzyme, which regulates the efficiency of serotonin neurotransmission and is the target of many antidepressant medications, is a protein. Although our genetic code is critical for life, not everyone has the same DNA code at a given location in the genome. Rather, there is substantial inter-individual variability in the make-up of our genes. Genes that show differences in structure across people are called genetic *polymorphisms* or *variants*.

Furthermore, we have two copies of any gene that is not transmitted on a sex chromosome: one copy is inherited from our mother and one from our father. These copies are also called *alleles*. Therefore, at any given location on the genome, three *genotypes* are possible (i.e. two copies of allele *X*, two copies of allele *Y*, or one copy of each). Individuals who have two copies of the same allele for a given gene are said to be *homozygous* for that genotype, whereas persons with one copy of each allele are called *heterozygous*. These individual differences in genotypes often correspond to differences in protein production, which can in turn produce phenotypic differences, such as varying rates of serotonin neurotransmission in the case of the serotonin transporter protein previously described.

With this background information in mind, we now turn to recent research implicating individual genetic variants in prosociality. To make the interpretation of the findings easier, we have organized this part of the review into three *candidate gene* pathways. Candidate genes are those genetic variants that are theorized to be involved in a given phenotype given their role in biological systems that are thought to support the phenotype. Since we are interested in the genetic bases of prosociality, we focus here on genes relating to (a) the oxytocin and vasopressin neuropeptides, (b) dopamine neurotransmission, and (c) serotonin neurotransmission. Each of these systems has been associated with prosociality and related traits in animal model and human research, so we now examine the extent to which the genes regulating activity in each of these systems predict prosocial physiological, cognitive, and behavioral outcomes.

Oxytocin and arginine vasopressin

Oxytocin (OT) and arginine vasopressin (AVP) are neuropeptides that are often studied in tandem. Together, they are thought to regulate the propensity to engage in affiliative behaviors involving compassion, perspective taking, empathy, and trust (see Ebstein, Knafo, Mankuta, Chew, & San Lai, 2012). Intensive human research on OT and AVP was inspired by early animal studies showing that endogenous (i.e. naturally occurring) levels of these hormones are correlated with the strength of pair bonding in prairie voles (e.g. Insel & Shapiro, 1992).

Human research examining these neuropeptides has found that intranasal administration of OT and AVP influences social interactions in the laboratory (e.g. Tabak et al., 2015). For instance, temporarily boosting OT produces increases in empathy, trust, identification of others' affective states, and limbic reactivity to emotional cues in laboratory settings (for a review, see Striepens, Kendrick, Maier, & Hurlemann, 2011). In light of the wide-ranging effects of naturally occurring OT and AVP on social cognition and behavior, several studies have investigated how prosociality is influenced by genetic polymorphisms that are responsible for the structure and activity of these hormones.

A main focus of this work has been on examining links between prosociality and polymorphisms in the gene that encodes the oxytocin receptor, which is responsible for binding OT to the postsynaptic neuron and thus terminating the neurochemical communication process among neurons. There are many locations in the oxytocin receptor gene (abbreviated OXTR) where the DNA code varies across people. Analogously, there are two polymorphisms in the gene carrying the information for an AVP receptor protein (called AVPR1a) that are usual suspects in molecular genetic research on prosocial outcomes.

Correlational molecular genetic studies of oxytocin and arginine vasopressin

Turning first to self-reported prosocial behaviors, two studies have investigated these genes in relation to empathy. The first study found that individuals homozygous for the so-called G allele at the OXTR polymorphism (designated rs53576) endorsed more empathic attitudes than those who were heterozygous at that polymorphism or who had two copies of the A allele (Rodrigues, Saslow, Garcia, John, & Keltner, 2009). Additionally, these same G homozygotes demonstrated better inferences of others' affective states in a laboratory task. More recently, Uzefovsky and colleagues found this same rs53576 G allele to be linked with greater emotional empathy (i.e. empathic concern and personal distress over another's pain), but not cognitive empathy (i.e. perspective taking), in an undergraduate sample (Uzefovsky et al., 2015). Conversely, a polymorphism in the promoter region of the AVPR1a gene was associated with emotional, but not cognitive, empathy in this study. Specifically, those without a variant called the 327-repeat allele (to denote the increased length of the promoter region) at a polymorphism labeled RS3 reported less of an emotional response to others' distress. An independent study of mothers with two-year-old offspring corroborated this OXTR finding by showing that mothers carrying at least one rs53576 G allele were more responsive to their toddlers' cries than mothers without the G allele (Bakermans-Kranenburg & van Ijzendoorn, 2008).

Several large-scale studies have examined real-world prosocial behavior (i.e. as opposed to attitudes or personality traits). In the same female twin sample described earlier, Cherkas and colleagues (2004) found no evidence of an association between variation in the AVPR1a gene and marital infidelity. Similarly, after correction for multiple testing, a study of Finnish twins found no associations between polymorphisms in the AVPR1a gene (including the RS3 location mentioned above) and rates of marital fidelity (Zietsch et al., 2015). Finally, a study employing a nationally representative sample of unrelated individuals in the United States found no main effects of OXTR rs53576, AVPR1a RS1, or AVPR1a RS3 polymorphisms on participants' engagement in volunteer work or charitable activity (Poulin, Holman, & Buffone, 2012).

Experimental molecular genetic studies of oxytocin and arginine vasopressin

Complementing these correlational findings, an interesting line of experimental behavioral research has begun to explore compassion through individuals' economic behavior. For example, several studies have genotyped players in the Dictator Game, in which the first player (the "Dictator") decides what proportion of a fixed sum of money to keep and what proportion to donate to an anonymous "Recipient," without any consideration of reciprocity or retaliation. The donations can thus be considered completely altruistic insofar as they cannot benefit the Dictator in any way. In one study that employed this task, three out of the 15 polymorphisms examined predicted the size of the Dictators' donations (Israel et al., 2009). In a second study, Apicella et al. (2010) attempted to replicate this result but found no associations between any of the nine OXTR polymorphism tested and participants' donation rates. In a third study, Knafo et al. (2008a) examined variation in the AVPR1a gene and found that the RS3 (but not RS1) polymorphism predicted donation size, with the longer versions of RS3 (indicating larger promoter regions of AVPR1a) being associated with more generous Dictator Game allocations and higher self-reported altruism. Finally, Krueger and colleagues (2012) genotyped undergraduates at OXTR rs53576 and invited them to play a different economic game. In this "trust game," an investor and trustee both start with ten monetary units. Then, the investor donates some proportion of that amount to the trustee, at which point the donation amount is tripled and the trustee chooses how much of his or her money to return to the investor. Using this task, Krueger and colleagues found that G homozygote investors not only made larger initial transfers to trustees, but also had higher self-reported dispositional empathy.

Another useful paradigm for assessing prosocial behavior in the lab involves dyadic interactions, either between strangers or close relations. Using this approach, Feldman et al. (2012) coded minute-by-minute interactions between parents and infant offspring for instances of parental touch and gaze synchrony (i.e. parent-offspring eye contact). This study not only found that the OXTR rs1042778 polymorphism—one of those linked with Dictator donations by Israel et al. (2010)—predicted parental touch rates, but also implicated variation in the CD38 gene, which is partially responsible for brain OT secretion, in parenting behavior. No genetic effects were detected for gaze synchrony. Around the same time, an independent research group studied the gaze duration of unrelated undergraduates in a naturalistic conversation, and contradicting prior research on the OXTR rs53576 locus, this study found that undergraduates carrying an A allele maintained better eye contact with a conversation partner compared to G homozygotes (Verhagen, Engels, & Van Roekel, 2014). Other research with adults has found no direct effect of rs53576 variation on cognitive empathy tests or judgments of confederates' experience of pain (Laursen et al., 2014; Weisman et al., 2015). In a recent study of Chinese children, however, Wu and Su (2015) found that rs54576 G allele homozygotes exhibited more helping and comforting behaviors to experimenters than A allele carriers.

Along these same lines, several studies have focused on OXTR variation and romantic partner interactions. In one study, investigators observed a supportive interpersonal interaction and coded it for indices of empathic communication (Walter et al., 2012). They found that a risk score computed from variation at five OXTR polymorphisms correlated with poorer empathic support. A separate research team also found evidence of oxytocinergic involvement in prosocial romantic behavior (Algoe & Way, 2014). Specifically, this study examined CD38 variability— polymorphisms called rs6449182 and rs3796863 that underlie the expression of the CD38 protein and plasma OT levels—and found that these variants related to participants' positive responses to expressions of gratitude from their romantic partners.

Serotonin

The neurotransmitter serotonin has been associated with a vast array of behavioral phenotypes. These include such diverse processes as sleep, appetite, sexual behavior, and mood. Initial attention to the potential impact that serotonergic genetic variation might have on prosociality and antisociality was highlighted by early personality theories linking serotonin system function with aggression (Carver, Johnson, & Joormann, 2008), and a seminal demonstration of gene-environment interaction for violence and antisocial behavior involving a serotonergic gene (i.e. monoamine oxidase A; Caspi et al., 2002).

The body of research examining serotonin-related genes and prosocial behavior is far smaller than that involving OT and AVP. Moreover, nearly all of the studies on this topic involve variation in one gene that controls the transcription efficiency of the serotonin transporter gene. Specifically, there is a polymorphism (abbreviated 5-HTTLPR) in the promoter region of the serotonin transporter gene that corresponds to differences in the number of serotonin transporter enzymes on presynaptic neurons (Lesch et al., 1996). The short (S) allele of this polymorphism is less transcriptionally efficient than the long (L) allele and leads to fewer working serotonin transporters. This difference in the availability of transporter enzymes in turn translates into individual differences in rates of serotonin neurotransmission.

The S allele at 5-HTTLPR is best known for conspiring with environmental stressors to confer vulnerability to emotional disorders (e.g. Conway, Slavich, & Hammen, 2014; for a review, see Caspi et al., 2010). However, several studies have also examined its relation to prosociality. An early study (Hamer, Greenberg, Sabol, & Murphy, 1999) provided evidence supporting an association between the 5-HTTLPR S allele and lower self-reported cooperativeness (Cohen's $d = 0.35$), as assessed by the TCI. The direction of this effect is consistent with the S allele's implication in various forms of psychopathology that involve social deficits (Caspi et al., 2010).

Experimental molecular genetic studies of serotonin

Data linking the serotonin transporter gene and prosociality also come from laboratory studies of social cognition and interaction. In one study on utilitarian moral judgments (Marsh et al., 2011), healthy volunteers were asked about whether they would cause harm to one person to save the lives of others by changing the path of a hypothetical runaway train away from five people and toward one innocent victim. S allele carriers were less likely to endorse this type of harm and were also more averse to causing unintentional harm to innocent people. A more recent study examined associations between 5-HTTLPR and females' judgments of pain experience of another participant (Laursen et al., 2014). The authors assessed how accurately raters could sense the intensity of pain that their fellow participants were experiencing after an electric shock. However, genotype at 5-HTTLPR was unrelated to the accuracy of ratings and neural activity in relevant brain regions during the rating process. In sum, then, different research methodologies have yielded inconsistent findings linking 5-HTTLPR with prosociality.

Dopamine

Finally, like serotonin, the dopamine system is involved in a variety of different behavioral outcomes. Although dopamine neurotransmission is perhaps most commonly linked with personality traits like disinhibition, reward dependence, and extraversion, some studies have explored its association with prosociality. For example, Comings et al. (2000) invited undergraduates to complete the TCI and then analyzed their responses in relation to 59 candidate genes. Variation at the dopamine transporter gene (DAT), which performs an analogous function to 5-HTTLPR, was associated with responses on the TCI Cooperativeness scale, although only 3% of the variation in self-reported cooperativeness was accounted for by DAT. In a second study, Baeken, Claes, and De Raedt (2014) examined variation in the catechol-O-methyltransferase (COMT) gene as a predictor of novelty seeking, as measured by the TCI. Although the hypothesized association was not found, COMT genotype was strongly related to the TCI Cooperativeness scale. The authors argued that this finding is consistent with the hypothesis that people with lower resting dopamine levels are more empathic and compassionate and, in doing so, they cited an independent study on DAT genotype showing that higher dopamine availability corresponds to low TCI Cooperativeness scores (Pelka-Wysiecka et al., 2012). Corroborating this hypothesis, another study documented gender-specific effects of a dopamine receptor gene (DRD4) on self-reported empathy (Uzefovsky et al., 2014).

Experimental molecular genetic studies of dopamine

Several laboratory studies that are similar in design to those supporting the involvement of OT and AVP in prosociality have been conducted to examine dopaminergic genetic effects on objective prosocial behavior. Two such studies investigated genetic links to children's willingness to donate money to charity. In the first study, children earned money in two computer tasks and were then invited to donate as much of their endowment to a South American charity as they liked

(Reuter, Frenzel, Walter, Markett, & Montag, 2011). Children carrying at least one COMT Val allele (named after the amino acid valine encoded by the corresponding segment of DNA) donated approximately twice as much as children who were homozygous for the COMT Met (methionine) allele. This effect was in the same direction as the association between COMT and TCI Cooperativeness reported by Baeken et al. (2014). In a second study, Bakermans-Kranenburg and van Ijzendoorn (2011) examined associations between DRD4 genotype and altruism in seven-year-olds. They found no main effect of genotype on charitable donations, although there was a complex pattern of interaction between child attachment style and DRD4 genotype in predicting helping behavior. Specifically, securely attached children gave more money, but only if they carried a so-called 7-repeat allele at DRD4.

Finally, a few laboratory studies have examined dopaminergic effects on empathy in child samples. One study found that maternal negativity interacted with DRD4 genotype to predict children's reactions to an experimenter who was simulating physical pain (Knafo, Israel, & Ebstein, 2011). A second study examined associations between dopamine-related genes and *theory of mind*, which is the ability to understand others' mental states that is thought to underlie compassionate behavior and related phenotypes (Lackner, Sabbagh, Hallinan, Liu, & Holden, 2012). Here, children carrying the 7-repeat version of DRD4 demonstrated superior theory of mind capabilities, which is consistent with the results reported by Bakermans-Kranenburg and van Ijzendoorn (2011). However, variation at DAT and COMT in this study was unrelated to theory of mind performance.

Summary of molecular genetic studies

In summary, research on the molecular genetics of prosociality is in its infancy compared to that of other personality and clinical phenotypes. Although the data are still limited, several trends are apparent. First, the studies conducted to date have focused largely on the OT and AVP systems, in large part because of the long history of animal and human research linking naturally occurring levels of these hormones to affiliative behavior. The literature on genotypes that are related to monoamine neurotransmitter systems (i.e. serotonin, dopamine) is growing but is still comparatively small, and the literature linking genotypes with other biological systems is even smaller. Second, variation at any single location in the genome explains a surprisingly small proportion of prosocial phenotypic variance. Indeed, the largest effects rarely surpass more than a few percentage points of variability explained. The incongruity between the large overall genetic (i.e. entire genome) effects reported in quantitative genetic studies and the diminutive—sometimes vanishingly small—effect sizes emerging in molecular genetic studies is termed the *missing heritability* problem. This problem also highlights that quantitative and molecular genetic study designs have complementary strengths and weaknesses. Specifically, whereas quantitative genetics is capable of detecting robust genetic effects but cannot reveal the precise locations in the genome that are

Table 9.1 Key behavior genetic findings in research on prosocial behavior

Quantitative genetics	Molecular genetics
• Like other personality traits, prosociality is moderately heritable. • Heritability estimates range from about 0% to about 50%. • Like other cognitive and personality phenotypes, the heritability of prosocial behavior increases with age. • The shared environment, which includes parenting, appears to have a small influence on prosocial behavior, and this effect declines with age.	• Genes regulating oxytocin, vasopressin, serotonin, and dopamine are implicated in prosocial outcomes. • The influence that any single gene has on prosociality is small and sometimes infinitesimal. • As in other molecular genetic research areas, reproducibility of results for prosocial behavior is poor. • Through genome-wide association studies, researchers can now simultaneously examine associations between thousands of genetic polymorphisms and prosociality.

responsible for behavior, molecular genetics can pinpoint specific genes, but these genes seem to have only small—and perhaps not practically significant—effects on behavioral outcomes.

Third, readers may have noticed inconsistency across molecular genetic studies of a given phenotype. For instance, the G allele at OXTR rs53576 was found to be associated with both increased and diminished prosociality, and also to have no effects on prosociality. Failures to replicate are endemic to molecular genetic research in psychology (Duncan & Keller, 2011), and the track record of irreproducibility has inspired greater attention to good research practices (e.g. adequate statistical power, replication in independent samples). Perhaps the most prominent example of inconsistency in molecular genetic research is represented by the explosion of replication attempts for 5-HTTLPR gene-environment interaction in depression that has yielded many positive and negative results, along with contradictory meta-analytic results (Karg, Burmeister, Shedden, & Sen, 2011; Risch et al., 2009). These mixed results in genetic studies of prosociality, and the broader context of replication difficulties in molecular genetics, point to the importance of replication in studies on prosocial phenotypes and to exploring new avenues for genetic research, some of which are reviewed in the next section.

Future directions

What future developments can we expect in molecular genetic research on prosociality? One trend that is likely to advance research on prosocial phenotypes involves the simultaneous analysis of multiple polymorphisms in the same gene or across different genes. This practice is common in more mature genetic literatures and was inspired in part by the small effect sizes observed for any one polymorphism in isolation and, in addition, by the fact that genotypes at contiguous locations in the genome tend to be correlated (due to Mendel's law of segregation). As a result, some researchers are creating *haplotypes*, or combinations of nearby polymorphisms, to try and explain more variation in prosocial phenotypes. Other researchers are simply adding up the number of "risk" alleles in a given gene—or across a number of genes in the same biological pathway, such as the OT system—to create a *polygenic risk score* (e.g. Schneiderman, Kanat-Maymon, Ebstein, & Feldman, 2014; Tabak et al., 2014).

The ultimate example of analyzing multiple polymorphisms at the same time is the *genome-wide association study* (GWAS). Compared with hypothesis-based candidate gene research, which is driven by existing theory about the biological systems that support a given phenotype, GWAS is atheoretical. Because the cost of conducting genetic assays is falling quickly, researchers can now examine associations between thousands of polymorphisms and a particular phenotype. At the same time, though, the GWAS approach requires very large samples and oftentimes data sharing within a large research consortium. As a result, this method is starting to yield replicable genetic risk markers for cognitive ability and some psychiatric disorders (e.g. Plomin & Deary, 2015), but we are not presently aware of any studies that have used this methodology for studying the genetic bases of prosocial attitudes or behaviors.

Like GWAS, meta-analysis offers a way to enhance power to detect small genetic effects. Meta-analysis combines data from various original empirical studies to establish an effect size estimate based on all available data. This technique has been important for making sense of molecular genetic literatures for other personality and clinical phenotypes (e.g. Karg et al., 2011). However, we are aware of only one meta-analysis of molecular genetic effects on prosocial outcomes. Specifically, Bakermans-Kranenburg and van Ijzendoorn (2014) summarized evidence relating OXTR rs53576 and rs2254298 to prosocial outcomes in biological, subjective, and behavioral domains. This analysis included more than 17,000 participants for rs53576 and 13,000 participants for rs2254298, and it revealed that the overall effect size estimates are not significantly different from zero for any domain. This result calls into question the importance of OXTR variation for real-world prosocial outcomes. It also suggests that additional meta-analyses involving OXTR and other relevant genes are warranted.

Finally, to fully understand how genes cause prosocial phenotypes, it will be necessary to elucidate the entire biological pathway underlying these phenotypes. Specifically, researchers will need to identify the full set of psychological and biological mechanisms in the causal chain from distal genes to proximal prosocial outcomes. Fully integrated, multi-level models have been proposed for other outcomes, such as stress-related disorders and depression (e.g. Slavich & Cole, 2013; Slavich & Irwin, 2014), but not yet for prosocial phenotypes.

Critical for advancing this scientific strategy is the identification of intermediary processes, sometimes called *endophenotypes*, which occur downstream of gene action (Kendler & Neale, 2010). Prior molecular genetic work has identified some possible endophenotypes for prosocial behavior. For example, Tost et al. (2010) correlated the OXTR rs53576 A allele, which in other research predicted social deficits associated with diminished empathy, with amygdala responses to images of emotional faces. Because the amygdala is involved in socioemotional information processing, altered neural dynamics in this brain region that are mediated by OXTR could potentially account for genetic effects on amygdala-dependent social behaviors and attitudes. Similarly, in the study reviewed here that asked participants to judge the pain experiences of live confederates (Laursen et al., 2014), variation at OXTR was associated with activation in the superior temporal sulcus during the appraisal of others' pain. The implication, therefore, is that OXTR may influence empathic cognitions and behaviors through its regulation of activity in the superior temporal sulcus.

Sympathetic nervous system activity is another possible mechanism linking OXTR with downstream cognitive and behavioral prosocial phenotypes. Evidence supporting this link comes from a study that examined participants' electrodermal activity (i.e. galvanic skin response) while they watched a violent mixed martial arts fight (Smith, Porges, Norman, Connelly, & Decety, 2014). Specifically, participants with the rs53576 G allele exhibited greater electrodermal activity during the fight compared to A allele homozygotes, indicating greater relative sympathetic arousal. A second study of OXTR and indices of the sympathetic nervous system presented females with the sounds of infants crying (Riem, Pieper, Out, Bakermans-Kranenburg, & van Ijzendoorn, 2011). Here, women with the rs53576 G allele exhibited greater heart rate responses to the cry sounds than A homozygotes.

In sum, the molecular genetic literature provides important new information about the exact genetic variants underlying large omnibus genetic effects documented in twin studies. Nonetheless, an imperfect track record of replication and consistently small effect sizes highlight the importance of exploring complementary and alternate methodologies. Haplotype analysis, GWAS, and meta-analysis all promise to enhance gene-hunting efforts, and the greatest advancements will likely be realized by integrating information from each of these strategies. Finally, establishing endophenotypes for prosocial behavior can simultaneously maximize genetic effect sizes and help delineate the mechanisms linking candidate genes and prosocial behavior. In this context, though, new models of prosociality are needed that identify the full set of psychological and biological mechanisms that link specific genes with prosocial behavior.

Summary and conclusions

In summary, decades of quantitative genetic research have revealed that compassion and closely related prosocial phenotypes are moderately heritable. Thus, some (but not most) individual differences in prosocial behavior are attributable to genetic differences. Perhaps unexpectedly, one of the main lessons learned from this body of quantitative genetic research involves the importance of environmental experiences in shaping prosocial attitudes and behavior. The most important sources of environmental effects, however, may be surprising. Specifically, twin studies have shown that the influence of the home environment (including parenting styles) on prosocial behavior is small, whereas environments not shared across siblings (e.g. distinct friendship groups, romantic partnerships) typically explain the lion's share of the non-genetic variation in prosocial outcomes.

Molecular genetic research, in turn, has implicated several neurotransmitter systems in prosociality. Polymorphisms in genes regulating oxytocin and arginine vasopressin have been associated with prosocial outcomes, although the effect size estimates are variable and usually small. Genes supporting serotonin and dopamine neurotransmission have also been linked to prosocial behavior. To resolve the missing heritability problem, new molecular genetic techniques and larger sample sizes will very likely be prioritized in future research on the genetics of compassion and other prosocial behaviors.

References

Algoe, S. B., & Way, B. M. (2014). Evidence for a role of the oxytocin system, indexed by genetic variation in CD38, in the social bonding effects of expressed gratitude. *Social Cognitive and Affective Neuroscience*, 9, 1855–1861.

Ando, J., Suzuki, A., Yamagata, S., Kijima, N., Maekawa, H., Ono, Y., & Jang, K. L. (2004). Genetic and environmental structure of Cloninger's temperament and character dimensions. *Journal of Personality Disorders*, 18, 379–393.

Apicella, C. L., Cesarini, D., Johannesson, M., Dawes, C. T., Lichtenstein, P., Wallace, B., . . . Westberg, L. (2010). No association between oxytocin receptor (OXTR) gene polymorphisms and experimentally elicited social preferences. *PLOS ONE*, 5, e11153.

Baeken, C., Claes, S., & De Raedt, R. (2014). The influence of COMT Val158Met genotype on the character dimension cooperativeness in healthy females. *Brain and Behavior*, 4, 515–520.

Bakermans-Kranenburg, M. J., & van IJzendoorn, M. H. (2008). Oxytocin receptor (OXTR) and serotonin transporter (5-HTT) genes associated with observed parenting. *Social Cognitive and Affective Neuroscience*, 3, 128–134.

Bakermans-Kranenburg, M. J., & van Ijzendoorn, M. H. (2011). Differential susceptibility to rearing environment depending on dopamine-related genes: New evidence and a meta-analysis. *Development and Psychopathology*, 23, 39–52.

Bakermans-Kranenburg, M. J., & van IJzendoorn, M. H. (2014). A sociability gene? Meta analysis of oxytocin receptor genotype effects in humans. *Psychiatric Genetics*, 24, 45–51.

Briley, D. A., & Tucker-Drob, E. M. (2017). Comparing the developmental genetics of cognition and personality over the life span. *Journal of Personality*, 85, 51–64.

Carver, C. S., Johnson, S. L., & Joormann, J. (2008). Serotonergic function, two-mode models of self-regulation, and vulnerability to depression: What depression has in common with impulsive aggression. *Psychological Bulletin*, 134, 912–943.

Caspi, A., Hariri, A. R., Holmes, A., Uher, R., & Moffitt, T. E. (2010). Genetic sensitivity to the environment: The case of the serotonin transporter gene and its implications for studying complex diseases and traits. *American Journal of Psychiatry*, 8, 398–416.

Caspi, A., McClay, J., Moffitt, T. E., Mill, J., Martin, J., Craig, I. W., . . . Poulton, R. (2002). Role of genotype in the cycle of violence in maltreated children. *Science*, 297, 851–854.

Cherkas, L. F., Oelsner, E. C., Mak, Y. T., Valdes, A., & Spector, T. D. (2004). Genetic influences on female infidelity and number of sexual partners in humans: A linkage and association study of the role of the vasopressin receptor gene (AVPR1A). *Twin Research*, *7*, 649–658.

Cloninger, C. R., Przybeck, T. R., & Svrakic, D. M. (1991). The tridimensional personality questionnaire: US normative data. *Psychological Reports*, *69*, 1047–1057.

Comings, D. E., Gade-Andavolu, R., Gonzalez, N., Wu, S., Muhleman, D., Blake, H., . . . MacMurray, J. P. (2000). A multivariate analysis of 59 candidate genes in personality traits: The temperament and character inventory. *Clinical Genetics*, *58*, 375–385.

Conway, C. C., Slavich, G. M., & Hammen, C. (2014). Daily stress reactivity and serotonin transporter gene (5-HTTLPR) variation: Internalizing responses to everyday stress as a possible transdiagnostic phenotype. *Biology of Mood & Anxiety Disorders*, *4*, 2.

Duncan, L. E., & Keller, M. C. (2011). A critical review of the first 10 years of candidate gene-by-environment interaction research in psychiatry. *American Journal of Psychiatry*, *168*, 1041–1049.

Ebstein, R. P., Knafo, A., Mankuta, D., Chew, S. H., & San Lai, P. (2012). The contributions of oxytocin and vasopressin pathway genes to human behavior. *Hormones and Behavior*, *61*, 359–379.

Falconer, D. S., & MacKay T.F.C. (1996). *Introduction to Quantitative Genetics, Fourth Edition*. Essex, UK: Longmans Green.

Feldman, R., Zagoory-Sharon, O., Weisman, O., Schneiderman, I., Gordon, I., Maoz, R., . . . Ebstein, R. P. (2012). Sensitive parenting is associated with plasma oxytocin and polymorphisms in the OXTR and CD38 genes. *Biological Psychiatry*, *72*, 175–181.

Gillespie, N. A., Cloninger, C. R., Heath, A. C., & Martin, N. G. (2003). The genetic and environmental relationship between Cloninger's dimensions of temperament and character. *Personality and Individual Differences*, *35*, 1931–1946.

Hamer, D. H., Greenberg, B. D., Sabol, S. Z., & Murphy, D. L. (1999). Role of the serotonin transporter gene in temperament and character. *Journal of Personality Disorders*, *13*, 312–328.

Harris, J. R. (1998). *The Nurture Assumption: Why children turn out the way they do*. New York: Simon and Schuster.

Insel, T. R., & Shapiro, L. E. (1992). Oxytocin receptor distribution reflects social organization in monogamous and polygamous voles. *Proceedings of the National Academy of Sciences of the United States of America*, *89*, 5981–5985.

Israel, S., Lerer, E., Shalev, I., Uzefovsky, F., Riebold, M., Laiba, E., . . . Ebstein, R. P. (2009). The oxytocin receptor (OXTR) contributes to prosocial fund allocations in the dictator game and the social value orientations task. *PLOS ONE*, *4*, e5535.

Karg, K., Burmeister, M., Shedden, K., & Sen, S. (2011). The serotonin transporter promoter variant (5-HTTLPR), stress, and depression meta-analysis revisited: Evidence of genetic moderation. *Archives of General Psychiatry*, *68*, 444–454.

Kendler, K. S. (1996). Parenting: A genetic-epidemiologic perspective. *American Journal of Psychiatry*, *153*, 11–20.

Kendler, K. S., & Neale, M. C. (2010). Endophenotype: A conceptual analysis. *Molecular Psychiatry*, *15*, 789–797.

Knafo, A., Israel, S., Darvasi, A., Bachner-Melman, R., Uzefovsky, F., Cohen, L., . . . Nemanov, L. (2008a). Individual differences in allocation of funds in the dictator game associated with length of the arginine vasopressin 1a receptor RS3 promoter region and correlation between RS3 length and hippocampal mRNA. *Genes, Brain and Behavior*, *7*, 266–275.

Knafo, A., Israel, S., & Ebstein, R. P. (2011). Heritability of children's prosocial behavior and differential susceptibility to parenting by variation in the dopamine receptor D4 gene. *Development and Psychopathology*, *23*, 53–67.

Knafo, A., Zahn-Waxler, C., Van Hulle, C., Robinson, J. L., & Rhee, S. H. (2008b). The developmental origins of a disposition toward empathy: Genetic and environmental contributions. *Emotion*, *8*, 737–752.

Knafo-Noam, A., Uzefovsky, F., Israel, S., Davidov, M., & Zahn-Waxler, C. (2015). The prosocial personality and its facets: Genetic and environmental architecture of mother-reported behavior of 7-year-old twins. *Frontiers in Psychology*, *6*, 112.

Koenig, L. B., McGue, M., Krueger, R. F., & Bouchard, T. J. (2007). Religiousness, antisocial behavior, and altruism: Genetic and environmental mediation. *Journal of Personality*, *75*, 265–290.

Krueger, F., Parasuraman, R., Iyengar, V., Thomburg, M., Weel, J., Lin, M., . . . Lipsky, R. H. (2012). Oxytocin receptor genetic variation promotes human trust behavior. *Frontiers in Human Neuroscience*, *6*, 66.

Krueger, R. F., Hicks, B. M., & McGue, M. (2001). Altruism and antisocial behavior: Independent tendencies, unique personality correlates, distinct etiologies. *Psychological Science*, *12*, 397–402.

Lackner, C., Sabbagh, M. A., Hallinan, E., Liu, X., & Holden, J. J. (2012). Dopamine receptor D4 gene variation predicts preschoolers' developing theory of mind. *Developmental Science*, *15*, 272–280.

Laursen, H. R., Siebner, H. R., Haren, T., Madsen, K., Grønlund, R., Hulme, O., & Henningsson, S. (2014). Variation in the oxytocin receptor gene is associated with behavioral and neural correlates of empathic accuracy. *Frontiers in Behavioral Neuroscience*, *8*, 423.

Lesch, K. P., Bengel, D., Heils, A., Sabol, S. Z., Greenberg, B. D., Petri, S., . . . Murphy, D. L. (1996). Association of anxiety-related traits with a polymorphism in the serotonin transporter gene regulatory region. *Science*, *274*, 1527–1531.

Losoya, S. H., Callor, S., Rowe, D. C., & Goldsmith, H. H. (1997). Origins of familial similarity in parenting: A study of twins and adoptive siblings. *Developmental Psychology*, *33*, 1012–1023.

Marsh, A. A., Crowe, S. L., Henry, H. Y., Gorodetsky, E. K., Goldman, D., & Blair, R. J. R. (2011). Serotonin transporter genotype (5-HTTLPR) predicts utilitarian moral judgments. *PLOS ONE*, *6*, e25148.

Matthews, K. A., Batson, C. D., Horn, J., & Rosenman, R. H. (1981). "Principles in his nature which interest him in the fortune of others . . . ": The heritability of empathic concern for others. *Journal of Personality*, *49*, 237–247.

Pedersen, O. B., Axel, S., Rostgaard, K., Erikstrup, C., Edgren, G., Nielsen, K. R., . . . Hjalgrim, H. (2015). The heritability of blood donation: A populationbased nationwide twin study. *Transfusion*, *55*, 2169–2174.

Pełka-Wysiecka, J., Zieztek, J., Grzywacz, A., Kucharska-Mazur, J., Bienkowski, A., & Samochowiec, J. (2012). Association of genetic polymorphisms with personality profile in individuals without psychiatric disorders. *Biological Psychiatry*, *39*, 40–46.

Plomin, R., & Deary, I. J. (2015). Genetics and intelligence differences: Five special findings. *Molecular Psychiatry*, *20*, 98–108.

Plomin, R., DeFries, J. C., Knopik, V. S., & Neiderhiser, J. M. (2016). Top 10 replicated findings from behavioral genetics. *Perspectives on Psychological Science*, *11*, 3–23.

Poulin, M. J., Holman, E. A., & Buffone, A. (2012). The neurogenetics of nice receptor genes for oxytocin and vasopressin interact with threat to predict prosocial behavior. *Psychological Science, 23*, 446–452.

Reuter, M., Frenzel, C., Walter, N. T., Markett, S., & Montag, C. (2011). Investigating the genetic basis of altruism: The role of the COMT Val158Met polymorphism. *Social Cognitive and Affective Neuroscience, 6*, 662–668.

Rice, F., Harold, G. T., & Thapar, A. (2002). Assessing the effects of age, sex and shared environment on the genetic aetiology of depression in childhood and adolescence. *Journal of Child Psychology and Psychiatry, 43*, 1039–1051.

Riem, M. M., Pieper, S., Out, D., Bakermans-Kranenburg, M. J., & van IJzendoorn, M. H. (2011). Oxytocin receptor gene and depressive symptoms associated with physiological reactivity to infant crying. *Social Cognitive and Affective Neuroscience, 6*, 294–300.

Risch, N., Herrell, R., Lehner, T., Liang, K. Y., Eaves, L., Hoh, J., . . . Merikangas, K. R. (2009). Interaction between the serotonin transporter gene (5-HTTLPR), stressful life events, and risk of depression: A meta-analysis. *Journal of the American Medical Association, 301*, 2462–2471.

Rodrigues, S. M., Saslow, L. R., Garcia, N., John, O. P., & Keltner, D. (2009). Oxytocin receptor genetic variation relates to empathy and stress reactivity in humans. *Proceedings of the National Academy of Sciences of the United States of America, 106*, 21437–21441.

Rushton, J. P. (2004). Genetic and environmental contributions to pro-social attitudes: A twin study of social responsibility. *Proceedings of the Royal Society of London B: Biological Sciences, 271*, 2583–2585.

Rushton, J. P., Chrisjohn, R. D., & Fekken, G. C. (1981). The altruistic personality and the self report altruism scale. *Personality and Individual Differences, 2*, 293–302.

Rushton, J. P., Fulker, D. W., Neale, M. C., Nias, D. K., & Eysenck, H. J. (1986). Altruism and aggression: The heritability of individual differences. *Journal of Personality and Social Psychology, 50*, 1192–1198.

Scarr, S., & McCartney, K. (1983). How people make their own environments: A theory of genotype greater than environment effects. *Child Development, 54*, 424–435.

Schneiderman, I., Kanat-Maymon, Y., Ebstein, R. P., & Feldman, R. (2014). Cumulative risk on the oxytocin receptor gene (OXTR) underpins empathic communication difficulties at the first stages of romantic love. *Social Cognitive and Affective Neuroscience, 9*, 1524–1529.

Scourfield, J., John, B., Martin, N., & McGuffin, P. (2004). The development of prosocial behaviour in children and adolescents: A twin study. *Journal of Child Psychology and Psychiatry, 45*, 927–935.

Slavich, G. M., & Cole, S. W. (2013). The emerging field of human social genomics. *Clinical Psychological Science, 1*, 331–348.

Slavich, G. M., & Irwin, M. R. (2014). From stress to inflammation and major depressive disorder: A social signal transduction theory of depression. *Psychological Bulletin, 140*, 774–815.

Smith, K. E., Porges, E. C., Norman, G. J., Connelly, J. J., & Decety, J. (2014). Oxytocin receptor gene variation predicts empathic concern and autonomic arousal while perceiving harm to others. *Social Neuroscience, 9*, 1–9.

Son, J., & Wilson, J. (2010). Genetic variation in volunteerism. *The Sociological Quarterly, 51*, 46–64.

Striepens, N., Kendrick, K. M., Maier, W., & Hurlemann, R. (2011). Prosocial effects of oxytocin and clinical evidence for its therapeutic potential. *Frontiers in Neuroendocrinology*, *32*, 426–450.

Tabak, B. A., Meyer, M. L., Castle, E., Dutcher, J. M., Irwin, M. R., Han, J. H., . . . Eisenberger, N. I. (2015). Vasopressin, but not oxytocin, increases empathic concern among individuals who received higher levels of paternal warmth: A randomized controlled trial. *Psychoneuroendocrinology*, *51*, 253–261.

Tost, H., Kolachana, B., Hakimi, S., Lemaitre, H., Verchinski, B. A., Mattay, V. S., . . . Meyer Lindenberg, A. (2010). A common allele in the oxytocin receptor gene (OXTR) impacts prosocial temperament and human hypothalamic-limbic structure and function. *Proceedings of the National Academy of Sciences*, *107*, 13936–13941.

Turkheimer, E. (2000). Three laws of behavior genetics and what they mean. *Current Directions in Psychological Science*, *9*, 160–164.

Uzefovsky, F., Shalev, I., Israel, S., Edelman, S., Raz, Y., Mankuta, D., . . . Ebstein, R. P. (2015). Oxytocin receptor and vasopressin receptor 1a genes are respectively associated with emotional and cognitive empathy. *Hormones and Behavior*, *67*, 60–65.

Uzefovsky, F., Shalev, I., Israel, S., Edelman, S., Raz, Y., Perach-Barzilay, N., . . . Ebstein, R. P. (2014). The Dopamine D4 receptor gene shows a gender-sensitive association with cognitive empathy: Evidence from two independent samples. *Emotion*, *14*, 712–721.

Verhagen, M., Engels, R., & Van Roekel E. (2014). The oxytocin receptor gene (OXTR) and gazing behavior during social interaction: An observational study in young adults. *Open Journal of Depression*, *3*, 136–146.

Walter, N. T., Montag, C., Markett, S., Felten, A., Voigt, G., & Reuter, M. (2012). Ignorance is no excuse: Moral judgments are influenced by a genetic variation on the oxytocin receptor gene. *Brain and Cognition*, *78*, 268–273.

Weisman, O., Pelphrey, K. A., Leckman, J. F., Feldman, R., Lu, Y., Chong, A., . . . Ebstein, R. P. (2015). The association between 2D: 4D ratio and cognitive empathy is contingent on a common polymorphism in the oxytocin receptor gene (OXTR rs53576). *Psychoneuroendocrinology*, *58*, 23–32.

Wu, N., & Su, Y. (2015). Oxytocin receptor gene relates to theory of mind and prosocial behavior in children. *Journal of Cognition and Development*, *16*, 302–313.

Zahn-Waxler, C., Robinson, J. L., & Emde, R. N. (1992). The development of empathy in twins. *Developmental Psychology*, *28*, 1038–1047.

Zietsch, B. P., Westberg, L., Santtila, P., & Jern, P. (2015). Genetic analysis of human extrapair mating: Heritability, between-sex correlation, and receptor genes for vasopressin and oxytocin. *Evolution and Human Behavior*, *36*, 130–136.

Part III

Compassion and relationships

Chapter 10

Evolution, child raising, and compassionate morality

Darcia Narvaez

Introduction

Compassion has an evolutionary history that involves the development of caring (Gilbert 2015; Chapter 1, this volume). The focus of most scholarship on compassion is adults and adulthood, yet according to what will be discussed here, we should be paying attention to the effects of early life experience on its development (see Gilbert, 2009, 2014; Mikulincer & Shaver, Chapter 11, this volume). Moreover, a human-centric compassion is incomplete. Compassion must also be directed to more-than-human life. In fact, this inclusivity is a part of humanity's ecological inheritance of cooperation, but which requires the evolved developmental niche or nest (EDN) to develop properly. With the EDN humans develop an organic morality, relational attunement with the natural world, grounding ego-self in common self, the whole of life.

The setting

Although many Western scholars and media journalists assume human nature to be naturally selfish and aggressive, following Hobbes and Thucydides, this is an unusual assumption in the history of human societies (where most presume divine origins and cooperative natures after childhood; Sahlins, 2008). What is misunderstood by those holding the Hobbesian view is that much of human personality is epigenetic (see Conway & Slavich, Chapter 9, this volume). In fact, child development is a rapidly shifting epigenetic, plastic undertaking that arises from the interaction among such things as built-in basic needs, cultural press on parents and their caregiving skills, and the ongoing emergent characteristics and maturational schedule of the child. Children develop as if in a 3D printer: thousands of layers upon layers of multiple systems and subsystems are built moment-by-moment from social and other lived interactions, shaping the person and the trajectory of development. Moreover, for every complex behavior, hierarchical layers of systems have interacting sensitive periods during development (Knudsen, 2004)—if care is inappropriate during these times, the system may never be properly established (e.g. anxiety controls, Meaney, 2001). If early layers are mislaid, through maltreatment or even under-care, the individual will have gaps or misshaped systems (e.g. misreactive stress response, Lupien, McEwen, Gunnar, & Heim, 2009).

I believe under-care happens routinely in "civilized" societies, like the United States, because the culture (shared practices and beliefs) aims to control babies instead of providing for their evolved needs. Such cultures often thwart instinctive caregiving practices through parental shaming and lack of support. The result is the feared and dismaying selfishness and aggression presumed to be genetic (Wrangham & Peterson, 1996). But, as noted, these characteristics too are primarily epigenetic in the broadest sense. Thus, the type of human that these Western scholars consider normal, is *abnormal* in many ways. But what is normal? To determine baselines for normality and potential, we need to understand human heritages (also see Spikins, Chapter 2, this volume).

Evolutionary inheritances

To comprehend how our baselines have shifted, it is important to understand humanity's inherited nature, its setting and its plasticity. We must examine humanity's inheritances, which include not only genetic material but things that are transferred across generations outside of genes (extra-genetic) (Jablonka & Lamb, 2005; Oyama, Griffiths & Gray, 2001). Although there are multiple extra-genetic inheritances, three are mentioned here: cooperation in Nature; the evolved developmental niche; and human biosocial plasticity.

Cooperation in nature

Animal and plant life on the planet are built around layers and layers of cooperation and companionship. Every life form exists in a web of memory from the past and mutual support in the present. Even humans are "symbionts on a symbiotic planet" (Margulis, 1998, p. 5). Humans are alive because their bodies are filled with trillions of bacteria, carrying many more bacterial genes than human genes (Dunn, 2011). Everywhere in the natural world, cooperation is commonplace. For example, forests are a complex "exquisite symbiosis among living tree, living fungus, dead tree, burrowing mammals and even . . . insects of the soil," and the normal biodiversity is adaptive—forests with more mycorrhizal fungi in root systems are better protected from acid rain (Luoma, 1999, pp. 111, 128). Although we may not want to call natural dynamic systems like this compassionate, they do represent what is called mutualism, the ongoing give-and-take-and-give of the natural world (Kropotkin, 2006; Worster, 1994). Human embodiment, from gut to brain, fits cooperatively into the social and natural world.

Species-typical nest

The anthropologist Colin Turnbull (1984) contrasted what he called his spirit-killing British upbringing with the life-enhancing upbringing of the Mbuti, whom he studied. The Mbuti follow the species-typical nest noted around the world among small-band hunter-gatherer societies, the type of society in which the human genus spent 99% of its history. What is the species-typical nest for human young?

First, it must be noted that humans are highly immature at birth and should be in the womb another 9–18 months compared to other animals whose bone growth is complete and are mobile at birth (Trevathan, 2011). As a result many human brain and body systems set their parameters and thresholds *postnatally* (e.g. stress response) in interaction with expected experience. Child-raising practices are notably similar around the world in SBHG societies. Here is the brief list of components of the human nest, what my colleagues and I call the Evolved Developmental Niche:

- *Soothing perinatal experiences* (e.g. no separation from mother; no induced pain).
- *Breastfeeding on request*: nursed frequently (2–3 times/hr initially) for 2–5 years.
- *Affectionate touch*: babies[1] are held, carried and kept nearby virtually all of the time.
- *Responsivity*: baby's needs and interactions warmly responded to; companionship throughout life.
- *Free play*: self-directed free play in natural world with multi-age playmates.
- *Positive social support*: high social embeddedness including being frequently cared for by responsive individuals other than mothers (allomothers such as fathers and grandmothers, in particular).

See the first column in Table 10.1 for a list of common effects. Converging evidence suggests that the species-typical nest provides the type of experiences that a baby's body/brain expects for developing species-typical capacities. Why do the EDN components have such effects?

Human biosocial plasticity

Humans are dynamic systems who are born with many psychobiosocial propensities that are shaped by experience after birth. Humans come from a tree of life where emotion systems are ancient. Capacities to deliberate and think linearly are recent developments in the tree of life. Although many of us may think of ourselves as *thinking creatures* that *feel*, biologically we are *feeling creatures* that *think* (Taylor, 2008, p. 19).

Emotions evolved as "psychobehavioral potentials" whose functions are shaped by experience, and for humans, particularly by caregivers (Panksepp, 1998). The infant and the caregiver's attachment systems provide a mechanism by which the rudimentary nervous system of the infant can be co-constructed by the caregiver. As an "external psychobiological regulator," the caregiver helps shift external into internal regulation, increasing the complexity of maturing brain

Table 10.1 The effects of the evolved development niche on child outcomes

Evolved Developmental Niche (EDN) with samples of general effects[1]	Sample effects on young children's moral development[2]
PERINATAL EXPERIENCES Vaginal childbirth (instead of cesarean section) Baby can initiate breastfeeding and cascade of hormones in mother (Trevathan, 2011)	Empathy, conscience, self-regulation
BREASTFEEDING Immune system, non-depression, intelligence, perception, less cancer and diabetes, all-round better health (USDHHS, 2011)	*Initiation*: conscience, intelligence *Length*: conscience, inhibitory control
TOUCH Growth, self-regulation, genes turned on to control anxiety (not turned on with lack of touch) (Meaney, 2001)	Empathy, self-regulation, conscience, intelligence, relational attunement, (lack of) social opposition, (lack of) social withdrawal
RESPONSIVENESS Calm brain, low stress reactivity, instigates calming hormones (e.g. oxytocin) which in early life significantly affect neurobiological development. Vagus nerve well established (Porges, 2011)	Cooperation, non-depression, non-aggression, self-regulation, relational attunement, (lack of) social opposition, (lack of) social withdrawal
PLAY Self-regulation, social skills, no ADHD (Panksepp, 2007)	Empathy, self-regulation, relational attunement, (lack of) social opposition, (lack of) social withdrawal
POSITIVE SOCIAL SUPPORT Overall child outcomes better (Hrdy, 2009)	Competence, cooperation, non-aggression, intelligence, relational attunement, (lack of) social opposition, (lack of) social withdrawal

Notes
1   For expert reviews and more references, see Narvaez, Panksepp, Schore, & Gleason, 2013; Narvaez, Valentino, Fuentes, McKenna, & Gray, 2014; Narvaez, Braungart-Rieker, Miller, Gettler, & Hastings, 2016.
2   Unless otherwise noted, findings are from our studies: Narvaez, Gleason, Wang, Brooks, Lefever, Cheng, & Centers for the Prevention of Child Neglect, 2013; Narvaez, Wang, Gleason, Cheng, Lefever, & Deng, 2013; Gleason, Narvaez, Cheng, Wang, & Brooks, 2016.

systems as they learn to adaptively regulate interactions between the baby-self and the social environment, particularly the mother (Schore, 2001, p. 202). During prenatal and perinatal life, brain stem neuroendocrine and neuromodulatory systems that govern the HPA axis and regulate the maturation of the neocortex are developing rapidly (Aitken & Trevarthen, 1997; Bear & Singer, 1986; Durig & Hornung, 2000; Schore, 1994; Osterheld-Haas, Van der Loos, & Hornung, 1994). Under good care conditions, by four months postnatally the connections between the amygdala and sites mediating motor activity and distress have become mature

(Weber, Watts, & Richardson, 2003). Before that time, reactions to unfamiliar events are not patterned clearly, though loud noises can trigger fear.[2]

Daniel Stern (1993, 1999) described the delicate matchings of expression between mother and infant as an attunement of *vitality contours*, the "essential musicality of intuitive parenting communication," signaled through modulations of the intensity of movement (Papousek, 1996, p. 65). Their relationship is dynamic, guided by affection and disaffection, with displays and evaluations of shared purposes and interests. This rich, positive social experience results in the child's secure attachment and capacities for mutual responsiveness and reciprocity, social intersubjectivity (self to self), dyadic meaning making and repair (Tronick & Beeghly, 2011). One can say that *what babies practice is what they become.* When raised in a species-typical manner, babies develop a deep sense of reciprocity with others which facilitates moral functioning.

Moral development

Early life is an apprenticeship for social and cognitive development. Thus, when babies are treated with compassion and interact with empathic, emotionally present others, they are practising the dances of empathy and prosociality while their brains are sensitive to establishing the neurobiological underpinnings of those systems which will be used throughout life (e.g. Carter, 2003; Porges, 2011; oxytocin system; vagal tone). In the EDN, the baby practises the precursors of compassion: presence, empathy, intersubjectivity, reciprocity, perspective taking, playful co-construction of narratives, and reverence—the *beholding* of the other. Babies construct the foundations for expertise (knowhow) in sociality, using their emotion and cognitive systems to get along with others with agility and nuance (Aristotle's "social fittedness"). They learn to "resonate" with the treatment they receive and the varying intersubjectivities they encounter and co-construct in social relations. The child builds a biosocial personal grammar for the social life that will underlie all future relations (Narvaez, 2011; Stern, 2010; Trevarthen & Delafield-Butt, 2013).

Early experiences shape different life narratives (Schore, 1994). Personal guiding narratives are embedded in biology. Every organism has a story grammar written into its being, formed by early experience: patterns of need-response-outcome. These are biologically engraved and difficult to change later. If the need-response-outcome patterns become frequent and predictable, the child takes the internalized narrative into his/her personality. Thus, a baby learns its habitual life-guiding social narratives from caregiver treatment (called "internal working models" by Bowlby, 1951). When the baby's needs are trusted and satisfied, guided gently towards calm prosociality, the child develops a sense of trust in self and the world. The internal impulses are reliable; the world is worthy of trust; I can relax. Warmly responsive caregivers, providing companionship care, gently shape the impulses towards self-control and prosociality. So for example, as demonstrated in SBHG, when surges for autonomy occur in toddlerhood, the child is not discouraged but redirected away from aggression, supported in their prosocial self-development (Hewlett & Lamb, 2005; Narvaez, 2014). There is no punishment or coercion. Instead, the child learns to move *with* community values because mother and caregivers embrace the child's needs without complaint. The EDN, whose effects we have noted, provides what we might call a *Compassion Acquisition Support System*. Under conditions of the EDN, human nature naturally grows in cooperative ways.

Children raised in the evolved nest tend to show the characteristics of Darwin's (1871) moral sense: social pleasure, empathy, concern for the opinion of others and habit development in response. These characteristics are less apparent in societies where the EDN is degraded (Narvaez, in press). Adults in EDN-providing societies also demonstrate Darwin's moral sense and are generous, egalitarian, honest, and cooperative (for a review see Narvaez, 2013). They demonstrate flexible relational attunement, which emerges from the layers of sociality capacities built from the beginning of life. I call this an engagement ethic (Narvaez, 2008, 2014, 2016).

Engagement involves the ability to employ emotions well—emotional intelligence—such as the ability to recognize, regulate, and express emotions effectively (Brackett & Mayer, 2003). But more than that, an active engagement ethic involves relational commitment and attunement to the other in the present moment. There is a sense of fellow feeling that encompasses the same concern for the other as for self in terms of justice, care, mercy, and reciprocity. Me + me becomes we. Positive social emotions are activated, including empathy/sympathy, generosity, and charity. An engagement ethic means that the welfare of the other who is present is taken equally into account when action is taken. It's a no-self approach to social relations as a shape-shifting social self is newly co-constructed with the other in a responsive dance. These capacities are mostly tacit and shaped by experience during sensitive periods (e.g. early life, adolescence, emerging adulthood).

EDN provision also influences higher-order capacities (abstract thought, imagining possibilities) which build on these relational capacities to bring about a communal imagination. Communal imagination allows one to move agilely within appropriately representational processing and content spaces, integrating controlled-automatic and specific-abstract aspects appropriate for the situation (the iCASA framework; Koutstaal, 2013). Communal imagination emphasizes the common good (Daly & Cobb, 1994) and ecological interdependence (Worster, 1994), fitting with notions of universalism, tolerance and democratic processes. Communal imagination fosters the collective coordination of building moral institutions (Narvaez, 2010).

This is the species-typical story of organic morality, a morality embedded in the tree of life and grown with an acceptance of human animal needs and grounded in earth-based living systems. This orientation of providing for children's built-in needs and living with the earth is still apparent in some traditional societies (e.g. Bolin, 2010; Mendoza, 2016). Species-typical personalities lead to compassionate and communally imaginative morality.

Although the discussion to this point emphasizes individual capacities, humans are social creatures throughout life. Human nature and personality are malleable. They can shift based on the choices individuals and communities make. The brain/mind requires appropriate environmental support for its optimal development until adult maturity (around age 30). After that it still requires positive, supportive social experience that keeps the mind attuned to the community and the brain awash in prosocial hormones (see Colonnello, Petrocchi, & Markus, Chapter 6, this volume). Otherwise, morality can go awry, as evidenced in faulty cognitive or affective processes, resulting in violence to self or others.

But what happens when upbringing is species atypical? Not only neurobiology is affected but also sociality. Moral development and moral functioning go awry when the EDN is degraded. The deep moral core of humanity's heritages may never develop.

Undercare

Growing a child with a degraded nest is like growing a plant in the closet. The plant will be weak and easily stressed. But of course it is worse because of the complex epigenetic factors that are scheduled to occur in a human's early life. Hofer (1987, 1994; Polan & Hofer, 1999) tested eight physiological systems in rat infants and found that the presence of the mother coordinated each one, corroborating Lewis and colleagues' (2000) point that the mammalian nervous system cannot build itself alone but requires the caregiver's "hidden" regulation of infant development across sensory systems (e.g. olfactory, tactile). Without appropriate care in early life, mammals grow up with erratic biological systems that are easily thrown into disarray when unpredictable things happen (Meaney, 2001). Lacking limbic regulation, mammals can slip toward physiological chaos. Indeed, mammalian maternal touch can lower an infant's heart rate during a distressing experience, which trains the infant's systems for adaptive responding to stress (Calkins & Hill, 2007). Isolated monkeys may survive isolation from caregivers, but not very well. Their systems become lastingly discoordinated, preventing them from socializing (and reproducing). Abused and neglected children develop in disorganized ways similar to those of isolated monkeys. In both cases, "interlocking neural barriers to violence do not self-assemble," resulting in "a limbically damaged" being that is "deadly"; severe neglect results in "a functionally reptilian organism armed with the cunning of the neocortical brain" (T. Lewis et al., 2000, p. 218). These are extreme cases, but how much damage is caused by an unloving early life? We can all tell the difference between a child who is well loved and one who is not. Knowledgeable loving care provides extensive experiences of intersubjectivity, critical for establishing conscious and unconscious capacities for relational communication and connection. Experiential deficits may damage capacities for empathizing and sympathizing. With poor early care, self-regulatory mechanisms in multiple systems may not develop properly. When overactivated for any period of time, stress hormones melt synapses, change gene expression (Kang et al., 2012), and undermine long term physiological and mental health, especially when this occurs during the rapid development in early childhood. As a result, the stress response systems can be faulty for life.

Triune ethics

Triune ethics meta-theory (TEM; Narvaez, 2008, 2014, 2016) describes humanity's moral heritages and the ways morality develops in species-typical and species-atypical circumstances. Our human moral heritages include engagement and communal imagination but toxic stress in early life can undermine their development. A child misdeveloped or undercared for develops stress reactivity. The nature of the stress response is that when it is triggered, there is a shift in blood flow away from higher-order thinking and toward mobilization for flight-fight-freeze-faint. The survival systems of the brain take over, impairing complex, nuanced thinking (like perspective taking) and undermining openness to others. Too much personal distress can promote social panic, social withdrawal, internalizing, or externalizing, undermining sociality. Contrary to relational attunement, these represent enhanced survival systems. When guiding behavior they become an ethic and can become dispositional protectionist ethics.

We study aspects of the EDN in my lab, relating its characteristics to well-being and morality in children and adults.[3] By investigating the precursors of these TET orientations, we hoped to illuminate the relation between EDN and moral capacities. The right column of Table 10.1 shows some of our findings, demonstrating that characteristics of the EDN are related to children's moral development, from self-regulation to empathy. It is not surprising that sociomoral functioning depends on biological functioning because the development of a well-functioning neurobiology means that social systems also function flexibly in response to changing situations. Humans are embodied creatures who are biosocially constructed by experience, especially in early life when the child is highly immature but dynamically flexible.

Culture

Our indigenous cousins, and most societies in human existence, have high expectations for virtue—skills and motivations for living well with others in ways that promote flourishing. But their virtue is inclusive of the local landscape, of other-than-humans—an ecological mindfulness that considers humans to be one member of a biodiverse, mutually related community. Ecological virtue requires embeddedness in one's landscape and the development of *ecological attachment*. It represents moving *with* rather than *against* Nature. Within the hunter-gatherer worldview, "characteristics of [individuals] . . . are not so much expressed as *generated* in the course of development, arising as emergent properties of the fields of relationship set up through their presence and activity within a particular environment" (Ingold, 2011, p. 4). That is, development of the self is "understood relationally as a *movement along a way of life*, conceived not as the enactment of a corpus of rules and principles (or a 'culture') received from predecessors, but as the negotiation of a path through the world" (p. 146). Civilized cultures that divorce themselves from ecological systems and the more-than-human world have forgotten this way of being.

The ecological mindfulness that our indigenous cousins display resembles Jill Bolke Taylor's description of the right-hemisphere dominance she experienced after having a stroke in her left cerebral hemisphere: "Our right hemisphere is designed to remember things as they relate to one another. Borders between specific entities are softened, and complex mental collages can be recalled in their entirety as combinations of images, kinesthetic, and physiology. To the right mind, no time exists other than the present moment, and each moment is vibrant with sensation. . . . the moment of *now* is timeless and abundant . . . The present moment is a time when everything and everyone are connected together as *one*. As a result, our right mind perceives each of us as equal members of the human family. It identifies our similarities and recognizes our relationship with this marvelous planet, which sustains our life. It perceives the big picture, how everything is related, and how we all join together to make up the whole. Our ability to be empathic, to walk in the shoes of another and feel their feelings, is a product of our right frontal cortex" (pp. 30–31). Iain McGilchrist (2009) points out how the Western world has suppressed the wisdom of the right hemisphere and instead is governed by the bureaucratic/scientific mode of the left hemisphere (which prefers static dead things and absolute control). In societies governed by this Western mindset, individual self-control and grounded sociality are underdeveloped and so must rely on external braces throughout life such as ideologies, many of which endanger other humans and particularly the more-than-human world.

Among civilized nations, but especially in the United States, EDN-consistent care has diminished. And the consequences are becoming more and more apparent. Here are a few examples. Measures of attachment preference indicate that insecure attachment is rising in the United States (Konrath, Chopik, Hsing, & O'Brien, 2014) along with single-adult households, suggesting that social capacities and pleasure in sociality are fraying.[4] At the same time empathy is significantly decreasing in college students (Konrath, O'Brien, & Hsing, 2011). This is not a surprise because when a child's developmental trajectory is redirected by lack of the EDN, he or she shifts toward self-protection, orthogonal to the relational attunement that underlies empathy and compassion in the moment (Gleason, Narvaez, Cheng, Wang, & Brooks, 2016). Neocortical capacities for abstraction, planning and imagination are also redirected toward protectionism and away from a communal imagination. Instead, the externalizing force is shaped into a "vicious" imagination of control over others and the internalizing force into a "detached" imagination of relational disengagement.

Virtue is something that seems to have deteriorated in Westernized societies, especially the United States (Derber, 2013), perhaps because of generations of EDN-inconsistent care. Too often, virtue has been narrowed down to anthropocentric, protectionist values. Ecological virtue has been shut out of dominant, civilized cultural narratives, practices, and institutions. Instead, humans consider themselves separate and superior to the rest of Nature (Jensen, 2016).

Regrowing ourselves

Very few of us were raised with a species-typical nest, which means that as adults we have aspects of ourselves to repair. A fundamental aspect of therapy is trying to reawaken or activate the right hemisphere (Siegel, 1999).

Before right hemisphere development can occur, the survival systems must be calmed down and become less reactive. Self-calming techniques such as deep breathing, meditation, and visualization can help. Compassionate mind-training facilitates self-healing (Gilbert, 2009, 2014). Self-compassion therapy fosters kindness towards the self, understanding one's common humanity, and mindful acceptance of painful experience (Neff, 2011).

The second step is to build social relational capacities and enjoyment. When a person is fully enjoying the present moment with others, the right hemisphere can grow new connections. Immersion in fun prosocial group activities, in and collaboration with the natural world, and social expression (e.g. folk dancing, spontaneous play) can be taken up to regrow the right hemisphere and sociality.

The third step is to build communal imagination by repairing compassion for the more-than-human, honoring and respecting natural processes; speaking up with concern for all entities as partners. We can find ways to support a sense of a Common Self even through such simple acts of supporting animals and plants on the land we tend.

Conclusion

From an evolutionary perspective we can see that human relational responsiveness, directed both at humans and other-than-humans, has been key to human adaptation (Narvaez, 2014; Spikins, Chapter 2, this volume).[5] Although such reciprocal responsiveness forms the social patterns of planetary life generally, humans have potential for more deliberate and organizational reciprocity with one another and the more-than-human. But only when properly developed. If one is aiming to develop compassionate people, one must attend to the dynamism that is human development and to humanity's species-typical nest.

Notes

1 Babies refers to children under age 2.5.
2 Kagan and Fox (2006) argue that reactivity is not a *fear* reaction (unless the stimulus is a known danger) but a *surprise* reaction—surprise in response to the unfamiliar. Of course, these reactions can be linked if a child is not helped with self-regulation, so that as an adult the unfamiliar is frightening.

3 Morality refers to the ways we cooperate and get along with one another. Normal moral development includes basic characteristics like self-control and social attunement but also empathy, perspective taking, moral reasoning, and other characteristics.

4 Some say that attachment style "should be" based on cultural needs because parents prepare their children for a particular culture. But then one must argue that misdevelopment from a violent family is good. Misdevelopment is not good for humanity or for the planet.

5 Of course this is true for any earth creature—it must fit into a network of community relations or it will eventually perish if it does not cooperate. Dominant "weed" species eventually die out (modern human culture is categorized this way). In recent history, human culture has trumped biology so that natural selection is undermined and people who are raised to be functionally maladapted are kept alive and reproduce, though in the past they would have died, leading to a host of humans who are not representative of our adapted ancestors.

References

Aitken, K.J., & Trevarthen, C. (1997). Self/other organization in human psychological development. *Development and Psychopathology, 9*, 653–677.

Atwood, J. B. (1999). Early warning and prevention of genocide and crimes against humanity. *Journal of Intergroup Relations, 26*, 33–39.

Bear, M.F., & Singer, W. (1986). Modulation of visual cortical plasticity by acetylcholine and noradrenaline. *Nature, 320*(6058), 172–176.

Bolin, I. (2010). Chillihuani's culture of respect and the circle of courage. *Reclaiming Children and Youth Worldwide, 18*(4), 12–17.

Bowlby, J. (1951). *Maternal Care and Mental Health*. New York: Schocken.

Brackett, M. A., & Mayer, J. D. (2003). Convergent, discriminant, and incremental validity of competing measures of emotional intelligence. *Personality and Social Psychology Bulletin, 29*, 1147–1158.

Bystrova, K., Ivanova, V., Edhborg, M., Matthiesen, A.S., Ransjö-Arvidson, A.B., Mukha medrakhimov, . . . Widström, A.M. (2009). Early contact versus separation: Effects on mother-infant interaction one year later. *Birth, 36*(2), 97–109.

Calkins, S.D., & Hill, A. (2007). Caregiver influences on emerging emotion regulation: Biological and environmental transactions in early development. In J. J. Gross (Ed.), *Handbook of Emotion Regulation* (pp. 229–248). New York: Guilford Press.

Carter, C.S. (2003). Developmental consequences of oxytocin. *Physiology & Behavior, 79*(3), 383–397.

Daly, H.E., & Cobb, J. (1994). *For the Common Good: Redirecting the Economy Toward Community, the Environment, and a Sustainable Future, 2nd Ed.* New York: Beacon Press.

Darwin, C. (1871/1981). *The Descent of Man*. Princeton, NJ: Princeton University Press.

Derber, C. (2013). *Sociopathic Society*. Boulder, CO: Paradigm Press.

Dunn, R. (2011). *The Wild Life of Our Bodies: Predators, Parasites, and Partners That Shape Who We Are Today*. New York: Harper.

Durig, J., & Hornung, J.P. (2000). Neonatal serotonin depletion affects developing and mature mouse cortical neurons. *Neuroreport, 11*(4), 833–837.

Gershoff, E.T., Lansford, J.E., Sexton, H.R., Davis-Kean, P.E., & Sameroff, A.J. (2012). Longitudinal links between spanking and children's externalizing behaviors in a national sample of White, Black, Hispanic, and Asian American families. *Child Development, 83*, 838–843.

Gilbert, P. (2009). *The Compassionate Mind.* Oakland, CA: New Harbinger.

Gilbert, P. (2014). The origins and nature of compassion focused therapy. *British Journal of Clinical Psychology, 53,* 6–41. doi:10.1111/bjc.12043

Gilbert, P. (2015). The evolution and social dynamics of compassion. *Journal of Social & Personality Psychology Compass, 9,* 239–254. doi: 10.1111/spc3.12176

Gleason, T., Narvaez, D., Cheng, A., Wang, L., & Brooks, J. (2016). The relation of nurturing parenting attitudes to flourishing in preschoolers. In D. Narvaez, J. Braungart-Rieker, L. Miller, L. Gettler, & P. Hastings (Eds.), *Contexts for Young Child Flourishing: Evolution, Family and Society* (pp. 166–184). New York: Oxford University Press.

Gottlieb, G. (1991). Experiential canalization of behavioral development: Theory. *Developmental Psychology, 27,* 4–13.

Gross, J. J. (Ed.) (2007). *Handbook of Emotion Regulation.* New York: Guilford.

Hewlett, B. S., & Lamb, M. E. (2005). *Hunter-Gatherer Childhoods: Evolutionary, Developmental and Cultural Perspectives.* New Brunswick, NJ: Aldine.

Hofer, M. (1987). Early social relationships: A psychobiologist's view. *Child Development, 58,* 633–647.

Hofer, M. A. (1994). Hidden regulators in attachment, separation, and loss. In N. A. Fox (Ed.), Emotion regulation: Behavioral and biological considerations. *Monographs of the Society for Research in Child Development, 59,* 192–207.

Hrdy, S. (2009). *Mothers and Others: The Evolutionary Origins of Mutual Understanding.* Cambridge, MA: Belknap Press.

Ingold, T. (2011). *The Perception of the Environment: Essay on Livelihood, Dwelling and Skill.* London: Routledge.

Jablonka, E., & Lamb, M. J. (2005). *Evolution in Four Dimensions: Genetic, Epigenetic, Behavioral, and Symbolic Variation in the History of Life.* Cambridge, MA: MIT Press.

Jensen, D. (2016). *The Myth of Human Supremacy.* New York: Seven Stories Press.

Kagan, J., & Fox, N. A. (2006). Biology, culture, and temperamental biases. In W. Damon & R. M. Lerner (Series Eds.) & N. Eisenberg (Vol. Ed.), *Handbook of Child Psychology, Vol. 3* (pp. 167–225). New York: Wiley.

Kang, H.J., Voleti, B., Hajszan, T., Rajkowska, G., Stockmeier, C. A., Licznerski, P., . . . Duman, R. S. (2012). Decreased expression of synapse-related genes and loss of synapses in major depressive disorder. *Nature Medicine 18*(9), 1413–1417.

Knudsen, E. I. (2004). Sensitive periods in the development of the brain and behavior. *Journal of Cognitive Neuroscience, 16*(8), 1412–1425.

Kochanska, G. (2002). Mutually responsive orientation between mothers and their young children: A context for the early development of conscience. *Current Directions in Psychological Science, 11*(6), 191–195. doi:10.1111/1467-8721.00198

Konrath, S. H., Chopik, W., Hsing, C., & O'Brien, E. H. (2014). Changes in adult attachment styles in American college students over time: A meta-analysis. *Personality and Social Psychology Review, 18*(4), 326–348. doi: 10.1177/1088868314530516

Konrath, S. H., O'Brien, E. H., & Hsing, C. (2011). Changes in dispositional empathy in American college students over time: A meta-analysis. *Personality and Social Psychology Review, 15,* 180–198.

Koutstaal, W. (2013). *The Agile Mind.* New York: Oxford University Press.

Kropotkin, P. (2006). *Mutual Aid: A Factor of Evolution.* Charleston, SC: BiblioBazaar.

Lewis, T., Amini, F., & Lannon, R. (2000). *A General Theory of Love.* New York: Vintage.

Luoma, J.R. (1999). *The Hidden Forest: The Biography of an Ecosystem.* New York: Henry Holt and Co.

Lupien, S. J., McEwen, B. S., Gunnar, M. R., & Heim, C. (2009). Effects of stress throughout the lifespan on the brain, behaviour and cognition. *Nature Reviews Neuroscience*, *10*(6), 434–445. doi:10.1038/nrn2639

McGilchrist, I. (2009). *The Master and His Emissary: The Divided Brain and the Making of the Western World*. New Haven, CT: Yale University Press.

Margulis, L. (1998). *Symbiotic Planet: A New Look at Evolution*. Amherst, MA: Sciencewriters.

Marinoff, L. (2007). *The Middle Way: Finding Happiness in a World of Extremes*. New York, Sterling Publishing.

Meaney, M. J. (2001). Maternal care, gene expression, and the transmission of individual differences in stress reactivity across generations. *Annual Review of Neuroscience*, *24*, 1161–1192.

Mendoza, S.L. (2016). Doing "indigenous" ethnography as a cultural outsider: Lessons from the Four Seasons. *Journal of International and Intercultural Communication*, http://dx.doi.org/10.1080/17513057.2016.1154181

Narvaez, D. (2008). Triune ethics: The neurobiological roots of our multiple moralities. *New Ideas in Psychology*, *26*, 95–119.

Narvaez, D. (2009). Triune ethics theory and moral personality. In D. Narvaez & D.K. Lapsley (Eds.), *Personality, Identity and Character: Explorations in Moral Psychology* (pp. 136–158). New York: Cambridge University Press.

Narvaez, D. (2010). Moral complexity: The fatal attraction of truthiness and the importance of mature moral functioning. *Perspectives on Psychological Science*, *5*(2), 163–181.

Narvaez, D. (2011). The ethics of neurobiological narratives. *Poetics Today*, *32*(1): 81–106.

Narvaez, D. (2013). The 99 Percent—Development and socialization within an evolutionary context: Growing up to become "A good and useful human being." In D. Fry (Ed.), *War, Peace and Human Nature: The Convergence of Evolutionary and Cultural Views* (pp. 643–672). New York: Oxford University Press.

Narvaez, D. (2014). *Neurobiology and the Development of Human Morality: Evolution, Culture and Wisdom*. New York: W.W. Norton.

Narvaez, D. (2016). *Embodied Morality: Protectionism, Engagement and Imagination*. New York: Palgrave Macmillan.

Narvaez, D. (in press). Evolution, early experience and Darwin's moral sense. In R. Joyce (Ed.), *Routledge Handbook of Evolution and Philosophy*. London: Routledge.

Narvaez, D., Braungart-Rieker, J., Miller, L., Gettler, L., & Hastings, P. (Eds.) (2016). *Contexts for Young Child Flourishing: Evolution, Family and Society*. New York: Oxford University Press.

Narvaez, D., Gleason, T., Wang, L., Brooks, J., Lefever, J., Cheng, A., & Centers for the Prevention of Child Neglect (2013a). The Evolved Development Niche: Longitudinal effects of caregiving practices on early childhood psychosocial development. *Early Childhood Research Quarterly*, *28*(4), 759–773. doi: 10.1016/j.ecresq.2013.07.003

Narvaez, D., Panksepp, J., Schore, A., & Gleason, T. (Eds.) (2013b). *Evolution, Early Experience and Human Development: From Research to Practice and Policy*. New York: Oxford University Press.

Narvaez, D., Valentino, K., Fuentes, A., McKenna, J., & Gray, P. (Eds.) (2014). *Ancestral Landscapes in Human Evolution: Culture, Childrearing and Social Wellbeing*. New York: Oxford University Press.

Narvaez, D., Wang, L., Gleason, T., Cheng, A., Lefever, J., & Deng, L. (2013). The Evolved Developmental Niche and sociomoral outcomes in Chinese three-year-olds. *European Journal of Developmental Psychology*, *10*(2), 106–127.

Neff, K. (2011). *Self-compassion*. New York: William Morrow.

Osterheld-Haas, M. C., Van der Loos, H., & Hornung, J. P. (1994). Monoaminergic afferents to cortex modulate structural plasticity in the barrelfield of the mouse. *Brain Research. Developmental Brain Research, 77*(2), 189–202.

Oyama, S., Griffiths, P.E., & Gray, R.D. (2001). *Cycles of Contingency: Developmental Systems and Evolution*. Cambridge, MA: MIT Press.

Panksepp, J. (1998). *Affective Neuroscience: The Foundations of Human and Animal Emotions*. New York: Oxford University Press.

Papousek, M. (1996). Intuitive parenting: A hidden source of musical stimulation in infancy. In I. Deliege & J. Sloboda (Eds.), *Musical Beginnings: Origins and Development of Musical Competence* (pp. 88–112). Oxford: Oxford University Press.

Polan, H.J., & Hofer, M.A. (1999). Psychobiological origins of infants' attachment and separation responses. In J. Cassidy & P. Shaver (Eds.), *Handbook of Attachment: Theory, Research, and Clinical Applications* (pp. 162–180). New York: Guilford.

Porges, S. W. (2011). *The Polyvagal Theory: Neurophsiologial Foundations of Emotions, Attachment, Communication, Self-Regulation*. New York: W.W. Norton.

Sahlins, M. (2008). *The Western Illusion of Human Nature*. Chicago, IL: Prickly Paradigm Press.

Schore, A. (1994). *Affect Regulation*. Hillsdale, NJ: Erlbaum.

Schore, A. N. (2001). Effects of a secure attachment relationship on right brain development, affect regulation, and infant mental health. *Infant Mental Health Journal, 22*(1–2), 7–66.

Siegel, D. (1999). The *Developing Mind: How Relationships and the Brain Interact To Shape Who We Are*. New York: Guilford Press.

Stern, D. N. (1993). The role of feelings for an interpersonal self. In U. Neisser (Ed.), *The Perceived Self: Ecological and Interpersonal Sources of Self-knowledge* (pp. 205–215). New York: Cambridge University Press.

Stern, D. N. (1999). Vitality contours: The temporal contour of feelings as a basic unit for constructing the infant's social experience. In Rochat, P. (Ed.), *Early Social Cognition: Understanding Others in the First Months of Life* (pp. 67–90). Mahwah, NJ: Erlbaum.

Stern, D. N. (2010). *Forms of Vitality: Exploring Dynamic Experience in Psychology, the Arts, Psychotheraphy, and Development*. Oxford: Oxford University Press.

Taylor, J. B. (2008). *My Stroke of Insight*. New York: Viking.

Trevarthen, C., & Delafield-Butt, J. T. (2013). Biology of shared experience and language development: Regulations for the inter-subjective life of narratives. In M. Legerstee, D. Haley, & M. Bornstein (Eds.), *The Infant Mind: Origins of The Social Brain* (pp. 167–199). New York: Guilford Press.

Trevathan, W. R. (2011). *Human Birth: An Evolutionary Perspective, 2nd ed.* New York: Aldine de Gruyter.

Tronick, E., & Beeghly, M. (2011). Infants' meaning-making and the development of mental health problems. *American Psychologist, 66*(2), 107–119.

Turnbull, C. (1984). *The Human Cycle*. New York: Simon and Schuster.

Weber, M., Watts, N., & Richardson, R. (2003). High illumination levels potentiate the acoustic startle response in preweanling rats. *Behavioral Neuroscience, 117*(6), 1458–1462.

Worster, D. (1994). *Nature's Economy: A History of Ecological Ideas*. New York: Cambridge University Press.

Wrangham, R. W., & Peterson, D. (1996). *Demonic Males: Apes and The Origins of Human Violence*. Boston, MA: Houghton, Mifflin and Company.

Chapter 11

An attachment perspective on compassion and altruism

Mario Mikulincer and Philip R. Shaver

Introduction

For centuries, compassion has been a central virtue in all major religious traditions. It has also appeared – sometimes indirectly – in the literature on social psychology under headings such as empathy, altruism, and prosocial behavior (see Gilbert, Chapter 1, this volume). In psychotherapy, compassion has been viewed as crucial, but again, often under different names – empathy, unconditional positive regard, containment or holding, client-therapist rapport, and working alliance attachment-informed focused therapy (Gilbert, 2010, 2014). Compassion appears, partially embedded, in the extensive literature on good parenting, under headings such as availability, sensitivity, and responsiveness. In recent years compassion has become visible in its own right, partly because of the growing emphasis in educated circles on Buddhism, which highlights compassion (Dalai Lama, 2002), and partly because of the tendency for compassion to wear thin in cases of "compassion fatigue" (e.g. Pardess, Mikulincer, Dekel, & Shaver, 2014).

When considering compassion from the standpoint of attachment theory (Bowlby, 1982; Cassidy & Shaver, 2016), the theoretical framework in which our own research is conducted (see Mikulincer & Shaver, 2016, for an overview), compassion is associated with what Bowlby called the "caregiving behavioral system" – an innate behavioral system in parents and other caregivers that responds to the needs of dependent others, especially (but not limited to) children. This behavioral system is thought to have evolved mainly to complement the "attachment behavioral system," which governs people's (especially young children's) emotional attachments to their caregivers (Gilbert 1989; Mikulincer & Shaver, 2016).

Much of the research based on extensions of Bowlby's child-oriented theory into adolescence and adulthood focuses on attachment, and individual differences in attachment, in the context of peer relationships, including romantic relationships. In recent years, however, increasing attention has been given to caregiving, and to individual differences in caregiving, including caregiving that extends well beyond close personal relationships. In particular, we have found that being secure with respect to attachment – either dispositionally secure or momentarily secure because of experimental interventions – is associated with empathy and willingness to help others (see Mikulincer & Shaver, 2016, for a review).

The purpose of the present chapter is to summarize what we have learned about the two behavioral systems that govern support seeking and support provision, the attachment and caregiving systems. We begin this chapter by explaining the behavioral system construct in more detail and showing how individual differences in a person's attachment system affect the functioning of the caregiving system. We then review adult attachment studies that show how individual differences in attachment orientations explain variations in compassion for, and caregiving to, needy relationship partners (e.g. one's own children, aging parents, spouses). Finally, we review empirical evidence that extends the study of attachment-caregiving links to global prosocial tendencies, the provision of help to strangers in distress, and the phenomenon of compassion fatigue in clinical settings.

A behavioral systems perspective on attachment and caregiving

In explaining human behavior, Bowlby (1982) borrowed from ethology the concept of *behavioral system*, a species-universal neural program that organizes an individual's behavior in ways that increase the likelihood of survival and reproductive success. Each behavioral system is organized around a particular goal (e.g. attaining a sense of security, providing support to a needy other) and includes a set of interchangeable, functionally equivalent behaviors that constitute the *primary strategy* of the system for attaining its goal (e.g. proximity seeking, empathically understanding another person's needs). These behaviors are automatically activated by stimuli or situations that make a particular goal salient (e.g. a signal of danger) and terminated by other stimuli or outcomes that signal attainment of the desired goal.

Bowlby (1973) believed that although behavioral systems are innate, experience shapes their parameters and strategies in various ways, resulting in systematic individual differences. According to Bowlby, the residues of such experiences are stored in the form of mental representations, or *working models of self and others*, that guide future attempts to attain a behavioral system's goal. With repeated use, these models become automatic and are important sources of within-person continuity in behavioral system functioning throughout development.

The attachment behavioral system

According to Bowlby (1982), the biological function of the attachment system is to protect a person from danger by ensuring that he or she maintains proximity to loving and supportive others (*attachment figures*). The proximal goal of the system is to attain a subjective sense of security (confidence that one is competent and lovable and that others will be responsive and supportive when needed), which normally terminates the system's activation. The goal of attaining security is made salient by perceived threats and dangers, which drive people to seek actual or symbolic proximity to attachment figures. During infancy, proximity seeking involves nonverbal expressions of need, such as crying and pleading, and locomotor behaviors (crawling, toddling) aimed at reestablishing and maintaining proximity to a caregiver (Ainsworth, 1991). In adulthood, this attachment strategy also includes many other methods of establishing contact (e.g. talking directly to or phoning an attachment figure) as well as activating soothing, comforting mental representations of attachment figures or even self-representations associated with these figures (e.g. Mikulincer, Gillath, & Shaver, 2002; Mikulincer & Shaver, 2004).

An abiding inner sense of attachment security (based on actual experiences) promotes general faith in other people's good will; a sense of being loved, esteemed, understood, and accepted by relationship partners; and optimistic beliefs about one's ability to handle challenges, frustration, and distress. Bowlby (1988) considered attachment security to be a mainstay of mental health and social adjustment throughout life. A host of cross-sectional and longitudinal studies strongly support this view (see Mikulincer & Shaver, 2016, for reviews).

However, when attachment figures are not reliably available, responsive, and supportive, a sense of attachment security is not attained, negative working models are constructed, worries about self-protection and lovability are heightened, and strategies of affect regulation (which Cassidy & Kobak, 1988, called *secondary attachment strategies*) other than appropriate proximity seeking are adopted. Attachment theorists (e.g. Cassidy & Kobak, 1988; Mikulincer & Shaver, 2016) emphasize two such secondary strategies: *hyperactivation* and *deactivation* of the attachment system. Hyperactivation is manifested in energetic attempts to gain greater proximity, support, and protection, combined with a lack of confidence that it will be provided. Deactivation of the system involves inhibition of proximity-seeking tendencies, denial of attachment needs, maintenance of emotional and cognitive distance from others, and compulsive reliance on oneself as the only reliable source of comfort and protection.

When studying these secondary strategies during adolescence and adulthood, attachment researchers have focused mainly on a person's *attachment style* – the chronic pattern of relational cognitions and behaviors that result from a particular history of attachment experiences (Fraley & Shaver, 2000). Beginning with Ainsworth, Blehar, Waters, and Wall's (1978) studies of infant attachment, and continuing through and beyond Hazan and Shaver's (1987) conceptualization of adult romantic attachment, many studies by social and personality psychologists (reviewed by Mikulincer & Shaver, 2016) have shown that variations in attachment can be measured along two continuous dimensions, avoidance and anxiety (Brennan, Clark, & Shaver, 1998). A person's position on the avoidance dimension indicates the extent to which he or she distrusts others' goodwill and relies on deactivating strategies for coping with threats and attachment insecurities. A person's position on the anxiety dimension indicates the degree to which he or she worries that relationship partners will be unavailable or unhelpful in times of need and relies on hyperactivating strategies. People who score low on both insecurity dimensions are said to be secure or securely attached. The two dimensions can be measured with reliable and valid self-report scales, and are associated in theoretically predictable ways with mental health, adjustment, and relationship quality (see Mikulincer & Shaver, 2016, for an extensive review).

The caregiving behavioral system

According to Bowlby (1982), human beings are born with a capacity to provide protection and support to others who are either chronically dependent or temporarily in need. Bowlby (1982) claimed that these behaviors are organized by a *caregiving behavioral system* that emerged over the long course of evolution because it increased the inclusive fitness of humans by increasing the likelihood that children, siblings, and tribe members with whom a person shared genes would survive to reproductive age and succeed in producing and rearing offspring (Hamilton, 1964). Although the caregiving system presumably evolved primarily to increase the viability of an individual's own offspring and close relatives, it may also have been more generally adapted to respond to the needs of other tribe members, and it can be extended through educational elaboration to include genuine concern for anyone in need (Wilson, 2014). Although most of us probably care more, and more easily, for people to whom we are closely related, either psychologically or genetically, we can experience empathy and compassion for all suffering human beings. Just as attachment-related motives, once they became universally present in a person's psychological repertoire, can affect a wide variety of social processes, caregiving motives can be applied more broadly than to one's immediate genetic relatives.

Following this reasoning, we (Shaver, Mikulincer, & Shemesh-Iron, 2010) proposed that if a person's caregiving system develops under favorable social circumstances, then compassion, empathy, loving-kindness, and generosity become common reactions to other people's needs. However, if the caregiving system does not develop under favorable circumstances, because of an absence of parental modeling, training, and support, or because of interactions with parents that engender insecurities and worries, a developing child is likely to become less compassionate and be less empathic with respect to other people's needs and suffering (see Shaver, Mikulincer, Gross, Stern, & Cassidy, 2016, for an extensive review).

According to Bowlby (1982), the goal of the caregiving system is to reduce other people's suffering, protect them from harm, and foster their growth and development. That is, the caregiving system is designed to serve two major functions: (1) meeting another person's needs for protection and support in times of danger or distress (which Bowlby, 1982, called "providing a safe haven"); and (2) supporting others' exploration, autonomy, and growth when exploration is safe and desirable (Bowlby, 1982, called this function "providing a secure base for exploration"). From this perspective, the goal of a care seeker's attachment system (to maintain a safe haven and secure base) is also the aim of his or her care provider's caregiving system. When a caregiver's behavioral system is activated by another person who needs help, the primary strategy of the system is to perceive the needy individual's problem accurately and provide effective aid. According to Collins, Guichard, Ford, and Feeney (2006), effective caregiving is characterized by two qualities emphasized by previous attachment researchers (e.g. Ainsworth et al., 1978): sensitivity (being attuned to, and accurately interpreting, another person's signals of need) and responsiveness (validating the other person's needs, perceptions, and feelings; respecting his or her beliefs and values; and providing useful assistance and support). As discussed by Gilbert (Chapter 1, this volume), "sensitivity and responsiveness" are at the core of compassion.

Although Bowlby (1982) assumed that everyone is born with the potential to become an effective care provider, effective functioning of the caregiving system depends on several factors. Effective caregiving can be impaired by feelings, beliefs, and concerns that dampen or conflict with motivation to help or with sensitivity and responsiveness. It can also be impaired by deficits in social skills, fatigue, and problems in emotion regulation that cause a caregiver to feel overwhelmed by a needy other's pain or to wish to distance oneself physically, emotionally, or cognitively from the person's problems and distress (Collins et al., 2006).

Interplay of the attachment and caregiving systems

Bowlby (1982) noticed that activation of the attachment system can interfere with the operation of the caregiving system, because potential caregivers may feel that obtaining safety and care for themselves is more urgent than providing a safe haven or secure base for others. At such times, people are likely to be so focused on their own vulnerability that they lack the mental resources needed to attend sensitively to others' needs; that is to say, when people are threat-focused, attention and resources are focused on their own protection and needs, not those of others (Gilbert, 2014). Only when a sense of attachment security (safeness) is restored can a potential caregiver perceive others to be not only potential sources of security and support, but also worthy human beings who themselves need and deserve sympathy and support.

Reasoning along these lines, attachment theorists (e.g. Collins et al., 2006; Kunce & Shaver, 1994) hypothesized that attachment security provides an important foundation for effective caregiving. Moreover, a person who is more secure with respect to attachment is likely to have experienced and benefited earlier in life from effective care provided by responsive attachment figures. This means that secure adults have mental representations of compassionate and generous caregivers when they themselves occupy the caregiving role. Moreover, secure individuals' comfort with intimacy and interdependence allows them to respond favorably when a relationship partner is vulnerable or in need of support. In addition, secure people's positive working models of others make it easier for them to perceive their relationship partner as deserving sympathy and support, whereas their positive self-representations allow them to feel confident that they can deal with their partner's needs or distress without being overwhelmed by their own needs and feelings.

In contrast, attachment insecurities are likely to interfere with responsive care provision (e.g. Collins et al., 2006). Attachment anxiety leads people to focus on their own distress and unmet attachment needs, which may draw mental resources away from attending accurately to a relationship partner's needs. Moreover, strong desire for closeness, support, and love related to attachment anxiety may taint caregiving motives with egoistic desires for acceptance and grateful approval, which can impair altruistic helping. The lack of comfort with closeness and negative working models of others that is associated with avoidant attachment may also interfere with the provision of sensitive and responsive care. People scoring high on avoidant attachment may back away rather than get involved with relationship partners whose needs for care and support are strongly expressed, preferring to detach themselves emotionally, cognitively, and physically.

In the remainder of this chapter, we review studies that test these theoretical ideas about the interplay of attachment and caregiving motives and processes. We particularly focus on studies that have measured individual differences in attachment orientations in adulthood or have contextually induced a sense of attachment security in adult participants and then have assessed feelings of compassion and effective supportive behavior for others who are in need.

Evidence concerning the attachment-caregiving link within close relationships

Parental caregiving

The hypothesized attachment-caregiving link has received extensive support in the context of parent-child relations. In studies observing actual parents' responses to their infants' signals of needs and distress, less secure parents have been found to be less attentive and responsive to their infants' needs, as well as more distressed and intrusive when interacting with their infants (e.g. Bernier & Matte-Gagné, 2011; Shlafer, Raby, Lawler, Hesemeyer, & Roisman, 2015). Similar effects have been reported in studies assessing the quality of support parents provide to their preschool children during challenging cognitive tasks (e.g. Shlafer et al., 2015; Whipple, Bernier, & Mageau, 2011). More secure parents were rated by independent judges as warmer and more supportive than insecure mothers. In addition, avoidant mothers were rated as more controlling and task-focused, and anxious mothers were rated as more distressed and intrusive when trying to help their children.

There is also evidence that insecure parents' difficulties in providing support are manifested during interactions with their adolescent offspring. In a recent observational study, Jones and Cassidy (2014) found that mothers scoring relatively high on attachment-related avoidance were less supportive and more hostile during a conflict management discussion with their adolescent offspring. Studies also show that less secure parents also have less knowledge about their adolescent offspring – being less aware of where their child is, with whom he or she is associating, and what he or she is doing (Jones, Ehrlich, Lejuez, & Cassidy, 2015). In addition, Jones, Brett, Ehrlich, Lejuez, and Cassidy (2014) found that mothers' avoidant attachment prospectively predicted more distressed and less supportive responses to their adolescent offspring's expression of negative emotions one and two years later.

Adult children's provision of care to parents

Adult attachment studies have also documented attachment-related differences in the ways adult children provide care and support to their aging parents. Cicirelli (1993) hypothesized that secure adult children would be more empathic regarding their parents' needs and would reciprocate their parents' earlier warmth, affection, and concern. In contrast, attachment insecurities were expected to cause children to react with emotional detachment or overwhelming distress when their early sources of safety became weak, needy, and vulnerable. In support of this view, several studies show that less secure children have more difficulties as caregivers (e.g. Carpenter, 2001; Chen et al., 2013), and express less willingness to care for aging parents (e.g. Karantzas, Evans, & Foddy, 2010).

Caregiving in romantic and marital relationships

To extend the construct of caregiving to romantic and marital relationships, Kunce and Shaver (1994) constructed a self-report questionnaire that assesses caregiving behaviors in such relationships. Several studies have used this scale and have shown that less secure people are less likely to provide support to a needy partner, less likely to be sensitive to his or her needs, and more likely to adopt a controlling or compulsive caregiving orientation (e.g. Kunce & Shaver, 1994; Millings, Walsh, Hepper, & O'Brien, 2013). Davila and Kashy (2009) obtained similar findings in a 14-day diary study: Self-reports of attachment insecurities were associated with less sensitive and less responsive provision of support to a needy partner throughout the 14-day period. Attachment insecurities have also been found to be associated with less sensitive and responsive care for a spouse suffering from cancer (e.g. Braun et al., 2012; Kim & Carver, 2007;). Similar findings were obtained in a longitudinal study of spousal caregiving in late life (Morse, Shaffer, Williamson, Dooley, & Schulz, 2012).

These problems in responsive caregiving are also evident in observational studies of caregiving behavior in the laboratory (e.g. Collins & Feeney, 2000; Monin, Feeney, & Schulz, 2012; Simpson, Rholes, & Nelligan, 1992). For example, Simpson et al. (1992) videotaped dating couples while the female partner waited to endure a stressful task and judges then rated the male partners' caregiving behavior. Whereas secure men recognized their partner's worries and provided greater support as their partner showed higher levels of distress, men who scored high on avoidance provided less support as their partner's distress increased. Collins and Feeney (2000) videotaped dating couples while one partner disclosed a personal problem to the other, finding that more anxiously attached participants were rated by judges as less supportive, less responsive, and more negative toward the distressed partner than participants who scored lower on attachment anxiety.

In another laboratory experiment, Feeney and Collins (2001) brought dating couples to the lab and informed one member of the couple (the "care seeker") that he or she would perform a stressful task – preparing and delivering a speech that would be videotaped. The other member of the couple (the "caregiver") was led to believe that his or her partner was either extremely nervous (high need condition) or not at all nervous (low need condition) about the speech task, and was given the opportunity to write a private note to the partner. In both studies, the note served as a behavioral measure of caregiving and was rated for the degree of support it conveyed. Less secure people wrote less emotionally supportive notes in both high and low need conditions, and provided less instrumental support in the high than in the low need condition, precisely when the partner most needed support. Moreover, they reported less empathic feelings toward their partner and were less willing to switch tasks with the partner.

The negative effects of attachment insecurities on caregiving behavior toward a relationship partner have also been observed when a partner is exploring new career opportunities or personal plans. In two observational studies of married couples interacting in a videotaped exploration activity (e.g. discussion of one partner's personal goals), Feeney and Thrush (2010) and Feeney, Collins, van Vleet, and Tomlinson (2013) found that insecurities reduced the provision of a secure base for a partner's exploration and impaired the partner's actual exploratory behavior (as judged by external observers). Specifically, spouses' avoidant attachment was predictive of less availability to their partner, and spouses' attachment anxiety was predictive of greater interference in a partner's explorations.

Although all of these findings confirm an attachment-caregiving link in couple relationships, the studies have all been based on dispositional measures of attachment and therefore cannot inform us fully about the causal effects of attachment security. Therefore, Mikulincer, Shaver, Sahdra, and Bar-On (2013) conducted a study, in both the United States and Israel, to see if experimentally augmented security would improve care provision to a romantic partner who was asked to discuss a personal problem. A second goal of the study was to examine the extent to which security priming would overcome barriers to responsive caregiving induced by mental depletion or fatigue. Dating couples came to the laboratory and were informed that they would be video-recorded during an interaction in which one of them (whom we regarded as the "care seeker") disclosed a personal problem to the other (the "caregiver"). Care seekers chose and wrote about any personal problem they were willing to discuss (except ones that involved conflict with the partner). And at the same time, caregivers were taken to another room where they performed a Stroop color-naming task in which we manipulated mental depletion and were subliminally exposed to either the names of security providers or the names of unfamiliar people. Following these manipulations, couple members were videotaped while they talked about the problem that the care-seeker wished to discuss, and then independent judges, viewing the video-recordings, coded participants' responsiveness to their disclosing partner.

Experimentally induced attachment security was associated with greater responsiveness to the disclosing partner. Moreover, security priming overrode the detrimental effects of mental depletion and of dispositional avoidance on responsiveness, and it counteracted the tendency of anxious caregivers to be less responsive following experimentally induced mental depletion. Overall, the findings emphasize that attachment security facilitates effective support provision, and that an experimental enhancement of security can counteract dispositional barriers (insecure attachment orientations) and situational barriers (mental depletion) to responsive caregiving.

Evidence concerning the attachment-caregiving link outside close relationships

The hypothesized attachment-caregiving link is also observable in one's prosocial reactions to other people's needs and one's actual reactions to suffering strangers. Studies assessing global self-report measures of prosocial virtues and tendencies have consistently found that higher attachment-related avoidance is associated with less empathic concern, less inclination to take the perspective of a distressed person, and less ability to share another person's feelings (e.g. Burke, Wang, & Dovidio, 2014; Joireman, Needham, & Cummings, 2002). Higher attachment anxiety scores have been found to be associated with more personal distress when witnessing others' distress (e.g. Monin, Schulz, Feeney, & Clark, 2010) and higher scores on measures of unmitigated communion and pathological concern, which tap a compulsive need to help others even when they are not asking for assistance and do not want it, and even when the help comes at the expense of one's own health and legitimate needs (e.g. Bassett & Aubé, 2013; Shavit & Tolmacz, 2014).

The contribution of attachment to acts of compassion outside romantic relationships has also been documented in observational studies that attempt to capture actual behavioral reactions to a suffering other. For example, Westmaas and Silver (2001) videotaped people while they interacted with a confederate of the experimenter whom they thought had recently been diagnosed with cancer. Whereas participants scoring higher on avoidant attachment were rated by observers as less verbally and nonverbally supportive, and as making less eye contact during the interaction, more anxiously attached participants reported greater discomfort while interacting with the confederate and were more likely to report self-critical thoughts after the interaction. These are clear signs of emotional over-involvement and self-related worries, which can sometimes interfere with caregiving. In another observational study, Feeney, Cassidy, and Ramos-Marcuse (2008) also found that more attachment insecurities were associated with the provision of less responsive support to an unfamiliar peer who was disclosing a personal problem and with more self-focus during the discussion (as coded by trained observers).

Beyond examining individual differences in self-reported attachment orientations, some studies have also manipulated a person's momentary sense of attachment security (security priming) and have found theoretically coherent effects on compassion-related feelings and behaviors toward needy people. In two sets of experiments Mikulincer, Gillath, and colleagues (Mikulincer et al., 2001; Mikulincer et al., 2003) found that contextual priming of names of security providers, as compared with neutral priming, increased empathic concern for a suffering stranger and endorsement of prosocial values (concern for close others and for all of humanity). In another experimental study, Mikulincer, Shaver, Gillath, and Nitzberg (2005, Study 1) examined the effects of security priming on the decision to help or not help a person in distress. Participants watched a confederate while she performed a series of aversive tasks. As the study progressed, the confederate became increasingly distressed, and the participant was given an opportunity to take her place, in effect sacrificing self for the welfare of another. Shortly before being exposed to the person's distress, participants were subliminally primed (for only 20 milliseconds) with either the name of a security provider (security priming) or a neutral name (neutral priming). We found that security priming, as compared with neutral priming, increased participants' compassion and willingness to take the distressed person's place. This effect occurred in both Israel and the United States, and also occurred when the priming was done supraliminally by asking participants to think about a familiar security provider (Mikulincer et al., 2005, Study 2).

In two additional studies, Mikulincer et al. (2005, Studies 3–4) tested whether contextual activation of mental representations of attachment security override egoistic motives for helping, such as mood-enhancement and empathic joy. Study participants were randomly assigned to one of two priming conditions (security priming, neutral priming), read a true newspaper article about a woman in dire personal and financial distress, and then rated their emotional reactions to the article in terms of compassion and personal distress. In one study, half of the participants anticipated mood-enhancement by means other than helping (e.g. expecting, immediately after this part of the experiment, to watch a comedy film). In the other study, half of the participants were told that the needy woman was chronically depressed and her mood might be beyond their ability to improve it (the "no empathic joy" condition). The findings indicated that expecting to improve one's mood by means other than helping or expecting not to be able to share a needy person's joy following the provision of help reduced compassion and willingness to help in the neutral priming condition, but not in the security priming condition. Instead, security priming led to greater compassion and willingness to help even when there was no egoistic reason for helping (i.e. no empathic joy or no mood relief).

In sum, the combined evidence from these experiments indicates that attachment security makes compassion and altruism more likely. Although there are other reasons for helping, the prosocial effects of attachment security do not depend on alternative egoistic motives such as a person's desire to improve his or her mood or the desire to share a suffering person's relief. We infer that a sense of attachment security reduces one's need for defensive self-protection and allows one to direct attention to others' needs, feel compassion toward a suffering other, and engage in altruistic behavior with the primary goal of benefiting others.

Attachment and compassion fatigue in therapeutic settings

Psychotherapists who work with special populations, such as victims of terrorism, abused children, disaster survivors, dying clients, and severely disturbed patients, sometimes neglect their own needs for care while focusing on the pressing needs of their clients. This kind of work can easily result in emotional depletion and professional burnout, which is sometimes called compassion fatigue (Figley, 2002). This unpleasant and destructive condition is marked by withdrawal and isolation from others, inappropriate emotionality, depersonalization, reduced life satisfaction, loss of boundaries with patients, and a sense of being overwhelmed (Figley, 2002). There is now evidence that compassion fatigue is more common among therapists who are insecure with respect to attachment and have problems regulating their distress while providing care to others (e.g. Tosone, Minami, Bettmann, & Jasperson, 2010; Zerach, 2013). Similar findings have been reported in studies of burnout and compassion fatigue among volunteers working with suffering others (e.g. Pardess et al., 2014; Romaniello et al., 2015). For example, Pardess et al. (2014) conducted a diary study assessing emotional reactions to actual helping encounters over a two-month period in a sample of volunteers working with traumatized individuals as well as a laboratory experiment examining the effects of security priming on reactions to a hypothetical helping encounter. As expected, attachment insecurities, both anxiety and avoidance, were associated with reports of compassion fatigue following actual helping encounters. Moreover, security priming reduced compassion fatigue in response to a hypothetical helping encounter.

Conclusions

Attachment theory and research provide good leads for fostering effective compassion in therapists, therapy clients, parents, and human beings more generally. Moreover, attachment theory suggests that the same caregiving behavioral system that evolved to assure adequate care for vulnerable, dependent children can be extended to include care and concern for other people in need, perhaps even compassion for all suffering creatures – an important Buddhist ideal (Shaver, Mikulincer, Sahdra, & Gross, 2016). Research clearly indicates that the condition of the attachment behavioral system affects the workings of the caregiving system, making it likely that heightening attachment security will yield benefits in the realm of compassionate caregiving. In addition, an increasing number of psychotherapies are placing the cultivation of caring for self and others central to the therapeutic process (Gilbert, 2014; Kirby & Gilbert, Chapter 15, this volume).

Research on attachment and caregiving suggests several ways to encourage this move toward attachment security and effective compassion. One is to care for children in ways that enhance their sense of security, which, besides having many benefits for the children themselves, makes it much more likely that they will be good parents and neighbors, and generous citizens of the world in later years. Another way to heighten a person's sense of security is to have him or her regularly recall times when beneficial support was provided, or to imagine similar situations, perhaps even ones depicted in religious stories or other inspiring works of art (Oman & Thoresen, 2003). Once a person has benefited from another's care, or deliberately imagined and emulated the kinds of care and concern for others exhibited by supportive parents (Jesus, the Buddha, or Gandhi) merely calling these exemplars to mind seems to have security-enhancing effects, as does exposure to pictures and drawings of examples of loving kindness. We suspect that many of these procedures foster compassionate caregiving in two ways: by enhancing a person's sense of security, and by providing models of good caregiving.

Our research has demonstrated that key constructs, propositions, and principles of attachment theory apply beyond the realm of close relationships to social life more generally. People who are relatively secure in the dispositional sense or are induced to feel secure in a particular context are less threatened than insecure people by novel information and in-group/out-group differences, and are more willing to tolerate diversity, more likely to maintain broadly humane values, and more likely to offer tangible help to others in need. It seems likely, therefore, that the earth would be a more compassionate place if a larger number of people were helped to become secure, both dispositionally and in the varied contexts of their daily lives.

References

Ainsworth, M. D. S. (1991). Attachment and other affectional bonds across the life cycle. In C. M. Parkes, J. Stevenson-Hinde, & P. Marris (Eds.), *Attachment Across the Life Cycle* (pp. 33–51). New York: Routledge.

Ainsworth, M. D. S., Blehar, M. C., Waters, E., & Wall, S. (1978). *Patterns of Attachment: Assessed in the Strange Situation and at Home*. Hillsdale, NJ: Erlbaum.

Bassett, R. L., & Aubé, J. (2013) "Please care about me" or "I am pleased to care about you!" Considering adaptive and maladaptive versions of unmitigated communion. *Journal of Psychology and Theology, 41*, 107–119.

Bernier, A., & Matte-Gagné, C. (2011). More bridges: Investigating the relevance of self-report and interview measures of adult attachment for marital and caregiving relationships. *International Journal of Behavioral Development, 35*, 307–316.

Bowlby, J. (1973). *Attachment and Loss: Vol. 2. Separation: Anxiety and Anger*. New York: Basic Books.

Bowlby, J. (1982). *Attachment and Loss: Vol. 1. Attachment* (2nd ed.). New York: Basic Books. (Original ed. 1969.)

Bowlby, J. (1988). *A Secure Base: Clinical Applications of Attachment Theory*. London: Routledge.

Braun, M., Hales, S., Gilad, L., Mikulincer, M., Rydall, A., & Rodin, G. (2012). Caregiving styles and attachment orientations in couples facing advanced cancer. *Psycho-Oncology, 21*, 935–943.

Brennan, K. A., Clark, C. L., & Shaver, P. R. (1998). Self-report measurement of adult romantic attachment: An integrative overview. In J. A. Simpson & W. S. Rholes (Eds.), *Attachment Theory and Close Relationships* (pp. 46–76). New York: Guilford Press.

Burke, S. E., Wang, K., & Dovidio, J. F. (2014). Witnessing disclosure of depression: Gender and attachment avoidance moderate interpersonal evaluations. *Journal of Social and Clinical Psychology*, *33*, 536–559.

Carpenter, B. D. (2001). Attachment bonds between adult daughters and their older mothers: Associations with contemporary caregiving. *Journals of Gerontology: Series B: Psychological Sciences and Social Sciences*, *56B*, 257–266.

Cassidy, J., & Kobak, R. R. (1988). Avoidance and its relationship with other defensive processes. In J. Belsky & T. Nezworski (Eds.), *Clinical Implications of Attachment* (pp. 300–323). Hillsdale, NJ: Erlbaum.

Cassidy, J., & Shaver, P. R. (Eds.) (2016). *Handbook of Attachment: Theory, Research, and Clinical Applications* (3rd ed.). New York: Guilford Press.

Chen, C. K., Waters, H. S., Hartman, M., Zimmerman, S., Miklowitz, D. J., & Waters, E. (2013). The secure base script and the task of caring for elderly parents: Implications for attachment theory and clinical practice. *Attachment & Human Development*, *15*, 332–348.

Cicirelli, V. G. (1993). Attachment and obligation as daughters' motives for caregiving behavior and subsequent effect on subjective burden. *Psychology and Aging*, *8*, 144–155.

Collins, N. L., & Feeney, B. C. (2000). A safe haven: An attachment theory perspective on support seeking and caregiving in intimate relationships. *Journal of Personality and Social Psychology*, *78*, 1053–1073.

Collins, N. L., Guichard, A. C., Ford, M. B., & Feeney, B. C. (2006). Responding to need in intimate relationships: Normative processes and individual differences. In M. Mikulincer & G. S. Goodman (Eds.), *Dynamics of Romantic Love: Attachment, Caregiving, and Sex* (pp. 149–189). New York: Guilford Press.

Dalai Lama (2002). *The Dalai Lama's Book of Love and Compassion*. Glasgow, UK: Thorsons Publications.

Davila, J., & Kashy, D. (2009). Secure base processes in couples: Daily associations between support experiences and attachment security. *Journal of Family Psychology*, *23*, 76–88.

Dawkins, R. (1976/1989). *The Selfish Gene*. New York: Oxford University Press.

Feeney, B. C., Cassidy, J., & Ramos-Marcuse, F. (2008). The generalization of attachment representations to new social situations: Predicting behavior during initial interactions with strangers. *Journal of Personality and Social Psychology*, *95*, 1481–1498.

Feeney, B. C., & Collins, N. L. (2001). Predictors of caregiving in adult intimate relationships: An attachment theoretical perspective. *Journal of Personality and Social Psychology*, *80*, 972–994.

Feeney, B. C., Collins, N. L., van Vleet, M., & Tomlinson, J. M. (2013). Motivations for providing a secure base: Links with attachment orientation and secure base support behavior. *Attachment & Human Development*, *15*, 261–280.

Feeney, B. C., & Thrush, R. L. (2010). Relationship influences on exploration in adulthood: The characteristics and function of a secure base. *Journal of Personality and Social Psychology*, *98*, 57–76.

Figley, C. R. (2002). Compassion fatigue: Psychotherapist's chronic lack of self-care. *Journal of Clinical Psychology. Special Issue: Chronic Illness*, *58*, 1433–1441.

Fraley, R. C., & Shaver, P. R. (2000). Adult romantic attachment: Theoretical developments, emerging controversies, and unanswered questions. *Review of General Psychology, 4*, 132–154.

Gilbert, P. (1989/2016). *Human Nature and Suffering*. London: Routledge.

Gilbert, P. (2010). *Compassion Focused Therapy*. London: Routledge.

Gilbert, P. (2014). The origins and nature of compassion focused therapy. *British Journal of Clinical Psychology, 53*, 6–41.

Hamilton, W. D. (1964). The genetical evolution of social behavior. I and II. *Journal of Theoretical Biology, 7*, 1–52.

Hazan, C., & Shaver, P. R. (1987). Romantic love conceptualized as an attachment process. *Journal of Personality and Social Psychology, 52*, 511–524.

Joireman, J. A., Needham, T. L., & Cummings, A. L. (2002). Relationships between dimensions of attachment and empathy. *North American Journal of Psychology, 4*, 63–80.

Jones, J. D., Brett, B. E., Ehrlich, K. B., Lejuez, C. W., & Cassidy, J. (2014). Maternal attachment style and responses to adolescents' negative emotions: The mediating role of maternal emotion regulation. *Parenting: Science and Practice, 14*, 235–257.

Jones, J. D., & Cassidy, J. (2014). Parental attachment style: Examination of links with parent secure base provision and adolescent secure base use. *Attachment & Human Development, 16*, 437–461.

Jones, J. D., Ehrlich, K. B., Lejuez, C. W., & Cassidy, J. (2015). Parental knowledge of adolescent activities: Links with parental attachment style and adolescent substance use. *Journal of Family Psychology, 29*, 191–200.

Karantzas, G. C., Evans, L., & Foddy, M. (2010). The role of attachment in current and future parent caregiving. *Journal of Gerontology: Psychological Sciences and Social Sciences, 65B*, 573–580.

Kim, Y., & Carver, C. S. (2007). Frequency and difficulty in caregiving among spouses of individuals with cancer: Effects of adult attachment and gender. *Psycho-Oncology, 16*, 714–728.

Kunce, L. J., & Shaver, P. R. (1994). An attachment-theoretical approach to caregiving in romantic relationships. In K. Bartholomew & D. Perlman (Eds.), *Advances in Personal Relationships* (Vol. 5, pp. 205–237). London: Kingsley.

Mikulincer, M., Gillath, O., Halevy, V., Avihou, N., Avidan, S., & Eshkoli, N. (2001). Attachment theory and reactions to others' needs: Evidence that activation of the sense of attachment security promotes empathic responses. *Journal of Personality and Social Psychology, 81*, 1205–1224.

Mikulincer, M., Gillath, O., Sapir-Lavid, Y., Yaakobi, E., Arias, K., Tal-Aloni, L., & Bor, G. (2003). Attachment theory and concern for others' welfare: Evidence that activation of the sense of secure base promotes endorsement of self-transcendence values. *Basic and Applied Social Psychology, 25*, 299–312.

Mikulincer, M., Gillath, O., & Shaver, P. R. (2002). Activation of the attachment system in adulthood: Threat-related primes increase the accessibility of mental representations of attachment figures. *Journal of Personality and Social Psychology, 83*, 881–895.

Mikulincer, M., & Shaver, P. R. (2004). Security-based self-representations in adulthood: Contents and processes. In W. S. Rholes & J. A. Simpson (Eds.), *Adult Attachment: Theory, Research, and Clinical Implications* (pp. 159–195). New York: Guilford Press.

Mikulincer, M., & Shaver, P. R. (2016). *Attachment in Adulthood: Structure, Dynamics, and Change* (2nd ed.). New York: Guilford Press.

Mikulincer, M., Shaver, P. R., Gillath, O., & Nitzberg, R. A. (2005). Attachment, caregiving, and altruism: Boosting attachment security increases compassion and helping. *Journal of Personality and Social Psychology, 89*, 817–839.

Mikulincer, M., Shaver, P. R., Sahdra, B. K., & Bar-On, N. (2013). Can security-enhancing interventions overcome psychological barriers to responsiveness in couple relationships? *Attachment & Human Development, 15*, 246–260.

Millings, A., Walsh, J., Hepper, E., & O'Brien, M. (2013). Good partner, good parent: Responsiveness mediates the link between romantic attachment and parenting style. *Personality and Social Psychology Bulletin, 39*, 170–180.

Monin, J. K., Feeney, B. C., & Schulz, R. (2012). Attachment orientation and reactions to anxiety expression in close relationships. *Personal Relationships, 19*, 535–550.

Monin, J. K., Schulz, R., Feeney, B. C., & Clark, T. B. (2010). Attachment insecurity and perceived partner suffering as predictors of caregiver distress. *Journal of Experimental Social Psychology, 46*, 1143–1147.

Morse, J. Q., Shaffer, D. R., Williamson, G. M., Dooley, W. K., & Schulz, R. (2012). Models of self and others and their relation to positive and negative caregiving responses. *Psychology and Aging, 27*, 211–218.

Oman, D., & Thoresen, C. E. (2003). Spiritual modeling: A key to spiritual and religious growth? *International Journal for the Psychology of Religion, 13*, 149–165.

Pardess, E., Mikulincer, M., Dekel, R., & Shaver, P. R. (2014). Dispositional attachment orientations, contextual variations in attachment security, and compassion fatigue among volunteers working with traumatized individuals. *Journal of Personality, 82*, 355–366.

Romaniello, C., Farinelli, M., Matera, N., Bertoletti, E., Pedone, V., & Northoff, G. (2015). Anxious attachment style and hopelessness as predictors of burden in caregivers of patients with disorders of consciousness: A pilot study. *Brain Injury, 29*, 466–472.

Shaver, P. R., Mikulincer, M., Gross, J. T., Stern, J. A., & Cassidy, J. (2016). A lifespan perspective on attachment and care for others: Empathy, altruism, and prosocial behavior. In J. Cassidy & P. R. Shaver (Eds.), *Handbook of Attachment: Theory, Research, and Clinical Applications* (3rd ed., pp. 878–916). New York: Guilford Press.

Shaver, P. R., Mikulincer, M., Sahdra, B., & Gross, J. T. (2016). Attachment as a foundation for kindness toward self and others. In K. W. Brown & M. R. Leary (Eds.), *The Oxford Handbook of Hypo-egoic Phenomena*. New York: Oxford University Press.

Shaver, P. R., Mikulincer, M., & Shemesh-Iron, M. (2010). A behavioral systems perspective on prosocial behavior. In M. Mikulincer & P. R. Shaver (Eds.), *Prosocial Motives, Emotions, and Behavior: The Better Angels of Our Nature* (pp. 73–92). Washington, DC: American Psychological Association.

Shavit, Y., & Tolmacz, R. (2014). Pathological concern: Scale construction, construct validity, and associations with attachment, self-cohesion, and relational entitlement. *Psychoanalytic Psychology, 31*, 343–356.

Shlafer, R. J., Raby, K. L., Lawler, J. M., Hesemeyer, P. S., & Roisman, G. I. (2015). Longitudinal associations between adult attachment states of mind and parenting quality. *Attachment & Human Development, 17*, 83–95.

Simpson, J. A., Rholes, W. S., & Nelligan, J. S. (1992). Support seeking and support giving within couples in an anxiety-provoking situation: The role of attachment styles. *Journal of Personality and Social Psychology, 62*, 434–446.

Tosone, C., Bettmann, J. E., Minami, T., & Jasperson, R. A. (2010). New York City social workers after 9/11: Their attachment, resiliency, and compassion fatigue. *International Journal of Emergency Mental Health, 12*, 103–116.

Westmaas, J., & Silver, R. C. (2001). The role of attachment in responses to victims of life crises. *Journal of Personality and Social Psychology, 80*, 425–438.

Whipple, N., Bernier, A., & Mageau, G. A. (2011). A dimensional approach to maternal attachment state of mind: Relations to maternal sensitivity and maternal autonomy support. *Developmental Psychology, 47*, 396–403.

Wilson, E. O. (2014). *The Meaning of Human Existence*. New York: Liveright/Norton.

Zerach, G. (2013). Compassion fatigue and compassion satisfaction among residential child care workers: The role of personality resources. *Residential Treatment for Children & Youth, 30*, 72–91.

Chapter 12

Broaden-and-build theory meets interpersonal neurobiology as a lens on compassion and positivity resonance

Barbara L. Fredrickson and Daniel J. Siegel

Barbara L. Fredrickson (BLF): I think the biggest points of connection between our work stem from my theorizing about a different view of love that unpacks its core phenomenon as being represented by micro-moments of what I call "positivity resonance" (Fredrickson, 2013a, 2013b, in press). These are collaborative, or joint experiences that unfold between two or more people. For linguistic convenience, I'll speak of dyads here. These are moments in which one person's positive emotion inspires and amplifies another person's positive emotion, which in turn inspires and amplifies the first person's positive emotion. Unpacking those exchanges of emotional experience from an affective science perspective, I see there are three key elements that form a temporal braid that unfolds between people.

The first element is a *shared positive affective experience*. This need not necessarily be the same identical positive affect experienced within each person. Rather, a strand of authentic emotional positivity emerges within each person that, when expressed through smiles, nonverbal behavior, or in words, also triggers the other person's authentic positive emotions (Niedenthal, Mermillod, Maringer, & Hess, 2010).

The second element is *a mutual care or concern*: a mutual orientation to be invested in the well-being of the other. Care and concern is, of course, at the heart of compassion too. Yet mutuality is key here. This element of positivity resonance is inspired by writings within the relationship science literature on perceived responsiveness and investment in well-being of the other (Hegi & Bergner, 2010; Reis, Clark, & Holmes, 2004). In certain moments, these two things emerge together in time. That is, at the same time that the self cares for, or invests in the well-being of another, that other person registers that the person they're with cares for them, and has been invested in their well-being, and that it's mutual, reciprocated. In such moments an emergent property arises that, in jargon terms, is called "mutual perceived responsiveness." This is considered to be the hallmark of intimacy. One way to describe that in more common terms is to say that you feel "seen" by the other; you feel understood, cared for, and validated. And at the same time they feel "seen" by you. This is not a role-governed "caretaking," but rather a just-noticeable concern for each other's well-being.

The third element is *biobehavioral synchrony*. I realize that's a big jargon mouthful, but with this term, I refer to two forms of synchrony. On the one hand is the synchrony that you can see – synchrony in their facial expressions, their postures, or nonverbal communications. This is not only mere mimicry or mirroring. Synchrony is a more encompassing term that means that expressions and gestures share a common tempo and rhythm (Vacharkulksemsuk & Fredrickson, 2012). On the other hand is the synchrony that we aren't privy to unless we're using more advanced instrumentation to measure the biological part of biobehavioral synchrony. There's intriguing initial evidence – more is definitely needed – that when two individuals are truly on the same page and sharing the same positive emotional experience, there's a biochemical synchrony in terms of shared rises and falls in oxytocin levels (Feldman, Gordon, & Zagoory-Sharon, 2010), and also a neural synchrony in terms of a whole-brain pattern of neural activity. This is not just in some isolated mirror neuron circuit of the brain, but whole-brain patterns (Stephens, Silbert, & Hasson, 2010).

What's interesting about these three intertwined facets is that they help us move "love" from an abstract concept to a momentary affective phenomenon that can emerge between any two or more individuals. And it has all the key components of an emotion process: a subjective experience component, a nonverbal communication component, and a physiological component, including a neural signature. Emotions, by definition, are a mind and body experience. Sometimes our definitions of love are somewhat disembodied. The bodily aspects are ignored when we conceptualize love as a status or category of relationship. I'm very interested in that momentary dance that's happening across nonverbal behavior, experience, and biology. I admit that it's difficult to take a scientific perspective on love because so many people have different views on what love is. Yet from an affective science perspective it's helpful to look at the momentary phenomena that drive the accrual of some of the other things that, culturally, we consider to be love, like loyalty, trust, commitment, and bonds. Micro-moments of positivity resonance can pave the way to these. This is where I bring in my "broaden-and-build" theory of positive emotion (Fredrickson, 1998, 2001, 2009, 2013b). This theory points out that even though positive emotions are subtle and fleeting, and sometimes very mild, they do have enduring consequences when repeated. Even mild positive emotions broaden our awareness, and such experiences, when recurrent, accumulate and compound to build people's enduring resources. Moments of positivity resonance have the signature of positive emotions from this "broaden and build" perspective. In the moment they broaden people's mindsets from thinking only in terms of "me versus you," to thinking in terms of "us" as a unit, or otherwise seeing oneness and connection between the self and the other. Those momentary experiences of greater unity, as they accumulate and compound, build our enduring loyalty, trust, bonds, and commitment. These are many of the things we take as synonyms of love or as definitions of love. I think these are actually the accumulated products of recurrent micro-moments of positivity resonance. We don't get loyalty, trust, bonds, and commitment out of thin air, but rather they emerge out of a shared positive emotional history (Fredrickson, 2013a, in press). Positivity resonance, by contrast, needs no history. It can emerge in first-time or one-time encounters, and in that sense is unlimited.

So that's an overview of my definition of positivity resonance, a very thumbnail sketch. Perhaps you have some connections and questions to connect it more to what you're up to, Dan.

Daniel J. Siegel (DJS): Absolutely. Well, Barb, that's really fantastic to hear the overview of not just positivity resonance and your wonderful work on love, but also hinting at the broader proposals about "broaden and build" and positive emotions. So from the position of where my professional work is, trained first in biochemistry, then moving to medicine, specializing initially in pediatrics and then psychiatry, and subsequently being trained as an attachment researcher looking to find ways of understanding the development of a healthy mind, the approach that seemed to be useful was to try to combine all the different disciplines of science together. And so anthropology, studying culture, and sociology, studying groups, and psychology, studying our mental life, including our relationships, biological studies including medicine, studying the way the body works, chemistry, studying molecules and their interactions, and physics, studying the physical properties of the world and even math, studying systems, for example, combining all these together into a field called interpersonal neurobiology (IPNB) is what I've been doing over these last 25 years (see Siegel, 2012a, 2012b, 2017). Other academics and clinicians have been active contributors as well to IPNB, and in our professional series we now have over 50 textbooks focusing on applying this synthesis of science to the clinical experience of healing. Broadly speaking, we examine how relationships, the embodied brain, and our mental lives are a part of one integrated system. The IPNB approach is a way we envision a few fundamental principles that I think have a potential to connect with your work in "broaden and build" views, in positive emotions, and also with the resonance you talk about in terms of love. Interpersonal Neurobiology also provides ways for thinking about compassion as a process of connectedness and coming together in the context of suffering rather than avoidance or moving away from each other.

You and I also collaborated the first time at the *Psychotherapy Networker* in Washington DC in 2014 because there was such a convergence of potential overlapping ideas, a process E. O. Wilson might call consilience (Wilson, 1998): independent pursuits that come up with parallel findings, and so I thought there was some consilience between your work and the work of interpersonal neurobiology. Here is a very brief summary of the take-home messages about that consilience. In interpersonal neurobiology, the first step we take is to discuss how the human mind is often described but very rarely defined, and so we actually offer a definition of one aspect of the mind that is beyond the descriptions. These common descriptions include, for example, information processing, subjective experience and consciousness. In IPNB we try to take a broad, multi-discipline scientific approach to keep things consistent with science but to try to also find these consilient elements that move beyond our often isolated scientific disciplines.

A proposal from the early 1990s suggested that we can view the mind as a process that is an emergent, self-organizing, embodied, and relational process that regulates the flow of energy and information (Siegel, 2012a). This self-organizing aspect of mind may overlap with consciousness, subjective experience, and information processing, or it may be independent. That is to say, our minds can be seen as an emergent property of energy and information flow – and this flow occurs both within our relationships as well as our whole bodies, including the brain. In this way, mental life is organized and textured by the interpersonal flow we find ourselves in in the "betweeness" of our relationships with others as well as by internal processes that occur in not only the skull-encased brain, but the entire body. Hence the joys, ambitions, fears, and suffering of others around us – part of the betweenness of our mind's origins – influence our own self-organization and interpersonal responses. Relationships, from this view, do more than "shape" the mind, they serve as part of the origin of the mind's emergence.

This proposed emergent self-organizing process is only one aspect of mind. This definition is derived by looking at how an anthropologist or sociologist or psychologist or psychiatrist or neuroscientist describes mental life. We see the common element across all those disciplines as the physics property of energy. Though many studying the mind seem to avoid using the concept of energy, the scientific study of energy, explored in the fields of physics, chemistry, and biology, for example, has profound empirically established findings that can be quite useful in exploring the nature of mind. Whether you are examining culture in shared patterns of energy with symbolic value we call information within communication in a society or patterns of energy flowing through the brain that create neural representations, neural processes that correlate with mental processes like feelings, emotions, thoughts, reasoning, memory, hopes, dreams, longings – all that mental life that we call "mental activities" – can be seen as patterns of energy flow within the body and its brain – and shared in our relational lives. This change in energy is called flow, and sometimes patterns of energy flow have a symbolic value and we call them "information," so you can have a unit of experience that can be simply called, "energy and information flow." Crucially, minds in interaction co-create patterns of flow in each mind. Flow can be positive and prosocial or not. Hence, the quality of flow will affect multiple processes within and between us.

Physicists see energy as the potential to do something. Information is a symbolic pattern of energy – something that stands for something else. And flow simply means "change." So we have this fundamental unit of *energy and information flow*. Where does this flow occur? Where is this system? In interpersonal neurobiology, we propose that this system is within your whole body, not just up in your head: This system of energy and information flow is not limited by the skull: it goes throughout the body. But energy and information flow are also not limited by the skin – they're happening right now between you and me, Barb, or between you and anyone else who might be reading these words. The patterns of flow are co-creations – it takes an orchestra to play a symphony that is the origin of mind. This reveals how mind is at once both an interpersonal and an internal process – between and within are part of one system though they may seem as if they are "two places at once." A systems view of mind enables us to see that neither skull nor skin are impermeable barriers to energy and information flow; the mind is an emergent property of this flow that occurs both within and between.

We can see how the co-creation of energy and information flow extends beyond skull and skin, and extends in a way that has certain properties as a system. This system has these three qualities: it's *open* to influences outside itself; it's *chaos-capable*, which means, roughly, it can be completely random; and it's *nonlinear*, meaning, on an initial look, it's not easy to predict what the result will be of an input that's placed into the system. When you're a nonlinear, chaos-capable, open system, then you're called a *complex system* – and complexity theory, which is derived as part of a division of probability theory of mathematics, tells us that complex systems have *emergent properties*. My suggestion is that mental life, maybe all of mental life, including subjective experience, consciousness, and information processing, might be emergent properties of energy and information flow. But one of these emergent properties of a complex system which may be distinct from or perhaps overlapping with those, as we mentioned, is *self-organization*.

What's so interesting about self-organization, and also what seems directly relevant to your work, Barb, is that to optimize the flow of this system, to optimized self-organization, what is needed is two processes: (1) to *differentiate* – that is, make unique or special, to make different; and (2) it needs to *link* those differentiated parts, to connect them to each other. And when differentiated elements are connected to each other, the self-organization of the system reaches a kind of movement that's called *optimal self-organization*, or maximizing complexity. And the human way of thinking about that, not just the math way, is that you've achieved a kind of *harmony*.

It's what resonance is based on. For example, when two elements, like two strings on a guitar, are resonating, they don't become each other, but they do influence each other in a deep way. This process of the *linkage of differentiated parts* in math does not have a name, but in common language, we can call it "*integration.*" Just like a symphony emerges from the differentiated musicians and their instruments of the orchestra, what is created is greater than simply the sum of the individual components. Integration, defined here as the linkage of differentiated parts, optimizes self-organization. With integrative harmony the system achieves the five qualities that complexity theory describes, in which it becomes: flexible; adaptive; coherent, which is holding well dynamically over time or being resilient; energized; and stable. And there's all sorts of qualities of what coherence really means – I'm an acronym nut, but you can spell the word "coherence" and you get some of those elements: it's *c*onnected and *o*pen; *h*armonious, it has a sense of being *e*mergent; *n*oetic – there's a sense of knowing, and all sorts of things that go along with that; and it has the qualities of being *c*ompassionate and *e*mpathic. These are fun ways of describing coherence and what integration creates.

When I was reading your work, I was revising the first edition of *The Developing Mind*, and I was blown away, because to me, the "broaden and build" approach seemed to be describing states that enhanced integration. It built on what I'd written about in the 1990s about emotion, which was one way of defining emotion as a shift in integration, so that you could interpret, for example, *negative emotions* (that is, of prolonged sadness, anger, fear, or shame) as decreases in how things are either differentiated or linked. Negative emotions would be down-shifts in states of integration. And *positive emotions* could be reinterpreted as increases in integration (like joy, gratitude, happiness, love, or awe) and in those ways, the "broaden and build" view of positive emotions would fit together with the idea that positive emotions were increases in integration.

As I was reading your work on love, what occurred to me was an idea that if you, Barbara Fredrickson, were open to thinking about the possibility that love could also embrace negative emotional states as well as the sharing of positive ones. For example, compassionate action involves someone tuning into the sadness or fear or anger or shame of another person, then you'd achieve a certain kind of resonance. With that resonance, with that joining of two differentiated individuals, even around a negative emotional state, the linking of them in compassionate communication would be creating more integration. Even though from an interpersonal neurobiology perspective the joining would be around a state of diminished integration (as negative emotions were being shared), the overall effect, even with resonating around a "negative" emotion, would actually be increasing integration of the dyadic system so it would feel deeply rewarding for both people. From a positive psychology perspective, the resonance around a negative emotion might lead to the positive emotional experience of being cared for by another, and caring for another, so that each individual would feel a positivity to the resonance, even though they became connected through a negative emotional state initially.

That's basically interpersonal neurobiology relevant to your notions of love as positivity resonance and a broaden-and-build view of positive emotions, in a nutshell.

To add one final little set of principles: amazingly, when a system is not integrated, it goes to either *chaos* or *rigidity*, and what's fascinating about that is you can go to the Diagnostic and Statistical Manual of Mental Disorders (DSM V, 2015) and you find that every disorder's symptoms can be reinterpreted as either chaos or rigidity. So for example, mania is chaos, depression (of manic-depressive illness) would be rigidity, and in individuals with schizophrenia, the same pattern can be described – one sees both chaotic and rigid symptoms. These are disorders that are not caused by what parents do; but in the case when researchers have examined experientially caused problems, such as severe abuse and neglect, called developmental trauma, and in fact, with any form of post-traumatic stress disorder, both chaotic and rigid symptoms are also revealed. What's also amazing are the studies of psychopathology and their correlation with brain structure and function; the research has now shown that there is impaired neural integration associated with individuals with manic-depressive illness, schizophrenia, and autism (Zhang and Raichle, 2010). And in studies of individuals with developmental trauma, such as abuse or neglect, there is also impaired integration in the brain (see Teicher et al., 2003). And what about in well-being? Recently, the International Human Connectome Project, which utilizes diffusion tensor imaging with which you can actually show the linkages among differentiated parts of the brain – called the connectome – has revealed that the best predictor of positive traits of life is how the separate areas are interconnected, basically a more integrated brain is the neural correlate of well-being (Smith et al., 2015). This is a connectome where there are more linkages of the differentiated parts. So it's an incredibly exciting moment to bridge this hypothesis about self-organization and integration as the underlying mechanism of well-being and health, with your wonderful work and to think about how compassion can be thought of as a form of love, because it's increasing the resonance of two individuals – increasing their way of being integrated beyond simply two separate individuals, but becoming a part of a "we." It's also exciting because, as a number of chapters in this volume show, there is increasing research suggesting that compassion training and cultivation can change a whole set of physical and neurophysiological processes in favor of integration.

So I want to just put this out there so we can see if the positivity resonance and "broaden and build" can be linked with the interpersonal neurobiology perspectives on self-organization and integration as health.

BLF: Well, one thing I'd add here, in keeping with our conversation in Washington DC, is that I do think it's quite reasonable to consider positivity resonance within the context of negativity and awareness of suffering. There's no part of my conceptualization of love as positivity resonance that says that the only emotions on the scene are positive. Just as an example of this, two people can be attuned to each other – showing shared positivity, mutual care, and biobehavioral synchrony – in the context of one person's awareness of the other's suffering. In this case, an element of negativity is woven in there as well. Certainly the suffering is negative and the empathic concern for another person's suffering can have a mixed quality that is poignant and a bit distressing, yet still the overarching feeling tone may be concern and care, which certainly has a positive element to it. I think that when somebody who is suffering registers that another person is concerned and caring, that suffering person is also feeling appreciative of that concern and caring, appreciative that somebody understands where they're at. That's a very different feeling than suffering and not feeling felt or seen, or not feeling understood. Expressing compassion is a way of registering that you care and you understand. The way I like to phrase it is that "compassion is what love (as positivity resonance) becomes when one individual is aware of the suffering of another" (Fredrickson, 2013a). So there is a continuum between love and compassion. They are not necessarily qualitatively different, except in the aspect of registering another person's suffering. Keep in mind that in defining love as an affective state of positivity resonance, I've disconnected it from any exclusive link to the people in your inner circle. In their most generous embodiments, love and compassion cross those boundaries freely.

My perspective is informed by affective science, social psychology, and evolutionary psychology. Part of what inspired this collaborative chapter – focusing on compassion – is that I shared your appreciation for the consilience between my work and your work. Each pointing to this dynamic, relational, and embodied state, and this idea that coherence or integration, or further whole-ism, emerges as a product of an accumulation of these sorts of positive experiences. I've found in my work, time and again, that people's resilience, their mental health, and even their physical health, is a product of their recent history – over the few months or so – of the positive emotions they've experienced, these micro-moments of uplift and warm-heartedness. When we tally those up they tend to predict people's health and well-being and their *sense of community and connection.* We've also used experimental designs, in which we've randomly assigned people to experience more positive emotions or not, to be able to make causal claims. In these we find that an increase in people's diet of positive emotions produces increases in physical health, in mental health, and so on (Fredrickson, Cohn, Coffey, Pek, & Finkel, 2008; Kok et al., 2013). So I think the work you're describing about the connectome in the brain is super-compatible and interesting here.

DJS: That's fascinating. A couple of things come to mind: I remember a patient once said to me – one of my first patients – after she had gotten better in therapy and I didn't understand why, so I said let's have an exit interview. She was going onto her post-doc, so I said, "What do you think helped you get better?" And she said, "Well, that's obvious," and I said, "Of course it's obvious, but how can you articulate it?" And she said, "Never in my life have I ever had the experience of feeling felt."

BLF: Yes!

DJS: And it was so simple and so elegant, and I'd like to give her credit (I can see her right now in my mind's eye). But this "feeling felt" description is exactly what you're talking about: being seen, being felt, resonating, not just being understood or analyzed, but that you exist within someone else's mental life. And here's what I want to ask you about, Barb: for this chapter, what to me is so exciting is in your work, you've really bridged some fantastic areas of not only social psychology, of positive psychology, but also of physiological issues, even looking at contemplation and meditative practice; in interpersonal neurobiology, what we try to do is look at ways to go deeply into fundamental questions, like "What is the mind?" and "What is a healthy mind?", and so I want to make sure that I'm hearing you right, that your sense of *love* is that it itself is a positive emotional state because it's involving resonance, and what I want to clarify for all of our understanding, is that on the one hand you can resonate with a person around their negative emotions in an act of compassion, and both of you may feel connected, resonating, grateful, and appreciative, so that's the positive side of it, yet it's resonating initially around negative emotional states. So I want to make sure I understand the phrase "positivity resonance" – how does that phrase go along with the notion of resonating with compassion around someone's negative affective states?

BLF: I would just rephrase that a bit. I don't think the resonance necessarily first happens over suffering and negative affect. In some cases it might, yet in other cases it might first emerge from sharing some form of positivity and the mutual concern and caring that comes with that. Say you're already connecting with another, and then, in that context, you become aware of their suffering. Here the resonating is on the positive, but as you learn about the suffering, then compassion emerges. This might actually be the way in which compassion is easiest to experience, when there is a resonance or a bond already built.

Or, when your very first encounter with somebody includes awareness of their suffering, then perhaps having a practised habit of care and concern for all people, without exception, could facilitate having that moment turn toward compassion rather than avoidance. So, I don't think that it's necessarily always the case that negativity resonance occurs first, and that it then transforms. Positivity resonance could come first, and then it could become more complex – because you're aware of the polarities of care and connection, on the one hand, and the fact that they're suffering, on the other. So compassion is not necessarily the regulation of a negative emotional experience.

DJS: What's really interesting about that is when I work with therapists – new therapists, especially, who are getting burnt out. I'll give you one example here. A daughter of a friend of mine was getting burnt out, and she came to me and I said, "Tell me what are you experiencing," and she said, "You know,

I'm in the clinic and there are a lot of abused young women, a little bit younger than me; they're becoming aware of their abuse, you know, child abuse when they were young." I then said, "Well, what do you do?" and she said, "Well, I'm empathic and compassionate." So I said, "What does that mean?" And she said, "You know, I try to imagine what it would be like to be them, like what if my father had done that to me?" And she was doing that over and over and over again, so she had been four or five months at this clinic, and now she was ready to quit and find another profession. So I said, "Let me tell you about a study and a general principle: the general principle is that integration depends on *differentiation* and *linkage*, and it sounds like you're losing your differentiation saying 'What if that were me?'" And she then asks, "Well isn't that being empathic?" So I said, "We'll talk about that in a moment," and I said, "Let me also tell you about a brain study where they show a person, for example, a photograph of a really terrible car accident, and in condition one, they say 'Imagine if that were you,' and in condition two, they say 'Imagine what the person in that car accident might feel like.'" In the two conditions the brain reacted completely differently. In condition one, the brain gets flooded with emotion and shuts down. And in condition two, it's activated, but then it activates the circuitry of compassion, which includes some of the medial prefrontal regions" (see Decety and Ickes, 2009).

After I told this to my friend's daughter, she asked, "But is that really being empathic?" I said, "That's being differentiated and being linked – being integrated." So she went back to work after our brief conversation, and I saw her several months later at a holiday party and she was glowing. I asked her how she was doing and she said, "Oh my God, that consultation completely turned everything around, and now I feel really excited to be a therapist." And what was so interesting, and this goes along with what you were saying, Barb, is that we need to find positivity even in connecting around painful emotions – or, perhaps especially around painful emotions.

BLF: Indeed.

DJS: Once, I was teaching a conference with Jon Kabat-Zinn and some others on becoming more aware of your inner emotional state, and at the end of the conference on the third day, a woman took the microphone and thanked us for such a powerful conference, and she said, "You know, I'm really angry at all of you." And we said, "Why are you angry?" And she said, "You're making me more empathic, and there's so much suffering in the world, now I feel completely burdened, and I feel horrible." And we talked to her about different things and one of the things I said was that I had heard someone asking the Dalai Lama this exact question – "How can you make us be more aware of our own internal state, you know, with more interoception, if the world is full of pain?" – and here's what I recall the Dalai Lama saying in response: "You know, the suffering in the world is so great; we are all vulnerable to losing our joy and our humor – but it's not in spite of the world's suffering; it's because of the world's suffering that we have to find and maintain the joy and the humor, because if we don't take that responsibility of being joyful and grateful, then the suffering will have won."

BLF: Yes, that's well put.

DJS: It was so clear, and she really responded to that and I said, "So, it isn't just to become more interoceptive, it's to find a way to transform your resonance with the pain and the negativity into a positive gratitude and appreciation that you're alive, that you can connect with someone, that there's always hope, that there's always the next breath that takes you more into the present moment, that you can let go of your expectations, all these we can imagine we can say, but the overarching thing in terms of positivity resonance that resonates with me, from the interpersonal neurobiology point of view, is that these are higher states of integration.

And I don't know specifically how that concept sits with you, but I'd love to know because whether you're looking at interpersonal integration with love, or looking at neural integration with either functional or structural studies of the connectome, what's so interesting about this is that you can show a kind of mutually causal link between internal neural integration and interpersonal dyadic or even larger cultural integration. I was just wondering how that sits with you?

BLF: I think it's definitely a very promising approach. One thing I've found to differentiate positive emotional experiences from negative emotional experiences is that positive emotional experiences widen our lens on our surroundings, and negative emotions narrow our perspective to just one key focal aspect of our richer context (Fredrickson & Branigan, 2005). This "taking in" of more information is one way to knit the individual to the context. By contrast, by narrowing our perception, negative emotions re-inscribe our sense of being separate and alone. Positive emotions help knit us together both with our context and with other people.

There are a few things I want to react to regarding what you were just mentioning: one is that I love this new emphasis on compassion and the other heart qualities – loving-kindness and sympathetic joy – within the contemplative science movement. Probably for practical concerns, contemplative approaches first introduced to the West primarily targeted their attentional, attunement qualities. This may be because stabilizing attention seems clearly a concept with gravity and importance in today's distracted world. If you're just starting to introduce meditation practices, you might not want to lead with the softer sides, the heart qualities.

There are parallels within emotion science. We had a decade or two of research on negative emotions before scientists warmed up to the science of the positive emotions (Fredrickson, 2013b). To get a new idea into a scientific mainstream, and then a popular mainstream, it's sometimes helpful to lead with the concepts that will have greater acceptance. We're now getting to a place within the contemplative sciences that the heart qualities are more integrated. We can balance awareness with appreciation. So it's not just about noticing everything, noticing all the suffering, it's equally about proactively cultivating the noble positive states.

The other thing I wanted to react to was the example from your former client of "feeling felt" and how that could be described as part of a therapeutic alliance between client and practitioner. One thing that can get in the way of "feeling felt" is – well, I'm not a clinician, so I can't speak to this from my own clinical experience, so I'll pitch this to you as a question – one thing that might be getting in the way is the habit of observing clients in a scholarly, affectively neutral way. You have your notepad and you write things down that you observe or hear. Then you have this interpersonal connection that is facilitated by eye contact and staying nonverbally present with the other. Every time you break that eye contact and presence – by focusing on your notes, your pen and paper, or your computer or whatever – when you look up again, you have to start over and create that connection anew. Whereas, if you consider that therapy session more as a "connection" session – as an opportunity to understand, and where appropriate, validate, and let somebody experience the quality of being understood, by giving up the notes and being present so that the most important thing is connection – that's what's going to be more healing. That might be the major "nonspecific treatment effect" that runs across all forms of therapy and that accounts for, regardless of treatment type, the benefits of the interpersonal context as a healing context.

DJS: That's beautifully said, and I couldn't agree more. I wrote a book called *The Mindful Therapist* (Siegel, 2010), which has an acronym of – and it's kind of the way the book is organized – the beginning of the acronym is PART, and it says you need to have *Presence*, so you're open to what's happening, *Attunement*, meaning you focus your attention on the internal world of other and the self, *Resonating*, just exactly like you described resonating, letting yourself stay differentiated but become influenced by the other, and that develops "T," *Trust*. I couldn't agree more that the nonspecific effects which have the most robust causal influence on positive outcomes, that's what the studies reveal, the meta-analyses shows (see Norcross, 2002), that is exactly I think what happens – and sadly, when people get lost in diagnostic categories or taking notes or in their computer – you lose exactly what you're saying is so important to create.

Even something as simple as going to an internist for a common cold, studies have revealed that if you get an empathic comment from your physician, you will actually get over your cold a day sooner and your immune system reaction will be more robust (Rakel et al., 2011). Imagine a brief empathic comment, like, "Oh, you know, this is April, final exams are coming up, and it must be so frustrating to have a cold when you're studying for exams." Whereas the "non-empathic" clinician offers exactly the same medical advice but no empathic comment. There's something about joining that, I think, as your work has beautifully shown – is what compassion and empathy are all about – but I think from the mind point of view, it's what makes the mind healthy, and just to underscore exactly what you summarized earlier, the studies of how long you live, how happy you are, your mental health, and your medical health, all relate to our social connections and our networks of social support. So we have this amazing reality that even your body, with its cardiovascular system and immune system, is affected by resonating with others in networks of social support that are mediated, I think, through a mental state of presence. And this presence is the gateway for connection and compassion. It's exactly what you're talking about: you're having this presence that's there, that allows you to resonate with another, there is that positivity resonance of love that you so beautifully articulated that I think is at the heart of developing trust, and I think as well for this "broadening and build" experience, which expands the integrated states so you no longer feel alone, so instead of just being an "I" and "you," it's a "we" that are together.

In the *Brainstorm* approach for adolescents (Siegel, 2013), I essentially say "Look, you know we have this moment in our history of thinking about our identity as separate in modern culture, as Einstein said many years ago that we have an 'optical delusion' of our separateness, and this delusion of our being isolated, separate individuals is really destructive." We can look at this from a positivity resonance point of view, as if people believe the self is completely encapsulated in the skin, that the self is just in the body, or even more, that the self is just in the head. In this way, the self is not resonating within anyone else, just a separate entity. This is parallel to the academic view commonly held that the "Mind is just brain activity alone," rather than a more interconnecting process. What is the outcome of such cultural or scholarly views of the self? Sadly the outcome of these perspectives can be the creation of isolation and a lot of misery. First of all, it's not consistent with the truth that self is as much relational as it is embodied. Secondly it's unhealthy – and all these studies are now affirming that when we feel membership to a larger whole, we are more whole, we are more healthy – that is, "whole" and "health" derive from the same root. A third point is this: A system is composed of nodes that allow interactions; we may have confused the node of the body as the self, rather than including the whole system as the self. When we believe the node of the body, or the node of the brain, is the whole origin of mind, we are left with a lonely life.

An integrated identity could be seen to embrace the reality of our internal life, a "me" that does live within the body, plus an interconnected source of mind, a "we." To integrate these important aspects of our whole identity, we can combine me with we as a MWe, our integrated identity. In this way, compassion and connection link us to one another in our integrated, co-created emergence of our interdependent lives. With positivity resonance, we create a more harmonious, more whole symphony of our lives, together.

Barb, I think we're at a great summary position and I think this is a powerful overview of both our work and a fun, interactive dialogue.

BLF: Yes, and I just want to add one thought: I think an important thing to add to this summary is that in the example of therapeutic alliance, of the clinician, the practitioner, expressing empathy to the other, it's not just something that's going to facilitate the healing and health of the client, it's also going to facilitate the healing and health – and resilience – of the practitioner. It's not only a way to give health or a better chance for health, but also to give oneself a better chance for resilience and health.

DJS: Beautiful, beautiful, absolutely. I love it.

References

Decety, J., & Ickes, W. (Eds.) (2009). *The Social Neuroscience of Empathy.* Cambridge, MA: MIT Press.

Feldman, R., Gordon, I., & Zagoory-Sharon, O. (2010). The cross-generation transmission of oxytocin in humans. *Hormones and Behavior, 58,* 669–676. doi: 10.1016/j.yhbeh.2010.06.005

Fredrickson, B. L. (1998). What good are positive emotions? *Review of General Psychology, 2,* 300–319. doi: 10.1037/1089-2680.2.3.300

Fredrickson, B. L. (2001). The role of positive emotions in positive psychology: The broaden-and-build theory of positive emotions. *American Psychologist, 56*(3), 218–226.

Fredrickson, B. L. (2009). *Positivity.* New York: Three Rivers Press.

Fredrickson, B. L. (2013a). *Love 2.0.* New York: Plume.

Fredrickson, B. L. (2013b). Positive emotions broaden and build. In E. Ashby Plant & P. G. Devine (Eds.), *Advances on Experimental Social Psychology, 47,* 1–53. Burlington, VT: Academic Press.

Fredrickson, B. L. (in press). *Love.* In L. F. Barrett, M. Lewis, & J. M. Haviland-Jones (Eds.) *Handbook of Emotions, 4th Ed.* New York: Guilford Press.

Fredrickson, B. L., & Branigan, C. (2005). Positive emotions broaden the scope of attention and thought-action repertoires. *Cognition & Emotion, 19*(3), 313–332.

Fredrickson, B. L., Cohn, M. A., Coffey, K. A., Pek, J., & Finkel, S. M. (2008). Open hearts build lives: Positive emotions, induced through loving-kindness meditation, build consequential personal resources. *Journal of Personality and Social Psychology, 95,* 1045–1062. doi: 10.1037/a0013262

Hegi, K. E., & Bergner, R. M. (2010). What is love? An empirically-based essentialist account. *Journal of Social and Personal Relationships, 27,* 620–636. doi: 10.1177/0265407510369605

Kok, B. E., Coffey, K. A., Cohn, M. A., Catalino, L. I., Vacharkulksemsuk, T., Algoe, S. B., Brantley, M., & Fredrickson, B. L. (2013). How positive emotions build physical health: Perceived positive social connections account for the upward spiral between positive emotions and vagal tone. *Psychological Science, 24,* 1123–1132. doi: 10.1177/0956797612470827

Niedenthal, P. M., Mermillod, M., Maringer, M., & Hess, U. (2010). The Simulation of Smiles (SIMS) model: Embodied simulation and the meaning of facial expression. *Behavioral and Brain Sciences, 33,* 417–480. doi: 10.1017/S0140525X10000865

Norcross, J. (Ed.) (2002). *Psychotherapy Relationships That Work: Therapist Contributions and Responsiveness to Patients.* Oxford: Oxford University Press.

Rakel, D., Barrett, B., Zhang, Z., Hoeft, T., Chewning, B., Marchand, L., & Scheder, J. (2011). Perception of empathy in the therapeutic encounter: Effects on the common cold. *Patient Education and Counseling, 85*(3), 390–397.

Reis, H. T., Clark, M. S., & Holmes, J. G. (2004). Perceived partner responsiveness as an organizing construct in the study of intimacy and closeness. In D. Mashek & A. Aron (Eds.), *Handbook of Closeness and Intimacy*, 201–225. Mahwah, NJ: Lawrence Erlbaum.

Siegel, D. J. (2010). *The Mindful Therapist: A Clinician's Guide to Mindsight and Neural Integration*. New York: W.W. Norton.

Siegel, D. J. (2012a). *The Developing Mind: How Relationships and the Brain Interact to Shape Who We Are, 2nd Ed*. New York: Guilford Press.

Siegel, D. J. (2012b). *Pocket Guide to Interpersonal Neurobiology: An Integrative Handbook of The Mind*. New York: W.W. Norton.

Siegel, D. J. (2013). *Brainstorm: The Power and Purpose of the Teenage Brain*. New York: Tarcher/Penguin.

Siegel, D. J. (2017). *Mind: A Journey to the Heart of Being Human*. New York: W.W. Norton.

Smith, S. M., Nichols, T. E., Vidaurre, D., Winkler, A. M., Behrens, T. E. J., Glasser, M. F., . . . Miller, K. L. (2015). A positive-negative mode of population co-variation links brain connectivity, demographics, and behavior. *Nature Neuroscience, 18*(11), 1567–1571.

Stephens, G. J., Silbert, L. J., & Hasson, U. (2010). Speaker-listener neural coupling underlies successful communication. *Proceedings of the National Academy of Sciences, 107,* 14425–14430. doi: 10.1073/pnas.1008662107

Teicher, M. H., Andersen, S. L., Polcari, A., Anderson, C. M., Navalta, C. P., & Kim, D. M. (2003). The neurobiological consequences of early stress and childhood maltreatment. *Neuroscience and Biobehavioral Reviews, 27*(1–2), 33–44.

Vacharkulksemsuk, T., & Fredrickson, B. L. (2012). Strangers in sync: Achieving embodied rapport through shared movements. *Journal of Experimental Social Psychology, 48,* 399–402. doi: 10.1016/j.jesp.2011.07.015

Wilson, E. O. (1998). *Consilience: The Unity of Knowledge*. New York: Vintage/Penguin.

Zhang, T., & Raichle, M. E. (2010). Disease and the brain's dark energy. *Nature Reviews Neurology, 6*(1) 15–28.

Part IV

Applying compassion

Chapter 13

Positive leadership, power and compassion

Daniel Martin and Yotam Heineberg

Compassion and leadership

Leadership has always been core to the social fabric of human societies across history, and accordingly manifested in various ways. Appreciation of compassion and compassionate leadership highlights acknowledgement for the need to shift from autocratic power and social rank oriented models of leadership to egalitarian collaboration based models of management (Gilbert, 2005a; West & Chowla, Chapter 14, this volume). While there are innumerable leadership models, development programs and efforts to provide insights into this ancient and complex endeavor, we will focus on perspectives that provide a potential underpinning and context for our approach towards compassionate leadership and its measurement.

Gilbert and Choden (2013) define compassion as "a sensitivity to suffering in self and others with a commitment to try to alleviate and prevent it," highlighting the important motivational dimensions of compassion (see Gilbert, Chapters 1 and 3, this volume). In addition, because compassion and compassion training focuses on the prevention of suffering, it focuses on needs and the awareness needs. For example, a parent who does not anticipate the needs of his/her child to be fed will end up with a hungry, suffering child. As we will see, transformational leadership involves an appreciation of the needs to be met in order to avoid suffering and promote flourishing in others and the organization. Given the above cognitive, affective, motivational and behavioral perspectives, we will show this framework links well with both the transformational and positive approaches to leadership discussed in the following sections.

Transformational leadership

In recognizing that leadership can take many forms, it is important to note that transformational leaders use their influence to ask followers to consider the good and welfare of others, the organization and society (Bass, 1985). Transformational leadership reflects meaningful and creative exchange between leaders and followers to facilitate vision-driven change in people and organizations (Bass, 1985). Transformational leaders are unique and stand out in the sense that they facilitate followers' problem-solving while developing employees so they are more open, creative and prepared to address future problems (Bass, Avolio, Jung, & Berson, 2003). They are also committed to facilitating potential opportunities for followers to become leaders themselves (Bass et al., 2003). Empirical evidence supports the relationship between transformational leadership and enhanced performance (Avolio, 1999; Bass, 1998; Bass et al., 2003). These findings have been further supported via several meta-analyses (DeGroot, Kiker, & Cross, 2000; Lowe, Kroeck, & Sivasubramaniam, 1996).

Transformational leadership often entails social charisma, as well as the genuine desire for employees to receive both intellectual stimulation and personalized consideration of their experience in the workplace, towards further growth in the system. Values are critical to the dissemination and linkage to the vision of the leader. Benevolence and self-direction are consistently selected as the most important values across cultures (Schwartz & Bardi, 2001). For example, people can be coerced into doing things because they are frightened of the consequences of not doing them (criticism, demotion or even losing one's job) or because they are positively inspired to do them. Transformational leaders understand this crucial distinction between reward-based and threat-based engagement with others – particularly important as the rewards can be valuable, positive social relating (see Stellar & Keltner, Chapter 7, this volume). These critical insights give us the opportunity to link compassion to transformational leadership via awareness of employee and organizational needs (awareness of suffering), feeling empathic (recognizing sympathetic feelings) and initiating action to solve the problem at hand (action). Transformational leaders want to be a source of the relief and prevention of suffering – not to use their position/ power to be a cause of it, either on purpose or through indifference!

Positive leadership

Amidst many view points on leadership, a set of principles has emerged from the fields of positive psychology and positive organizational scholarship, focusing on: (1) positively deviant performance, or an emphasis on moving from normalcy to excellence in organizations and individuals; (2) an orientation toward strengths rather than weaknesses in all aspects of orientation (communication, attitudes, and efforts); as well as (3) a chronic emphasis on the norms of positivity that are evident on a daily basis that are often glossed over given a negative bias (Cameron, 2008). Cameron (2008) identifies four strategies to manifest and develop positive leadership which are supported through the leadership literature including: (1) cultivation of positive climate; (2) developing and maintaining positive relationships; (3) establishing positive communication; and (4) ensuring clear and positive meaning.

While there is significant overlap in the narratives of positive leadership and the compassion literature, some gaps in foci suggest the two systems can become mutually enriched. For example, the caring attention, skills and capacities compassion brings to the issue of suffering and awareness of needs will add improved outcomes to leaders who are engaged with positive methods, yet are also synergistically committed to compassionately responding to suffering and challenge.

In attempting to further our understanding of leadership and other workplace-related constructs, we have operationalized leadership in some of our studies as consistent with the Values in Action Leadership scale (Peterson & Seligman, 2006) which manifests components of positive leadership – encouraging the group leader to get things done while maintaining good relations within the group; organizing group activities and ensuring task completion. Any and/or all of these components have the potential to advance well-being at the intra/interpersonal and organizational level. Ultimately, transformational leadership is concerned with both leader and follower. This also happens through recognition that high-performance leadership is closely linked with team development, and understanding the necessity of building high-quality relationships which entail caring and flexible responses to each individual's needs and struggles. This outlook leads us to anticipate a negative relationship between social dominance orientation and leadership as defined (Cameron, 2008).

The role of social mentalities in leadership

Central to our approach to leadership is understanding the motivational focus of leaders. While we can teach different competencies of leadership, it is the deeper motivational processing systems that are crucial, particularly whether leaders are self-focused, competitive and threat driven, in contrast to being cooperative, supportive and care-focused. As we will discuss, these are rooted in and arise from completely different evolved motivational systems that organize a range of emotional, cognitive, behavioral and self-focused processes in different ways (Gilbert 1989/2016, 2005a, 2014).

One way we can explore these issues is with social mentality theory (see Gilbert, 2005a, 2014 for reviews). Social mentality theory uses an evolutionary functional analysis of motivational processing. Evolution is basically driven by reproduction and survival. Over many millions of years these drivers have built a range of motivational systems for sexual competition and engagement, caring for offspring and alliances, forming in-groups and out-groups, cooperating and social hierarchical competing (Buss, 2014; Gilbert, 1989/2016). Gilbert (1989/2016, 2005a, 2014) highlighted five social mentalities focused on: (1) care eliciting; (2) care giving; (3) cooperation/alliance building; (4) competition/social rank; and (5) sexual relation forming. He referred to these as *social mentalities* to indicate they are highly sensitive to interpersonal communication and are secured via acting in dynamic, reciprocal, interactive social roles. So, for example, a particular set of signals communication and "dances" may lead to a sexual interaction whereas a very different set of social communication signals and interpersonal "dances" may lead to dominant subordinate interactions. Clearly, if a potential sexual partner is turned off by the signals s/he is receiving that's the end of that role formation; if subordinates do not submit to a dominant (but as can happen sometimes) they gang up against them, then the dominant role fails and s/he may be deposed and have to accept subordinate status. Individuals are therefore coding for social signals and sending social signals all the time in order to *co-create* particular kinds of social role and interactions that are actually linked to phenotypic strategies for survival and reproduction. Within any population there will be variation in these strategies, with some people manifesting strategies that are highly prosocial (possibly linked to the polymorphisms of the oxytocin gene; see Colonnello, Petrocchi, & Heinrichs, Chapter 6, this volume; Conway & Slavich, Chapter 9, this volume) whereas others will be manifesting strategies that are highly self-promoting, individualistic and threat-focused.

Also crucial is that competencies like empathy will be used in different ways according to an individual's activated motivational system or social mentality (Zaki, 2014). So the way we might use empathy to attract a sexual partner might be different to how we use it in caring for someone we love, which will be different from how we use it to win a competitive contest. The social signals we process, make sense of and send will be very different according to goals. We may be good in one area (reading people in a poker game) and poor in another (understanding the distress of a lover or child) (Liotti & Gilbert, 2011). The point is that our attention, ways of thinking/reasoning/aspiration, moral values, what gives us good or bad feeling, and our behaviors will be very different according to (say) whether we are orientated to be caring and supportive or to achieve status and power and control over others.

One of the core aspects of compassion is that it must *look into the causes of suffering*. Gilbert (1989/2016, 2005b, 2015; Gilbert & Choden, 2013) argued that central to bringing compassion to social problems in education and business, we need to be much more clear about the evolutionary causes of suffering in relation to our evolved minds with their survival and reproductive strategies. Compassionate leadership therefore must address the dark side of our minds (Gilbert, 2015). We explore this later in the chapter to advance our understanding of the *inhibitors of compassion* and the challenges that lie ahead to move organizations, and indeed human politics in general, towards more ethical and compassionate orientations (Gilbert & Mascaro, in press).

Social dominance orientation

We can now explore leadership through the lens of social mentalities starting with self-focused, competitive ones. Social dominance orientation (SDO) is an individual's level of "basic ruthlessness and a view of the world as a competitive, dog-eat-dog environment of winners and losers" (Sidanius et al., 2012) and an in-group's desire to be superior to out-groups (Pratto, Sidanius, Stallworth, & Malle, 1994). SDO theorists posit that there is a fundamental human desire (social motivation) to maintain group-based social hierarchies – such as cultural, racial, and ethnic groups – (Levin & Sidanius, 1999) despite the possible negative effects for the individual (Pratto et al. 1994; Sidanius & Pratto, 1999).

Those who score high in SDO measures want high social and economic status (Pratto, Stallworth, Sidanius, & Siers, 1997; Sidanius & Pratto, 1999) and are tougher-minded, less other concerned, less warm and sympathetic, compared with people lower in SDO (Duckitt, 2001; Heaven & Bucci, 2001; Lippa & Arad, 1999; Pratto et al., 1994).

High SDOs prefer to be dominant in normal relationships, are immoral (Georgesen & Harris, 2006, p. 453), lacking in empathy (Duriez 2004) and benevolence (Cohrs, Moschner, Maes, & Kielmann, 2005), scoring high in Machiavellianism and psychoticism (see "The dark triad" later in this chapter; Altemeyer 1998; Heaven & Bucci, 2001). The potential ramifications for leadership of high SDO individuals who seek social, political and economic status at all costs (Duriez & Van Hiel, 2002; Duriez, Van Hiel, & Kossowska, 2005; Pratto et al., 1997; Sidanius & Pratto, 1999); strive for leadership positions (Altemeyer, 2003, p. 165) and are willing to use unethical means such as exploitation to achieve social or political gain (Son-Hing, Bobocel, Zanna, & McBride, 2007) are extensive. SDO is therefore clearly a compassion inhibitor.

Social dominance orientation, leadership and workplace distress

As previously described, leadership has immense influence on the lives of individuals in the system, as well as the collective as a whole. Given this, learning about different leadership styles, and the potential impact of high SDO leadership on organizations is obviously important. The negative impact of SDO perspectives on the world is especially relevant when trying to decipher systemic processes, and then conceptualize ways to enhance organizational functioning.

Higher SDO motivates interpersonal deviance and is indirectly related to interpersonal citizenship (Shao, Resick, & Hargis, 2011). With managers who are more likely to have higher levels of SDO, the relationships between subordinates may be undemocratic and possibly abusive (Shao et al., 2011). Supervisors with higher levels of SDO will be more likely to use hard power tactics with employees, like showing disapproval and reminding employees that the supervisor is in the position to help the subordinate get promoted (Aiello, Pratto, & Pierro, 2013). Increasing demands in the workplace are related to workplace burnout since they can contribute to distress (Demerouti, Bakker, De Jonge, Janssen, & Schaufeli, 2001; Demerouti, Bakker, Nachreiner, & Schaufeli, 2001). When employees experience uncertainty, conflicts in the workplace, and one harmful or hazardous experience, they are more likely to have absences (Böckerman & Laukkanen, 2010) or even find employment elsewhere (Böckerman & Ilmakunnas, 2009). SDO-oriented organizations may generate a culture that is unsupportive and lacking empathy, which may perpetuate the cycles of stress, depression and anxiety. These may become manifested in feelings of poor self-worth, high blood pressure from having to perform under harsh working conditions, and unprovoked nervousness in the presence of supervisors or others in power roles.

High scorers on SDO scales prefer disharmony to egalitarianism: those with higher SDO scale scores demonstrate higher scale scores on preferences for war, national hegemony and international disharmony and inequality. Dominant, power-oriented leaders have more sensitive stress responses and may use force and hierarchy legitimizing myths (Georgesen and Harris, 2006) when their social standing is threatened. This makes our integration of Gilbert's (2005a) social mentalities approach a novel theoretical lens with which to analyze potential leadership capacities, individual differences and their subsequent impact at the group and organizational level.

Keep in mind that social mentality theory focuses on the co-creation of social roles. Therefore in order for individuals to say play an aggressive dominant strategy, they have to be able to stimulate either (1) a fearful subordinate strategy in the minds of subordinates, or (2) address and appeal to subordinates' own fear systems (e.g. of the outsider) or "wants" and offer themselves as protective or providers, in order to maintain support for their personal power seeking and maintaining style and strategies. This is important because in Western beliefs the importance of competitiveness over prosocial values has become a dominant economic and political discourse, and has largely been the success of the dominating elite influencing the values and world views of ordinary working people through ownership of the media and support of political groups. To put it another way, SDO could not flourish in populations unless there were others supporting, or at least complicit in playing the reciprocal role of willing or fearful follower/subordinate. These processes have been identified in how aggressive leaders can set up movements and cults and attract followers from Hitler to Jim Jones (Lindholm, 1993) and get "good people to do bad things" (Zimbardo, 2008).

The dark triad

Furnham, Richards, & Paulhus (2013) offered a ten-year review of the literature on how certain personality traits, labeled *the dark triad* impact on leaders and followers/subordinates. The dark triad are: Machiavellianism, narcissism and (subclinical) psychopathy. They note that individuals who possess these personality traits are more likely to be drawn to power positions, as well as leadership positions in particular, driven by an up-rank focus, as opposed to an egalitarian collaborative stance. This will also impact how they might mentor others into positions of power; and cultivating future leaders into a competition mindset. "Dark triad" leaders are likely to help people "get ahead of" but not necessarily "get along with" others in the work place (Hogan, 2007). Not surprisingly, dark triad traits are also positively correlated with higher *levels* of SDO (Hodson, Hogg, & MacInnis, 2009). Recognizing these realities of leadership tendencies towards power and competitive, rank-focused mentalities is salient to our thinking of power in organizations, as well as to our recognition for the importance of devising methods to increase compassion and collaborative, alliance-building mentalities in organizations. Future research might add to our chapter's correlation outcomes by demonstrating how the dark triad might correlate and interact with other dimensions of power, leadership, compassion, individual and organizational well-being.

Bases of social power

The use of power for leadership positions is regarded as exercising influence over others by utilizing various bases of social power in order to achieve organizational objectives (Conger & Kanungo, 1998). There are six bases of powers (Raven, 1993), based on social norms, namely legitimate power; reward power; coercive power; expert power; referent power and information power. While the use of power is ubiquitous in the pursuit of organizational leadership, compassion covers multiple dimensions – affective, cognitive – and at the behavioral level can be observed at the individual, group and organizational level. Given the growing interest in compassionate leadership, the use of compassionate power is of interest, specifically as the term might seem counterintuitive.

Reward power is the ability to grant a reward and might be construed as compassion or favoritism, based on egalitarian norms within the organization. Using the social mentalities model, norms and standard operational procedures should be guided by an understanding of the four aforementioned mentalities. To effectively reward people, individuals must have an awareness of the needs and desires of their followers, as well as the valence of the reward. Of course compassion facilitates excellent interpersonal skills, enabling the effective use of active, empathic listening. Accordingly, compassion seems to be part of the basis for effective use of reward power.

Coercive power is the ability to take something away or punish someone for non-compliance. Coercive power often has a negative connotation, but it is part of the tools of an effective leader when used in limited but appropriate contexts. Compassion can enable a useful approach to facilitating an appreciation for the use of coercive power by examining the rationale behind its use (i.e. organizational, economic, individual or group problems, shortfalls, poor fits, etc.). A better way to think of this perhaps is that compassion is not submissive but assertive. Individuals who cause harm do need to be prevented from doing so. Importantly the appropriate use of coercive power can be seen as protective by observers – for example leaders who deal effectively with bullies and bullying can be regarded as deeply compassionate and supportive. Compassionate leaders however do not act out of rage or hostility but a desire to protect and be assertive – they may also offer (for example) accurate feedback and psychological help for bullies. Again and again the issue of motivation behind action is crucial. Individuals and organizations who are targets of coercive power are usually in a position that is negative and might cause stress and fear. So while leadership must occasionally use coercive power, there must also be an attempt to understand the motives behind it and to listen and empathize with people.

Expert power is established knowledge, abilities and skills. Compassionate leaders want to use their knowledge for the benefit of others; happy for others to collaboratively learn from them. Compassionate leaders take pleasure in being able to foster the development and learning of those around them; they use their own knowledge to support and help others, and in this way encourage others to turn to them for wisdom and mentoring. This means that compassionate leaders are motivated to acquire knowledge and the wisdom of how to lead in their own particular field effectively. So compassion inspires us to be at our best and therefore we can develop our own wisdom and knowledge. Non-compassionate leaders use their knowledge for personal gain and may withhold information if it could advance someone else in the organization. Inter-department concealment, competitiveness and non-cooperation are known to cause serious problems in organizations.

Referent power stems from personal characteristics of the leader. It is good to have referent power and have admiring followers, and is linked to charisma (Lindholm, 1993). However, we can only understand this process through the co-creation of roles – leaders do not exist in a vacuum – the degree to which others refer to them and follow them is dependent upon what the subordinate is looking for and wants a leader to do or provide (Lindholm, 1993). What gave Hitler his leadership power was his appeal as a strong leader responding to the anger and threat of certain sections of the general population. Nelson Mandela, on the other hand, had a completely different reference leadership profile. Compassionate leadership styles are often communicated through non-verbal communications such as friendliness, voice tones, facial expressions, body postures, taking an interest in others and humor. Whereas some leaders are seen by others as slightly angry and strident, even threatening (e.g. Hitler), others want to use their charisma to be seen as likeable leaders and easy to get on with; but charisma, friendly or otherwise, does not define a compassionate leader – motivation does. Sometimes charismatic leaders rely too much on referent power, leading them to abuse their power or be vulnerable to hubris (http://www.daedalustrust.com).

Information power is having special access to specific information. A few individuals holding the information that others need or want is of great value, and while specific/rare information is critical for competitive advantage, giving subordinates developmental opportunities to acquire this knowledge, empowering them to facilitate their needs as well as the needs of the organization, give the leaders an opportunity to continue their own development plans and expertise along with information power.

Thus, different forms of power affect individuals' leadership approach, follower compliance, motivation and the success of the power approach. In this, the relationship between power and compassion can be more powerful. The following three questions can help leaders and managers determine whether they are using power compassionately:

1   Does the behavior produce an outcome for people inside and outside the organization that reflects a desire to address and prevent suffering and promote flourishing?

2   Does the power behavior respect the long-term rights, needs and resources of all parties?

3   Does the power behavior treat all parties equitably and fairly; that is, is it rooted in a sound ethical basis?

Consider these three principles from the point of view of SDO or the dark triad! As with all areas of power and authority, individuals can use their power and act with compassion for themselves and for others via the three directions of compassion, receiving from others and for oneself (see Gilbert, Chapter 3, this volume). The three directions of compassion viewed through the "power dynamics" noted above might give us a new lens with which to view empowerment. The essence of empowerment resides in the four dimensions of meaning: competence; self-determination; impact and creating heightened motivation through the development of a strong sense of personal self-efficacy. In implementing compassionate empowerment, managers should:

- express awareness of challenges as well as confidence in employees' capabilities;
- set high performance expectations while providing resources to accomplish them;
- offer opportunities for employees to participate in decision making;
- remove constraints that stifle autonomy, compassion and awareness of linkages between jobs and positions;
- set inspirational goals.

Our current research

Our own current leadership research spans both basic and applied streams. In a study of 371 working business students we found a significant negative relationship of social dominance orientation (SDO) with compassion and positive leadership ability as well as a mediational impact of compassion (for others, self as well as fears of compassion). Our research also found that high levels of competitive and hierarchical world conceptualization were significantly, and sometimes strongly, negatively linked to compassion and leadership-related constructs (Martin et al., 2014). Our studies reveal that positive leadership scores were significantly negatively correlated with SDO and fear of compassion from others and for self. Given the positive relationship with compassion for others and leadership, this finding suggests that a powerful tool for self-awareness in leaders (and a crucial component of leadership development) is awareness and development of acceptance of compassion in three directions: towards others, from others, and towards self.

Consistent with the theoretical approach to compassionate leadership, and the recognition of the importance of both facilitators and inhibitors (fears) of compassion (Gilbert & Mascaro, in press) we found that the high levels of fears of compassion has detrimental impacts on the interpersonal skills of leaders, modeling inappropriate behavior across the organization. While it is very understandable that people can experience fears of engaging with compassion towards others, themselves, as well as receiving compassion from others; due to various evolutionary and attachment-related threats, trust dynamics and self-protection strategies (Gilbert, McEwan, Matos, & Rivis, 2011), it is important to highlight the problematic impact of these fears. A thorough compassion training model would be wise to address these fears through psycho-education, as well as practices to address these issues. This is likely to support improved leadership capacities, and overall well-being in organizations.

Also theoretically consistent is the significant positive correlation between compassion (compassion for others and fears of compassion) and positive leadership. When taken with the previously mentioned findings, this suggests that the higher an individual scores on positive leadership the less the preferences of social dominance orientation will be manifested, more compassion for others will be expressed, and less fear (inhibitors) of expressing compassion for others, receiving compassion from others, and expressing care and compassion toward oneself. While counter-intuitive in the dog-eat-dog world of enterprise (Martin & Heineberg, 2014), the emerging picture is clear: Leadership benefits (as do employees) from diminished levels of SDO via compassionate awareness and behavior. Ongoing research suggests strong and significant links between the high levels of SDO, lack of compassion and high levels of fears of compassion with the constructs of stress, anxiety and depression. SDO is inversely related to positive leadership, namely inspirational motivation, idealized influence, intellectual stimulation and individualized consideration.

Our studies have also shown that scores on the measure SDO are significantly negatively correlated with compassion, consistent with theoretical expectations and previous research (Martin & Heineberg, 2014). SDO was significantly negatively correlated with fear of expressing compassion for others, fear of receiving compassion from others and fear of expressing compassion toward oneself. This finding suggests that the higher one scores on the SDO scale the less compassion they might show for others, and they will be more fearful of expressing compassion for others and self as well as being more fearful of receiving compassion from others.

Given the similarity of the questions in the compassion measures we used, as well as the fact all other measures of compassion correlated significantly with SDO, we were surprised to find that the Self Compassion measure developed by Neff (2003) did not. Consistent with our theoretical concept, compassion for others correlated significantly with both fear of receiving compassion from others and fear of expressing compassion toward oneself. This finding suggests that the two constructs are tapping into similar elements of acceptance of compassion toward oneself (from others and self).

Of note then is the surprising lack of significant correlation between the Neff self-compassion scales in any of the other measures in the current research besides the measure of compassion for others. Though the scale is used frequently, previous research using the scale has found similar results (Martin et al., 2014), and it may reflect either multidimensionality in the construct or required reification of the scale/s. People with dark triad and SDO characteristics do not regard themselves as self-critical and if anything are quite "positively" self-focused. So here there might be instances where it is possible to have self-compassion without compassion for others.

Mediational analyses

Contrary to our expectations, self-compassion did not mediate the relationship between SDO and positive leadership. Additionally, the lack of a meditational role of self-compassion may be a function of the nature of leadership in that it is focused on the leader's relationship with others and not necessarily an intrapersonal capacity. As such, we would expect that transformational leadership capacity would be impacted more so by compassion in the context of the other over the self. While further replication is necessary to corroborate this claim, our study seems to provide initial support for it.

Consistent with our hypotheses, the relationship between SDO and positive leadership was mediated by compassion for others. As SDO is thought to be predictive of potentially negative interpersonal/group relationships, compassion for others seems to facilitate positive and beneficial social interactions. As such, this finding seems to suggest that a higher level of compassion for others is the key ingredient in the negative relationship between SDO and the values of leading positively.

Consistent with our hypotheses, a mediational role was found between fear of compassion from others and for self in the relationship between SDO and positive leadership. However, fear of compassion for others did not mediate the relationship between these constructs. While SDO is thought to be predictive of potentially negative interpersonal/group relationships, fears of compassion seem to prevent leaders from accessing the very tools they need to receive and offer assistance in the execution of organizational requirements.

Training and education

The findings outlined in this chapter suggests a need for intervention programs that facilitate an increase of compassion for others or a reduction in fears of compassion from others, for others and for self. Such outcomes are also likely to result in increased overall well-being, as well as increased positive leadership. In the last few years we have been developing and piloting a new Compassion Skills Training program for leaders and managers (Martin & Heineberg, 2014) based in part on training practices developed in therapeutic contexts called compassion focused therapy (CFT) and compassionate mind training (CMT) (Gilbert, 2009, 2010; Gilbert & Choden, 2013). Our approach is unique in that it is based on peer and regular dyadic interactions, sharing of compassion focused psycho-education (a different theme each week) with practices for instigating insight engrained into daily living. We have recently piloted our new program in hospitals and universities with positive results. For example, we found statistically significant pre and post differences in the aforementioned domains. While further data are being gathered and analyzed, and replication and controlled studies will be needed to establish the efficacy of our model, we believe our pilot studies act as initial proof for feasibility of compassion training for leaders.

Our compassion skills training program for leaders and managers provides participants handouts and other materials covering up-to-date evidence on the nature of the human mind and its inherent emotional conflicts and difficulties, and the value of cultivating well-being and compassion. Participants learn how the prosocial motives and emotions influence our bodies, brains and minds. They are then invited to engage with meaningful experiential growth-oriented peer-to-peer discussions on a weekly provided topic. The program relies on a rich fund of evidence-based literature that has been adapted to fit the online peer-to-peer format of the program, and the needs of the specific population with whom we intend to work. This is not a clinical program, and is not psychotherapy. Rather, lessons in this program are presented in the format of a psycho-educational class with the intention of increasing intellectual understanding and insights of topic matters, as well as experiential learning, in order to increase one's sense of resilience, empathy and compassion towards self and others.

Compassion skills training begins with a pre-training assessment, followed by eight sessions consisting of approximately 30–60 minutes of reading, followed by a 1-hour dyadic interaction conveniently scheduled at the discretion of the two participants using compassion development skills protocols. Participants gain access to various reflection opportunities and perspective-taking insights to engage with between sessions. The training ends with a post-training assessment. In total, 16 hours' worth of training occurs, with web-based participation evidence and outcomes provided by participants.

In previous applications of the CST with the working student population, significant effects were found in pre/post-test measures of the following scales for both genders:

1) Santa Clara Brief Compassion Scale.
2) Subjective Happiness Scale.
3) Values in Action Leadership Scale.
4) Acceptance and Action Scale.
5) Fear of Offering Compassion to Others Scale.

Specifically, for men:

6) Self-Compassion Scale (Neff).
7) Forms of Self-criticizing/Attacking and Reassurance Scale.
8) Functions of Self-criticizing/Attacking Scale.
9) Fear of Compassion from Others Scale.

While data collection is ongoing in multiple environments, industries and occupations, we anticipate similar responses from these studies with various populations, and with potentially more significant results, as pilots have been executed with working business students (undergraduate and graduate) who are not vocationally motivated to consider the intra and interpersonal criticality of compassion in meeting personal, social and organizational needs.

Discussion and conclusions

In this chapter we have spanned across various leadership related constructs. We explored the nature of positive and transformative leadership, as well as problematic leadership related to constructs such as Social Dominance Orientation, dark triad leadership and elements of power use and misuse by leaders. These styles act as powerful compassion inhibitors with serious consequences to employee well-being and eventually organization efficiency with negative social impacts. The framework of social mentalities is offered as a route to understand systemic processes in work places, with a special emphasis on the tension between compassion-related collaborative/alliance building social mentalities, and competition-oriented social mentalities, which often link up with social rank dynamics, and the power-based desire to "up-rank" others who are viewed as a competitive threat. We have reviewed multiple studies which clearly outline that the impact of negative attitudes in leadership can have a detrimental impact not only on individuals, but also on systems and whole human societies.

Drawing on these various constructs we shared some of our own research findings which demonstrate significant relationships that holding non-egalitarian views to the world (SDO), and lower levels of compassion are related to lower levels of positive leadership, as well as lower levels of overall well-being (e.g. stress, depression, anxiety). These findings act as a call for action, by way of further basic research, as well as the implementation of compassion-focused interventions in various systems.

We conclude by advocating additional basic research studies which will help map out the systemic landscape of organizations. Further drawing on the variables and data we presented here, we hope to conduct future studies which will identify relationships with additional constructs in workplace environments, towards increased systemic understanding. For example, identifying how the aforementioned variables relate with constructs such as job satisfaction, employee well-being, productivity, and various manifestations of social mentalities will help guide us towards productive routes of intervention. We believe that future trainings on compassionate leadership will benefit from attention to the issue of social mentalities and the co-construction of social roles, and supporting individuals in shifting from self-focused competitive to more collaborative mentalities.

On the program implementation side, we introduced our online model of Compassion Skills Training, which effectively strives to increase engagement with compassionate and positive leadership. We conclude by proposing that ongoing implementations of highly scalable compassionate leadership training can yield beneficial outcomes, both on the individual with organizations and collective levels of society. A commitment to this trajectory of work can significantly improve dimensions of resilience, compassion, ethical use of power and productive functioning in various societal domains such as healthcare, business, education and other core systems in our culture.

References

Aiello, A., Pratto F., & Pierro, A. (2013). Framing social dominance orientation and power. *Organizational Context, Basic and Applied Social Psychology*, *35*(5), 487–495, doi: 10.1080/01973533.2013.823614

Altemeyer, B. (1998). The other "authoritarian personality." *Advances in Experimental Social Psychology*, *30*, 48–92.

Altemeyer, B. (2003). What happens when authoritarians inherit the earth? A simulation. *Analyses of Social Issues and Public Policy*, *3*(1), 161–169.

Avolio, B. J. (1999). *Full Leadership Development: Building the Vital Forces in Organizations*. Thousand Oaks, CA: Sage.

Barsade, S. G., & Gibson, D. E. (2003). Why does affect matter in organizations? *The Academy of Management Perspectives*, *21*, 36–59. doi: 10.5465/AMP.2007.24286163

Bass, B. M. (1985). *Leadership and Performance Beyond Expectations*. New York: Free Press.

Bass, B. M. (1998). The ethics of transformational leadership. *Ethics, the Heart of Leadership*, 169–192.

Bass, B. M., Avolio, B. J., Jung, D. I., & Berson, Y. (2003). Predicting unit performance by assessing transformational and transactional leadership. *Journal of Applied Psychology*, *88*(2), 207–218.

Böckerman, P., & Ilmakunnas, P. (2009). Job disamenities, job satisfaction, quit intentions, and actual separations: Putting the pieces together. *Industrial Relations: A Journal of Economy and Society*, *48*, 73–96. doi: 10.1111/j.1468-232X.2008.00546.x

Böckerman, P., & Laukkanen, E. (2010). What makes you work while you are sick? Evidence from a survey of workers. *The European Journal of Public Health*, *20*(1), 43–46.

Buss, L. (2014). *The Evolution of Individuality*. Princeton, NJ: Princeton University Press.

Cameron, K. S. (2008). *Positive Leadership: Strategies for Extraordinary Performance*. Oakland, CA: Berrett-Koehler.

Cohrs, J., Moschner, B., Maes, J., & Kielmann, S. (2005). The motivational bases of right-wing authoritarianism and social dominance orientation: Relations to values and attitudes in the aftermath of September 11, 2001. *Personality and Social Psychology Bulletin*, *31*, 1425–1434.

Cosley, B. J., McCoy, S. K., Saslow, L. R., & Epel, E. S. (2010). Is compassion for others stress buffering? Consequences of compassion and social support for physiological reactivity to stress. *Journal of Experimental Social Psychology*, *46*(5), 816–823. doi: 10.1016/j.jesp.2010.04.008

DeGroot, T., Kiker, D. S., & Cross, T. C. (2000). A meta-analysis to review organizational outcomes related to charismatic leadership. *Canadian Journal of Administrative Sciences*, *17*, 356–371.

Demerouti, E., Bakker, A. B., De Jonge, J., Janssen, P. P. M., & Schaufeli, W.B. (2001). Burnout and engagement at work as a function of demands and control. *Scandinavian Journal of Work, Environment and Health*, *27*, 279–286.

Demerouti, E., Bakker, A.B., Nachreiner, F., and Schaufeli, W.B. (2001). The job demands-resources model of burnout. *Journal of Applied Psychology*, *86*, 499–512.

Duckitt, J. (2001). A dual-process cognitive-motivational theory of ideology and prejudice. *Advances in Experimental Social Psychology*, *33*, 41–113. doi: 10.1016/S0065-2601(01) 80004-6

Duriez, R. (2004). A research note on the relation between religiosity and racism: The importance of the way in which religious contents are being processed. *International Journal for the Psychology of Religion*, *14*, 175–189.

Duriez, R., & Van Hiel, A. (2002). The march of modern fascism: A comparison of social dominance orientation and authoritarianism. *Personality and Individual Differences*, *32*, 1199–1213.

Duriez, R., Van Hiel, A., & Kossowska, M. (2005). Authoritarianism and social dominance in Western and Eastern Europe: The importance of sociopolitical context and of political interest and involvement. *Political Psychology*, *26*, 299–320.

Dutton, J. E., Worline, M. C., Frost, P. J., & Lilius, J. (2006). Explaining compassion organizing. *Administrative Science Quarterly*, *51*(1), 59–96.

Furnham, A., Richards, S. C., & Paulhus, D. L. (2013). The dark triad of personality: A 10 year review. *Social and Personality Psychology Compass*, *7*, 199–221.

Georgesen, J., & M. J. Harris. (2006). Holding onto power: Effects of powerholders' positional instability and expectancies on interactions with subordinates. *European Journal of Social Psychology*, *36*, 451–468.

Gilbert, P (1989/2016). *Human Nature and Suffering*. London: Psychology Press and Routledge.

Gilbert, P. (2005a). Social mentalities: A biopsychosocial and evolutionary reflection on social relationships. In M. Baldwin (Ed.) *Interpersonal Cognition* (pp. 299–333). New York: Guilford Press.

Gilbert. P. (2005b). Compassion and cruelty: A biopsychosocial approach. In P. Gilbert (Ed.) *Compassion: Conceptualisations, Research and Use in Psychotherapy* (pp. 3–74). London: Routledge.

Gilbert, P. (2009). *The Compassionate Mind*. London: Constable-Robinson, and Oakland, CA: New Harbinger.

Gilbert, P. (2010). *Compassion Focused Therapy: The CBT Distinctive Features Series*. London: Routledge.

Gilbert, P. (2014). The origins and nature of compassion focused therapy. *British Journal of Clinical Psychology*, *53*, 6–41. doi: 10.1111/bjc.12043

Gilbert. P. (2015). The evolution and social dynamics of compassion. *Journal of Social & Personality Psychology Compass*, *9*, 239–254. doi: 10.1111/spc3.1217

Gilbert, P., & Choden. (2013). *Mindful Compassion*. London: Constable & Robinson.

Gilbert, P., McEwan, K., Matos, N., & Rivis, A. (2010). Fears of compassion: Development of three self-report measures. *Psychology and Psychotherapy: Theory, Research and Practice*, *84*(3), 239–255. doi: 10.1348/147608310X526511

Gilbert, P., McEwan, K., Matos, M., & Rivis, A. (2011). Fears of compassion: Development of three self-report measures. *Psychology and Psychotherapy*, *84*, 239–255. doi: 10.1348/147608310X526511

Gilbert, P., & Mascaro, J. (in press). Compassion: fears, blocks, and resistances: An evolutionary investigation. In E. Sappla & J. Doty (Eds.) *Handbook of Compassion*. New York: Oxford University Press.

Heaven, P. C., & Bucci, S. (2001). Right-wing authoritarianism, social dominance orientation and personality: An analysis using the IPIP measure. *European Journal of Personality*, *15*(1), 49–56.

Hodson, G. M., Hogg, S. M., & MacInnis, C. C. (2009). The role of "dark personalities" (narcissism, Machiavellianism, psychopathy), Big Five personality factors, and ideology in explaining prejudice. *Journal of Research in Personality, 43,* 686–690.

Hogan, R. (2007). *Personality and the Fate of Organizations.* Mahwah, NJ: Erlbaum.

Levin, S., & Sidanius, J. (1999). Social dominance and social identity in the United States and Israel: Ingroup favoritism or outgroup derogation? *Political Psychology, 20*(1), 99–126. doi: 10.1111/0162-895X.00138

Lindholm, C. (1993). *Charisma.* London: Wiley.

Liotti, G., & Gilbert, P. (2011). Mentalizing, motivation, and social mentalities: Theoretical considerations and implications for psychotherapy. *Psychology and Psychotherapy: Theory, Research and Practice, 84*(1), 9–25.

Lippa, R., & Arad, S. (1999). Gender, personality, and prejudice: The display of authoritarianism and social dominance in interviews with college men and women. *Journal of Research in Personality, 33*(4), 463–493.

Lowe, K. B., Kroeck, K. G., & Sivasubramaniam, N. (1996). Effectiveness correlates of transformational and transactional leadership: A metaanalytic review. *Leadership Quarterly, 7,* 385–425.

Martin, D., Seppala, E., Heineberg, Y., Rossomando, T., Doty, J., Zimbardo, P., & Zhou, Y. (2014). Multiple facets of compassion: The impact of social dominance orientation and economic systems justification. *Journal of Business Ethics, 129*(1), 237–249.

Neff, K. D. (2003). The development and validation of a scale to measure self-compassion. *Self and Identity, 2*(3), 223–250. doi: 10.1080/15298860309027

Peterson, C., & Seligman, M. E. (2006). The Values in Action (VIA) classification of strengths. In M. Csikszentmihalyi and I. Csikszentmihalyi (Eds.) *A Life Worth Living: Contributions to Positive Psychology*, pp. 29–48. New York: Oxford University Press.

Pratto, F., Sidanius, J., Stallworth, L. M., & Malle, B. F. (1994). Social dominance orientation: A personality variable predicting social and political attitudes. *Journal of Personality and Social Psychology, 67,* 741–763. doi: 10.1037/0022-3514.67.4.741

Pratto, F., Stallworth, L. M., Sidanius, J., & Siers, B. (1997). The gender gap in occupational role attainment: A social dominance approach. *Journal of Personality and Social Psychology, 72*(1), 37.

Raven, W. (1993) The bases of power: Origins and recent developments. *Journal of Social Issues, 49*(4), 227–251.

Schwartz, S. H., & Bardi, A. (2001). Value hierarchies across cultures taking a similarities perspective. *Journal of Cross-Cultural Psychology, 32,* 268–290.

Shao, P., Resick, C. J., & Hargis, M. B. (2011). Helping and harming others in the workplace: The roles of personal values and abusive supervision. *Human Relations, 64*(8), 1051–1078.

Sidanius, J., Kteily, N., Sheehy-Skeffington, J., Ho, A. K., Sibley, C., & Duriez, B. (2013). You're inferior and not worth our concern: The interface between empathy and social dominance orientation. *Journal of Personality, 81*(3), 313–323.

Sidanius, J., & Pratto, F. (1999). *Social Dominance: An Intergroup Theory of Social Hierarchy and Oppression.* Cambridge: Cambridge University Press.

Son-Hing, L. S., Bobocel, D., Zanna, M., & McBride, M. (2007). Authoritarian dynamics and unethical decision making: High social dominance orientation leaders and high right-wing authoritarianism followers. *Journal of Personality and Social Psychology, 92,* 67–81.

Zaki, J. (2014). Empathy: A motivated account. *Psychological Bulletin, 140*(6), 1608–1647.

Zimbardo, P. (2008). *The Lucifer Effect: How Good People Turn Evil.* London: Rider.

Chapter 14

Compassionate leadership for compassionate health care

Michael A. West and Rachna Chowla

Health care: context and cultures

Caring for the health and well-being of others is an intrinsically compassionate behaviour that is at once an act and an expression of a value. The people who work in health care have generally made a decision early in their adult lives to dedicate an enormous part of their precious lives to caring for others. Health care is a vocation that implies a core value of compassion amongst those who choose this path. Compassion is important to them and the extent to which their organisations also value compassion will influence the value 'fit' between health care workers and their organisations. The stronger the alignment of individual and organisational values, the higher the levels of staff members' commitment, engagement and satisfaction.

We draw particularly on the context of the UK's National Health Service (NHS) to illustrate our arguments here. The NHS was created in 1948 by a post-war government with a determination to provide health care free at the point of delivery to all in society, regardless of wealth, status, disability or background. It is still seen as a central element of English society, featuring strongly in the opening ceremony of the London Olympics in 2012 and in all national election political party manifestos. This reflects the national pride in a system that reflects a core societal value of compassion. It employs approximately 1.4 million staff spread across around 300 organisations in hospitals, community and primary care services, mental health, ambulance services, clinical commissioning groups and many ancillary bodies.

The aim of the NHS is to deliver high-quality, compassionate care which comprises clinically effective care, safe care and positive patient experiences. These aspirations are not easily achieved in a context characterised by high levels of stress, complexity, and workload, and where the possibilities of errors are many (Salas, Rosen, & King, 2007). Moreover, health care is a demanding context for the staff. The most detailed study of NHS staff stress showed that more than 26.8% of staff suffer damaging levels of stress, compared with 17.8% of the general population (Wall et al.,1997). Health professionals, in particular nurses, have among the highest rates of work-related stress, depression or anxiety every year (Health & Safety Executive, 2015). How are the demands and difficulties to be managed effectively?

Successive studies have demonstrated that the culture of organisations is key in creating the conditions where staff fulfil their purpose of delivering safe, high-quality, continually improving and compassionate care (Dixon-Woods et al., 2014). Culture is the combination of *'the values and beliefs that characterize organizations as transmitted by the socialization experiences newcomers have, the decisions made by management, and the stories and myths people tell and re-tell about their organizations'* (Schneider & Barbera, 2014). To the extent that health care organisations have values and beliefs that reflect a core commitment to compassionate care, the values of those who make up the workforce will be matched by organisational values. Consequently, their commitment and engagement will be high (Amos & Weathington, 2008) and they will demonstrate compassion in their interactions with patients.

But what factors most influence the culture of organisations? Culture is a consequence of all interactions that take place within organisations, but a recent review of the climate and culture research reveals that leadership plays the most powerful role in transmitting the core values and beliefs of organisations (Schneider, González-Romá, Ostroff, & West, in press). Every interaction by every leader, every day, shapes the culture of the organisation. Therefore, to the extent that leaders model compassion, the organisation will develop a culture of compassion. These norms and expectations, in turn, are communicated to staff creating the expectation that they should behave with compassion in all interactions (with patients and colleagues) at work.

What is compassionate leadership?

First we define leadership before addressing the question of what is meant by compassion in organisations and then proposing a model of compassionate leadership. Yukl (2013) says that most definitions of leadership conceptualise it as *'a process whereby intentional influence is exerted over other people to guide, structure, and facilitate activities and relationships in a group or organisation'* (p. 2). Leadership can therefore be seen as both a specialised role that an individual occupies and as a process of influence not confined to individuals. Thus we can distinguish between leaders and leadership, with leaders implied by the perspective towards understanding who leaders and who followers are, and why they occupy these roles. However, the influence process perspective assumes that anyone in a group or organisation may exercise leadership at any point and that the complex interactions between people and situation will affect the emergence of leadership processes. Compassion in the latter case is a characteristic of interactions rather than necessarily of individuals. We favour this latter perspective in what follows.

Now we turn to addressing the concept of compassion. This volume explores the concept of compassion in depth, so we do not propose to provide a detailed deconstruction of the construct (see Gilbert, Chapters 1 and 3, this volume). However, it is important to understand what is meant by compassion in the context of work organisations and, in particular, what is meant by the concept of compassionate leadership. There has been some growth in theory and related research activity in the concept of compassion at work in the last decade, with the Academy of Management Review dedicating a special issue to the topic in 2012 (Rynes, Bartunek, Dutton, & Margolis, 2012). Compassion (in an organisational context) can be understood as having four components: *attending, understanding, empathising* and *helping* (Atkins & Parker, 2012). In the context of an interaction between a health care professional and (for example) an elderly patient with a hip fracture, compassion involves:

1   Paying attention to the other and noticing his or her suffering – *attending.*
2   Understanding what is causing the other's distress, by making an appraisal of the cause – *understanding.*
3   Having an empathic response, a felt relation with the other's distress – *empathising.*
4   Taking intelligent (thoughtful and appropriate) action to help relieve the other's suffering – *helping.*

This operationalisation of the concept of compassion shares features with the definition offered by Gilbert & Choden (2013) and others (de Zulueta, 2016). Gilbert & Choden define compassion as 'a sensitivity to suffering in self and others with a commitment to try to alleviate and prevent it'. As a basic motivation (caring), it has both stimulus sensitivity and action components. So we are motivated to notice and become aware of the distress of the other, and pay attention to this distress (Cole-King & Gilbert, 2011), while having an empathic insight into the needs of others (Gilbert, this volume). It also implies having the motivation to help (Cole-King & Gilbert, 2011). The 'commitment to alleviate/prevent suffering' requires courage and wisdom (Cole-King & Gilbert, 2011), i.e. taking 'wise' action. De Zulueta views compassion as involving 'the motivation to relieve the suffering of another' (de Zulueta, 2016) and invokes the concept of cognitive empathy – 'stepping into someone else's shoes' which helps to guide an appropriate response (de Zulueta, 2016).

Compassion has facilitators and inhibitors. For example, it is easier to be compassionate to people we like than those we don't; those we think will appreciate us rather than people we think will not and people who share our values rather than those who do not. Inhibitors of compassion in health care include poor working conditions, poor leadership, role confusion, role conflicts and work overload. It is therefore important to identify both the inhibitors and facilitators of compassion in this context (Brown, Crawford, Gilbert, Gilbert, & Gale, 2014; Gilbert & Mascaro, in press).

Based on our exploration of the concept of compassion previously outlined, we suggest that compassionate leadership can be understood as having four components (see Figure 14.1).

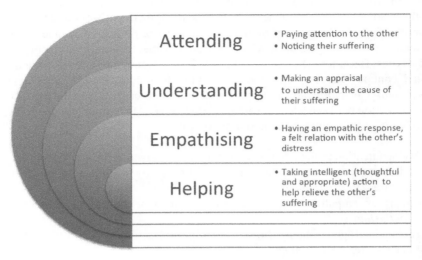

Figure 14.1 The elements of a compassionate response.

Source: Figure modified from Atkins & Parker (2012).

Attending

Since it is our motives that direct our attention, focused leaders will pay attention in a particular way to those they lead – what Nancy Kline (2002) calls 'listening with fascination'. In practice, this would involve leaders being motivated to take the time to listen to the accounts of the experiences of staff throughout their work – the challenges, obstacles, frustrations and hurts as well as the successes and delights. Staff in health services deal with situations where they witness pain, tragedy, suffering, fear and sometimes relief, happiness and even joy (consider the birth of a child in hospital). According to a model of compassionate leadership, the first task for leaders is to ensure they devote adequate time to listening deeply to those they lead in order that they have an appreciation of the situations they face and the abilities they have to face them.

Understanding

The second component involves leaders achieving an appraisal of the situation others face and arriving at an understanding of the causes of this distress. Simply responding to distress without exploring the underlying reasons may exacerbate the other's distress. For example, a ward sister may express strong frustration with a colleague because a particular task (e.g. completing the drug round), was taking longer than usual, resulting in the nurse colleague feeling angry and hurt. Exploration of the incident might reveal that the nurse had experienced a verbal attack from a patient's relative during the working day that led to her feeling threatened and overwhelmed. The second task of compassionate leadership is therefore appraising the causes of distress and arriving at an understanding of the causes. Ideally, this is best done in conjunction with the individual whose distress evokes compassion because a shared understanding is likely to be both more accurate and helpful for the distressed person. These first two elements may seem obvious prescriptions for leadership, but in the context of highly pressured work situations, staff often feel they are not listened to and that their leaders do not understand the situations they face (West, Dawson, Admasachew, & Topakas, 2011).

Empathising

The third component of compassionate leadership is empathising. In general empathising has two components: one that is linked to emotion, and the second component that is linked to perspective-taking, which is cognitive. Compassionate leaders are motivated and able to emotionally 'tune in' to the distress of the other – the frustration of the ward sister, the anger and hurt of her colleague, the anxiety of the patient's relative. In addition, perspective taking enables an understanding of the sources and context of these difficulties. We are uniquely enabled as a species to feel the distress of others because of our neurophysiological capacity to mirror observed emotion. Compassion as others have shown (see Gilbert, Chapter 3, this volume; Stellar & Keltner, Chapter 7, this volume; Vrtička et al., Chapter 8, this volume) has emotional, cognitive and behavioural responses that vary with context. Compassionate leaders are therefore emotionally in touch with, able to tolerate and not overidentify with, the distress of others. This mirroring of emotion, in part, enables leaders to arrive at a deeper understanding of the other's situation and thereby be able to more effectively work out how to take steps to help the other.

Helping

The fourth and final component is taking thoughtful and intelligent action to help the other. Leadership, according to all definitions, includes helping and supporting others. In the context of health care where staff face significant challenges on a daily or even hourly basis, supportive leadership is an important determinant of staff well-being and effectiveness. This fourth component is focused on taking action to help the person. Wisdom is needed to know what this actually involves – it could be by removing obstacles, supporting the implementation of solutions or otherwise taking thoughtful, appropriate action (it might simply be enough to listen). The helping element has four sub-components that are required for a competent compassionate response: *scope* – breadth of resources offered; *scale* – the volume of resources; *speed* – the timeliness of the response and *specialization* – the extent to which the response meets the real needs of the sufferer (Lilius, Kanov, Dutton, Worline, & Maitlis, 2011).

We propose that these four domains of compassionate leadership are particularly powerful in health care, where the workforce is largely composed of highly skilled and motivated professionals, intent on doing their jobs to the highest possible standard. Motivated as they are to help others by providing health care as their vocational orientation – and generally being highly trained and skilled – they require support rather than direction and enabling rather than controlling interventions from leaders. When leaders demonstrate compassionate responding they provide this support in a way that is consistent with the core value orientation of those they lead. But they also legitimate it as a valued and worthwhile endeavour, toward which to devote valuable time and organisational resources, thus encouraging and empowering those they lead to respond compassionately in the face of suffering (Worline & Boik, 2006). We propose therefore that compassionate leadership is the appropriate model of leadership for organisations that have compassion as a core value, as in health care organisations.

Emotion and compassion in health care

The 'shackles of routine and ritual' are compassion inhibitors and have been blamed for constraining compassion by hindering flexible, individualised and creative delivery of patient-centred care (Kelly, 2007). The complexity of the NHS environment with its demands created by factors such as regulation, governance protocols, political conflicts and the introduction of competition to stimulate innovation, can lead to a focus on chasing targets and to a sense of threat. Other barriers to compassion in health care include the fear of making errors; time pressure (Gilbert, 2013); excessive and often defensive bureaucracy (Cole-King & Gilbert, 2011); bullying (Cole-King & Gilbert, 2011; Gilbert, 2013); stress; depression; burnout (de Zulueta, 2016); rapid change (Gilbert, 2013); workload demands (de Zulueta, 2016); poor levels of staffing (Mannion, 2014); job insecurity (Gilbert, 2013); difficult patients and families; and complex clinical situations (de Zulueta, 2016).

De Zulueta (2013) argues that the emphasis across health care systems internationally on cost-efficiency and process-target driven and 'high-volume' care creates ever heavier workloads, more complex task variety and increased managerial pressure, thus over-stimulating sympathetic-based stress systems. Stressed leaders themselves often pass their stress downwards. When leaders in health care become preoccupied with non-patient centred tasks and targets, this can diminish staff motivation and performance (Dixon-Woods et al., 2014; West, Dawson, Admasachew, & Topakas, 2011). Moreover, De Zulueta suggests this shift from person to ritualised task, from sick people to diseases and bed capacity, can lead to a dehumanisation and disengagement of leaders and staff (de Zulueta, 2013).

In contrast, compassionate cultures can be nurtured by leaders behaving with compassion. While much of the research on emotions in organisations has focused on the personal impact of an individual's emotions, emotions have influence beyond the individual. For example, the affective states of individual group members can influence the general mood of the whole team, a phenomenon known as *mood linkage* or *emotional contagion* (Hatfield, Cacioppo, & Rapson, 1992; Totterdell, 2000; Totterdell, Kellett, Teuchmann, & Briner, 1998). Similarly, the moods and emotions of leaders, given their positions of power and influence within organisations, can influence the moods and behaviours of those with whom they work. Research shows that positive leader affect is associated with more positive affect among employees (Cherulnik, Donley, Wiewel, & Miller, 2001), enhanced team performance (George, 1995), and higher rates of prosocial behaviours (George, 1990).

The language used and stories told at work, and the feelings that leaders model and endorse in their members, can also have a significant impact across the organisation (Kanov et al., 2004). Leaders set an important tone for the value and legitimacy of noticing suffering at work (Dutton, Worline, Frost & Lilius, 2006). Kanov et al. (2004) argue that 'organisational compassion' can be developed where there is collective noticing or acknowledging of pain within a system that values such noticing. Similarly, staff can collectively feel concern and articulate such concern through narratives and emotionally expressive communication within an organisation. And collective helping or responding is more likely when responses to pain are legitimated and resourced within an organisation. Beyond the impact of compassion on individuals therefore, compassion has the potential to spiral out, where those receiving compassion are then better able, or more likely, to direct caring and supportive behaviours towards others (Lilius et al., 2011). And this may well replenish the emotional resources that care-givers need, especially in a caring environment, and cushion against stress and burnout (Dutton, Workman & Hardin, 2014; Lilius et al., 2011). The positive ripples of compassion can also affect witnesses and bystanders (beyond patients and carers), who may experience feelings of pride about the way people in the organisation behave, encouraging people to act more for the common good (Dutton et al., 2014; Lilius et al., 2011).

Experiencing compassion from others shapes individuals' appraisals about themselves (e.g. seeing oneself as more capable), their peers (e.g. viewing them as more kind) and the kind of organisation of which they are a part (Dutton et al., 2014). When staff feel valued and cared for (i.e. perceived organisational support), they tend to feel more satisfied in their jobs, and have increased affective commitment to their organisations (Lilius et al., 2011), and there is considerable evidence that this is true in the NHS and is associated with high levels of patient satisfaction, care quality and even financial performance of health care organisations (West et al., 2011).

Receiving compassion in the workplace has beneficial effects, both for staff and the organisation. It can lead to people experiencing more positive emotions such as gratitude, pride and inspiration, and can lead to upward emotional spirals that can enhance emotional well-being (Lilius et al., 2008). It can help communicate dignity and worth, and help people feel better psychologically connected with others (Dutton et al., 2014). The theory of positivity resonance explains how moments of connectivity (e.g. moments of interpersonal compassion) benefit people in an interaction through a natural synchronisation of bodies and brains, in ways that foster health and well-being (Fredrickson, 2013). Compassion also creates a sense of being valued at work (Dutton et al., 2014). This sense of being valued and worthy is not a state that is a given in work organisations; rather, it is something that is either created or destroyed by the way that people interact with one another at work (Dutton et al., 2014).

Having explored compassion based on four broad categories of compassionate leadership behaviours (attending, understanding, empathising and helping), we now turn to explore how compassion may manifest in the core behaviours of effective health care leadership.

Compassion and health care leadership behaviours

What does the literature indicate leaders are required to do? The formulation below is based on a review of the leadership literature generally and a review of the research on leadership in health care (West et al., 2015; see also Yukl, 2013). It also draws on consultations with leaders and practitioners within NHS provider organisations as well as leaders in the regulatory agencies and other national bodies. Ten constellations of leadership behaviours are described in Table 14.1.

We integrate these below with the notions of compassionate leadership previously described, revealing how there is a clear compatibility between compassionate leadership and the literature on what constitutes effective leadership behaviours. Since compassion is rooted in caring motivations it is useful to keep in mind some of the functions of caring; for example, in caring for the young. Attachment theory highlights that caring has three functions (among others):

1   Proximity maintenance.
2   Providing a secure base that offers encouragement for the child to try things out, move into the world and explore and build confidence.
3   A safe haven – as a source of comfort and calming when distressed (Mikulincer & Shaver, 2007).

Table 14.1 The essence of effective health care leadership

1	Support, trust and compassion
2	Valuing diversity and fairness
3	Building effective teams
4	Building relationships across boundaries
5	Promoting learning and innovation
6	Promoting others' development and leadership
7	Ensuring effective performance
8	Ensuring the necessary resources are available and used well
9	Ensuring direction and alignment
10	Developing positivity, pride and identity

These functions are also central in therapies such as compassion-focused therapy (Gilbert, 2010). While being clear about the distinction between leadership and therapy, we suggest that they are also central to compassionate leadership, because such leaders will provide these functions for their teams. Compassionate leaders stimulate proximity rather than avoidance; they provide a secure base for team members to work from and are a source of support and help when distress and difficulties occur in the workplace.

Support, trust and compassion

Compassionate leadership includes being supportive and caring to patients who are distressed or staff who are under pressure; understanding the difficulties staff face; taking practical action to help and encouraging others to support each other. This has 'safe haven' qualities. It underpins developing trust and cooperation between staff members because compassion results in a stronger felt connection between co-workers (Frost, Dutton, Worline, & Wilson, 2000). Supportive and compassionate leadership therefore emphasises collegial support, kindness and valuing others' contributions, which increases trust, compassion and cohesion. Necessarily, it requires helping to resolve conflicts quickly and fairly and building a strong sense of community. Trust is built and earned over time from the supportive actions of leaders.

Valuing diversity and fairness

While compassion focuses on suffering, failure to promote valuing of diversity and the promotion of fairness are sources of conflicts and suffering. Compassionate leaders focus on ensuring equality and valuing diversity (such as race, disability, religion or belief, age, gender, sexual orientation, professional background). This can be facilitated by modelling careful listening to others' contributions ('listening with fascination'); ensuring everyone's opinions are valued (staff and patients). The key to this is creating a secure base so that people feel comfortable to be honest and open. It also requires challenging aggressive or intimidating behaviours and dealing effectively with bullying, harassment or discrimination. These dimensions reflect concern with promoting social justice and morality: leadership that emphasises fairness and honesty in all dealings, and challenging unethical practices or social injustices. Compassionate leaders provide role models for ethical/moral behaviour, especially when it requires the sacrifice of personal interests.

Building effective teams

Leadership is ensuring the team has clear objectives and team members have helpful data on team performance; co-operative working; shared leadership so everyone contributes their expertise and ideas; and regular, protected time for collective reviews of team functioning and performance. These activities create collective identity through a positive vision of the team's work and promote a compassion-based approach to team working, thereby producing cohesion and a secure base. Compassionate leadership focuses also on creating a sense of pride in the team's performance and nurtures team identity through rituals, celebrations, humour and narrative so that people feel proud of who they work for and with. There is also 'sympathetic joy' where team members can take pleasure from the successes of others around them – rather than feeling envious or critical. Compassionate leaders direct attention to how their team's work makes a positive difference to patients and society.

Building relationships across boundaries

Compassionate leaders build trust across team boundaries, encouraging people to build trust, respect and cooperation across teams, departments and organisations, fostering the idea of 'teams of teams'. It involves describing and emphasising shared visions; building a sense of long-term continuity and stability in cross-boundary relationships; ensuring frequent contact with these others; surfacing and resolving cross-boundary conflicts swiftly and creatively; and promoting a 'How can we help you?' orientation of team members towards those in other teams (or organisations).

Promoting learning and innovation

Leadership behaviours in a health care system must be focused on creating a psychologically safe environment within which team members will share learning about errors and near misses, and avoid blaming unnecessarily; focus on improving the quality of their work through regular reviews of working methods; develop and implement ideas to improve quality; and support others in implementing ideas for new and improved ways of working. This learning involves a focus on both emotional and cognitive elements, and compassionate leadership involves helping teams to process negative emotions – pain and grief – where necessary. Such leadership ensures teams regularly take time out to review objectives, strategies and processes so they collectively learn and improve at work while ensuring team member personal well-being. Blaming cultures, in contrast, are fearful, inhibit compassion and prevent learning.

Promoting others' development and leadership

Leadership includes promoting continued learning and development for all, and ensuring all have freedom to work autonomously where appropriate rather than being restricted; all have the opportunity to participate in challenging projects and other development opportunities, and to lead in their work. It involves developing and empowering staff by enabling their continued growth and development, and their ability to function autonomously, which is fundamental to human health and well-being. Such leadership is manifested also in encouragement to followers to respond successfully to challenges while providing the necessary supports and resources (emotional as well as practical) to achieve this. Indeed, the promotion of growth and development is one of the functions of a secure base.

Ensuring effective performance

Leadership involves ensuring everyone is clear about each other's roles and responsibilities; organising and co-ordinating work efforts towards agreed goals; dealing with obstacles to the delivery high-quality work such as systems difficulties, challenges and coordination problems; and giving timely and balanced feedback about progress towards objectives. This involves compassion at a system level and a subsequent competent compassionate response that enables people to work together in a coordinated way to overcome these obstacles, but also in a way that enhances their well-being – thereby building alignment, connection and compassion. As with other domains, it reflects an inverted leadership style of working in support of staff enabling them, rather than directing them. Virtually all health care staff seek to provide high-quality and compassionate care but there can be many organisational inhibitors to people fulfilling their roles (Brown et al., 2014).

Ensuring the necessary resources are available and used well

Compassionate leaders try to ensure staff have the resources and supports needed to get their work done effectively, such as money, staff, IT or other specialist support and time, reducing the demands on staff when they are overwhelmed and ensuring resources are used as efficiently and effectively as possible. This involves political acumen and risk-taking in dealing with the wider organisation, patients and other stakeholders. It requires leadership that wins the necessary resources for the team/organisation and avoiding teams working in chronically under-resourced environments, which erode compassion.

Ensuring direction and alignment

Leadership requires a focus on seeking shared agreement on direction (the overall purpose and aims of the work, i.e. their role in enabling the delivery of high-quality, compassionate care) within teams/organisations and across teams; encouraging everyone to work together to ensure all are clear on the direction and strategy of their teams and of the organisation; seeking agreement and shared understanding about key priorities; and helping people to make sense of events in the organisation. Clarifying direction, strategy and the priorities for people's efforts helps staff to be clear about their roles and to prevent work overload – particularly important in the highly demanding environment of health care (Drath et al., 2008).

It includes defining the key priorities (few in number) and making clear what the team is not going to do, rather than overwhelming people with inspirational priorities. Good leadership results in clear, agreed, challenging, measureable objectives for all individuals and teams.

Developing positivity, pride and identity

Leadership includes celebrating the successes of the team and organisation; emphasising how the work makes a difference to patients and the community; encouraging others to be positive; expressing optimism, confidence, gratitude and humour; and building a sense of positivity about the future. Effective leaders support those they lead by creating an environment where people can freely express and discuss the way they feel, which in turn helps them make sense of their circumstances, seek or provide comfort, and imagine a more hopeful future (Dutton, Frost, Worline, Lilius, & Kanov, 2002). They help those they lead make sense of change, catastrophes, successes and the future by attending, understanding, empathising and responding to their reactions. They provide a helpful narrative which both makes sense to people and inspires them to give of their best. They encourage and model positive attitudes, experiences and compassion rather than cynicism, depersonalisation or defeatism and they do so with humour, empathy, kindness, belief and a sense of purpose. Leaders nurture this sense of commitment by being actively and compassionately committed to meeting the needs of their employees to support them in their work (Lilius et al., 2008).

Integrating compassion into our understanding of essential leadership behaviours is not difficult because the behaviours revealed by research implicitly require noticing or attending by leaders; their understanding of the situation faced by those they lead; empathising or understanding the feelings of others and helping or supporting. The role of leaders, particularly in health care, is to support and enable those providing health care rather than to direct or control them as numerous reports have made clear (e.g. Berwick, 2013). Compassionate leadership is therefore more consistent with our understanding of leadership behaviours and, as we have argued, particularly so in health care contexts. Moreover, reviews of the research on cultures and climates for health care excellence suggest that the opposite model – command and control – is inimical to creating cultures of high-quality, continually improving and compassionate care (West, Topakas, & Dawson, 2014).

Compassionate leadership for cultures of high-quality and compassionate care

How can compassionate leadership nurture cultures of high-quality, continually improving and compassionate care? Extensive research within the NHS context has identified five key cultural elements that leaders need to focus upon (Dixon-Woods et al., 2014; West, Lyubovnikova, Eckert, & Denis, 2014).

Inspiring visions, operationalised at every level

Leaders in the best-performing health care organisations prioritise a vision and develop a strategic narrative focussed on prioritising high-quality, compassionate care as opposed to emphasising productivity, cost efficiency or meeting the requirements of regulators (important though these factors are). In the best-performing health care organisations, all leaders (from the top to the front line) make it clear that high-quality, compassionate care is the core purpose and priority of the organisation (Dixon-Woods et al., 2014). Visions must be translated into leadership actions because the messages that leaders send about their priorities are communicated more powerfully through their actions than their words. Leadership authenticity is revealed by the extent to which leaders behave with compassion while advocating compassionate behaviour by those they lead (Avolio & Gardner, 2005). If leaders focus more on targets, cost efficiencies, productivity and costs (vital though these are) than patient experience, quality of care, patient safety and compassion, it undermines trust in the organisational vision and shapes the culture accordingly.

Performance, objectives and feedback

Staff in the English NHS report often feeling overwhelmed by tasks as well as unclear about their priorities, and there is robust evidence showing the effects on stress, inefficiency and poor-quality care (Dixon-Woods et al., 2014; Wall et al., 1997). Creating cultures that are focussed on high-quality, compassionate care requires good management of performance by ensuring clear, aligned and challenging objectives for all teams at all levels in the organisation, focused on the provision of such care (West, 2013). The key to this objective-setting process is that the objectives should be agreed rather than imposed and based on a well-developed mutual understanding of the work context and challenges faced by the team. This is therefore quite different from the institution of target-driven cultures to drive change – an approach that has limited success (Ham, 2014). It requires leadership that listens, understands and enables staff both to set and achieve challenging objectives.

People management, engagement and support

The NHS national staff survey, which has been run annually for 12 years, shows that if staff are to treat patients with compassion, respect and care, they themselves must be treated with compassion, respect and care. Where health service staff report that they are well led and they are satisfied with their leadership, patients report being treated with respect, care and compassion (Dawson, West, Admasachew, & Topakas, 2011). The English NHS national staff survey data, collected between 2004 and 2011, show that there is a strong relationship between staff satisfaction and commitment and patient satisfaction (Dawson et al., 2011). The more positive staff are about their working conditions, the more positive patients are about their care (confirmed in longitudinal analyses). Similar findings emerge from other studies examining the relationship between nurse leadership and patient outcomes (Wong & Cummings, 2007). Directive, brusque managers dilute the ability of staff to make good decisions, deplete their emotional resources and hinder their ability to relate effectively to patients, especially those who are most distressed or difficult (Carter & West, 1999; Mickan & Rodger, 2005; West, 2013).

Work engagement describes an experience of work as involving, meaningful, energising, stretching and connecting. It has three components: vigour (the energy we bring to our work); dedication (our commitment to the work and organisation) and absorption (the sense of loss of time and the experience of 'flow' while doing the work) (Schaufeli & Bakker, 2004). Health care staff who are engaged are likely to deliver high-quality care, to seek ways of improving care and to have more capacity for compassion (Bakker, 2011; Bakker, van Emmerik, & Euwema, 2006; Bakker, Schaufeli, Leiter, & Taris, 2008). The NHS staff survey reveals that staff engagement is the best overall predictor of hospital performance – care quality and financial performance (based on independent audit body ratings), staff health and well-being, patient satisfaction and (negatively) patient mortality, staff absenteeism and stress (West et al., 2011). Engagement is higher in health care organisations where leaders create a positive emotional climate for staff, with the result that they feel involved and have the emotional capacity to be compassionate towards others. The implication is that the fear, pain, anxiety, loss and uncertainty that patients inevitably and often experience, and that therefore characterise the culture of health care organisations, must be balanced by *positivity* – this requires leaders who create positive and compassionate emotional environments. This does not imply the avoidance or repression of negative emotion – quite the contrary. Engagement and creativity are also elicited when leaders show compassion and support staff to cope with the inevitable negative experiences of health care (e.g. patient fear, suffering, anger, grief). When leaders take the time to help staff process negative experiences, they enable staff to experience positive affect and greater work-focussed creativity (Bledow, Rosing, & Frese, 2013).

Learning and innovation

Research in the NHS has shown that learning and innovation, in the context of psychological safety rather than a blame culture, is vital for nurturing cultures of high-quality, continually improving and compassionate care. Following failures in health care organisations, a succession of reports (e.g. Berwick, 2013) advocated culture changes, with a strong emphasis on embedding learning and quality improvement throughout health care organisations. Moreover, the voice of the service user should be constantly heard by leaders. This requires that teams are led in a way that creates psychological safety and in which team members pay attention ('listen with fascination' to each other), develop mutual understanding, empathise and support each other (West & Markiewicz, 2016). In such psychologically 'safe' team environments, there are higher levels of learning and innovation (Edmondson, 1999). In effect, leadership and team member compassion create the context for learning and innovation. Given the challenges health services face in delivering care for patients, it is vital to encourage staff to apply their knowledge, skills and capacities for cooperation and coordination across boundaries. Creating the conditions for innovation requires giving front-line teams autonomy to experiment, discover and apply new and improved ways of delivering care (Liu, Chen, & Yao, 2011; Somech, 2006). Releasing the capacity for innovation is more likely to occur when staff are supported and given discretion, control and freedom for service improvement (Hirst, Van Knippenberg, Chen, & Sacramento, 2011).

Team working

Working in teams is vital for health care quality but there is also good evidence that supportive teams, with good team leadership, have significantly lower levels of stress than dysfunctional or pseudo teams in health care. The more staff work in such teams, the lower the levels of stress, errors, staff injuries, harassment, bullying and violence against staff, staff absenteeism and (in the acute sector) patient mortality (Carter & West, 1999; Lyubovnikova, West, Dawson & Carter, 2015). Teams with these characteristics ensure greater role clarity for team members, provide higher levels of social support and buffer members from the negative and depleting effects of wider organisational pressures. Good team leadership ensures connection and compassion across boundaries so that that health care staff work together across professions to deliver high-quality care (West, 2012; West & Lyubovnikova, 2012). Compassionate leadership of teams involves ensuring a climate of team members listening carefully to each other, understanding of all perspectives in the team, empathy and social support, and helping and supporting one another. Such teams are considerably more effective than teams that do not practise these simple team-working skills (West, 2012).

To the extent that leadership is focused on these key cultural elements, with a compassionate orientation, health care organisations (the evidence suggests) will be likely to deliver high-quality, continually improving and compassionate care. We have referred to leadership and leaders throughout this chapter but the prescriptions we offer have clear implications for the style of leadership if we are to create compassionate leadership in organisations and suggest the need for collective leadership cultures.

Collective and compassionate leadership

Collective leadership means the distribution and allocation of leadership power to wherever expertise, capability and motivation sit within organisations (West, Eckert, Steward, & Pasmore, 2014). The purposeful, visible distribution of leadership responsibility onto the shoulders of every person in the organisation is vital for creating the type of collective leadership that will nurture the right culture for health care (McCauley, 2011). This implies leaving behind traditional command and control, hierarchies and professional silos which create conditions for bullying and exclusion, and reduce compassion. The arguments above imply a collective approach to leadership: leadership of all, by all, for all. This is everyone taking responsibility for ensuring there is high-quality, continually improving and compassionate care; shared rather than dominating leadership in teams; interdependent leadership with leaders working together across boundaries prioritising patient care overall and not only their area of responsibility; and consistent approaches to leadership across organisations characterised by authenticity, openness, curiosity, kindness, appreciativeness and, above all, by compassion (West et al., 2014). Such collective leadership is characterised by constant changes in leadership and followership, dependent on the task at hand or the unfolding situational challenges. There is still a formal hierarchy but the ebb and flow of power is dependent on expertise at each moment. There is a growing literature demonstrating that shared leadership in teams consistently predicts team effectiveness, particularly but not exclusively within health care (Aime et al., 2014; Carson et al., 2007). In summary, we suggest that collective leadership creates the culture in which high-quality, compassionate care can be delivered because all staff accept the distribution and allocation of leadership power to wherever expertise, capability and motivation sit within organisations.

This perspective proposes therefore that it is not simply the number or quality of individual leaders that determine organisational performance, but the extent to which formal and informal leaders work collectively to implement the five elements described above, achieve organisational goals focused primarily on continually improving, high-quality and compassionate care, and model the values of the desired culture (West et al., 2014). Leadership is therefore both the leaders themselves and the relationships among them, including how they demonstrate compassion, cooperate and coordinate efforts to nurture compassionate leadership, and thereby a compassionate organisational culture.

However, organisations and individuals do not exist in isolation in their work. They are part of wider systems that create a powerful context. We turn finally to the wider context of health care and, in particular, compassion in the context of inter-organisational relationships.

Compassionate leadership across the health care sector

The need for compassionate leadership cooperation across boundaries is not only intra-organisational. Governments, practitioners and policy makers are increasingly agreed that health and social care services must be integrated in order to meet the needs of patients, service users and communities both efficiently and effectively (Ferlie, Fitzgerald, McGivern, Dopson, & Exworthy, 2010; Huerta, Casebeer, & Vanderplaat, 2006; Lemieux-Charles et al., 2005). Health care has to be delivered by an interdependent network of organisations. This requires that leaders work together, spanning organisational boundaries both within and between organisations, prioritising overall patient care rather than the success of their component of it. That means leaders working collectively and building a cooperative, integrative leadership culture – in effect collective leadership at the system level. This requires a shared vision of high-quality, compassionate and continually improving care; frequent and supportive contact across boundaries between leaders; a long-term commitment to cooperative working; quick, creative and fair resolution of conflicts; and an orientation of helping the other – elements of cross-boundary working that are fundamentally underpinned by compassion.

The broader national-cultural context, of which the organisation is a part, is likely to influence how compassion unfolds in the workplace (Dutton et al., 2014), and this too can either support or impede compassion. For compassionate cultures to be developed, leaders at all levels must model compassion. In a national context such as the UK NHS, compassion must be modelled by government ministers down through national regulatory agencies in how they operate both in relation to the health care provider organisations they oversee and in their interactions with other national organisations. If these agencies interact with the system in ways that are (or are perceived as) directive, controlling, punitive, threatening or uncaring, then compassion will be weakened systemically and replaced by directive and bullying leadership across health care cultures.

Conclusion

Caring for the health of others requires compassion – attending, understanding, empathising and helping. Health care organisations must therefore nurture cultures of compassion and their leadership plays the crucial role in developing and sustaining compassionate values, norms and behaviours. If they are to model compassion, however, previous research and practice suggests they must ensure they are compassionate towards themselves. The ability to be compassionate in interactions with others depends on the extent to which we can pay attention to ourselves; to understand our own life situations; to turn the light of empathy on to ourselves and to compassionately take wise and kind action to help ourselves. Through such self-compassion we develop the resources and wisdom to be compassionate towards others. In health care organisations, such wise and compassionate leadership is essential for nurturing cultures where all are focused on providing compassionate care, high-quality care and continually improving care for those the health care system serves. And, in so doing, we progressively increase the strength of compassion in our society as a whole.

References

Aime, F., Humphrey, S., DeRue, D. S., & Paul, J. B. (2014). The riddle of heterarchy: Power transitions in cross-functional teams. *Academy of Management Journal, 57*(2), 327–352.

Amos, E. A., & Weathington, B. L. (2008). An analysis of the relation between employee-organisation value congruence and employee attitudes. *The Journal of Psychology, 142*, 615–632.

Atkins, P. W. B., & Parker, S. K. (2012). Understanding individual compassion in organisations: The role of appraisals and psychological flexibility. *Academy of Management Review, 37*(4), 524–546.

Avolio, B. J., & Gardner, W. L. (2005). Authentic leadership development: Getting to the root of positive forms of leadership. *The Leadership Quarterly, 16*(3), 315–338.

Bakker, A. B. (2011). An evidence-based model of work engagement. *Current Directions in Psychological Science, 20*(4), 265–269.

Bakker, A. B., Schaufeli, W. B., Leiter, M. P., & Taris, T. W. (2008). Work engagement: An emerging concept in occupational health psychology. *Work & Stress, 22*(3), 187–200.

Bakker, A. B., van Emmerik, H., & Euwema, M. C. (2006). Crossover of burnout and engagement in work teams. *Work and Occupations, 33*(4), 464–489.

Berwick, D. (2013). *A Promise to Learn – A Commitment to Act: Improving the Safety of Patients in England.* London: Department of Health.

Bledow, R., Rosing, K., & Frese, M. (2013). A dynamic perspective on affect and creativity. *Academy of Management Journal, 56*(2), 432–450.

Brown, B., Crawford. P., Gilbert, P., Gilbert, J., & Gale, G. (2014). Practical compassion: Repertoires of practice and compassion talk in acute mental healthcare. *Sociology of Health & Illness, 36*, 383–399.

Carson, J. B., Tesluk, P. E., & Marrone, J. A. (2007). Shared leadership in teams: An investigation of antecedent conditions and performance. *Academy of Management Journal, 50*(5), 1217–1234.

Carter, A. J. W., & West, M. A. (1999). Sharing the burden: Teamwork in health care settings, in Firth-Cozens, J. & Payne, R. (Eds.), *Stress in Health Professionals: Psychological Causes and Interventions* (pp. 191–202). Chichester: Wiley.

Cherulnik, P. D., Donley, K. A., Wiewel, T. S. R., & Miller, S. R. (2001). Charisma is contagious: The effect of leaders' charisma on observers' affect. *Journal of Applied Social Psychology, 31*(10), 2149–2159.

Cole-King, A. & Gilbert, P. (2011). Compassionate care: The theory and the reality. *Journal of Holistic Healthcare, 8*(3), 29–37.

Dawson, J. F., West, M. A., Admasachew, L. and Topakas, A. (2011). *NHS Staff Management and Health Service Quality: Results from the NHS Staff Survey and Related Data.* Department of Health, London, available at: www.dh.gov.uk/health/2011/08/nhs-staff-management/.

de Zulueta, P. (2013). Compassion in 21st century medicine: Is it sustainable? *Clinical Ethics, 8*(4), 119–128.

de Zulueta, P. C. (2016). Developing compassionate leadership in health care: An integrative review. *Journal of Healthcare Leadership, 8*, 1–10.

Dixon-Woods, M., Baker, R., Charles, K., Dawson, J., Jerzembek, G., Martin, G.,. . .West, M. (2014). Culture and behaviour in the English National Health Service: Overview of lessons from a large multimethod study. *British Medical Journal Quality and Safety, 23*(2), 106–115.

Drath, W. H., McCauley, C. D., Palus, C. J., Van Velsor, E., O'Connor, P. M., & McGuire, J. B. (2008). Direction, alignment, commitment: Toward a more integrative ontology of leadership. *The Leadership Quarterly, 19*(6), 635–653.

Dutton, J. E., Frost, P. J., Worline, M. C., Lilius, J. M., & Kanov, J. M. (2002). Leading in times of trauma. *Harvard Business Review*, *80*(1), 54–61.

Dutton, J. E., Workman, K. M., & Hardin, A. E. (2014). Compassion at work. *Annual Reviews of Organisational Psychology and Organisational Behaviour*, *1*(1), 277–304.

Dutton, J. E., Worline, M. C., Frost, P. J., & Lilius, J. (2006). Explaining compassion organizing. *Administrative Science Quarterly*, *51*(1), 59–96.

Edmondson, A. (1999). Psychological safety and learning behavior in work teams. *Administrative Science Quarterly*, *44*(2), 350–383.

Ferlie, E., Fitzgerald, L., McGivern, G., Dopson, S., & Exworthy, M. (2010). *Networks in Health Care: A Comparative Study of Their Management, Impact and Performance, SDO-NHS*. London: Queen's Printer and Controller of HMSO.

Fredrickson, B. (2013). *Love 2.0: How Our Supreme Emotion Affects Everything We Feel, Think, Do, and Become*. New York: Hudson Street Press.

Frost, P. J., Dutton, J. E., Worline, M. C., & Wilson, A. (2000). Narratives of compassion in organisations. *Emotion in Organisations*, *2*, 25–45.

George, J. M. (1990). Personality, affect, and behavior in groups. *Journal of Applied Psychology*, *75*(2), 107.

George, J. M. (1995). Leader positive mood and group performance: The case of customer service. *Journal of Applied Social Psychology*, *25*(9), 778–794.

Gilbert, P. (2010). *The Compassionate Mind (Compassion Focussed Therapy)*. London: Constable.

Gilbert, P. (2013). *Compassion into Practice: Understanding Some Challenges*, available at: https://www.england.nhs.uk/wp-content/uploads/2013/12/paul-gil-pres.pdf

Gilbert, P., & Choden. (2013). *Mindful Compassion*. London: Robinson.

Gilbert, P., & Mascaro, J. (in press). Compassion fears, blocks, and resistances: An evolutionary investigation. In E. Sappla & J. Doty (Eds.), *Handbook of Compassion*. New York: Oxford University Press.

Ham, C. (2014). *Reforming the NHS from Within: Beyond Hierarchy, Inspection and Markets, The King's Fund, London*, available at: http://www.kingsfund.org.uk/sites/files/kf/field/field_publication_file/reforming-the-nhs-from-within-kingsfund-jun14.pdf.

Hatfield, E., Cacioppo, J. T., & Rapson, L. R. (1992). Primitive emotional contagion. In M. S. Clark (Ed.), *Review of Personality and Social Psychology: Emotion and Social Behavior* (Vol. 14, pp. 151–177). Newbury Park, CA: Sage.

Health & Safety Executive. (2015). *Work Related Stress, Anxiety and Depression Statistics in Great Britain 2015*, available at: http://www.hse.gov.uk/statistics/causdis/stress/stress.pdf

Hirst, G., Van Knippenberg, D., Chen, C. H., & Sacramento, C. A. (2011). How does bureaucracy impact individual creativity? A cross-level investigation of team contextual influences on goal orientation–creativity relationships. *Academy of Management Journal*, *54*(3), 624–641.

Huerta, T. R., Casebeer, A., & Vanderplaat, M. (2006). Using networks to enhance health services delivery: Perspectives, paradoxes and propositions. *Healthcare Papers*, *7*(2), 10–26.

Kanov, J. M., Maitlis, S., Worline, M. C., Dutton, J. E., Frost, P. J., & Lilius, J. M. (2004). Compassion in organisational life. *American Behavioral Scientist*, *47*(6), 808–827.

Kelly, J. (2007). Barriers to achieving patient-centered care in Ireland. *Dimensions of Critical Care Nursing*, *26*(1), 29–34.

Kline, N. (2002). *Time to Think: Listening to Ignite the Human Mind.* London: Cassell.

Lemieux-Charles, L., Chambers, L. W., Cockerill, R., Jaglal, S., Brazil, K., Cohen, C., LeClair, K., Dalziel, B., & Schulman, B. (2005). Evaluating the effectiveness of community-based dementia care networks: The dementia care networks' study. *The Gerontologist, 45*(4), 456–464.

Lilius, J. M., Kanov, J., Dutton, J. E., Worline, M. C., & Maitlis, S. (2011). Compassion revealed: What we know about compassion at work (and where we need to know more), in K. Cameron & G. Spreitzer (Eds.), *The Oxford Handbook of Positive Organisational Scholarship.* New York: Oxford University Press.

Lilius, J. M., Worline, M. C., Maitlis, S., Kanov, J. M., Dutton, J. E., & Frost, P. (2008). The contours and consequences of compassion at work. *Journal of Organisational Behavior, 29,* 193–218.

Liu, D., Chen, X. P., & Yao, X. (2011). From autonomy to creativity: A multilevel investigation of the mediating role of harmonious passion. *Journal of Applied Psychology, 96*(2), 294–309.

Lyubovnikova, J., West, M. A., Dawson, J. F., & Carter, M. R. (2015). 24-Karat or fool's gold? Consequences of real team and co-acting group membership in healthcare organisations. *European Journal of Work and Organisational Psychology, 24*(6), 929–950.

McCauley C. (2011). *Making Leadership Happen.* Greensboro, NC: Center for Creative Leadership.

Mannion, R. (2014). Enabling compassionate health care: Perils, prospects and perspectives. *International Journal of Health Policy & Management, 2*(3), 115–117.

Mickan, S. M., & Rodger, S. A. (2005). Effective health care teams: A model of six characteristics developed from shared perceptions. *Journal of Interprofessional Care, 19*(4), 358–370.

Mikulincer, M., & Shaver, P. R. (2007). *Attachment in Adulthood: Structure, Dynamics, and Change.* New York: Guilford Press.

NHS Staff Survey (2015). *Briefing Note: Issues Highlighted By The 2015 NHS Staff Survey In England* (*updated March 22nd 2016*), available at: http://www.nhsstaff surveys.com/Page/1006/Latest-Results/2015-Results/.

Rynes, S. L., Bartunek, J. M., Dutton, J. E., & Margolis, J. D. (2012). Care and compassion through an organisational lens: Opening up new possibilities. *Academy of Management Review, 37*(4), 503–523.

Salas, E., Rosen, M. A., & King, H. (2007). Managing teams managing crises: Principles of teamwork to improve patient safety in the emergency room and beyond. *Theoretical Issues in Ergonomics Science, 8*(5), 381–394.

Schaufeli, W. B., & Bakker, A. B. (2004). Job demands, job resources, and their relationship with burnout and engagement: A multi-sample study. *Journal of Organisational Behavior, 25*(3), 293–315.

Schneider, B., & Barbera K.M. (Eds.) (2014). *The Oxford Handbook of Organisational Climate and Culture.* Oxford: Oxford University Press.

Schneider, B., González-Romá, V., Osstroff, C., & West, M. (in press). Organisational climate and culture: Reflections on the history of the constructs in JAP. *Journal of Applied Psychology.*

Somech, A. (2006). The effects of leadership style and team process on performance and innovation in functionally heterogeneous teams. *Journal of Management, 32*(1), 132–157.

Totterdell, P. (2000). Catching moods and hitting runs: Mood linkage and subjective performance in professional sport teams. *Journal of Applied Psychology, 85*(6), 848.

Totterdell, P., Kellett, S., Teuchmann, K., & Briner, R. B. (1998). Evidence of mood link-age in work groups. *Journal of Personality and Social Psychology*, *74*(6), 1504.

Wall, T. D., Bolden, R. I., Borrill, C. S., Carter, A. J., Golya, D. A., Hardy,. . .West, M. A. (1997). Minor psychiatric disorder in NHS trust staff: Occupational and gender differ-ences. *The British Journal of Psychiatry*, *171*(6), 519–523.

West, M. A. (2012). *Effective Teamwork: Practical Lessons from Organisational Research (3rd edition)*. Oxford: Blackwell.

West, M. A. (2013). Creating a culture of high-quality care in health services. *Global Economics and Management Review*, *18*(2), 40–44.

West, M. A., Armit, K., Loewenthal, L., Eckert, R., West, T., & Lee, A. (2015). Leadership and leadership development in health care. London: FMLM and The King's Fund/ Brussels: Center for Creative Leadership.

West, M. A., Dawson, J. F., Admasachew, L., & Topakas, A. (2011). *NHS Staff Management and Health Service Quality: Results from the NHS Staff Survey and Related Data.* Report to the Department of Health, available at: http://www.dh.gov.uk/ health/2011/08/nhs-staff-management/.

West M.A., Eckert R., Steward, K., & Pasmore, B. (2014). *Developing Collective Leadership for Health Care*, The King's Fund, available at: http://www.kingsfund. org.uk/sites/files/kf/field/field_publication_file/developing-collective-leadership-kingsfund-may14.pdf

West, M. A., & Lyubovnikova, J. (2012). Real teams or pseudo teams? The chang-ing landscape needs a better map. *Industrial and Organisational Psychology*, *5*(1), 25–28.

West, M., Lyubovnikova, J., Eckert, R., & Denis, J. L. (2014). Collective leadership for cultures of high quality health care. *Journal of Organisational Effectiveness: People and Performance*, *1*(3), 240–260.

West, M. A. & Markiewicz, L. (2016). Effective team work in health care. In E. Ferlie, K. Montgomery, & R. Pedersen (Eds.), *The Oxford Handbook of Health Care Management* (pp. 231–252). Oxford: Oxford University Press.

West, M.A., Topakas, A., & Dawson, J.F. (2014). Climate and culture for health care performance. In B. Schneider & K. M. Barbera (Eds.), *The Oxford Handbook of Organisational Climate and Culture* (pp. 335–359). Oxford: Oxford University Press.

Wong, C. A., & Cummings, G. G. (2007). The relationship between nursing leader-ship and patient outcomes: A systematic review. *Journal of Nursing Management*, *15*(5), 508–521.

Worline, M. C., & Boik, S. (2006). Leadership lessons from Sarah: Values based lead-ership as everyday practice. In K. Cameron & E. Hess (Eds.), *Leading with Values: Positivity, Virtue, and High Performance* (pp. 108–131). Cambridge: Cambridge University Press.

Yukl, S. (2013). *Leadership in Organisations (8th edition)*. Harlow, UK: Pearson Education Limited.

Chapter 15

The emergence of the compassion focused therapies

James N. Kirby and Paul Gilbert

Where from and where to?

Two and a half thousand years ago, an Indian Prince, Siddhartha, had been closeted in a golden palace by his father, with all the pleasures on hand to protect him from the realities of suffering outside the palace walls. One day, dissatisfied with this limited life, Siddhartha persuaded a servant to sneak him outside the palace. To his shock he encountered disease, ageing and death for the first time (what is traditionally called the 'four messengers', the fourth being a meeting with a holy man who was seeking answers to suffering and set Siddhartha on the path to enlightenment). For most of us these fearful discoveries would have sent us back to the wine, sex and songs, but he was so taken by the suffering all around him, and aware this was his destiny too, that he became preoccupied with the nature of human suffering and was determined to find a solution for the human condition (Leighton, 2003; Vessantara, 1993). On his quest he encountered many philosophies, insights, yoga and contemplative practices to address suffering, eventually arriving at the famous Bodhi tree. For many hours, if not days, he sat quietly observing the rising and falling of his own, different mental phenomena. From this deep, personal experience he became aware that our minds can be filled with conflicting and difficult motives and passions – ones of not-wanting (aversions) and wanting (grasping after what is impermanent). Emotions and passions bounce us about like corks on a restless sea, causing suffering to ourselves and others as they control our preoccupations and actions. Sitting in silent but intense observation, he realised it was possible to focus on his own *observing knowing consciousness* itself, observing its arising and falling, to become mindful. He made a very clear distinction between the experience of observing (consciousness of consciousness; the awareness of awareness) and the mind's content – the 'what' is observed. Moving attention increasingly into the observer position creates mindful wisdom, discernment and insight, not only into the contents of mind (created by our biological forms) but also the subtleties of mind and consciousness. He recognised that without mindful clarity and insight we are easily taken over by whatever motives and passions happen to be stimulated within us (Vessantara, 1993).

Mindfulness opens the potential for a 'mindful brake' on the link of feeling into action. Without this we can be non-mindful actors for the archetypal dramas of life, acting out their scripts.

His solution was twofold. First, train the conscious, deliberate, observational competencies of mind, cultivating sharp awareness of our mind's contents as they arise, so that we can become mindful rather than 'mindless' in our thoughts and actions. The practices of mind-settling mindfulness also give insight into the subtle levels of mind and ultimately allow us to see into the illusions of the separate self, the snowflake that mistakes its individual separateness until it hits the sea. The Buddha's second solution was *motivation training*; of all the motives, passions and desires in us, the one that can offset grasping, greed and aversion, and balance the mind and bring true calmness and transformation is the motive of *compassion* – the desire to see all beings free of suffering and the causes of suffering – and then work for that outcome (Ricard, 2015). So the contents of mind can be given a focus. Mindfulness can bring stability to mind and compassion transforms it, freeing us from egoistic pursuits (Dalai Lama & Ekman, 2009; Germer & Siegel, 2012; see Germer & Barnofer, Chapter 4, this volume).

Over 2,000 years later Freud's observations, from encouraging free association in his patients, and analysing his own thoughts and dreams, married with the then rise of Darwinian thinking, generated similar insights (Ellenberger, 1970). Freud recognised, as had Siddhartha, that our minds are beset by complex and conflicting desires and passions, especially in the domains of yearnings, sex and violence. Unlike Siddhartha however, he argued that many of the darker sides of our minds are kept hidden by processes of defence (e.g. repression, denial, dissociation, sublimation) that can serve useful purposes but also make us vulnerable to mental distress. His solutions were quite different to Siddhartha's. He argued for the need to bring these conflicts into consciousness and resolve them, not via mindfulness or cultivating compassion (indeed, he viewed compassion with suspicion) but via therapist-guided free association. Indeed, both Freud and Jung argued that simply allowing unconscious contents to emerge without guidance or a therapeutic relationship could be dangerous for some people (Clark, 1994; Jung, 1984; see Farias & Wikholm, 2015). So for Siddhartha, without concepts of evolved motives and emotions, unconscious processes and defence mechanisms, the problem was a lack of insight-awareness of the nature of mind, for which training in 'observing the mind' was part of the solution. Today we can make a distinction between how to pay attention moment by moment, *mindfulness* in contrast to *mind awareness* which arises from scientific study of mind, various psychotherapies, and everyday interactions with people who provide feedback to us.

As the years unfolded an increasing varied melange of therapies for mind awareness, insight and change emerged – some seeing the mind as 'meaning seeking', especially around the existential life issues of loneliness, freedom, meaning and death (Yalom, 1980). Others moved from Freud's focus on (thwarted) drives to a focus on interpersonal psychodynamic processes (Greenberg & Mitchell, 1983), and the role of attachment (Bowlby, 1960, 1973, 1980; Holmes, 2001). Gestalt and emotion focused therapists concentrated on emotion processing (Greenberg & Safran, 1987). Others, such as George Kelly (1963), saw the human mind like a scientist constantly generating and testing theories about the world and developing 'personal constructs'. Albert Ellis (Ellis, 1962) and Aaron Beck (1985), both trained psychoanalysts, made a different set of observations. It is not unconscious conflicts, a lack of mindful insight/enlightenment, compassion, or existential struggles that cause us problems, but the conscious interpretations we make, and beliefs we hold. Their focus was on the processes of reasoning, 'stream of conscious thinking', automatic thoughts, beliefs and interpretations as responsible for mental distress and harmful behaviour. One could therefore intervene on these directly and *alter their content*; central to this was evidence testing. With the innovations of computers, our minds became described as information-processing systems, with feedback and feed-forward loops. Subsequently new therapies arose that focused on changing our relationship with our thoughts, rather than the contents, with increased body awareness noted particularly in mindfulness approaches, such as Acceptance Commitment Therapy and Dialectical Behaviour Therapy (Hayes, Follette, & Linehan, 2004).

The other major tradition, behaviourism, disavowed the internal world altogether, exploring instead the contingencies of behaviour. Both classical and operate conditioning approaches were interested in how animals adapt to their environments in order to better survive and exploit them, and, especially for classical conditioning, are physiologically changed in the process of adapting. We now know that adapting to environments can even influence the expression of genes (see Conway & Slavich, Chapter 9, this volume). The way our physiologies are changed via associative learning, especially classical conditioning, is now central to many therapies, especially body-based therapies (e.g. Van der Kolk, 2015) and Compassion Focused Therapy (CFT). What's also important is the social context in which classical conditioning takes place, for example, whether we experience fear in the context of aloneness or in the context of receiving soothing support and care it is easier to face things we are frightened of whom we feel supported by others then when we feel completely alone. For example, when veterans return from combat situations they are conditioned to be sensitive to the presence of their 'buddies' as safeness signals and when they are not present (as in the home environment) this can create feelings of disconnection and vulnerability.

The medical model

Many Western psychotherapies are also located within medical approaches to mind (Gilbert, 1995). These convey the idea that there is nothing fundamentally wrong with our mind as designed (i.e. nothing inherently bad or tricky about its evolved construction) and it is only 'when things go wrong' that we have a mental 'disorder', requiring therapies 'to correct' and 'fix' (Brune et al., 2012). So the therapies tended to cluster around 'disorders' of anxiety, depression and paranoia; with thoughts being 'distorted' and attitudes and behaviours being 'dysfunctional'. Whereas the Buddha highlighted that our *normal unenlightened* states were problematic – that the mind is, in a way, inherently crazy (Vessantara 1993), especially if it lacks compassion (Dalai Lama, 1995), the medical model took a different view, and psychotherapy to some degree followed this, particularly with the rise of DSM classifications and empirically supported treatments (Gilbert, 1995).

Evolution approaches to both physical and mental health problems have been critical of the medical model for failing to understand the difference between genuine pathology, reactions and evolved adaptations of innate strategies (Brune et al., 2012; Gilbert 1998a; Nesse & Ellsworth, 2009; Nesse & Williams, 1995). Indeed, we have known for a long time that in certain social contexts humans are naturally and easily prone to irrationalities, riddled with conscious and unconscious conflicts, tribal violence, nepotism and mental health problems (Buss, 2014; Gilbert, 1989/2016, 2009; Nesse & Williams, 1995). We are now beginning to understand why, and as we better understand why we can better understand 'how' to change things.

Today psychotherapy stands at an important developmental point. Before medicine understood the sophisticated physiology of how the heart works or how cells become cancerous, it relied on observations and engaging in 'trial and error' interventions. But as the scientific understanding of basic physiological systems improved, so did our capacity to develop improved interventions that target specific physiological processes. Psychotherapy is beginning to grapple with our better understanding of how humans evolved as biological, gene-built systems that (phenotypically) adapt to their environments and operate a range of evolved strategic and motivation- and emotion-processing systems (Barash, 2013; Conway & Slavich, Chapter 9, this volume; Gilbert, Chapter 3, this volume; Narvaez, Chapter 10, this volume). We recognise that as an evolved species (Siddhartha did not know this) many of our basic motives and emotions, and their genetic polymorphisms, are products of the challenges of survival and reproduction (Conway & Slavich, Chapter 9, this volume). This has important implications not only for our understanding of mental health difficulties but for their prevention and alleviation. It also warns us that assumptions like '*all is well until something goes wrong*' are unhelpful, misleading and basically often wrong (Brune et al., 2012; Gilbert, 1998a; Nesse & Williams, 1995). Crucial too is that we're moving away from the idea of humans as 'autonomous minds' to ones of 'information flow' and mutual influence (see Gilbert, Chapter 3, this volume; Frederickson & Siegel, Chapter 12, this volume; Siegel, 2016).

Rooting ourselves in our evolved minds, Table 15.1 provides a few basic building blocks showing some of its problematic trade-offs and glitches (Gilbert, 1998a). Establishing the origins of how our brains have evolved can help us identify and focus on core evolutionary archetypal themes and motives, such as status, attachment, sense of belonging and connectedness, fears of rejection and shame. These are important for humans because of our evolved history and how the brain evolved to be choreographed.

Viewing mental distress through an evolutionary lens, particularly the evolution of social connectedness, mutual influence and our social intelligences, supports many of the basic tools of psychotherapy, such as the importance of the therapeutic relationship, the value of guided discovery and reflection and behavioural

Table 15.1 Evolution informed psychotherapy in CFT

	Description	Implications	Therapy

1. Human brain as an evolved organ	• Like all living beings we are part of the flow of life.
	• We have a human brain we did not design, but evolved through millions of years of evolution, which has inbuilt emotion and motivational systems.
		• Our evolved brains' primary motivations are to survive and reproduce.
		• Our brains have inbuilt motives and motive conflicts:
		  ○ Harm avoidance, food, sex, competitive, caring, status.
		• Motives organise our minds:
		  ○ Attention, thinking, behaviour, imagery, emotion, sensory.
			• As therapists, with the help of our clients, we aim to discover how our clients are primarily motivated to be in the world, and how that changes/shifts in different social contexts (e.g. work, family, friends, romantic partner).
			  ○ For example, guided discovery, Socratic questioning.
			• Over the course of therapy the therapist then focuses on exploring how particular motives impact and organise our minds.

2. Brain capacities	• As a result of evolution, our brain has; 'trade-offs', constraints and many built-in biases.
	• Old Brain Functions are focused on survival and reproduction.
	• New Brain Functions, especially those supporting social intelligence (see Gilbert, Chapter 3, this volume), are focused on awareness and meta-awareness.
		• Old Brain Functions:
		  ○ Motives: harm avoidance, food, sex, caring, status.
		  ○ Emotions: anger, anxiety, sadness, joy.
		  ○ Behaviours: fight, flight, shut down, courting, caring.
		• New Brain Functions and competencies:
		  ○ Language/symbols, self-monitoring/ awareness, self-criticism, imagination, planning, rumination, worry, shame, integration.
		• We get caught in '*old brain–new brain*' loops.
		  ○ We have the new capacity of thinking, but run on 'old' psychological systems, whereby external 'threat' stimulus is brought inside our minds (e.g., imagination, rumination, worry, self-blame).
			• Psychodynamic and Jungian therapies focused on old-brain capacities (e.g. motives and archetypes, sex, aggression). Cognitive therapies focused on new-brain capacities (e.g. automatic thoughts, reasoning).
			• As therapists we can focus on both, as in reality it is a two-way street, where we can attend to the interaction between old brain–new brain processing loops.
			  ○ For example, this could be demonstrated with the analogy of the 'Zebra in the Savannah'. If the Zebra senses a predator it will run away for safety (better safe than sorry), then go back to eating. Put a human brain in the Zebra, despite being safe, thoughts will continue such as "*suppose I get caught tomorrow, dying would be terrifying!*" Thus, external threat stimulus taken into the mind, and continues physiological threat response in the body, an 'old brain–new brain' loop.
			• Therapists then focus on developing a case formulation of the client based on Evolutionary Functional Analysis (EFA, see Gilbert, 2014; Chapter 3, this volume).

3. Brain/ mind shaped by social contexts	• A genetic lottery for how our brains are built. • The environments in which we grow and the parenting we receive influence our genetic expression and our developing phenotypes. • Phenotypes are the expressed or manifest traits/outputs that are observable or measurable (e.g., styles of language or attachment).	• Born with a pre-determined set of genes we have inherited from parents. • Epigenetics and the process of methylation influences genetic expression. Stressful environments, in contrast to safe and predictable environments, turn genes on and off in different ways as the child is developing his/her phenotypes that prepare them for the environmental niche in which s/he is growing. • We are socially shaped, from gene expressions to our sense of self and values.	• This permits a de-shaming for our clients, as so much of what has happened to them is not of their choosing, and is not their fault. o For example, ask yourself, *"Would you be the same person if you had been kidnapped as a three-day old baby and raised by the Mafia?"* • Focus of therapy becomes what version of ourselves have we become and in what contexts, and what versions of ourselves are possible that we wish to cultivate (e.g., compassionate self, angry self, anxious self; for more see Gilbert, 2010, 2014).
4. Brain and biases	• We have biases that shape how we see the world.	• Biased learning (e.g., fear of snakes but not electricity). • Self-focused (grasping and aversion). • Kin preferences (nepotism). • In-group preferences (tribalism). • Negativity (better safe than sorry) bias.	• These biases can lead to inner (mental anguish, such as self-criticism) and outer conflicts (interpersonal), which can lead humans to engage in great cruelty, bringing suffering to ourselves and to others (both mentally and physically). • Therapists can explore with their clients how these biases were not 'chosen' by them, and how they operate in their daily life, which informs the ongoing EFA for the client, then how to counteract them with different forms of compassion focusing. o To indicate threat, therapists could provide clients the example of the 'Christmas Shopper'. The person who goes into 10 shops, in 9 of which he/she is greeted in a friendly and helpful manner, but in the 10th shop he/she is greeted by a rude and unhelpful shop assistant. When the Christmas Shopper gets home, what does he/she tell their partner about? The negative experience: an example of negativity bias.

(continued)

Table 15.1 (continued)

	Description	Implications	Therapy
5. Brain and caring motivation	• Parental investment (care for offspring – supporting allies). • Distress Signal/Distress Response. • Humans mammals evolved for forming (and needing) attachment and social lives	• Humans are have few offspring, cared for many years. Parental care involves moving towards distress signals from young to soothe and calm (emotion regulation for child), and this forms attachments. • Attachment system: 　○ Proximity seeking – desire closeness. 　○ Secure base – source of security and guidance to explore. 　○ Safe haven – source of comfort and emotion regulation. 　○ Later in life, close friends and partners take on these roles and suffering can arise if they don't.	• The therapist aims to create an internalised, secure base and safe haven for the client by activating the compassionate self as an organising process and focus for self-identity. • The therapist also acts as a model for compassion to the client in therapy, and seeks to create a secure base and safe haven enabling clients the opportunities to explore difficult memories, situations, thoughts, emotions in a therapeutic context of safeness. • Understanding how the client has developed safety behavioural strategies is crucially important at this stage, which also informs the EFA. • Therapist makes the distinction between safety (threat focused/preventive) and safeness (open, explorative and growth focused) (see Gilbert, 2014).
6. Brain and affect system	• The brain has emotion regulation systems that impact how we interact with the world and ourselves.	• Threat and self-protect system: 　○ Focus on protection and safety-seeking, it activates and inhibits. 　○ Emotions: anger, anxiety, disgust • Drive and achievement system: 　○ Incentive/resource focused, wanting, pursuing, achieving, activating. 　○ Emotions: drive, excite, vitality. • Affiliative/soothing system: 　○ Non-wanting, affiliative focused, safeness-kindness, soothing. 　○ Emotions: content, safe connected.	• The therapist with the client explore how we can operate from various emotion systems, and how each system can impact how we view ourselves and interact with others. 　○ Process of psycho-education, guided discovery, Socratic questioning. • The information ascertained further informs ongoing EFA for client. • The therapist with the help of the client, aims to develop a balance between these affect systems.

(exposure) practices which will remain the bedrock of therapeutic interventions. However, new models of how to facilitate change are also working out how to change neurophysiological pathways directly due to neurogenesis and neuroplasticity (Klimecki, Leiberg, Ricard, & Singer, 2013) and epigenetics (Conway & Slavich, Chapter 9 this volume; Fredrickson et al., 2013). We are moving towards a kind of 'psycho-physiotherapy'. These approaches themselves, however, are contextualised in greater appreciation of the sociality of our species, and that our neuroplasticity and phenotypic variations are especially sensitive to social relationships, and are the cornerstone for understanding mental distress and its healing. It has been the research highlighting how prosocial, caring, supportive, helpful, altruistic and compassionate behaviour, both given and received (explored in the chapters of this book), impacts on such a wide range of physiological and psychological processes, that underpins CFT (Gilbert, 2000, 2009, 2014). So there is growing awareness of the importance of understanding how and why recruiting and cultivating evolved, care-focused motivational systems and affiliative emotions need to become central to the therapeutic process (Gilbert, 2000, 2014, 1989/2016; Chapter 3, this volume). Tibetan Buddhism has always placed the cultivation of compassion (Bodhicitta) central to the integration and organisation of mind, but science is beginning to show how and why this is so important (see Gilbert, Chapter 3, this volume). Indeed, much of this book, especially Part II, is dedicated to exploring how powerful compassion-focused social mentalities are in actually organising, choreographing and patterning the brain and body – even at the genetic level (see also Seppala & Doty, in press).

The compassion focused therapies

Most psychotherapies follow unfolding and progressive (not necessarily linear) stages. For example, assessment, developing a formulation and building a therapeutic relationship for collaborative work are central components. Beyond these common themes, different therapies will structure their tasks and goals around their models. One core feature that varies is psychoeducation. Different therapies have different psychoeducations. For example, behaviour therapists educate about contingencies of behaviour and how to change those with action; cognitive therapists teach the link between our appraisals and interpretations to feeling and behaviours; body-based therapies focus on postures and body awareness. Some therapists prefer hardly any psychoeducation, believing it should all be via direct experience. As an evolution-informed therapy, CFT focuses psychoeducation a lot on the fact that the human brain 'evolved' in a piecemeal fashion and is riddled with trade-offs, compromises and quite serious 'glitches', whilst also being inherently social, and socially needy (Gilbert, 1998a, 1998b); we call it 'tricky brain' (described in Table 15.1). Part of the reason for focusing on the problems nature has handed us, with how our brain evolved is not only to provide a framework for the work to be constructed, but also as a process of de-shaming (Gilbert, 2007, 2009, 2010). As people begin to see their human mind as riddled with complexities, conflicts and competencies – that they did not choose and often do not want, but which can be sources of suffering to themselves and others – they can begin to gradually depersonalise. We are all just 'one' of many possible versions (see Table 15.1). As this process unfolds individuals are able to recognise that at the core of what we want: food, love, sex and status, what we feel if we achieve them or do not achieve them (happy, or sad, anxious and angry) and what threatens us (physical harm and social harms), is an evolutionary setup, and that is not our fault! The senses and bodily functions we have, and the contents and preoccupations of our minds, emerge from gene-built physiological systems interacting with historically created social contexts, in relation with the bodies and minds of others created the same way.

This links us to some sense of common humanity; just like other people we are actors in the dramas of life's archetypal motivations; suffering is part of it (Vessantara, 1993). We differ from animals though, in that we have the potential to gain insight into this and begin to choose and cultivate versions of ourselves that are conducive to ours and other people's well-being; we have a range of complex social intelligences to help us (see Gilbert, Chapter 3, this volume). So we move from blaming (because we did not choose the genes that made us nor the contexts that shaped us) to taking responsibility for the inner patterns we want to cultivate and the person we want to become (Gilbert, 2009). Similarly, we begin to see others through the same lens, which gives us the courage and insight for forgiveness and letting go of anger that can block compassion (Worthington et al., 2005). We may come to recognise that some of our anger (rage), fear and sadness can be linked to parental figures and can become a focus in therapy (Gilbert, 2010). The emergence of these unprocessed emotions may be one reason why mindfulness by itself can be traumatic for some people without a therapeutic safe haven, containment and guidance. Siddhartha had no insight into the evolutionary dynamics at the heart of life and mind, but clearly his solution is in tune with them. So this psychoeducation process is about increasing not reducing responsibility taking, and this is more likely when we give up a blaming and shaming approach, and rather gain insight into how to cultivate coping with suffering and what is conducive to well-being for us and others.

Clients become able to recognise that we are all particular versions of multiple potentials (phenotypes), the vast majority of which we will never know or live out. As Table 15.1 describes in point three, if we had been kidnapped as three-day-old babies into violent drug gangs then this current 'version' of ourselves would not exist, and even our genetic expression would be different – we are socially created versions of phenotypes (Conway & Slavich, Chapter 9, this volume). We are also made up of multiple potentials of motives and emotions, each with its own view of the world, talents and priorities (e.g. angry self, anxious self, joyful self, competitive self; Gilbert, 2014; Ornstein, 1986). These patterns arise moment by moment according to how our current physiological states interact with social contexts – for good and bad (see Narvaez, Chapter 10; Zimbardo, 2006). So it is an important realisation that we all have *very tricky brains* for which schools and society ill-prepares us to understand or train. Nothing has necessarily gone wrong for people who suffer or who harm others – rather it can be the mind 'naturally' reacting to the context in which it is operating.

Another stage of the compassion focused therapies is rooted in the understanding of what brings out well-being and the best in us; that is to say, if the natural state of the human condition is not necessarily a happy or healthy one, what can we do to advance that? (Dalai Lama, 1995). In addition to more than 2,500 years of the contemplative and spiritual traditions emphasising compassion for self and others as the path to happiness, wisdom and growth, scientific studies over the last 20 or 30 years have revealed much about human needs and optimal functioning (Singer & Bolz, 2012). As many chapters in this book and others (Seppala & Doty, in press) indicate, there is now considerable evidence that the mammalian reproductive strategies, to have small numbers and high investment, 'to care for the kids' and support friends and allies (Gilbert 1989/2016; MacLean, 1985; Mayseless, 2016; Narvaez, Chapter 10, this volume), along with other forms of conspecific caring, had a major impact on the evolution of our ancestral bodies and brains (Dunbar, 2010; Spikins, Chapter 2, this volume). 'Caring' gave rise to physiological systems being highly sensitive to distress signals, with oxytocin (Carter, 2014; Colonnello, Petrocchi & Henrichs, Chapter 6, this volume) and changes in the autonomic system, such as the vagal system, playing major roles (Mascaro & Raison, Chapter 5, this volume; Porges, 2007; Stellar & Keltner, Chapter 7, this volume) in brain development (Vrtička, Favre & Singer, Chapter 8, this volume). In a study conducted by Mascaro, Rilling, Negi, and Raison (2013), in comparison with a control group, Cognitively Based Compassion Training was associated with increased theory of mind, mentalising and motivation. As an indicator of the interconnected importance of the flow of compassion (see Gilbert, Chapter 3, this volume), Hermanto et al. (2016) found that, in a sample of 701 participants, the ability to receive compassion buffeted the effects of self-criticism on depression.

Forms of compassion focused interventions

With the rise of an awareness of the power of prosocial, compassionate interactions for well-being, and how their opposite (criticism and neglect) is linked to mental distress, there has been a growth of different approaches to help people cultivate compassion for themselves and others. They differ in various ways, however. For example, CFT distinguishes between therapy and compassionate mind training. Therapy aspects include formulation, the therapeutic relationship and the skills of moment-by-moment therapeutic engagement. Compassionate mind training is the provision of a series of practices to cultivate core qualities of compassion. Many of the newer approaches to cultivating compassion are primarily compassionate mind trainings of various forms, rather than therapies designed to train therapists conceptualise the therapeutic process and be used in therapeutic interactions and contexts with complex mental health problems as CFT was originally developed to do.

Different compassion approaches include Mindful Self-Compassion (MSC; Neff & Germer, 2013); Compassion Cultivation Training (CCT; Jazaieri et al., 2013); Cognitively Based Compassion Training (CBCT; Pace et al., 2009); Cultivating Emotional Balance (CEB; Kemeny et al., 2012); Compassion and Loving-Kindness

Table 15.2 Common and specific features of compassion-based trainings and therapy

Common features

- Designed to be secular in approach, utilising Western psychology science and therapies but also informed, to greater or lesser degrees, by contemplative traditions.
- Define what compassion is, with each intervention having a different definition.
- Attention and Mindfulness-based training components.
- Compassion focused visualisations and meditation practices.
- Some form of psychoeducation where rationale provided for intervention.
- Active experiential components.
- Focus on intention or values.
- Homework exercises and regular practice.

Specific features

CFT	MSC	CBCT	CCT	CEB
• Compassion definition includes two psychologies, (1) engagement and (2), alleviation and prevention, each with six trainable competencies. • Psychoeducation of evolved 'tricky mind' due to 'old' and 'new' brain interactions. • Evolved function of emotions of threat/protection, drive/ acquisition and soothing/ contentment, and the links to (neuro)physiological processes and emotional balance.	• Based primarily on Neff's conceptualisation of self-compassion using bipolar constructs of: (1) kindness v. self-judgement; (2) common humanity v. isolation; (3) mindfulness v. over-identifying. • Informed by various approaches including self-experiences of life difficulties, Insight Meditation, CFT and other mindfulness-based interventions such as MSBR.	• Based primarily on Buddhist *lojong* tradition. • Examines compassion as aspirational and active. • Focus on four immeasurables: equanimity, loving-kindness, appreciative joy and compassion.	• Based on definition of compassion by Jinpa involving four constructs: cognitive, affective, intentional and motivation. • Begin and end each session with a meditation practice, which includes breath focus meditation. • Inclusion of *tong-len*.	• Compassion more focused on others as a prosociality. • Concentration and directive practice meditations. • Recognising emotions. • Understanding emotional patterns. • Recognising emotions in others (face, verbal) as a way to promote empathy.

- The concept of multiple (phenotypic) versions of self arising from gene and social context – focus on cultivating phenotypes for de-shaming, de-personalising and building compassionate intentions.
- Breath and posture training, creating a friendly tone in one's thinking and thoughts; stimulate vagal tone.
- Cultivating compassion for others, open to compassion from others and self-compassion.
- Developing compassionate imagery and sense of self using acting techniques of becoming and then 'acting from' constructed self-role.
- Developing and using the compassionate mind to address difficulties such as shame, self-criticism and relational conflicts (Figure 15.1).
- Developing the 12 competencies of compassion.

- Inclusion of the self-compassion break exercise, based on self-compassion definition.
- Breaks meditations into core, other and informal practices.
- Focus on savouring and positive psychology.
- Includes letter-writing.
- Working with backdraft problems with compassion blocks.
- **Training program components:**
  1. Introduction and review of self-compassion.
  2. Mindfulness training.
  3. Application of self-compassion to daily life.
  4. Developing a compassionate inner voice.
  5. Living in accordance with values.

- Teaches active contemplation of loving-kindness, empathy and compassion towards loved ones, strangers, and enemies.
- Integrates cognitive interventions
- **Follows eight steps:**
  1. Developing attention and stability of Mind.
  2. The nature of mental experience.
  3. Developing self-compassion.
  4. Developing equanimity for others.

- Primary focus is on meditative practices to cultivate compassion and loving-kindness towards self and others.
- **Follows six steps:**
  1. Settling and focusing the mind.
  2. Loving-kindness and compassion for a loved one.
  3a. Compassion for self.
  3b. Loving-kindness for oneself.
  4. Embracing shared common humanity and developing appreciate of others.
  5. Cultivating compassion for others.

- Yoga and movement practices.
- Knowledge of functions, sensations, triggers, appraisals and cognitions associated with affective states.
- **Training program components:**
  1. Concentration training.
  2. Mindfulness training.
  3. Promotion of empathy and compassion.
  4. Yoga and other movement practices.
  5. Conceptual discussion including a focus on values, life meaning.

(continued)

Table 15.2 (continued)

Specific features

CFT	MSC	CBCT	CCT	CEB
• Compassion-focused letter-writing and flash card exercises. • Expecting and addressing fears, blocks and resistances to positive and affiliative emotions and the three orientations of compassion. • **Therapy approach:** 1. Individualised and group interventions based on client's presentation and case conceptualisation. 2. Various (clinical and non-clinical) compassionate Mind Training programmes under development including an eight-week intervention, one being piloted. **Initial development** • Complex clinical problems of high shame and self-criticism. Clients being major contributors to development. **Source** • Gilbert, P. (2000, 2010, 2014).	6. Dealing with difficult emotions. 7. Dealing with challenging interpersonal relationships. 8. Relating to positive aspects of oneself and one's life with appreciation. 9. A mid-program, four-hour retreat often included. **Initial development** • The general population who struggle with self-criticism. **Source** • Neff, K., & Germer, C. (2013).	5. Developing appreciation and gratitude for others. 6. Developing affection and empathy. 7. Realising, wishing and aspirational compassion. 8. Realising Active Compassion for Others. **Initial development** • University students and adolescents at risk to develop emotional resilience. **Source** • Ozawa-de Silva, B., & Dodson-Lavelle, B. (2011).	6. Active compassion practice (*tong-len*) and integrated daily compassion cultivation practice. **Initial development** • The general population to help with emotion regulation and cultivate compassion. **Source** • Jazaieri, H. et al., (2014).	6. Knowledge of functions, sensations, triggers, automatic appraisals and cognitions associated with specific affective states (e.g. anger, fears). 7. Recognising one's own emotions. 8. Understanding one's own emotional patterns. 9. Recognising emotion in others (face, verbal) to promote empathy. **Initial development** • The general population to reduce destructive enactment of emotions and enhance prosocial responses. **Source** • Kemeny, M. et al., (2012).

Meditations (e.g. CM & LKM; Hoffmann, Grossman, & Hinton, 2011) and Compassion-Focused Therapy (CFT; Gilbert, 2000, 2007, 2014; Kirby, 2016).

Hybrids are also constantly appearing, such as the mindful compassionate living course that combines CFT with more intense mindfulness training (Bartels-Velthuis et al., 2016; van der Brink & Koster, 2012) or the integration of CFT with therapies like Acceptance Commitment Therapy (Tirch, Schoendorfe, & Silberstein, 2015). We cannot review all of them but Table 15.2 offers a brief description of some of the elements that are similar and different across some of these compassion-based approaches.

To date, there has only been one meta-analysis conducted on compassion-based interventions (Kirby, Tellegen, & Steindl, 2015), which included 23 randomised controlled trials (RCTs) over the last 10 years. Results found significant short-term moderate effect sizes for compassion ($d = 0.559$), self-compassion ($d = 0.691$) and mindfulness ($d = 0.525$). Significant moderate effects were also found for reducing suffering-based outcomes of depression ($d = 0.656$) anxiety ($d = 0.547$), and small to moderate effects for psychological distress ($d = 0.374$). Significant moderate effects were also found for well-being ($d = 0.540$).

While such meta-analyses are important and useful, it is wise to keep in mind that they bring together models from different definitions of compassion, different theoretical underpinnings and different compassion practices (see Kirby, 2016 for a critique of the similarities and differences). To date CFT was developed for, and with, people with severe mental health problems. CFT has been helpful for individuals suffering from a range of difficulties including, but not limited to, psychotic disorders (Braehler et al., 2013), eating disorders (Kelly & Carter, 2015), personality disorders (Lucre & Corten, 2013) and traumatic brain injury (Ashworth, Gracey, & Gilbert, 2011). A recent systematic review of CFT, in a range of clinical settings and with different clinicians, showed good outcomes to support funding for further controlled randomised controlled trials (Leaviss & Uttley 2015). Although CFT was designed for clinical populations, the compassionate mind training practices that have been developed have been found to be helpful for non-clinical populations (McEwan & Gilbert, 2016), including producing changes in compassion and positive emotions, and at improving heart-rate variability (Matos et al., under review). Over time CFT and therapies and interventions will seek to develop the evidence base of the individual *ingredients* of their approach and build better interventions from evidence of specific ingredients or processes (Kirby, 2016).

Common cross-therapy interventions that target process

There exist over 150 different kinds of psychotherapies that all share a common purpose: to help individuals cope with the varied difficulties of suffering they are experiencing, prevent future ones where possible and come to terms with ones that are not changeable (e.g. one's own death). Many also help patients in their search for personal meaning. Not surprisingly there are many common evidence-based ingredients that are key to CFT, including the therapeutic relationship; psychoeducation (e.g. affective regulatory systems); guided discovery (which can include Socratic dialogues and guided practices); structured formulations and functional analysis (using EFA and identifying safety behaviours); thinking and reasoning strategies (e.g. thought monitoring, reappraisal, mentalising); body-focused exercises (e.g. breathing, voice tone, posture); behavioural experiments and exposure; imagery; attention/mindfulness/meditation; letter writing; distinguishing shame-based criticising from compassionate self-correction and homework (Gilbert, 2010). We would like to offer an important note to this in regard to the therapeutic relationship and therapist development. Here, and in Chapter 3, we highlight the Bodhicitta principle and motivation of developing 'self-enlightenment' to help others. This has implications for a therapist's preparedness to understand and work with their own minds (Gale, Schroder & Gilbert, 2015), especially mindfully (Katzow & Safran, 2007). Needing to have insight into one's mind was of course central to early psychodynamic training and is a basis of 'mind awareness'. Certainly, many caution against the idea that therapy is simply learning a mechanical set of techniques (Bennett-Levy & Haarhoff, in press; Bennett-Levy & Thwaites, 2007). The more we understand our own minds in relationship to others (e.g. clients) the less chance we have of simply acting as rescuers, engaging in dissociation or denial, getting caught in complex transference and counter-transference issues, acting out, and justifying or allocating blame to therapeutic ruptures (Gilbert & Leary, 2007). Since CFT was developed as a psychotherapy, embedded in research into affiliative caring motivational systems (social mentalities) these are central issues in building and sustaining a therapeutic relationship (Gilbert, 2007; Gilbert & Leary, 2007).

Using evolutionary insights to fashion therapy

A cornerstone of CFT is rooted in the evolution of caring and affiliative motives and behaviours, and in particular attachment, friendship formation and sense of belonging and connectedness. These all contribute to a sense of safeness in the world and provide resources for regulating and integrating our minds (Gilbert, 2014). In his attachment triology Bowlby (1969, 1973, 1980) emphasised that there are three core qualities and resources that are fundamental to the infant's growth and development: (1) the ability to be in close physical *proximity* with each other, vigilant to each other's whereabouts/availability; (2) the provision of a *secure base*, which supports the infant's growth, maturation, exploration and development of a separate but connected self-identity and confidence and (3) to provide a *safe haven*, which provides competent soothing for distress. As a secure base, parents facilitate *courage* through encouraging the child to face, at times, difficult or risky things, for example riding a bike or going to school (e.g. using voice tone, touch, and eye contact). Many therapies see these as crucial to therapeutic relationships (Liotti, 2007).

The self psychologist, Kohut (1977) added the role of parents as approving, admiring others, noting it is important for children to have their own self-worth reflected back, a process he referred to as 'mirroring'. The facial expressions or what he called '*gleam in mother's eye*' stimulates positive emotion about the child's sense of self. In addition, parental mirroring means that as a child achieves small development steps there is a joyful audience. Indeed, for children, successes need to matter to others not just themselves. Imagine growing up, cared for, but with nobody having time or interest or joy in seeing if you do well or not.

Another key function is for the parent to 'hold the child in mind', attentive of the need to recover or rescue. The experiences of 'another coming' when one is lost or distressed provides fundamental learning about the safeness and helpfulness of others. For children who have not received this, when they were distressed and no-one came, the world seemed a dangerous and lonely place. The need to 'feel' there is someone there 'looking over me or out for me' is central to many forms of relating, including religious forms. Archetypal fears of aloneness (which in young primates and mammals would mean probable death via predation or dehydration) can be an archetypal terror and these can sometimes reappear in the therapy. For example, one patient described it as a feeling of separateness and aloneness terror 'as if cast adrift in the dark, silent emptiness of outer space'. Having an evolutionary lens enables the therapist to be aware of the possible terror of disconnection/aloneness.

Once the parent arrives or responds to a distress signal then their capacity to provide soothing and grounding in times of stress or threat becomes central. For example, a parent who returns to a distressed child but is critical of, or irritated with, the child for the distress is not soothing. The capacity to be *available* and *effective* in times of need builds the child's emotion regulation competencies. The *strength* and *wisdom* of the parent provides support for the emerging emotions and motive conflicts of the child's mind.

Important too, for social beings like humans, who are highly socially connected and regulated (Keltner, Kogan, Piff, & Saturn, 2014), is the ability to understand the minds and intentions of others. Intersubjectivity (different to empathy) is a core competency in relating to other minds, creating a sharing of experience and awareness, and it too is a competency that develops through childhood, especially compassionate childhood (Cortina & Liotti, 2010). Recent evidence suggests that our capacities to trust and have an accurate awareness of others is influenced by the early experiences of receiving empathic care (Cortina & Liotti, 2010). So there is a vast range of inputs that caring figures provide to the child that enable them to become a confident, self-regulating, interacting social agent, with physiological infrastructures, such as the parasympathetic vagal system, to support them (see Colonnello et al., Chapter 6, this volume; Davidson, 2012; Depue & Morrone-Strupinsky, 2005; Dunbar, 2010; Porges, 2007; Thayer & Lane, 2000). These are the basis of compassionate care and building a compassionate mind.

Sadness and grief

Another key attachment question is how a child experiences sadness, loss and grief, and others' responses to them when they do. Crying is one of the most dangerous emotions because one is unable to see, one's breathing is affected and muscles become lower in tone. This could only have evolved in the context of being cared for – otherwise one could be in extreme danger. It is one of the most important emotions linked to a desire for interpersonal (re)connection. The more unsafe we feel, or feel or express that sadness is inappropriate in some way, the less able we may be to feel sadness and grief. In fact, the ability to feel sadness and sorrow is essential to Buddhist models of compassion (Gilbert & Choden, 2013) and has recently been identified as a seriously neglected process for people with mental health problems; indeed some therapies seem to have an avoidance of engaging with painful grief processing (Horwitz & Wakefield, 2007). As noted by Gilbert and Irons (2005), grieving, in the context of a caring other, can have major implications for the reorganisation of inner working models. Gilbert (Chapter 3, this volume) notes too that an inability to grieve for losses in one's own life (e.g. for the loving/protecting parent one wanted and yearned for but never had) can block processes like guilt. CFT therefore facilitates the ability to engage with past losses and work with the associated emotions like anger and fear – but also with sadness and grief – and to see grief not as a vulnerability, weakness or danger but as a very important evolved human process that can have many therapeutic effects.

Building the compassionate mind in CFT

CFT seeks to create the conditions in the therapy, *and within the patient*, to provide for the stabilising experiences of the secure base and safe haven, feeling valued (mirroring), with the competencies for empathy and intersubjectivity that enable individuals to understand their own minds and that of others (see Figure 15.1). As discussed in earlier chapters (e.g. Gilbert, Chapter 3, this volume), compassion stimulates and cultivates care-focused *motivations and intentions*. Therefore, we wish for the client to experience the *compassionate intentionality of the therapist* and to some degree elements of the 12 competencies of compassion (Gilbert 2010, Chapter 3, this volume). How these are used clinically are very briefly given in Table 15.3.

Ideally then, the client comes to experience the therapist as sensitive, moved by their experience, emotionally/distress tolerant, empathic and non-judgemental with the commitment and wisdom of knowing how to work together.

There are a range of practices that texture CFT to help build the compassionate competencies within the client. These include formulation in the evolutionary model, attention, awareness and mindfulness training; developing a sense of grounding and slowing linked to the balance of the sympathetic and parasympathetic systems partly provided by practices such as how to use the breath to slow the mind and stimulate the vagal system (approximately five breaths per minute); how to create and use friendly postures, facial expressions and inner voice tones to texture one's thoughts rather than hostile self-criticisms; cultivate self and other-focused empathy and mentalising training and build the characteristics of a compassionate self and mind.

CFT compassion practices focus on the *flow of compassion*. There is the compassion we experience *from* others, the compassion we have *for* others and

Table 15.3 The 12 competencies of compassion in CFT

Engagement	Action
Care for well-being: Is focused on building the desire-intention to begin the process of cultivating compassion and caring motivation. For people who are struggling, fears, blocks and resistances can be related to over-self-monitoring and self-doubt, shame and negative beliefs and early life experiences. Clarify the definition of compassion, including that it is a (building of) courage for a descent into pain/suffering, not an ascent away from it in order to heal or cope with it.	**Attention:** Recognise how to tune attention and focus to 'what would help you/me at this time to work on this issue' (e.g. creating in mind the pattern of compassionate self, or recalling coping memories or skills).
Sensitivity: Attentional sensitivity is tuned to noticing the presence of suffering in self and others as it arises. Many psychological therapies offer 'mindful' attention and awareness training in different ways; helping people to become more aware of their emotions, automatic thoughts, (difficulty with) bodily experiences. Sometimes this is direct training (e.g. mindful awareness); sometimes it's therapist-guided, 'bringing to the client's attention key issues as they arise.' 'I notice that when you say "that" your body curls up or your faces changes; I notice when we touch on your feelings about X you change the subject/go blank/seem disorientated/become angry etc. . . .'	**Imagery:** Many therapies use forms of imagery to do a range of different things including exposure, stimulating coping rehearsals, through to stimulating physiological systems. Many aspects of imagery in CFT include compassion-focused visualisations and meditations (compassionate self and compassionate-other images) through to imagining compassion focused behaviour rehearsals. **Reasoning:** Compassion is wisdom-based. Using insights from the evolution model and also a range of cognitive (CBT and ACT) reappraisal practices – but in CFT these are rooted and textured in compassionate *intention* and motives with appropriate emotions.
Sympathy: As attention moves towards suffering for self and others, we become emotionally moved/engaged by what comes into focus and into mind. This can generate emotions like sadness or fear linked to this awareness. These then require distress tolerance and empathic insight.	**Behaviour:** Considerable evidence shows that changing behaviour is often essential for change. CFT is a very behavioural therapy in many ways. Sometimes this is developing the courage to face threat (e.g. the agoraphobic goes out, the shy person practises assertiveness). Given that some can be fearful of compassion, compassion behavioural rehearsals are important. Fear of compassion and friendly, affiliative emotions can be treated very similarly to the behavioural treatment of any fear. CFT also utilises classical conditioning models.

(continued)

Table 15.3 (continued)

Engagement	Action
Distress tolerance: Many therapies enable clients to stay with (become tolerant of) distress, and thus to turn towards problems rather than experientially avoid, repress, deny or dissociate. Sometimes this is with specific training and guidance (e.g. graded tasks/exposures, knowledge, mindfulness). It often needs to be contextualised with the use of the secure base and safe haven of the therapeutic relationship. **Empathy:** In CFT empathy is an umbrella term for a range of mind-reading processes such as emotional attuning/recognising, through to cognitive perspective taking and mentalisation. Understanding both what and why we (and others) are thinking, feeling and behaving. It emphasises the cognitive and emotional understanding, and appreciation of the experience of another and flexibly engaging with their perspective. It also draws upon wisdom and insight, e.g. our tricky human brain. Any sense of common humanity can only come from empathic abilities. **Non-judgement:** This refers to being open and holding experience in mind rather than condemning and criticising one's experience.	**Sensory focusing:** This involves using body posture, grounding, soothing rhythm breathing, practising friendly voice tone to one's inner thoughts to create bodily states that are conducive to compassion focusing and changing mental states. **Feeling and emotion:** Feelings and emotions are often an emergent property of changes in stimulus valence and also behaviour change. Some practices such as loving-kindness and gratitude practices can generate friendly affiliative feelings. For some, though, stimulating these emotions can trigger feared or painful attachment memories and/or a grief process. The feelings and emotions of compassion are also context-dependent. The client's ability to experience caring emotions motives from the therapist can be very important. Affiliative emotions may arise slowly or not at all, e.g. we do not need to feel affaliative in order to forgive.

Note: We draw attention to the fact that these 12 characteristics (6 for engagement and 6 for action) are highly interdependent, and help cultivate the compassionate motives and intentions. For example, the more tolerant of distress we are the more we will be able to pay attention to distress and if we can hold it in mind we can begin to have more guided discovery and empathic insights. These also build courage and help with our reasoning. In CFT, therefore, the therapist is working and using the relationship, and teaching the client how to experience these different characteristics. CFT is an integrative therapy but the key focus is to pull together these characteristics within the context of compassionate motivation, which partly creates a secure base, safe haven and mirroring, and allows integration of beliefs, emotions and memories.

self-compassion. As discussed in Chapter 3 of this volume, these are interdependent and build and support each other. Developing experiences of compassion 'coming in' can be through gratitude and appreciation exercises (practising noticing the helpfulness of others) but also through imagery and meditation work. For example, people are guided into how to generate images of compassionate others/minds relating to them with wisdom (that we all just find ourselves here with a tricky brain), strength and complete commitment to them. There is a guided discovery element to this for the client because some recognise they prefer one gender for their image over another; some recognise they struggle even to imagine interacting with a wise, committed caring other, and sometimes they can experience a sense of aloneness, separateness rather than compassion (Rockliff, Gilbert, McEwan, Lightman, & Glover, 2008). Some clients fear that '*if others (even my compassionate image) really knew what goes on in my mind they would not like or care for me*'. Others find even trusting or relating to an inner image to be difficult. Nonetheless, these images are designed to stimulate physiological systems. This is no different, in principle, to imagining a happy memory or lying in bed with erotic fantasies that will create a cascade of hormones from the pituitary and sexual arousal. Equally, fantasising compassion from and for others stimulates affiliative physiological systems including the frontal cortex and with repeated practice is a focus for neuroplasticity (Klimecki et al., 2014).

CFT also uses practices of empathy training and taking actions that are going to *be helpful to others*, for example, taking an empathic interest in other people, mentalising, thinking what one can do that would be helpful and doing it, but also at times assertive training, because compassion is not submissive. Appreciative awareness of the helpfulness of others is also key. Again, the concepts of Bodhicitta are salient here (Gilbert, Chapter 3, this volume)

Core to CFT and the compassionate mind is building the *compassionate self*, imagining stepping into it and thinking and acting for the perspective of 'one's ideal compassionate self', 'imagining ourselves as we would ideally like to compassionately be', with the qualities of wisdom, strength, and commitment (Gilbert, 2010; Gilbert & Choden, 2013). CFT utilises acting training techniques to help people see that we are made up of multiple possibilities or mini-selves. In a conflict situation, for example, we might be regulated by the angry self or inner pattern that thinks and wants to behave in certain ways, or perhaps the anxious-self that thinks, feels and behaves in different ways. People can discover that these mini-selves are often in conflict. Angry-self may not like anxious-self, while anxious-self/pattern can be frightened of angry-self/pattern. However, when we notice this we can deliberately stand back and switch to the compassionate self, by slowing the breath, grounding with compassion body postures and remembering our compassion intention and identity that brings wisdom, strength and commitment to any life situation.

The compassionate self can also be used as a focus for working with situations where self-criticism is common. People can learn to recognise self-criticism, its forms and functions, and with functional analysis and guided discovery look at how self-criticism is often hostile, unhelpful and depressing rather than inspiring

(Gilbert, 2010). In contrast, compassionate self-encouragement and self-correction, underpinned by compassion motivation, motivates us to try to be at our best in whatever we do and take joy from that. We may feel guilt if we fail but not shame, and hostile self-criticism (Gilbert 2010; see Chapter 3, this volume).

The compassionate self and compassion image act like an internalised, secure base and safe haven with mirroring and mentalising functions (as previously discussed). When we deliberately create these conditions in our mind, and try and function from this inner position, we are in a much better place to be able to work with our threat emotions and integrate them. This process of providing the contexts and conditions for differentiation and integration is central to growth (Siegel, 2016). We can better differentiate our emotions from one another, enabling a better understanding of what we are feeling and what is being triggered in us and how one emotion can suppress others. This in turn enables us to integrate and to hold these differing emotions without suppression, avoidance or dissociation, thus integrating them so we can be better at ease with them. The compassionate mind brings insight (from the wisdom of CFT psychoeducation) and can therefore empathise and mentalise the inner emotions – a source for coming to understand ourselves as the evolved and social constructed being we are. This is depicted in Figure 15.1.

As these skills and competencies develop people realise others are like this too (we are all made up of multiple potentials of motives and emotions; we are all gene-socially constructed versions of minds; see Table 15.1), so we can extend these

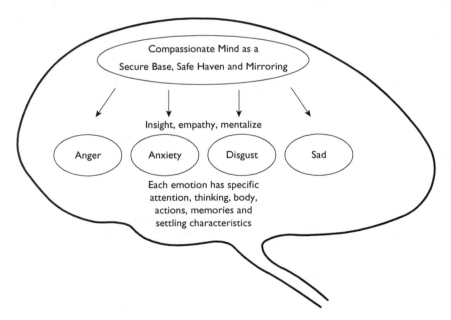

Figure 15.1 Representation of the integrated and therapeutic effects of building the compassionate mind. © Paul Gilbert.

compassionate insights to others too. There is growing evidence for this way of working (Kirby, 2016; Leaviss & Uttley, 2015) and a recent study of a relatively short compassionate mind training intervention found significant reductions in self-criticism and shame, and major increases in compassion for self and others, and positive affect with improvement in heart-rate variability (Matos et al., under review).

Fears of compassion

One of the most important therapeutic CFT challenges can be because people experience *fears* of compassion (e.g. wanting to be compassionate but feeling they don't deserve it or are frightened of the feelings it ignites – especially the fear of sadness and grief), feeling blocked (e.g. struggling to find time to practise or remember) and resistance (seeing compassion as weak and undesirable, known collectively as fears, blocks and resistances (FBRs) (see Gilbert & Mascaro, in press, for a review). Highly self-critical people can even respond to compassion with physiological indicators of threat as measured with fMRI (Longe et al., 2010), heart-rate variability (Rockliff et al., 2008) and salivary alpha amylase (Duarte et al., 2015). Gilbert, McEwan, Matos, & Rivis (2010) developed measures to explore metacognition of fears of compassion *to others*, fears of *receiving* compassion from others and *self-* compassion. Not surprisingly these are linked to mental health problems, fears of happiness in general and problems in emotions processing (Gilbert et al., 2013). Importantly, however, compassion training can reduce the fears of compassion (Jazaieri et al., 2013; Lawrence & Lee, 2014; Matos et al., under review). Importantly, not all resistances to compassion are based on fears. Indeed there are many complex factors that produce compassion resistance (Gilbert & Mascaro, in press)

Some of the emotional difficulties that arise when engaging with compassion motives and emotions can sometimes be explained in classical conditioning terms. For example, images and fantasies of a holiday will trigger positive affect for most people. But if one has experienced a recent holiday were one was robbed or injured then holiday stimuli could activate (classically conditioned) trauma memory and be unpleasant. If the people one has looked to for caring have been hostile and abusive then, when we stimulate the attachment system, what are released are trauma memories not affection ones. Hence, these can be the first experiences of individuals when they begin compassion work – the return of abuse-type feelings. So therapist and client work to 'detoxify' the attachment-linked trauma memories that are creating the fears and blocks to compassion, and enable a sense of social connectedness to emerge (Gilbert, 2010). Also not uncommonly, in people who have experienced emotional neglect, as they begin to open the affiliative and attachment systems, they can experience a sense of loneliness with a yearning and grief for the connectedness and love they wanted but did not get. Partly because crying is the most vulnerable state we can experience, and also because it requires a sense of connectedness, it is one of the most feared emotions by some people. This is why in CFT therapists need to be able to work with attachment trauma of various kinds and profound grief (Gilbert & Irons, 2005). Healing these process, especially fears of compassion, have their own therapeutic sequence (Lawrence & Lee, 2014).

Conclusion

The human brain evolved in a piecemeal fashion, subject to many constraints from what had evolved previously, and with many trade-offs. As such it is full of conflicting motives and emotions in pursuit of survival and reproductive strategies. These have recently been equipped with a whole range of newly evolved, socially intelligent competencies (Gilbert, Chapter 3, this volume). While these give rise to modern cultures of science and art, and the pursuit of knowledge and meaning, they also underpin many mental health problems, not to mention difficulties with violence and tribalism.

One problem with current psychotherapy is that it can see mental health problems as 'errors and disorders' that can be categorised according to DSM or ICD. Obviously there are genetic polymorphisms and structural processes that do give rise to mental health vulnerabilities. However, it is clear that many mental health problems, not to mention domestic and tribal violence that are undesirable (and harmful to others), are variations in phenotypes, adaptions and reactions to life histories and social contexts.

This is what makes compassion such a powerful process to focus on in therapy for social change in general, and the integration of mind(s) (Siegel, 2016). As we recognise the tragedy of the human condition, with our tricky, poorly integrated minds, and lives of threat, loss, decay and death, we can look to common processes on how to cope together. The evolution of caring and then human socially intelligent competencies fundamentally changes how minds work, are soothed and find purpose and meaning. The core focus of the compassion focused therapies therefore is less trying to remove or correct something than trying to develop and cultivate the best of us – conducive to the flourishing and well-being in all.

References

Ashworth, F., Gracey, F., & Gilbert, P. (2011). Compassion focused therapy after traumatic brain injury: Theoretical foundations and a case illustration. *Brain Impairment*, *12*, 128–139.

Barash, D. P. (2013). *Buddhist Biology: Ancient Eastern Wisdom Meets Modern Western Science*. New York: Oxford University Press.

Bartels-Velthuis, A. A., Schroevers, M. J., van der Ploeg., K., Koster, F., Fleer, J., & van der Brink, E. (2016). A Mindfulness-Based Compassionate Living Training in a heterogeneous sample of psychiatric outpatients: A feasibility study. *Mindfulness, 7*, 809–818. doi: 10.1007/s12671-016-0518-8

Beck, A. T. (1985). Cognitive therapy, behavior therapy, psychoanalysis, and pharmacotherapy: A cognitive continuum. In M. J. Mahoney & A. Freeman (Eds.), *Cognition and Psychotherapy* (pp. 325–347). New York: Plenum.

Bennett-Levy, J., & Haarhoff, B. (in press). Why therapists need to take a good look at themselves: Self-practice/self-reflection as an integrative training strategy for evidence-based practices. In S. Dimidjian (Ed.), *Evidence-based Practice in Action*. New York: Guilford.

Bennett-Levy, J., & Thwaites, R. (2007). Self and self-reflection in the therapeutic relationship. A conceptual map and practical strategies for the training supervision and self supervision of interpersonal skills. In P. Gilbert & R. L. Leary (Eds), *The*

Therapeutic Relationship in the Cognitive Behavioural Therapies (pp. 255–281). London: Routledge.

Bowlby, J. (1969). *Attachment: Attachment and Loss, Vol. 1*. London: Hogarth Press.

Bowlby, J. (1973). *Separation, Anxiety and Anger: Attachment and Loss, Vol. 2*. London: Hogarth Press.

Bowlby, J. (1980). *Attachment and Loss, Vol. III: Loss, Sadness and Depression*. London: The Hogarth Press and the Institute of Psycho-Analysis.

Braehler, C., Gumley, A., Harper, J., Wallace, S., Norrie, J., & Gilbert. P. (2013). Exploring change processes in compassion focused therapy in psychosis: Results of a feasibility randomized controlled trial. *British Journal of Clinical Psychology, 52*, 199–214.

Brune, M., Belsky, J., Fabrega, H., Feierman, J. R., Gilbert, P., Glantz, K., . . . Wilson, D. R. (2012). The crisis of psychiatry: Insights and prospects from evolutionary theory. *World Psychiatry, 11*, 55–57. doi: 177/0146167212445599

Buss, D. M. (2014). *Evolutionary Psychology: The New Science of the Mind*, Fifth Edition. London: Psychology Press.

Carter, C. S. (2014). Oxytocin pathways and the evolution of human behavior. *Annual Review of Psychology, 65*, 17–39.

Clark, J. J. (1994). *Jung and Eastern Thought: A Dialogue with the Orient*. London: Routledge.

Cortina, M., & Liotti, G. (2010). Attachment is about safety and protection, intersubjectivity is about sharing and social understanding the relationship between attachment and intersubjectivity: The relationships between attachment and intersubjectivity. *Psychoanalytic Psychology, 27*, 410–441.

Crocker, J., & Canevello, A. (2012). Consequences of self-image and compassionate goals. In P. G. Devine & A. Plant (Eds.), *Advances in Experimental Social Psychology* (pp. 229–277). New York: Elsevier.

Dalai Lama (1995). *Awakening the Mind, Lightening the Heart*. New York: HarperCollins.

Dalai Lama, & Ekman, P. (2009). *Emotional Awareness: Overcoming the Obstacles to Psychological Balance and Compassion*. New York: Hold Paperbacks.

Davidson, R. J. (2012). The biology of compassion. In C. Germer & D. Siegel (Eds.), *Wisdom and Compassion in Psychotherapy: Deepening Mindfulness in Clinical Practice* (pp. 111–118). New York: Guildford Press.

Depue, R. A., & Morrone-Strupinsky, J. V. (2005). A neurobehavioral model of affiliative bonding. *Behavioral and Brain Sciences, 28*, 313–395.

Duarte, J., McEwan, K., Barnes, C., Gilbert, P., & Maratos, F. A. (2015). Do therapeutic imagery practices affect physiological and emotional indicators of threat in high self-critics? *Psychology and Psychotherapy: Theory, Research and Practice, 88*, 270–284.

Dunbar, R. I. M. (2010). The social role of touch in humans and primates: Behavioural function and neurobiological mechanisms. *Neuroscience and Biobehavioral Reviews, 34*, 260–268. doi: 10. 1016/j.neubiorev.2008.07.001

Ellenberger, H. F. (1970). *The Discovery of the Unconscious: The History and Evolution of Dynamic Psychiatry*. New York: Basic Books.

Ellis, A. (1962). *Reason and Emotion in Psychotherapy*. New York: Lyle Stuart.

Farias, M., & Wikholm, C. (2015). *The Buhdda Pill: Can Meditation Change You?* London: Watkins.

Fredrickson, B. L., Grewen, K. M., Coffey, K. A., Algoe, S. B., Firestine, A. M., Arevalo, J. M. G., . . . Cole, S. W. (2013). A functional genomic perspective on human well-being. *Proceedings of the National Academy of Sciences, 110*, 13684–13689. doi: 10.1073/pnas.1305419110

Gale, C., Schroder, T., & Gilbert, P. (2015). Do you practice what you preach? A qualitative exploration of therapists' personal practice of Compassion Focused Therapy. *Clinical Psychology and Psychotherapy*, doi: 10.1002/cpp.1993

Germer, C. K., & Siegel, R. D. (2012). *Wisdom and Compassion in Psychotherapy*. New York: Guilford Press.

Gilbert, P. (1989/2016). *Human Nature and Suffering*. London: Routledge.

Gilbert, P. (1995). Biopsychosocial approaches and evolutionary theory as aids to integration in clinical psychology and psychotherapy. *Clinical Psychology and Psychotherapy*, *2*, 135–156. doi:10.1002/cpp.5640020302

Gilbert, P. (1998a). Evolutionary psychopathology: Why isn't the mind better designed than it is? *British Journal of Medical Psychology*, *71*, 353–373.

Gilbert, P. (1998b). What is shame? Some core issues and controversies. In P. Gilbert & B. Andrews (Eds.), *Shame: Interpersonal Behavior, Psychopathology and Culture* (pp. 3–36). New York: Oxford University Press.

Gilbert, P. (2000). Social mentalities: Internal 'social' conflicts and the role of inner warmth and compassion in cognitive therapy. In P. Gilbert & K. G. Bailey (Eds.), *Genes on the Couch: Explorations in Evolutionary Psychotherapy* (pp.118–150). Hove, UK: Psychology Press.

Gilbert, P. (2007). *Psychotherapy and Counselling for Depression (3rd edition)*. London: Sage.

Gilbert, P. (2009). *The Compassionate Mind: A New Approach to the Challenge of Life*. London: Constable & Robinson.

Gilbert, P. (2010). *Compassion Focused Therapy: The CBT Distinctive Features Series*. London: Routledge.

Gilbert, P. (2014). The origins and nature of compassion focused therapy. *British Journal of Clinical Psychology*, *53*, 6–41. doi: 10.1111/bjc.12043

Gilbert, P., & Choden (2013). *Mindful Compassion*. London: Constable & Robinson.

Gilbert, P., & Irons, C. (2005). Focused therapies and compassionate mind training for shame and self-attacking. In P. Gilbert (Ed.), *Compassion: Conceptualisations, Research and Use in Psychotherapy* (pp. 263–325). London: Routledge.

Gilbert, P., & Leary, R. L. (Eds.) (2007). *The Therapeutic Relationship in the Cognitive Behavioural Therapies*. London: Routledge.

Gilbert, P., McEwan, K., Gibbons, L., Chotai, S., Duarte, J., & Matos, M. (2013). Fears of compassion and happiness in relation to alexithymia, mindfulness and self-criticism. *Psychology and Psychotherapy*, *84*, 239–255. doi: 10.1348/147608310X526511

Gilbert, P., McEwan, K., Matos, M., & Rivis, A. (2010). Fears of compassion: Development of three self-report measures. *Psychology and Psychotherapy: Theory, Research and Practice*, *84*, 239–255. doi: 10.1348/147608310X526511

Gilbert, P., & Mascaro, J. (in press). Compassion: Fears, blocks, and resistances: An evolutionary investigation. In E. Sappla & J. Doty (Eds.), *Handbook of Compassion*. New York: Oxford University Press.

Greenberg, J. R., & Mitchell, S. A. (1983). *Object Relations in Psychoanalytic Theory*. Boston, MA: Harvard University Press.

Greenberg, L. S., & Safran, J. (1987). *Emotion in Psychotherapy*. New York: Guilford Press.

Hayes, S. C., Follette, V. M., & Linehan, M. N. (2004). *Mindfulness and Acceptance: Expanding the Cognitive Behavioral Tradition*. New York: Guilford Press.

Hermanto, N., Zuroff, D.C., Kopala-Sibley, D.C., Kelly, A.C., Matos, M., Gilbert, P., & Koestner, R. (2016). Ability to receive compassion from others buffers the depressogenic effect of self-criticism: A cross-cultural multi-study analysis. *Personality and Individual Differences*, *98*, 324–332.

Hoffmann, S. G., Grossman, P., & Hinton, D. E. (2011). Loving-kindness and compassion meditation: Potential for psychological intervention. *Clinical Psychology Review*, *13*, 1126–1132. doi: 10.1016/j.cpr.2011.07.003

Holmes, J. (2001). *The Search for a Secure Base: Attachment Theory and Psychotherapy*. London: Routledge.

Horwitz, A.V., & Wakefield, J.C. (2005). *The Loss of Sadness: How Psychiatry Transformed Normal Sorrow Into Depressive Disorder*. Oxford: Oxford University Press.

Jazaieri, H., McGonigal, K., Jinpa, T., Doty, J. R., Gross, J. J., & Goldin, P. R. (2013). A randomized controlled trial of compassion cultivation training: Effects on mindfulness, affect, and emotion regulation. *Motivation and Emotion*. doi: 10.1007/s11031-013-9368

Jazaieri, H., McGonigal, K., Jinpa, T., Doty, J. R., Gross, J. J., & Goldin, P. R. (2014). A randomized controlled trial of compassion cultivation training: Effects on mindfulness, affect, and emotion regulation. *Motivation and Emotion*, *38*, 23–35. doi: 10.1007/s11031-013-9368-z

Jung, C. G. (1984). *Memories, Dreams, Reflections*. London: Routledge.

Katzow, A.W., & Safran, J.D (2007). Recognising and resolving ruptures in the therapeutic alliance. In P. Gilbert & R. L Leary (Eds.), *The Therapeutic Relationship in the Cognitive Behavioural Therapies* (pp. 90–105). London: Routledge.

Kelly, A. C., & Carter, J. C. (2015). Self-compassion training for binge eating disorder: A pilot randomized controlled trial. *Psychology and Psychotherapy*, *88*, 285–303. doi: 10.1111/papt.12044

Kelly, G. (1963). *A Theory of Personality: The Psychology of Personal Constructs*. Norton: New York.

Keltner, D., Kogan, A., Piff, P. K., & Saturn, S. R. (2014). The sociocultural appraisals, values and emotions (SAVE) framework of prosociality: Core processes from gene to meme. *Annual Review of Psychology*, *65*, 425–460. doi: 10.1146/annurev-psych-010213-115054

Kemeny, M. E., Foltz, C., Cavanagh, J. F., Cullen, M., Giese-Davis, J., Jennings, P., & Ekman, P. (2012). Contemplative/emotion training reduces negative emotional behavior and promotes prosocial responses. *Emotion*, *12*, 338–350. doi: 10.1037/a0026118.

Kirby, J. N. (2016). Compassion interventions: The programs, the evidence, and implications for research and practice. *Psychology and Psychotherapy: Theory, Research, and Practice*. doi: 10.1111/papt.12104

Kirby, J. N, Tellegen, C. L., & Steindl, S. R. (2015). Cultivating compassion: A systematic review and meta-analysis of compassion-based interventions. *PROSPERO: International Prospective Register of Systematic Reviews, 2015*, CRD42015024576. Retrieved from http://www.crd.york.ac.uk/PROSPERO/display_record.asp?ID=CRD42015024576

Klimecki, O.M., Leiberg, S., Ricard, M., & Singer, T. (2014). Differential pattern of functional brain plasticity after compassion and empathy training. *Social Cognitive and Affective Neuroscience*, *9*, 873–879. doi: 10.1093/scan/nst060

Kohut, H. (1977). *The Restoration of the Self*. New York: International Universities Press.

Lawrence, V., & Lee, D. (2014) An exploration of people's experiences of Compassion Focused Therapy for trauma, using interpretative phenomenological analysis. *Clinical Psychology and Psychotherapy*, *6*, 495–407.

Leaviss, J., & Uttley, L. (2015). Psychotherapeutic benefits of compassion-focused therapy: An early systematic review. *Psychological Medicine*, *45*, 927–945. doi: 10.1017/S0033291714002141

Leighton, T. D. (2003). *Faces of Compassion: Classic Bodhisattva Archetypes and their Modern Expression*. Boston, MA: Wisdom Publications.

Liotti G. (2007). Internal working models of attachment in the therapeutic relationship. In P. Gilbert & R. L. Leary (Eds.), *The Therapeutic Relationship in the Cognitive Behavioural Therapies* (pp. 141–161). London: Routledge.

Longe, O., Maratos, F.A., Gilbert, P., Evans, G., Volker, F., Rockliffe, H., & Rippon, G. (2010). Having a word with yourself: Neural correlates of self-criticism and self-reassurance. *NeuroImage, 49*, 1849–1856.

Lucre, K. M, & Corten, N. (2013). An exploration of group compassion-focused therapy for personality disorder. *Psychology and Psychotherapy, 86*, 387–400.

McEwan, K., & Gilbert, P. (2016). A pilot feasibility study exploring the practising of compassionate imagery exercises in a nonclinical population. *Psychology and Psychotherapy, 89*, 239–243.

MacLean, P. (1985). Brain evolution relating to family, play and the separation call. *Archives of General Psychiatry, 42*, 405–417.

Mascaro, J. S., Rilling, J. K., Negi, L. T., & Raison, C. L. (2013). Compassion meditation enhances empathic accuracy and related neural activity. *Social Cognitive and Affective Neuroscience, 8*, 48–55.

Matos, M., Duarte, C., Duarte, J., Pinto-Gouveia, J., Petroscchi, N., Basran, J., & Gilbert, P. (under review). Psychological and physiological effects of compassionate mind training: A randomised controlled trial.

Mayseless, O. (2016). *The Caring Motivation: An Integrated Theory*. New York: Oxford University Press.

Neff, K. D., & Germer, C. K. (2013). A pilot study and randomized controlled trial of the mindful self-compassion program. *Journal of Clinical Psychology, 69*, 28–44. doi: 10.1002/jclp.21923

Nesse, R. M., & Ellsworth, P. C. (2009). Evolution, emotions, and emotional disorders. *American Psychologist, 64*, 129–139. doi: 10.1037/a0013503

Nesse, R. M., & Williams, G. C. (1995). *Evolution and Healing*. London: Weidenfeld & Nicolson.

Ornstein, R.E. (1986). *Multimind*. New York: Houghton Mifflin.

Ozawa-de Silva, B., & Dodson-Lavelle, B. (2011). An education of heart and mind: Practical and theoretical issues in teaching cognitive-based compassion training to children. *Practical Matters, 1*, 1–28.

Pace, T. W., Negi, L. T., Adame, D. D., Cole, S. P., Sivilli, T. I., Brown, T. D., . . . Raison, C. L. (2009). Effect of compassion meditation on neuroendocrine, innate immune and behavioral responses to psychosocial stress. *Psychoneuroendocrinology, 34*, 87–98. doi: 10.1016/j.psyneuen. 2008.08.011

Porges, S.W. (2007). The polyvagal perspective. *Biological Psychology, 74*, 116–143.

Ricard, M. (2015). *Altruism: The Power of Compassion to Change Itself and the World*. London: Atlantic Books.

Rockliff, H., Gilbert, P., McEwan, K., Lightman, S., & Glover, D. (2008). A pilot exploration of heart rate variability and salivary cortisol responses to compassion-focused imagery. *Journal of Clinical Neuropsychiatry, 5*, 132–139.

Sepalla, E., & Doty, J.R. (in press). *Handbook of Compassion Science*. Oxford: Oxford University Press.

Siegel, D. J. (2016). *Mind: A Journey to the Heart of Being Human*. New York: W. W. Norton.

Singer, T., & Bolz, M. (Eds.) (2012). *Compassion: Bridging practice and science*. http://www.compassion-training.org/

Thayer, J. F., & Lane, R. D. (2000). A model of neurovisceral integration in emotion regulation and dysregulation. *Journal of Affective Disorders*, *61*, 201–216.

Tirch, D., Schoendorfe, B., & Silberstein, L. R. (2015). *ACT Practitioner's Guide to the Science of Compassion: Tools for Fostering Psychological Flexibility.* Oakland, CA: New Harbinger.

Van den Brink, E., & Koster, F. (2012). *Mindfulness-Based Compassionate Living: A New Training Programme to Deepen Mindfulness With Heartfulness*. London: Routledge.

Van Der Kolk, B. (2015). *The Body Keeps the Score: Brain, Mind, and Body in the Healing of Trauma*. London: Penguin.

Vessantara (1993). *Meeting the Buddhas: A Guide to Buddhas, Bodhisattvas and Tantric Deities*. Birmingham: Windhorse Publications.

Worthington, E. L., O'Connor, L., Berry, J. W., Share, C., Murray, R., & Yi, E. (2005). Compassion and forgiveness: Implications for psychotherapy. In P. Gilbert (Ed.), *Compassion: Conceptualisations, Research and Use in Psychotherapy* (pp. 168–192). London: Routledge.

Yalom, I. D. (1980). *Existential Psychotherapy*. New York: W. W. Norton.

Zimbardo, P. (2006). *The Lucifer Effect: Understanding How Good People Turn Evil*. Random House: New York.

Index